BACKCOUNTRY SKI & SNOWBOARD ROUTES

COLORADO

BACKCOUNTRY SKI & SNOWBOARD ROUTES

COLORADO

BRITTANY WALKER KONSELLA
AND FRANK KONSELLA

FOREWORD BY CHRIS DAVENPORT

MOUNTAINEERS BOOKS

MOUNTAINEERS BOOKS

Mountaineers Books is the publishing division of The Mountaineers, an organization founded in 1906 and dedicated to the exploration, preservation, and enjoyment of outdoor and wilderness areas.

1001 SW Klickitat Way, Suite 201, Seattle, WA 98134
800.553.4453, www.mountaineersbooks.org

Printed in China
Distributed in the United Kingdom by Cordee, www.cordee.co.uk
First edition: first printing 2017, third printing 2025

Copyeditor: Paula Thurman
Design: Peggy Egerdahl
Layout: McKenzie Long
Cartographer: Pease Press Cartography
The background maps for this book were produced using the online map viewer CalTopo. For more information, visit caltopo.com.
All photographs by the authors unless otherwise noted
Cover photograph: *A skier milks the edge of the trees on Mount Shimer. (Photo by Jordan White)*
Back cover photograph: *A steep descent on the upper reaches of Dragon's Tail Couloir*
Frontispiece: *You will find beautiful views while climbing up the Y Couloirs of Maroon Peak.*

Library of Congress Cataloging-in-Publication Data
Konsella, Brittany Walker, author. | Konsella, Frank, author.
Backcountry ski & snowboard routes : Colorado / Brittany Walker Konsella and Frank Konsella.
Backcountry ski and snowboard routes
First edition. | Seattle, Washington : Mountaineers Books, [2017] | Includes index.
LCCN 2017016912 | ISBN 9781594858826 (paperback) | ISBN 9781594858833 (ebook)
LCSH: Cross-country skiing—Colorado—Guidebooks. | Snowboarding—Colorado—Guidebooks. | Cross-country ski trails—Colorado—Guidebooks. | Outdoor recreation—Colorado—Guidebooks. | Colorado—Guidebooks.
LCC GV854.5.C6 K66 2017 | DDC 796.93/209788—dc23
LC record available at https://lccn.loc.gov/2017016912

Mountaineers Books titles may be purchased for corporate, educational, or other promotional sales, and our authors are available for a wide range of events. For information on special discounts or booking an author, contact our customer service at 800-553-4453 or mbooks@mountaineersbooks.org.

Printed on FSC®-certified materials

FSC www.fsc.org MIX Paper | Supporting responsible forestry FSC® C188448

ISBN (paperback): 978-1-59485-882-6
ISBN (ebook): 978-1-59485-883-3

CONTENTS

MOSQUITO AND TENMILE RANGES

GORE RANGE

ELK MOUNTAINS

SANGRE DE CRISTO MOUNTAINS

SAWATCH RANGE

SAN JUAN MOUNTAINS

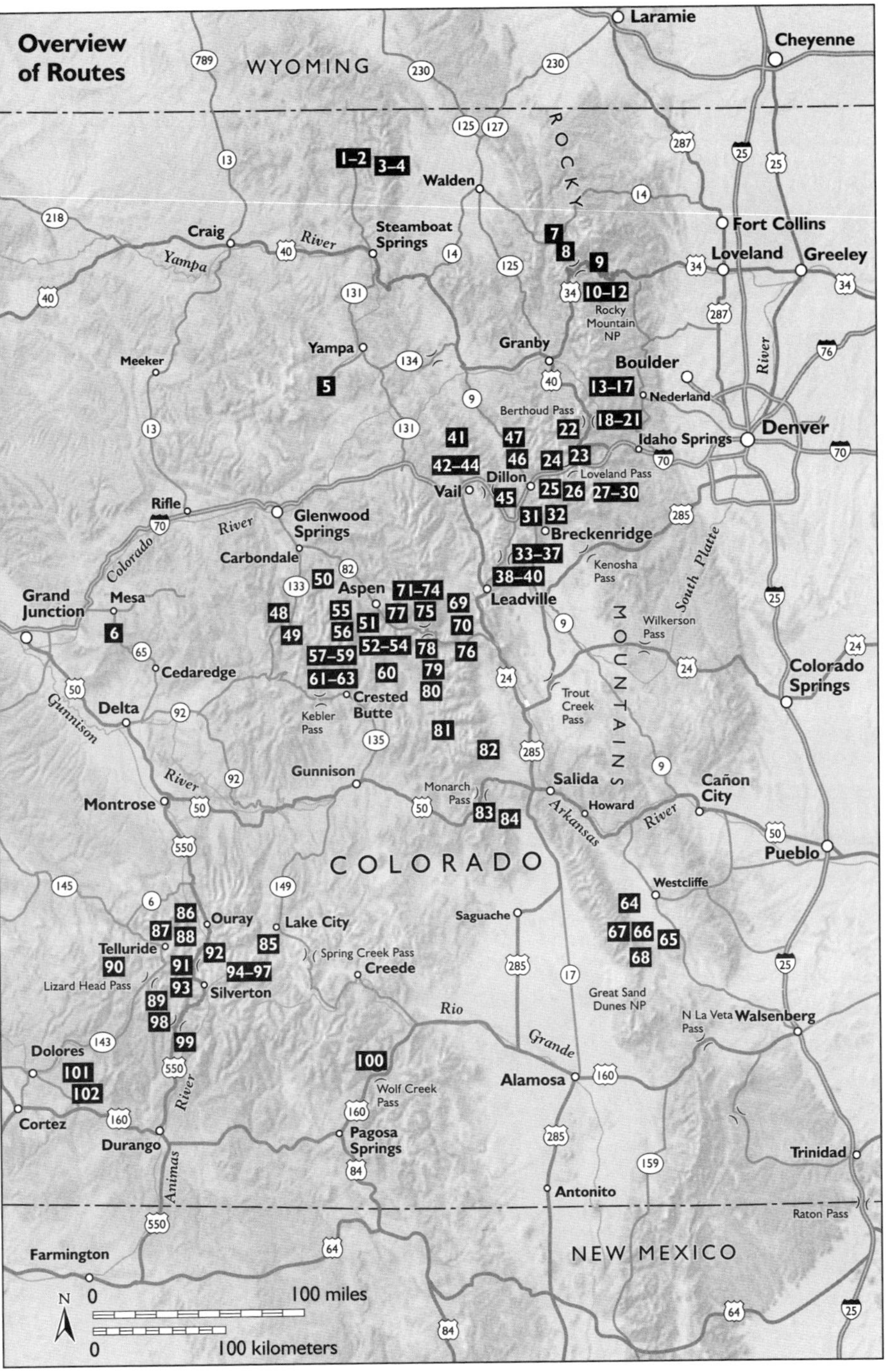
Overview of Routes
WYOMING
COLORADO
NEW MEXICO
ROCKY MOUNTAINS
Laramie
Cheyenne
Walden
Fort Collins
Loveland
Greeley
Craig
Steamboat Springs
Yampa River
Rocky Mountain NP
Granby
Yampa
Meeker
Boulder
Nederland
Berthoud Pass
Denver
Idaho Springs
Dillon
Vail
Loveland Pass
Rifle
Colorado River
Glenwood Springs
Carbondale
Breckenridge
Kenosha Pass
Aspen
Leadville
Grand Junction
Mesa
Cedaredge
Wilkerson Pass
South Platte River
Colorado Springs
Delta
Gunnison River
Crested Butte
Kebler Pass
Trout Creek Pass
Gunnison
Salida
Monarch Pass
Montrose
Howard
Arkansas River
Cañon City
Pueblo
Westcliffe
Saguache
Ouray
Lake City
Telluride
Spring Creek Pass
Creede
Lizard Head Pass
Silverton
Great Sand Dunes NP
Rio Grande
N La Veta Pass
Walsenberg
Dolores
Alamosa
Wolf Creek Pass
Cortez
Durango
Animas River
Pagosa Springs
Trinidad
Antonito
Raton Pass
Farmington
0 100 miles
0 100 kilometers
N
1–2
3–4
5
6
7
8
9
10–12
13–17
18–21
22
23
24
25
26
27–30
31
32
33–37
38–40
41
42–44
45
46
47
48
49
50
51
52–54
55
56
57–59
60
61–63
64
65
66
67
68
69
70
71–74
75
76
77
78
79
80
81
82
83
84
85
86
87
88
89
90
91
92
93
94–97
98
99
100
101
102

TOURS AT A GLANCE

No.	Tour	Approximate Vertical (feet)	Best Months	Ski Skills Required
PARK RANGE, FLAT TOPS, AND GRAND MESA				
1	Hahns Peak: West Side	2200+	December to mid-March	Easy with options up to difficult
2	Farwell Mountain: South Face and Chutes	3000	December to mid-March	Easy with options up to difficult
3	Little Agnes: West and Northeast Sides	4000+	December to April	Easy with options up to difficult
4	Big Agnes: West Face	4500+	March to early June	Difficult
5	Flat Top Mountain: Northeast Slopes	2900	April through June	Difficult
6	Grand Mesa: Former Mesa Creek Ski Area	1000+	December to early March	Moderate
NORTHERN FRONT RANGE				
7	North and South Diamond Peaks: East Faces	1600+	Mid-February through April	Moderate to difficult
8	Nokhu Crags: Three Sisters, Grand Central, and Nokhouloir	2800+	Mid-March to early May	Moderate to difficult
9	Sundance Mountain: North Face	2200	Late May to July	Easy to difficult
10	Flattop Mountain: Dragon's Tail Couloir	2500	March and April	Very difficult
11	Tyndall Gorge: Tyndall Glacier and Couloir	2900 to 3000	March to June	Moderate to very difficult
12	Bear Lake: Terrain Park	2000+	January to early April	Easy to difficult
13	Mount Audubon: Crooked Couloir	2900	April to June	Difficult
14	Mount Toll: Southeast Face	2700	April to June	Moderate to difficult
15	Apache Peak: Queen's Way and Apache Couloir	3400	April to June	Difficult
16	North Arapaho Peak: Northstar Couloir	4300	May and June	Difficult
17	South Arapaho Peak: Skywalker Couloir	3277	May and June	Extremely difficult
SOUTHERN FRONT RANGE				
18	Skyscraper Peak: Skyscraper Glacier	1450	June and July	Moderate to very difficult
19	Radiobeacon Mountain: East Cirque	1300 to 2900	May and June	Moderate to very difficult

No.	Tour	Approximate Vertical (feet)	Best Months	Ski Skills Required
20	James Peak: North and East Couloirs	3650	April and May	Easy to very difficult
21	Mount Eva: Eva Bowl and Southeast Face	3600	April to June	Easy to difficult
22	Berthoud Pass	1980	December to April	Moderate
23	Hagar Mountain	2600	March to early June	Difficult
24	Mount Trelease: South and Northeast Faces	1100+	December to April	Easy to moderate
25	Loveland Pass: Hippie Trees	1200	December to April	Moderate to difficult
26	Black Mountain: Shit for Brains Couloir	1900 to 2200	March to April	Very difficult
27	Grizzly Peak: Grizzly Couloir	3050	March to early June	Difficult
28	Torreys Peak: Tuning Forks	4467	March to early June	Difficult
29	Square Top Mountain: East Bowl	3000	March through May	Moderate to difficult
30	Argentine Peak: Waldorf Bowl	3500	April and May	Difficult to very difficult
MOSQUITO AND TENMILE RANGES				
31	Mount Victoria: Victoria Trees and J Chute	2200 to 2700	January to March	Moderate to difficult
32	Royal Mountain: Coin Slot Couloir	1360	February to March	Difficult to very difficult
33	Crystal Peak: North Face	3500/3700	April to mid- to late May	Difficult
34	Pacific Peak: North Chutes	3600	April and May	Difficult to extremely difficult
35	Mayflower Gulch: Mayflower Hill	1000 to 1450	December to February	Easy to moderate
36	Fletcher Mountain: Northwest Face	3001	March to May	Difficult to very difficult
37	Mount Tweto: Northeast Face	2620	March to May	Very difficult
38	Quandary Peak: Cristo Couloir	3400	March to May	Difficult
39	North Star Mountain: Polaris Couloir	2200 to 2750	April and May	Very difficult to extremely difficult
40	Mount Democrat: North Face	3250-	April and May	Difficult to very difficult

No.	Tour	Approximate Vertical (feet)	Best Months	Ski Skills Required
GORE RANGE				
41	Peak C: CC Rider Couloir	4000+/-	June	Difficult
42	Outpost Peak: South Side	4200	February and March	Moderate to difficult
43	Pitkin Creek Drainage: Birthday Chute	3900	March and April	Moderate to difficult
44	Pitkin Creek Drainage: West Skiers Point	4300	March and April	Difficult to very difficult
45	Uneva Peak: West/Southwest Aspects	1950+/-	December to February	Easy to moderate
46	Buffalo Mountain: Silver Couloir	3100	March to May	Moderate
47	Red Peak: Big Bad Wolf	4400	April to early June	Very difficult
ELK MOUNTAINS				
48	Huntsman Ridge	2300+/-	December to March	Moderate to difficult
49	Marble Peak	2414	December to April	Moderate
50	Mount Sopris: The Elbow	4600	April and May	Difficult
51	Ski Hayden Peak	4375	February to April	Difficult
52	Greg Mace Peak	3130	March to early May	Difficult
53	Castle Peak: East Face	4815	April to May	Very difficult
54	Conundrum Peak: Conundrum Couloir	8750 feet or less	May and June	Very difficult
55	Pyramid Peak: The Landry Line	5268+/-	April to early May	Extremely difficult
56	Maroon Peak: East Face to the Bell Cord	4700	April to early June	Extremely difficult
57	Unnamed 13,253: White Widow Couloir	3653	April to May	Very difficult
58	White Rock Mountain: West Face	3940	April to May	Difficult
59	Gothic Mountain: Gothic Spoon and West Chutes	3518	March to May	Difficult
60	Teocalli Mountain	4258	March to May	Difficult
61	Coneys	1500	November to April	Moderate
62	Mount Emmons: Red Lady Bowl	3200	December to March	Moderate
63	Mount Emmons: Redwell Basin	3300	December to March	Moderate

No.	Tour	Approximate Vertical (feet)	Best Months	Ski Skills Required
SANGRE DE CRISTO MOUNTAINS				
64	Eureka Mountain: Eureka Couloir	4007+/-	March to early May	Difficult
65	Broken Hand Peak: Broken Dogleg Couloir	3623	March to early May	Very difficult
66	Crestone Needle: South Couloir	4247	March to early May	Very difficult
67	Mount Adams: West Face	5031	March to April	Difficult
68	Unnamed 13,020: Juice Box Couloir	4620	March to April	Very difficult
SAWATCH RANGE				
69	Mount Oklahoma: Northeast Face	3350	April through June	Difficult
70	Mount Elbert: Northwest Gullies	4200	April to June	Difficult
71	Twining Peak: Southeast Face	1650/2900	End of May to June	Difficult to very difficult
72	Mount Champion: West Face and North-east Chutes	2100 to 3500	End of April to June	Difficult
73	Unnamed 13,736: West Face	2950	End of May and June	Difficult
74	Lackawanna Peak: South Gully and West Face	3400	February to mid-May	Moderate to difficult
75	Independence Pass: Mountain Boy Gulch	1600/2200	End of May to early June	Moderate
76	La Plata Peak: Southeast Couloir and North Face	6000	March to May	Moderate
77	Mount Shimer (a.k.a. Sunshine)	3350	January to May	Moderate
78	Anderson Peak: North Face	2660	May to June	Very difficult
79	Jenkins Mountain: Steeple Couloir	5000	May to early June	Difficult
80	Park Cone	2900	December to April	Moderate to Difficult
81	Emma Burr Mountain: Northeast Face	2200 +/-	May and June	Difficult
82	Tabeguache Peak: North Face	5300	April and May	Difficult
83	Monarch Pass: Perfect Trees	900	January and February	Moderate
84	Mount Ouray: Devil's Armchair	4311	March to May	Difficult

No.	Tour	Approximate Vertical (feet)	Best Months	Ski Skills Required
SAN JUAN MOUNTAINS				
85	Unnamed 13,299: Dead Squirrel Couloir	3680	March to early May	Difficult
86	Mount Sneffels: Snake Couloir	4300	March to May	Very difficult
87	Chicago Peak: Lightning Bolt Couloir	3185+/-	March to early May	Difficult
88	Ajax Peak: The Dream Stream	5400	March to early May	Moderate
89	Sheep Mountain: Sheep Chute	2938	March to early May	Difficult
90	Gladstone Peak: North Face	4200	April to early June	Very difficult
91	Sam's Trees	1550	December to March	Moderate to difficult
92	Red Mountain No. 3: West Face	1760	Late March to April	Difficult
93	Clear Lake: South Lookout Peak and V2	3500	May to June	Moderate to very difficult
94	Tower Mountain: North Face	3002+	April to early June	Difficult
95	King Solomon Mountain: North Face	3310	March to early May	Difficult
96	Hazelton Mountain: Turkey Chute	2800	November; March to early May	Difficult
97	Kendall Peak: Northwest Couloir	3951	March to early May	Difficult
98	Grand Turk: Zipper Couloir	2450	March to April	Very difficult
99	Snowdon Peak: Naked Lady Couloir	2402	March to May	Extremely difficult
100	Wolf Creek Pass	2000+/-	November to April	Easy to moderate
101	Tomahawk Basin	3150	May	Difficult
102	Babcock Peak: South Couloir	3750	May	Difficult

FOREWORD

THE COLORADO MOUNTAINS HAVE LONG BEEN a source of inspiration and pride to the people who see them. Today, about 95 percent of all people living in Colorado enjoy a vista of the Colorado mountains from at or near their homes. These mountains call to us, as they did the intrepid miners of the nineteenth century and the early climbers of the twentieth century, like Albert Ellingwood and Carl Melzer.

My own history with Colorado's mountains began with my parents, who both attended the University of Denver in the late 1960s and brought our family out from New Hampshire each winter to ski at Arapahoe Basin and Keystone. In the summers, we hiked and camped in the mountains, and I fell in love with the adventures the peaks and valleys provided. On my first "fourteener" ski descent of Torreys Peak in 1990, I realized that my skiing and climbing upbringing back East formed a perfect foundation for a "graduate" degree in mountaineering right here in Colorado.

Upon moving to Colorado in 1989, I promptly purchased *Dawson's Guide to the Colorado Fourteeners* by Lou Dawson. This newly published book was the first Colorado guidebook with a focus on skiing the high peaks, and it also set the stage for what would be a twenty-seven-year (and counting) obsession for me with ski mountaineering. The Colorado mountains, when covered with a white mantle of snow, provide a dynamic, ever-changing challenge. Unlike the more static personality of these peaks in the summer, in winter and spring conditions they change by the day, oftentimes by the hour. Timing is everything, and to succeed in this environment I had to educate myself in the practices, or perhaps art forms, of snow safety, backcountry travel, risk management, and advanced ascent and descent techniques, just as all aspiring ski mountaineers must do.

In 2006, I took on a project that would in some ways come to define me as a skier. There are fifty-four official 14,000-foot summits in Colorado. During the winter and spring of that year, I undertook to climb and ski them all. My inspiration for this effort came from Lou Dawson himself, his seminal guidebook that I had purchased as a teenager, and the personal challenges these peaks presented to me. In climbing and skiing these high mountains, I was challenged physically while also learning what I was capable of in life. As the American poet T. S. Eliot said, "Only those who will risk going too far can possibly find out how far they can go." In taking on this challenge and accepting and managing the risks involved, not only was I able to finish the project the following winter, but I certainly learned a ton about myself and the mountains of Colorado.

The authors of this guidebook, Frank and Brittany Konsella, have undergone a similar journey. Both have spent many hundreds of days over the years seeking out skiing adventures on our high peaks, and both can count ski descents of all fifty-four Colorado fourteeners on their résumés—a feat fewer than twenty people have accomplished.

Heading up the skin track on a cloudy yet beautiful day with Shimer's summit (Route 77) visible on the right

If there is one thing we all have learned through these experiences, it's that many lifetimes' worth of adventures exist out there. It's just up to us to seek them out.

To be a backcountry skier or ski mountaineer in Colorado means we must accept a certain level of risk and learn advanced methods to manage that risk. The more days spent out in the mountains skiing means a higher level of understanding of the conditions but also a greater degree of exposure to the risks involved. I've spent more than twenty years attempting to master these methods, only to realize that one never truly knows enough. Ski mountaineering becomes a daily exercise in humility when one accepts that it's always okay to switch to plan B or turn around when red flags present themselves.

When you head out to climb and ski one of the many excellent routes in *Backcountry Ski & Snowboard Routes: Colorado*, I think you'll find that you won't just check one route off your list, but you'll end up gazing out from the summit and adding many more to it. And that's exactly what ski mountaineering is all about. So invest the time in learning the skills necessary. Find a mentor and some great partners. Practice with your gear. And most of all, set your goals high.

Here's to smooth climbs, epic summits, and graceful descents.

—Chris Davenport, US Ski Hall of Fame member

Two-time World Champion skier Chris Davenport is widely regarded as one of the premier big mountain skiers in the world today. Among his many ski mountaineering achievements, in 2007 Chris became the first person to ski all fifty-four of Colorado's 14,000-foot peaks in less than one year. He has numerous first descents of peaks around the globe under his belt, and he recently guided and skied on Mount Everest. When not traveling the globe, Chris resides in Aspen, Colorado, with his wife and three boys.

Skiing the Marble area (Route 49) on a Pacific Northwest–style day

INTRODUCTION

EVERY STATE IS KNOWN FOR SOMETHING. In Wisconsin, it's cheese. In New York, it's skyscrapers. Here in Colorado, we're known for our mountains. Depending on how one counts, we have nearly 2000 summits higher than 12,000 feet in Colorado. And where there are mountains, there's skiing.

Skiing is what we do. When we embarked on our journey to ski all the "fourteeners," one of the great side benefits of that project was that we began to learn the intricacies of this great state. There are, of course, the famous ski towns such as Crested Butte, Telluride, and Aspen, but our travels also took us to the lesser-known gems such as Lake City, Westcliffe, and Creede. Beyond that, the varied geography of our state kept us entranced as we explored the highest peaks of Colorado's greatest ranges such as the Elks and the San Juans. The greatest gift of all was that for each peak we skied, we spied five more peaks that we knew we wanted to come back for. After our fourteener project was finished, the subsequent seasons lacked a little something—mostly a lack of exploration while we stayed close to home, skiing our favorite backyard peaks near our home in Crested Butte.

When Mountaineers Books approached us to write this book, we knew our exploratory itch was about to reach another level. Unlike our fourteeners project, we were not bound by elevation and could instead seek out the lower ranges in addition to the big boys. Of course, we also wanted to go back and ski some of those lines we'd viewed while skiing the fourteeners. That's what this book represents—a chance to explore this great state filled with mountains. Hopefully, you'll have as much fun exploring as we did. And like us, we're sure you will spy hundreds of other lines to come back to on your journeys as well.

EDUCATION

Becoming a knowledgeable backcountry skier is a lifelong process. It is important to become educated in avalanche awareness, navigation, and wilderness medicine through classes and books and through constant practice. We also recommend that you seek the advice of a mentor. We recommend the following:

- **Take an avalanche course:** Before tackling any of these routes, we strongly recommend that you take an avalanche fundamentals course (Level 1). Avalanche education does not stop there, however. The American Avalanche Association (www.americanavalancheassociation.org) has designed a continuing education track for both recreationists and professionals, and as you progress in the sport, you may consider additional courses.
- **Practice your avalanche skills:** Another good habit is to practice with your avalanche rescue equipment often enough that a beacon search feels as natural as brushing your teeth or any other day-to-day activity.

- **Take a mountain skills course:** Beyond an avalanche course, you may also want additional instruction in mountain skills. These skills include navigation as well as the use of specialized climbing equipment, such as crampons, ice axes, and ropes, which are required for many of the routes in this book.
- **Practice your mountain skills:** Practice your ski skills at one of Colorado's many ski areas—you can usually ski more vertical in an hour than you can in a full day of backcountry skiing. Hiring an instructor is a great way to take your skiing to the next level.
- **Take a wilderness first-aid course:** Finally, a wilderness first-aid course is also a wise decision that your backcountry partners will surely appreciate in the event of an accident.

EQUIPMENT

While researching this book, we perused a number of other guidebooks and if there was one thing they all had in common, it was that the equipment introduction was hopelessly outdated. Therefore, we won't be spending much time telling you what pieces of equipment to get because the advice will seem utterly antiquated in just a few years' time. Besides, differences in skiing styles and abilities play a big part in gear choices as well.

Clothing

The type of clothes you wear somewhat depends on how your body copes in a cold environment, but the general idea is to dress in layers. Oftentimes a thin polypro or wool base layer is more than enough while climbing a mountain, even when the temperatures are in the single digits. One of the nicest layers to carry in your pack is a lightweight down coat with a hood, no matter if it's midwinter, spring, or even summer. It's amazing how much warmth this layer can give you, and you'll be glad to have it should you unexpectedly spend a night out or go into shock after an accident.

The Basics and the Ten Essentials

For the purposes of the route introductions, "the basics" are skis (or snowboard), ski boots (or snowboard boots), poles, skins, backpack, avalanche shovel, beacon, probe, helmet (skiing or climbing, depending on route), gloves and/or mittens, hat, sun hat, cell phone, and the following Ten Essentials:

- Navigation (maps, compass, GPS device)
- Sun protection (sunscreen, sunglasses, sun hat)
- Insulation (extra clothing layers)
- Illumination (headlamp and spare batteries)
- First-aid kit
- Fire (firestarter and matches)
- Repair kit (including multitool)
- Nutrition (extra food)

Enjoying some of the moderate slopes at Wolf Creek Pass (Route 100)

- Hydration (extra water)
- Emergency shelter

Optional Basics

Optional basics would include a personal locator beacon, airbag backpack, and ski crampons. We have become quite accustomed to using airbag packs, and while they are a bit heavier and more expensive, we feel as though it is a small price to pay to stack the deck slightly more in our favor in the event of a slide. (An airbag is an inflatable backpack that, thanks to physics, makes it more likely for someone caught in an avalanche to end up on top of the slide when it stops. Visit your local shop for more information or even a demonstration.) Ski crampons attach to your bindings and can make springtime ascents on hard moderate snow far easier.

A skier kicks his way up CC Rider Couloir (Route 41).

Crampons and Ice Axe

Beyond the basics, many of the routes in this book suggest bringing crampons and an ice axe. We strongly recommend using aluminum crampons. The weight differential is significant compared to steel ones, and the downsides are minimal in Colorado where the probability of finding long stretches of water ice is low. Trust us; it's a lot easier to throw aluminum crampons in your pack "just in case" than it is for the steel variety. When choosing an ice axe, we suggest an axe with a straight spike rather than one that is formed at a 45-degree angle. On some of the more moderate routes, you may want to use a whippet-style pole rather than an ice axe. Whippets are ski poles with the pick end of an ice axe attached at the grip. Just remember that ice axes are more functional overall, so don't get caught bringing a knife to a gun fight.

Routefinding Tools

Maps: We have made every effort to provide accurate and worthwhile maps for every route in this book, but we recommend that you also carry a map with you. USGS quadrangles are listed for every route and can be purchased online or at your favorite local backcountry shop. Keep in mind that many of these USGS quads have not been updated in years, so trail locations may have changed significantly. GPS maps utilize these same quads, so your GPS device may have outdated information as well.

Online route-planning tools: Online, two excellent resources when route planning include caltopo.com and Google Earth. Both of these tools allow you to draw routes, save those routes, and even print them out. As an added bonus, they're both great ways to find new terrain if you're looking to get out and explore.

Smartphones versus GPS devices: When we started researching routes for this book, we were using a GPS device by a well-known GPS manufacturer. By the end, however, we were mostly using our smartphones because we found them to be more user friendly. Our phone app of choice is Gaia, and it's worth every penny. A pro account allows you to do slope-angle overlays to see how steep the terrain is and, therefore, helps you travel safer in avalanche terrain. The downside of using your phone as your GPS device is battery usage, especially if you're also taking photos, checking emails, and tweeting your ascent as you go. Our advice is to download the maps at home, and then switch your phone to airplane mode while you tour. Our phones allow spare batteries to be used, so we can instantly go from 1 percent power to 100 percent. If you don't have a phone that supports extra batteries, you will want to carry an extra battery pack to ensure you don't lose your GPS capabilities. As with any electronic device, make sure to keep your phone away from your beacon, as electronic devices can interfere with avalanche beacons.

Equipment weight: There has been a trend in recent years for backcountry skiers to pay extra attention to the weight of their gear. While there are benefits to lightweight gear, we feel they are often exaggerated and many skiers can do themselves a favor by not counting the number of grams of every last piece of gear in their kit. If a pair of skis or boots is a couple of ounces lighter, but the performance is cut by 50 percent, is that really worth it—especially over the course of an eight- or ten-hour day? In our view, the answer is a resounding no. Go with gear that works and performs, instead of gear that looks good on a scale. Finding the perfect balance between weight and performance is key.

PERMITS AND FEES

Generally speaking, day-use permits are not needed for most of the routes in this book; however, rules change all the time. Overnight usage may require a permit, especially in wilderness areas or Rocky Mountain National Park. You will find useful listings in Resources at the back of this book to help you determine whether or not a permit is needed for your intended destination.

Most of our public lands do not require fees. However, certain state-run forests as well as national parks require admittance or parking fees. If fees are associated with accessing a route, these fees are discussed in the introduction of each route.

ROAD CONDITIONS

For general highway conditions, consult Colorado's Department of Transportation website (www.cotrip.org). This site is especially useful to determine highway openings, such as Independence Pass.

Many of the routes in this guidebook do not have an exact trailhead. In many cases, where you start will depend on snowmelt and/or how quickly crews clear the roads in the springtime. Also, many of the routes are most easily accessed with a four wheel drive (4WD) vehicle. While we have done our best to describe the difficulty of reaching a trailhead, road conditions can change quickly. Therefore, we suggest planning on starting below many of the trailheads, and if you are able to drive to our suggested trailhead or even farther up the road, consider it a bonus.

Road information status can sometimes be found by calling the county road department or the local forest service. In our experience, this information may still be difficult to ascertain depending on whom you talk to. Some people will know exactly what road you're asking about, while others will have no clue. Other times, the information is just plain wrong. Too often we've shown up to find roads open that we were told were not, and vice versa. If at all possible, try to reach the trailhead the day before, so you

Stream crossings in spring can be quite treacherous.

A skier enjoys perfect conditions in the Eureka Couloir (Route 64).

will know your starting point. You may even need to change plans or go with a super-early alpine start if you are unable to reach the starting point you were hoping for.

MOUNTAIN SAFETY

Every single route in this book has some degree of avalanche danger, and Colorado has a notoriously dangerous and tricky snowpack. Avalanche education never stops—there is always more to learn, no matter how experienced you are. Learning from mentors, reading avalanche-related literature, and being an observant traveler are all great ways to hone your skills.

- **Avalanche information:** Avalanche information can most easily be found at Colorado Avalanche Information Center (CAIC, http://avalanche.state.co.us/). In the Crested Butte zone, the Crested Butte Avalanche Center (CBAC) has its own excellent website (http://cbavalanchecenter.org/). Like the CAIC, the CBAC provides thought-provoking discussion in its daily forecasts, while also servicing an area known for highly variable snowfall. (It isn't uncommon for the town of Crested Butte to receive an inch or two while the mountains to the west receive two feet.)
- **Avalanche forecasts:** We make it a habit of reading the online CAIC avalanche forecasts every day. These forecasts provide details on the

day's avalanche dangers and problems as well as useful travel advice if you're traveling in the mountains. Their discussions are often filled with helpful tips and tricks, and the website has other useful resources, such as user-submitted observations, weather stations, and weather forecasts. Reading the forecasts on a daily basis is far more helpful for developing an understanding of how the snowpack is progressing through the course of the week or even the year, rather than simply checking the CAIC on your way to the mountains.

- **Weather forecasts:** CAIC and CBAC websites tend to have very good weather forecasts. Beyond that, our favorite weather information comes from the National Oceanic and Atmospheric Administration (NOAA) website (www.weather.gov). NOAA offers point forecasts, so you can plan your ski tour based on the forecast for the exact area you're heading to. Additionally, reading the "forecast discussion" tab is an excellent way to learn more about meteorology.
- **Timing:** We have suggested certain months that we feel may be ideal for every route, but every winter will be different. Snow and avalanche conditions fluctuate daily, and sometimes on a minute-to-minute basis. You'll have to use your best judgment. For many of the routes in this book you should wait for springtime after the snow has consolidated into a more manageable and predictable snowpack. With a solid springtime snowpack, your main concern will be timing, for both snow quality and avoiding wet avalanches. Following a good overnight refreeze, easterly aspects tend to warm up first, and you should be off of those early in the morning. South faces will "corn up" next, followed by west-facing terrain. With a handful of routes in this book, you can even follow the sun around the compass for a full day of skiing!

TRAIL ETIQUETTE AND BACKCOUNTRY ETHICS

Respecting other trail users is the simplest way to practice trail etiquette. Following the golden rule is a good strategy in life and in the backcountry. At the trailhead, this means keeping your volume levels at a minimum while other groups are getting ready for their day. A friendly discussion is never a bad idea, either, in case multiple groups are heading to the same area. No one wants another group endangering their lives in avalanche terrain.

Our public lands are just that—public. This means that you may encounter other user groups in the backcountry, including snowmobilers, fat bikers, and snowshoers. In most cases outside of wilderness areas, these other groups have just as much right to be there as a backcountry skier. So smile, wave, and be courteous. Who knows, maybe you'll even get a ride from an equally friendly snowmobiler. If you're accessing terrain on snowshoes or a fat bike, remember that those activities can quickly wreck a skin track, so make your own trail.

Descending the lower stretches of the long Cristo Couloir on Quandary Peak (Route 38)

On the environmental side, be conscientious about what you're doing. Carpool to the trailhead whenever possible, especially in areas where parking lot crowding can endanger future access. Follow Leave No Trace principles (https://lnt.org/). Human waste is one of the biggest problems in the backcountry, so try to "take care of business" before you reach the trailhead, and pack it out, including your toilet paper, if you have to go.

Winter is a difficult time for most animals in the mountain environment. Try to leave a wide berth so you'll be less likely to disturb wildlife. Human food may be tasty, but don't feed the wildlife, which trains wild animals to develop bad habits. Pack out everything you pack in. Alpine tundra is fragile—after all, it's a short growing season. Try to travel on snow or established trails above tree line, and if you must travel over tundra, stay on rocks as much as possible.

Respecting Private Land and Mining Claims

Mining is part of the rich history of Colorado. Because of this, the remains of many mines and claims can still be found scattered throughout the mountains of our state.

The Mining Law of 1872 set the standards for turning federal lands into mining claims. There are two types of claims: patented and unpatented. Patented mining claims are private land. Unpatented claims are land that is leased, where mining is permitted.

Descending the Sheep Chute (Route 89)

A number of mining claims exist scattered throughout wilderness areas, Bureau of Land Management land, and Forest Service lands where many of our routes pass through. We have taken care to label any claims that we are aware of on the maps, and we include mining claim boundaries if we know them.

It would be impractical for us to look up every mining claim to determine whether the claim is patented or unpatented, thus determining if the mine is technically private property or not. To be safe, it is better to assume that all mining claims are patented and, therefore, private property.

However, many of these mines have also been abandoned and there is no sign of active use. It's common for backcountry skiers to be completely unaware they are even passing over a mining claim as all signs have been erased, especially under the cover of snow. When mines are abandoned and owners seem to have forgotten that their property even exists, then determining whether these mining claims are public or private starts to become more difficult.

To complicate matters more, there are also other cases where commonly used trails and climbers' routes pass right through mining claims. Our routes are not immune to this.

While we have taken care to try to plan our routes so that they do not pass over mining claims, it is not always possible to do so, nor does it always make sense. If a route passes through a mining claim that we know of, we will bring it to your attention and you can make the decision to adjust the route accordingly.

However, should you see any signs of someone residing on a mining claim, or observe any "No Trespassing" signs, we advise you to consider that land as private property. Do not trespass on their land.

Last, where applicable, we have mentioned any active mines that are located near our routes and described how best to avoid them in your tour. Please obey private property laws and adhere to any easement rules that have been placed on these mining claims.

HOW TO USE THIS BOOK

THIS BOOK IS INTENDED TO BE USED by backcountry skiers and snowboarders who have an avalanche education. In order to simplify wording, we have used the term "backcountry skiers" to encompass *both* backcountry skiers and backcountry snowboarders.

ORGANIZATION

This book is organized based on mountain ranges. Some ranges are larger than others, so when necessary, we have divided or combined mountain ranges. Generally speaking, we organized the routes in each range from north to south. Terms that you may see mentioned in this book include "fourteeners," which refers to mountains over 14,000 feet in elevation, as well as "centennials," which refers to the highest one hundred summits in Colorado.

Naming

The naming of peaks is somewhat subjective compared to many other geological features like lakes or rivers. If a peak is named on a USGS map, we have used that as the name. However, some peaks are listed as points on USGS maps but have more common unofficial names. If a peak has a name, unofficial or not, we have included it.

Routes that lie on peaks also have names. Some of these are not well documented or may vary depending on the source. In this case, we have often gone with the name that is most common in the backcountry skiing and ski mountaineering community.

Route Selection

All routes in this book are intended for backcountry skiers and snowboarders. Many of the routes in this book would be unsafe for alpine climbers wanting to glissade, as they are often too steep or do not have a clean line on the descent.

We have included a variety of routes to encompass many different types of backcountry skiers as well as the conditions as they change throughout the season. Some routes are intended for midwinter, while others are best sought out in spring. Additionally, we have a wide range of route lengths within the book.

Note about Elevation Figures

Elevation figures cannot possibly always be to the exact foot. Furthermore, reported elevations for peaks have changed through the years as technology has improved. Our data was gathered based on USGS maps, CalTopo maps, Google Earth imagery, and GPS waypoints. It is not uncommon for certain points to vary by twenty feet or more between resources. In our route descriptions, we have stated elevations to the best of our knowledge. But you may find that they vary slightly with your resources and devices.

ROUTE INFORMATION

Each route contains useful information to help you compare routes and plan your trip.

Starting Elevation: The elevation at the parking lot or trailhead. For some routes, access can vary depending on snow cover. In this case, starting elevation is given at the most common access point.

High Point: The uppermost point of the ski tour, which may or may not be at the summit of a particular peak. Some peaks are not always skiable from the summit due to lack of snow cover. In this case, further details are usually included in the route description.

Vertical Gain/Loss: Usually calculated by the difference between the high point and the low point. However, some complex routes may have a descent in the ascent or a climb in the descent. In this case, those additional climbs are included. Since elevations are somewhat inexact, we have often rounded this number to the nearest fifty feet.

Ascent Distance: The approximate mileage from the starting point to the high point. If multiple ascent options are given, we have included distances for the alternate ascent routes in the route description. Since distances can often change with small variations in route, distances have been rounded to the nearest half mile.

Descent Distance: The approximate mileage from the high point back to the starting point. In many of our routes, the best descent is different from the ascent. For this reason, we felt the need to separate the descent distance from the ascent. Similar to the ascent distance, we have included distances for alternate descent routes in the route description and have rounded distances to the nearest half mile.

Time: The approximate roundtrip time. This time is very much a generalization and will depend on snow conditions, snow cover, fitness level, acclimatization, weather, number of stops, group dynamics, group size, ability to follow the route, and many other factors. It also does not include the time it may take to do multiple laps or for any prolonged stops. Our times assume that you can climb at a rate of about 1000 feet of elevation in an hour and cover about 2 miles an hour on approaches.

Ski Skills: Based on the typical maximum slope angle of the route. Slope angle can change depending on melting patterns, winds, weather patterns, and how the snow fills in to the line, especially at the entrance, so descriptions are approximate.

Easy: less than 30 degrees

Moderate: between 30 and 34 degrees

Difficult: between 35 and 45 degrees

Very Difficult: between 46 and 50 degrees

Extremely Difficult: over 50 degrees

Please note that conditions can make routes appear easier or more difficult. For example, an icy 40-degree slope can quickly become very difficult or even extremely difficult. A powder day can make the same 40-degree slope seem moderate. Exposure can also add to the relative difficulty of a route. The descriptions given are based on average conditions for the optimal months listed.

Fitness Level: A measure of the effort required for the tour. In general, we have categorized routes based on vertical gain as well as distance. However, some routes have been bumped up to higher levels due to steepness of the route.

Not very strenuous: up to 2000 feet of vertical gain or under 4 miles total distance

Moderately strenuous: from 2000 to 3500 feet of vertical gain or between 4 and 8 miles total distance

Strenuous: from 3500 to 5000 feet of vertical gain or between 8 and 11 miles total distance

Very strenuous: from 5000 to 6000 feet of vertical gain or between 11 and 14 miles total distance

Extremely strenuous: more than 6000 feet of vertical gain or over 14 miles total distance

Technical Skills: Describes the difficulty, typically on the ascent. But the rankings can also apply to a descent if a downclimb or rappel is needed.

Low: requires basic skinning and ski touring

Moderate: involves technical skinning or easy bootpacking. Ice axe and crampons may be advisable for some climbers during certain conditions

High: steeper bootpacking where an ice axe and crampons are recommended. Possible class 3 terrain. Strong navigation skills needed

Very High: requires the use of an ice axe and crampons. May include class 4 climbing or a rappel. Potentially difficult routefinding

Gear: Describes the gear that is typically needed for the route. In most cases "The basics" are required. (See The Basics and the Ten Essentials listed above.)

Best Months: The best months to ski the route in an average year. Typically, this is when the route is in its best condition. This can vary depending on the amount of snowfall or average temperatures in a given year. When describing these months, we have also taken into consideration typical seasonal snowpack stability as well as the best times for access.

USGS Map: The recommended USGS quadrangle. In the case that the tour is not encompassed within one map, we will list all quadrangles needed.

Introduction: Each tour description begins with an overview of the route and why it is appealing to backcountry skiers.

Getting There: This section describes how to get to the starting point of each tour. In many cases, we have given descriptions from a nearby town, ski area, or other significant point. Access can vary depending on season, and we have described any nuances for each route.

The Route: In this section, we describe the ascent and descent. In many cases, there is no set trail, and routes can vary. We have done our best to try to describe each route so that average backcountry users can follow the tour, meaning that it is a general description that includes details when necessary, but not every detail. Some routes are complex and difficult to describe. We always recommend checking the route descriptions ahead of time with additional topographic maps and Google Earth imagery to gain a better understanding of the routefinding involved in each tour.

Route Maps: The maps in this book are intended to help guide you, but they are very general and are by no means intended to be your sole source of navigation. While the maps we've included give a good overview of the route and surrounding area, they lack detailed topographic information and are limited in scope. We highly recommend that you purchase or download the USGS topographic maps for the area you plan to visit to act as a supplement for the maps in the book. We also recommend using them in conjunction with a compass or GPS device, especially for more complex and involved routes.

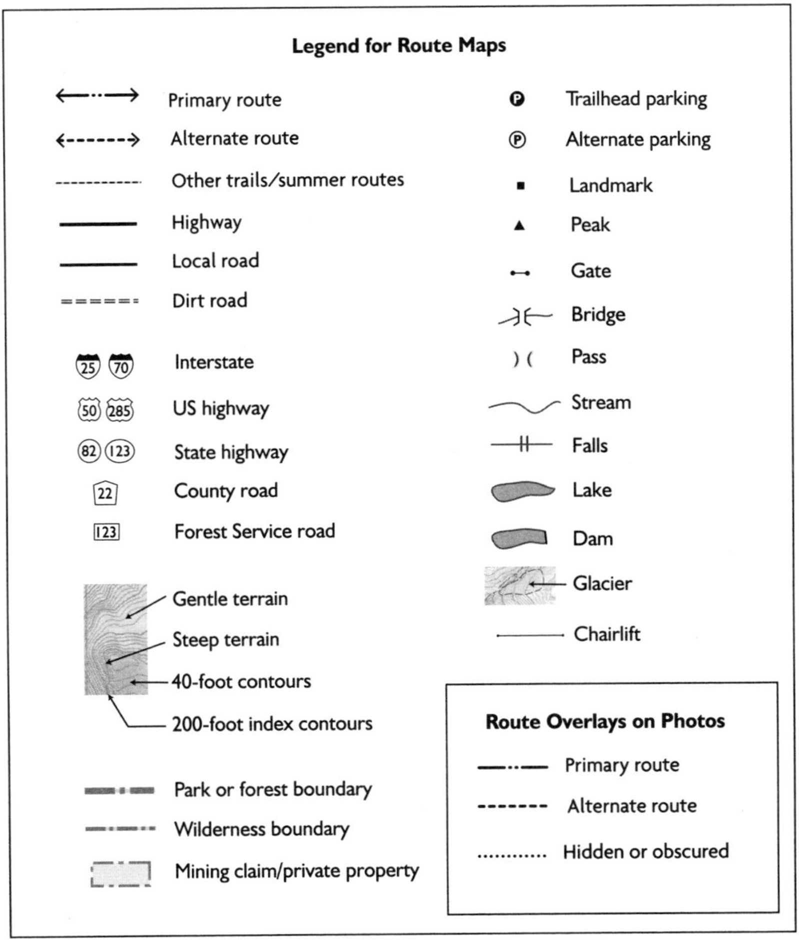

Extra Credit

Backcountry skiing is a progressive sport. As you use this guidebook, you will undoubtedly hone in on your planning and routefinding skills. The next step in that progression is to begin planning to ski routes where the details are lesser known. The Extra Credit alternatives mentioned in this book are for this purpose. Our goal is to entice you but leave the research, details, and route planning up to you! We hope you will take this opportunity to grow your skills.

Opposite: Dead trees on Little Agnes (Route 3) make for a surreal scene.

PARK RANGE, FLAT TOPS, AND GRAND MESA

THE PARK RANGE, FLAT TOPS, AND GRAND MESA are distinct regions, but for the purposes of this book's organization, we have combined them.

The Park Range encompasses what would generally be considered the Steamboat Springs zone, at least as far as skiing is concerned. While the peaks of the Park Range aren't lofty by Colorado standards, the range is known for its prodigious amounts of snow. When storms roll in from the northwest and favor the northern part of the state, the Steamboat area will often have the most snow in Colorado. With its slopes full of trees, the combination makes the Park Range a powder-hound mecca. Some of the highest peaks in the area, such as those found in the Zirkel Wilderness are difficult to access without a snowmobile or an overnight trip until late in the spring, but a trip here is full of rewards for the adventurer. Too often overlooked due to the lack of alpine summits, the Park Range and the welcoming western town of Steamboat Springs are worth the trip.

Like the Park Range, the Flat Tops receive heavy snowfall with storms favoring the north. As the name suggests, the Flat Tops feature flat summits, but surprisingly rugged cirques guard the mesas, often capped with cornices. The cirques usually feature a couloir or two, and while the vertical tends to be short, the remoteness and unique topography make the area worth a trip. Heavy snow stays later into the summer than the modest 12,000-foot summits would suggest. Few backcountry skiers even know where the Flat Tops are located, let alone can claim to have made turns on them. For that reason alone, a trip to the Flat Tops is highly recommended. And if someone asks, you can tell them the Flat Tops are located north of Glenwood Springs, east of Meeker, and southwest of Steamboat Springs.

The Grand Mesa is often described as the largest flat-topped mountain in the world. Whether that is the case or not, it certainly qualifies as one of the most interesting zones in Colorado. Floating high above the desert near Grand Junction, a ski tour on the Grand Mesa can end with some mountain biking in the desert or perhaps wine tasting at the vineyards of Palisade. Grand Mesa receives more modest snowfall than the Flat Tops or the Park Range, although it is in line with most other areas of Colorado.

1 Hahns Peak: West Side

Starting Elevation	8700 feet
High Point	10,839 feet
Vertical Gain/Loss	2200+ feet
Ascent Distance	3+/- miles
Descent Distance	3+ miles
Time	2.5 to 4.5 hours
Ski Skills	Easy with options up to difficult
Fitness Level	Moderately strenuous
Technical Skills	Low
Gear	The basics
Best Months	December to mid-March
USGS Map	Hahns Peak

Although this summit stands nearly 200 feet short of 11,000 feet, Hahns Peak is one of the most iconic features of northern Routt County, or North Routt. Donning a nearly perfect cone-shaped appearance, Hahns is capped with a geological laccolith that keeps the upper half of the mountain as a dominant feature in the landscape and makes this peak particularly inviting to skiers. Which range Hahns Peak lies in is a subject of debate. Some sources list it as the easternmost point of the Elkhead Range, while others classify Hahns Peak as part of the Park Range.

Visitors to the summit of Hahns Peak can take a closer look at the fire-lookout tower that was originally built in 1912 and reconstructed in 1942. The tower still stands today as a historic structure and is regularly maintained.

Dominating the North Routt landscape, Hahns Peak is actually a fairly simple ski. Options for more difficult routes are included for those who want more of a challenge.

GETTING THERE

From the north end of Steamboat Springs on US Highway 40, turn right (north) onto County Road 129 toward the town of Clark. Follow CR 129 north for about 29 miles, passing through the small towns of Clark and Hahns Peak Village to the town of Columbine.

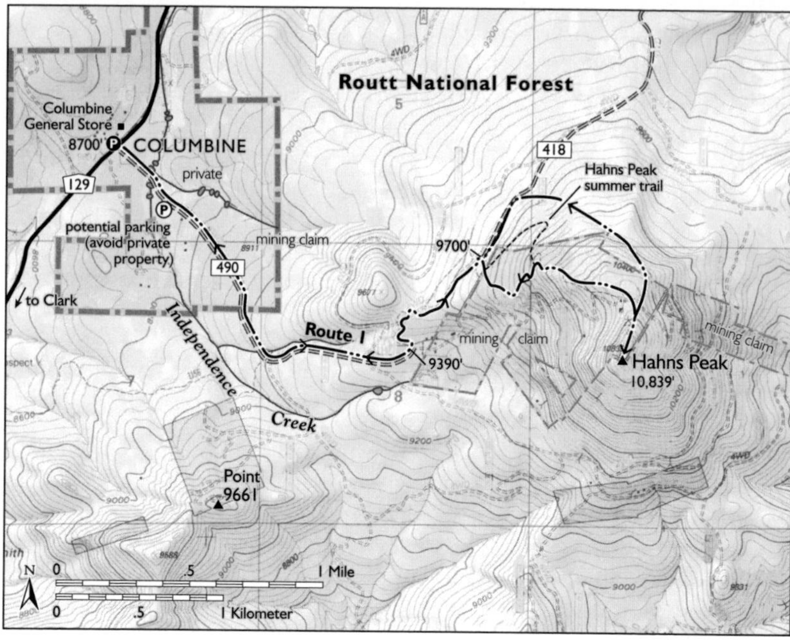

In the winter, you may want to park in Columbine, perhaps at the General Store. Alternatively, from Columbine turn right (southeast) onto CR 29 (Forest Road 490). The road is typically plowed here for about the first half mile. You may find some pull-outs where you can park, but there is no established parking here. Please make sure to respect private property when you choose your place to park. Later in the winter, lower segments of the road can be melted out and you may be able to drive farther up FR 490.

THE ROUTE

Hahns Peak is laden with mining claims and private property. While easements exist to allow access to the summit, please be respectful of any private property signs you may encounter.

From the town of Columbine, travel southeast and then east on FR 490 about 1.5 miles to the Hahns Peak summer trailhead at roughly 9390 feet. This trail sees use in winter as well, so you will likely find that the snow is compacted here. Follow this trail as it heads northeast up the mountain. Around 9700 feet, you may find it more efficient to leave the trail and begin heading more directly east up the northwest slopes of Hahns Peak. At tree line (10,300 feet), you'll find the ridge beginning to narrow and the route to the summit becomes obvious. Follow the ridge southeast, and then south, to reach the summit. Enjoy the views and the shelter of the lookout tower!

Descent. Generally you'll want to descend your skin track. However, as you reach tree line, you may find better skiing in the trees that face more directly north. If you choose this option, descend to about 9700 feet where you'll find FR 418. Follow this road southwest, and it will meet back up with the summer trail. Follow your ascent route back to your vehicle.

Extra Credit. For those wanting a little more challenge, another option is to ski the obvious east-facing avalanche gully directly off the summit. Be wary of possible cornices at the top as well as avalanche conditions. Make proper snow stability assessments before you drop in. Descend this about 1500 feet to an elevation between 9400 or 9200 feet. Then reascend through the trees and ridge looker's left of the gully to once again gain the summit, which will add approximately 1.5 miles to your tour. Follow the instructions in the paragraph above to return to your vehicle.

2 Farwell Mountain: South Face and Chutes

Starting Elevation	8060 feet
High Point	10,860 feet
Vertical Gain/Loss	3000 feet
Ascent Distance	3.5+/- miles
Descent Distance	4 miles
Time	3 to 5 hours
Ski Skills	Easy with options up to difficult
Fitness Level	Moderately strenuous
Technical Skills	Low
Gear	The basics
Best Months	December to mid-March
USGS Maps	Farwell Mountain and Hahns Peak

Standing just southeast of Hahns Peak (Route 1) and only 20 feet less in elevation, Farwell Mountain is a little less noticeable than its more dominant neighbor. Yet Farwell Mountain is actually a much broader mountain, with many backcountry skiing options, and it does not have the private property issues that plague Hahns Peak. Farwell has a variety of line choices that accommodate a wide range of conditions and suit the desires of backcountry skiers of many levels.

GETTING THERE

From the north end of Steamboat Springs on US Highway 40, turn right (north) onto County Road 129 toward the town of Clark. Follow CR 129 north, passing through the small town of Clark. After about 22 miles (6 miles north of Clark), turn right (east) onto CR 209. After 1.3 miles, you'll encounter an intersection. Stay right, remaining on CR 209 toward Pearl Lake State Park. Travel another 0.6 mile to a parking area with a fee station just before a hill that is the winter parking zone. A fee is required to park here. At the time of writing, it was $7 for one vehicle. As

A skier enjoys a fun zone on Farwell Mountain's south chutes.

snow melts later in the year, it may be possible to drive your vehicle farther up the road in the park.

THE ROUTE

From the winter parking area, head east up the road a few feet. Then leave the road, continuing directly east, up to a small ridge, which flattens. Here you'll likely see some yurts, which are available for rent (see Resources), and you should also be able to see Pearl Lake in front of you. In the distance, you'll have a good glimpse of Farwell Mountain. If the lake is adequately frozen, you may want to cross over it in a northeast direction. Otherwise, follow along the shores of Pearl Lake to the north and east. The property boundaries of the state park are tight here, so make sure to not veer too far away from the shoreline.

At the northeast corner of the lake, you should see an obvious gully that continues northeast. Follow this gully upward. Be careful not to go to the slightly more east gully of Lester Creek if you can avoid it. The northeast gully provides more efficient travel.

Around 8600 feet, the gully will begin to fade and you'll see the southwest slopes of Farwell Mountain before you. Ascend through the aspen forest, continuing to travel northeast. You'll reach tree line around 10,000 feet where you'll see a ridge in front of you. Ascend to this ridge, and then turn east to reach the summit.

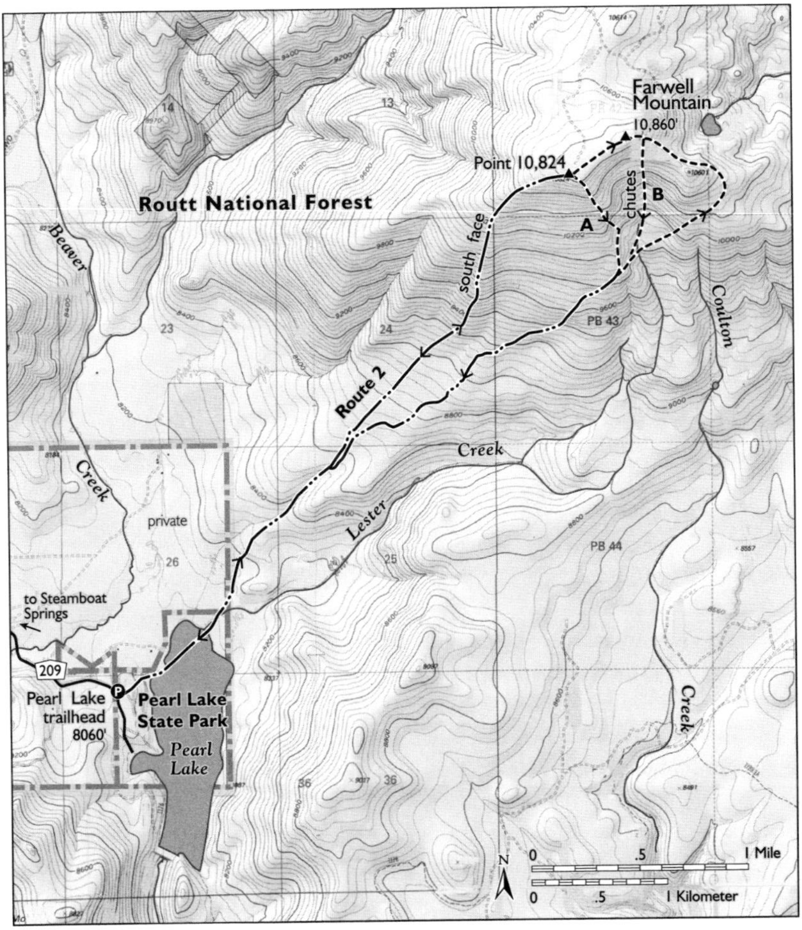

On USGS maps, the summit is labeled as a point with an elevation of 10,824 feet. But the true summit lies just a little farther northeast at 10,860 feet. Reaching the true summit may not be necessary depending on the line you want to ski. You may see some snowmobilers at the top as there is a road to the north that they use to ascend to the top.

Descent. The primary route of your descent is the same as your ascent route. The aspen grove has some fantastic skiing! This is also the easiest route.

Alternate Descent A. From Point 10,824, ski slightly southeast into some chutes that go through rock bands. Descend to roughly 9900 or 10,000 feet before beginning to traverse to your right. Traverse right as you descend across Farwell's south slopes to eventually meet up with your ascent route. Follow your ascent route back to the winter parking at Pearl Lake State Park. This route is moderate to difficult and is approximately 0.25 mile longer than the ascent route. Take into account the southeast-facing nature of this route and the potential for wet slides before you drop in.

Alternate Descent B. If conditions are stable and it's not too late in the day, you may want to descend via the south chutes, which has terrain in the mid-40-degree range. From the true summit at 10,860, descend into one of the many chutes that surround a small bowl just south of the summit. Descend to about 9900 or 10,000 feet. From here, you have a choice to go back up and lap the area or continue down. If you want to do another lap, traverse skier's left into the trees. Make your skin track up the ridge, looker's right of the bowl you just descended. This extra lap will add approximately 2 miles to your tour. If you want to continue down, from about 9950 feet, begin traversing right as you descend across Farwell's south slopes to meet up with your ascent route. This option adds about 0.5 mile to your tour. Follow your ascent route back to the winter parking at Pearl Lake State Park.

3 Little Agnes: West and Northeast Sides

Starting Elevation	7670 feet
High Point	11,497 feet
Vertical Gain/Loss	4000+ feet
Ascent Distance	10.75+/- miles
Descent Distance	10.75+ miles
Time	8 to 12 hours or multiday
Ski Skills	Easy with options up to difficult
Fitness Level	Extremely strenuous
Technical Skills	Moderate
Gear	The basics
Best Months	December to April
USGS Maps	Mount Zirkel and Farwell Mountain

The peak of Little Agnes straddles the boundary for the Mount Zirkel Wilderness. This wilderness area is known for two primary peaks: Mount Zirkel and Big Agnes. But in the shadows of the "bigs" stand the little, and Little Agnes is one magnificent mountain that is packed with a bunch of good ski lines on all sides.

The forest on the west side of Little Agnes was plagued by beetle kill, fires, and blowdowns in the late 1990s and early 2000s. This misfortune transformed the forest but has created a magnificent skiing zone as it recovers. With perfectly spaced trees for making fast turns, this area has been called Burn Trees or Spooky Trees by some.

Other side aspects of Little Agnes provide more challenges. The north and northeast aspects provide steeper terrain that ranges between 40 and 50 degrees. These lines should only be skied in stable conditions, but the challenge awaits if the timing is right.

Curiously, USGS and Forest Service maps have two peaks that bear the name Little Agnes. The smaller one is located just northwest of Big Agnes and has an elevation of 11,233 feet. The larger one, and the one we are referring to for this route, has an elevation of 11,497 feet and lies directly west of Big Agnes.

The Spooky Trees on the west side of Little Agnes are a great ski in many conditions.

GETTING THERE

From the north end of Steamboat Springs on US Highway 40, turn right (north) onto County Road 129 toward the town of Clark. Follow CR 129 north for 18 miles, passing through the small town of Clark. At mile 18, turn right (east) onto Seedhouse Road (CR 64). Follow this road for 4.5 miles to a big parking lot at Hinman Park that is the winter parking area. You will also see buildings for a snowmobile tour company on the right. During late spring, it may be possible to drive farther up the road.

THE ROUTE

Little Agnes is quite remote during the winter road closure, but access becomes easier by a series of groomed roads. Some skiers may find it easier to use a snowmobile to travel on these groomed roads to improve access and efficiency. Keep in mind that snowmobiles are not allowed in wilderness areas.

From the winter parking area, continue east on the groomed road. Here the road name changes from CR 64 to Forest Road 400. Travel on this road for 3.7 miles and then take a hard left onto FR 433 (Lost Dog Road). At this intersection, you'll notice a few buildings that belong to the Forest Service, including the Seedhouse Guard Station, which can be rented. If you're not using a snowmobile, this cabin may make a good place to set up a home base to explore the area for a few days (see Resources).

From the intersection, travel about 3.5 miles north on the groomed FR 433 to an elevation of about 9000 feet. Here you'll see Little Agnes above you and to your right.

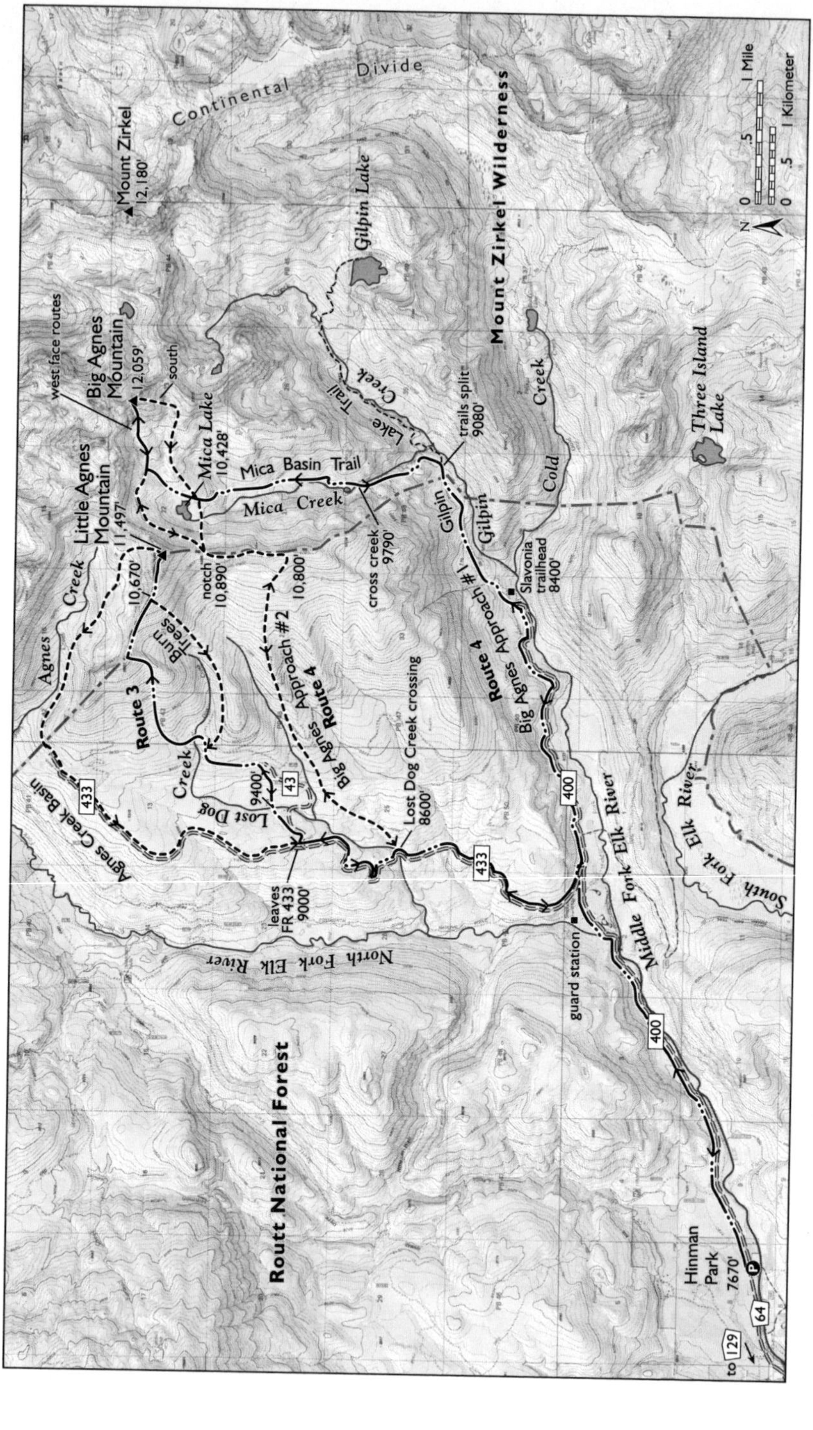

Continental Divide
Mount Zirkel 12,180'
Gilpin Lake
Mount Zirkel Wilderness
west face routes
Big Agnes Mountain 12,059'
south
Mica Lake 10,428'
Lake Creek Trail
Mica Basin Trail
Mica Creek
trails split 9080'
Creek
Cold
Little Agnes Mountain 11,497'
notch 10,890'
cross creek 9790'
Gilpin
Gilpin
Slavonia trailhead 8400'
10,670'
10,800'
Agnes
Creek
Burn trees
Approach #2
Route 4
Big Agnes
Approach #1
Route 4
Big Agnes
Route 3
Creek
Lost Dog
9400'
43
433
Agnes Creek Basin
Lost Dog Creek crossing 8600'
400
433
leaves FR 433 9000'
Middle Fork Elk River
South Fork Elk River
Three Island Lake
North Fork Elk River
guard station
400
Routt National Forest
Hinman Park 7670'
P
64
to 129
N
0 .5 1 Mile
0 .5 1 Kilometer

You may also notice signs of a road that is FR 43. At this point, you'll want to leave the road and begin heading northeast toward Little Agnes. Cross Lost Dog Creek around 9400 feet. Continue traveling northeast for a few hundred feet before veering more directly east toward the northwest ridge of Little Agnes. Stay to the looker's left of a ridge feature that comes down from the main ridge. Gain the ridge around 10,670 feet. Follow the ridge southeast another 0.75 mile and 830 vertical feet to the summit.

Descent. From the summit, you have plenty of descent options. Nearly all aspects of Little Agnes are skiable, two of which are discussed below.

The Burn Trees are a very desirable descent for many backcountry skiers. From the summit, you may find it best to descend down the northwest ridge a few hundred feet before descending down the west side and into the trees. You'll find plenty of selection in the Burn Trees just about anywhere off of the northwest ridge. From the ridge, enjoy your turns and ski to about 9500 feet near Lost Dog Creek. If you have the time, it's worth your while to go back up for another quick lap or two. From Lost Dog Creek, follow your ascent route back to the winter parking at Seedhouse Road.

Alternate Descent. The northern aspects, descending into Agnes Creek Basin, provide much more challenging terrain than the west side. Furthermore, Agnes Creek Basin can also be a great place to set up an overnight camp for a multiday trip, allowing more time to explore the area. On your ascent, you will be able to catch a glimpse of what the north side has to offer. However, this terrain tends to be wind loaded and laden with cornices. The easiest route that descends into Agnes Creek Basin is one that faces northeast. From the summit, follow the ridge slightly farther southeast, and then descend northeast into the upper reaches of the obvious Agnes Creek Basin. Eventually, the natural terrain will cause you to descend slightly north. At an elevation of 10,600 feet, begin traveling down the valley as it heads northwest. It's best not to follow the valley all the way to the bottom. You will save some time by contouring to your left around 9800 feet to wrap around the northwest ridge of Little Agnes to reach its west side around 9400 feet. Traverse as you descend, eventually meeting up with groomed FR 433 (Lost Dog Road). Follow this southwest to the intersection with FR 400 where you'll turn right (west). Follow FR 400 back to the winter parking at Seedhouse Road. This option will add just under 5 miles to your tour.

4 Big Agnes: West Face

Starting Elevation	7670 feet
High Point	11,970 to 12,059 feet
Vertical Gain/Loss	4500+ feet
Ascent Distance	11+/- miles
Descent Distance	11+ miles
Time	8 to 12 hours or multiday
Ski Skills	Difficult
Fitness Level	Extremely strenuous

Technical Skills : High
Gear : The basics, plus ice axe and crampons
Best Months : March to early June
USGS Maps : Mount Zirkel and Farwell Mountain

Ranking as the third highest summit in Routt County and the Park Range, Big Agnes is one of the most intriguing peaks of the Zirkel Wilderness. Skiable on nearly all sides, Big Agnes offers much terrain for backcountry skiers who are willing to go the distance to explore. From the summit, you can catch a glimpse of the west face of Mount Zirkel (the tallest peak in the Park Range at 12,180 feet) and the rest of the wilderness area and begin dreaming of more ski lines.

Big Agnes Mountain is the namesake of the popular outdoor retailer Big Agnes, whose home base is in nearby Steamboat Springs. Historians say the mountain was named in 1875 by the gold prospector Robert McIntosh, but why he chose the name remains a mystery.

Big Agnes Mountain can be easily linked with Little Agnes Mountain (Route 3) in a multiday trip. Mica Lake Basin makes a great area to set up a base camp for your explorations of Big Agnes Mountain.

GETTING THERE

From the north end of Steamboat Springs on US Highway 40, turn right (north) onto County Road 129 toward the town of Clark. Follow CR 129 north for 18 miles, passing through the small town of Clark. At mile 18, turn right (east) onto Seedhouse Road (CR 64). Follow this road for 4.5 miles to a big parking lot at Hinman Park that is the winter parking area. You will also see buildings for a snowmobile tour company on the right. During late spring, it may be possible to drive farther up the road.

THE ROUTE

Big Agnes is quite remote during the winter road closure, but access becomes easier by a series of groomed roads. Some skiers may find it easier to use a snowmobile to travel on these groomed roads to improve access and efficiency. Keep in mind that snowmobiles are not allowed in wilderness areas.

From the winter parking area, continue east on the groomed road. Here the road name changes from CR 64 to Forest Road 400. Travel on this road for 3.7 miles until you reach the intersection with Forest Road 433 (Lost Dog Road). At this intersection, you'll notice a few buildings that belong to the Forest Service, including the Seedhouse Guard Station, which can be rented. If you're not using a snowmobile, this cabin may make a good place to set up a home base to explore the area for a few days (see Resources).

From the intersection, you have two options for your approach described below. Both are about the same distance.

Approach 1: From the intersection of FR 400 and FR 433, continue east on FR 400 another 3 miles to the Slavonia trailhead at 8400 feet. Late in the spring you may be able to access this by car. Follow the Gilpin Lake Trail No. 1161 about 1.5 miles

east along the north side of Gilpin Creek to an elevation of 9080 feet. Here the trail will split. Take the left fork bearing north onto the Mica Basin Trail No. 1162. This trail climbs another 4 miles directly to Mica Lake at 10,428 feet. If the trail is difficult to follow due to snow cover, remain on the west side of Mica Creek. Travel north for about 1 mile to an elevation of 9790 feet. Cross Mica Creek here, and follow the creek north, remaining on the west side all the way to Mica Lake.

Approach 2: Take a hard left and travel north on groomed FR 433 for about 2 miles. Just before the road crosses Lost Dog Creek at an elevation of 8600 feet, leave the road and bear northeast. You will see Little Agnes before you, and you'll be heading for its south ridge. Follow a gentle ridgeline northeast and then east up to the ridge, staying clear of steeper terrain and rock bands that are obvious on the west side of the ridge. You should gain the ridge around 10,800 feet.

From the top of the ridge, you can see the west and south sides of Big Agnes. You can begin planning your ascent and descent routes from the ridge. However, you'll need to descend east-facing terrain into Mica Lake Basin first. To reach one of the safest places to descend into Mica Lake Basin, travel north on the ridge toward Little Agnes for about two-thirds of a mile to an obvious notch at 10,890 feet. Descend northeast into the basin. Bear in mind that the east-facing nature of this descent could make it more susceptible to wet slides earlier in the day, and this same aspect must be reclimbed on your return unless you descend via Mica Creek. It may be best to establish a multiday base camp in Mica Lake Basin to allow for more time for exploration and safer timing for your exit.

As you drop into Mica Lake Basin, you have two choices. The first is to descend all the way to the lake at 10,428 feet. The other is to descend only about 100 feet and then traverse northeast and then east, remaining around 10,800 feet. Both are close to the same distance, but the first involves more sidehill travel while the second involves more vertical gain and loss.

From Mica Lake Basin, ascend your intended descent route on the west side. There are three main routes on the west side, and not all of them lead to the summit. The center line leads to an obvious notch at 11,970 feet. The couloir-shaped line to the looker's left of that is sometimes called the Hourglass, for its obvious shape, and tops out at a rock band around 11,850 feet. A right traverse under this rock band will lead you to the same notch as the center line. Another option is looker's right of the center, leading to one of Big Agnes's twin summits. The last 200 vertical feet of this line involve climbing over an exposed cliff. You will not be able to reach the center line notch from here as there is a vertical cliff between them.

Alternatively, the south face can also be used to reach the summit. This is the easiest ascent and descent route on Big Agnes Mountain, considered a moderate ski with terrain typically remaining below 35 degrees.

All routes are very similar in distance, depending on your approach.

Descent. From the summit, admire the views of Mount Zirkel to the east and then descend your ascent route. If you are concerned about wet slides on east-facing zones, it may be best for you to avoid reascending the east-facing terrain on the south ridge of Little Agnes. Alternatively, you can exit by following Mica Creek south to Slavonia at 8400 feet. Use the ascent descriptions to help you on your descent route.

5 Flat Top Mountain: Northeast Slopes

Starting Elevation	9530 feet
High Point	12,354 feet at Flat Top summit to 12,145 at subpeak summit
Vertical Gain/Loss	2900 feet
Ascent Distance	5 miles
Descent Distance	5 miles
Time	5 to 7 hours
Ski Skills	Difficult
Fitness Level	Strenuous
Technical Skills	Moderate
Gear	The basics; ice axe and crampons may be needed
Best Months	April through June
USGS Map	Orno Peak

The namesake of the Flat Tops Wilderness, Flat Top Mountain, is the tallest peak of the Flat Tops subrange, standing at 12,354 feet. Often confused with Flattop Mountain in Rocky Mountain National Park, this peak is aptly named for its shape. The

Flat Tops are indeed an elevated plateau with steep sides in some places, and a very flat top.

A beetle infestation during the 1940s attacked many of the spruce and fir trees in the Flat Tops. Although cold weather killed the beetles in 1951, the event left many of the trees dead. As they fall, forest travel has become increasingly difficult. Traveling through the forest during snow cover is recommended over traveling through it when it is dry.

The Flat Tops are not a common area for backcountry skiers to venture. With access issues and an overall short vertical, many backcountry enthusiasts choose to spend their time elsewhere. But the Flat Tops also hold some great, albeit short, ski lines. For those wanting to explore or for more of an adventure, the Flat Tops hold the key. Flat Top Mountain is just a small preview of what the range has to offer.

GETTING THERE

This area of the Flat Tops is best accessed from the small town of Yampa, which is roughly 27 miles south of Steamboat Springs on Colorado Highway 131. From the south end of Yampa on CO 131, turn west onto County Road 7. At the turn, you will likely see a sign that says "National Forest Access." Continue west for about 6.5 miles until the road becomes dirt. During the winter months, you may find the road closure here at 8680 feet. Some backcountry users choose to travel the remaining miles of road via snowmobile during this time frame.

Typically in mid-April, the road opens up all the way to Yamcolo Reservoir. To inquire about road conditions, contact the Yampa Ranger District (see Resources). Past the typical winter road closure, the road name changes to Forest Road 900. Continue west on this road about 5 miles until you are near the bottom of the spillway for

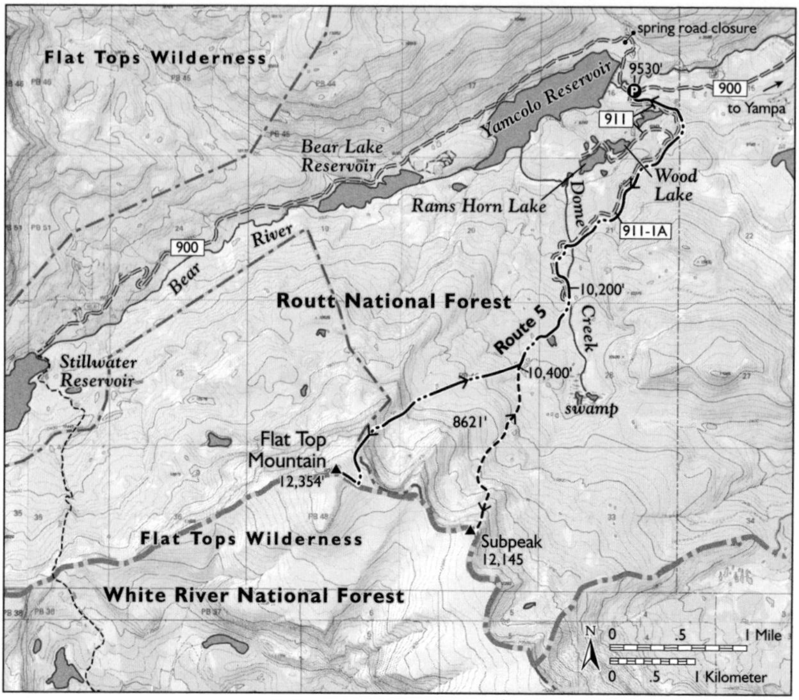

Yamcolo Reservoir. FR 900 will veer right to head north around the spillway, and the typical spring closure is about a half a mile from this corner. Just before FR 900 bears north, look for FR 911 to the left (south). You may see a sign referring to Rams Horn Lake. In spring, this road will typically have too much snow to drive on. When it is clear, it's a 4WD road. You'll likely want to park at the start of this road at 9530 feet.

Beginning in early June when the snow clears, the last 5 miles of FR 900 open all the way to its end at Stillwater Reservoir, allowing access to the summer trail for Flat Top Mountain.

THE ROUTE

From the intersection of FR 900 at FR 911 at 9350 feet, follow FR 911 as it heads southeast and then south. After traveling a little over half a mile, you'll encounter an intersection. A sharp right turn (north) keeping on FR 911 heads to Rams Horn Lake. Instead, continue straight, following FR 911-1A southwest. Two miles later, this road fades out at 10,200 feet, after running parallel with Dome Creek. Here, begin veering to your right in a southwest direction, likely passing a few different ponds along the way.

At 10,400 feet, you'll have to decide which route you want to take. The primary, ot summit route, requires both climbing and descending an east face above exposed cliffs with potentially dangerous cornices. In spring, these cornices commonly fall with warming temperatures and sun exposure. You'll want to make sure that your timing and conditions are right before attempting this route. Alternatively, a second route that typically does not go to the summit but heads toward Subpeak 12,145 keeps you on more north-facing terrain that is less susceptible to solar warming.

Clearings near 10,400 feet should provide you with a view of the summit of Flat Top Mountain that stands a few hundred feet above the obvious plateau. Look for a ridge that comes down from the plateau below the summit. The left side of the ridge is relatively gentle overall, but it is east facing. The right side of the ridge, which faces north, is laden with cliffs. You'll want to ascend the east-facing part of this ridge.

To reach the summit of Flat Top Mountain from 10,400 feet, begin heading southwest toward this ridge. By the time you reach tree line at 11,200 feet, you'll be just below the ridge. You'll likely want to plan your route up the ridge to avoid climbing cornices. However, this may cause you to veer farther to looker's left, causing you to climb over exposed cliffs. Take care to make sure that conditions are safe for an ascent with these high-risk consequences.

At 12,000 feet, you'll reach the plateau and have a good view of your route to the summit. You'll notice cornices on the east ridge. Veer slightly climber's left to gain the east ridge at a gentle point around 12,150 feet to avoid cornices. Follow the east ridge another 200 vertical feet westward to the summit.

Alternate Route. If conditions and timing are not right for an exposed east-facing ascent and descent, you can ski off Subpeak 12,145 of Flat Top, remaining mostly on north-facing terrain. Although this option provides a little less vertical, the distance remains the same. From viewpoints near 10,400 feet during the ascent, you can see the summit of Flat Top Mountain. From the plateau below the summit, there are a series of ridges and bowls that extend in either direction. You'll be aiming for the one that is two ridges looker's left (east) of the summit. The north-facing terrain off of this ridge does have cliffs, but there should be a snow route that avoids them.

From 10,400 feet, begin heading mostly south and slightly west to reach the bottom of this ridge. Aim a little more for the bowl that is on the looker's right of this ridge, as the safest way to access the ridge is actually from the bowl. Once in the bowl, head southeast to gain the ridge. Follow the north-facing snow route upward along the side of the ridge. You may find it difficult to reach the high point at 12,145 feet because of steep climbing for the last 200 feet and a cornice, which might be difficult to climb over. An obvious flat point on the ridge at 11,940 feet can make a good stopping point.

Descent. Reverse your ascent route.

6 Grand Mesa: Former Mesa Creek Ski Area

Starting Elevation: 8750 feet
High Point: 9750 feet

Vertical Gain/Loss	1000+ feet
Ascent Distance	0.7 to 1+ miles
Descent Distance	0.7 to 1+ miles
Time	1 to 2 hours
Ski Skills	Moderate
Fitness Level	Not very strenuous
Technical Skills	Low
Gear	The basics
Best Months	December to early March
USGS Map	Mesa Lakes

The Grand Mesa is one of the most prominent geologic features in Colorado, rising 6000 feet above the surrounding valleys. With such a rise in vertical feet and with the nearest range to the west quite far away, the Grand Mesa often recieves good snowfall. It's only natural that a ski area would be built here. In 1940, the Mesa Creek Ski Area was formed. The ski area expanded and featured two Poma lifts. But in the 1960s, frequent visitors were looking for more challenging terrain and more vertical to ski. In 1966, Powderhorn Mountain Resort, just 2.1 miles down the road, began spinning its lifts for the first time, thus closing the chapter to the ski area at Mesa Creek.

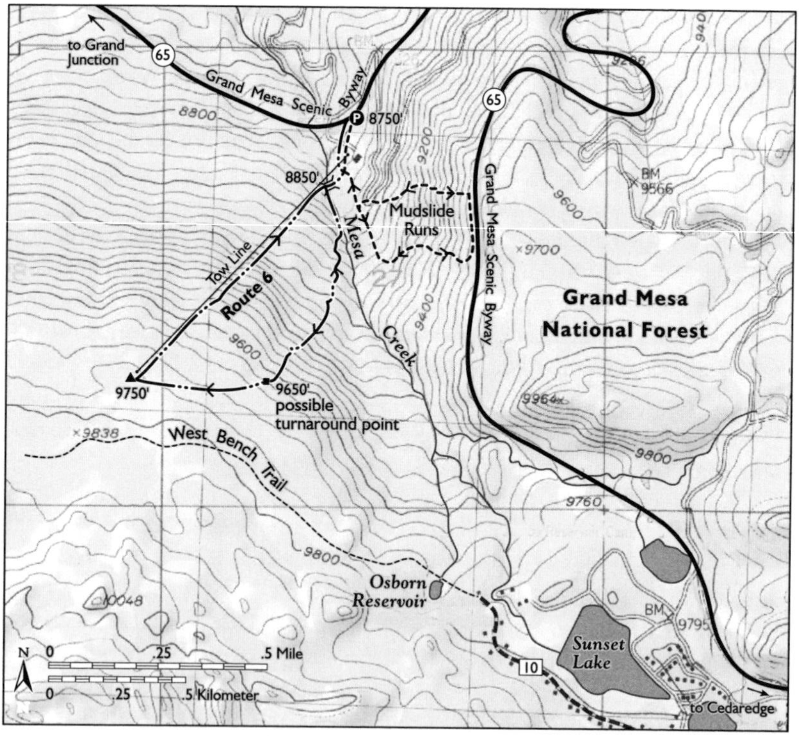

These days, the former Mesa Creek Ski Area is popular for local backcountry skiers. Its gentle slopes make great terrain for midwinter backcountry skiing.

GETTING THERE

The Grand Mesa stands just southeast of Grand Junction. If you are approaching the mesa from the north, take exit 49 off Interstate 70. Off the exit ramp, head south on Colorado Highway 65 (Grand Mesa Scenic Byway). Follow this 19 miles to the turnoff for Powderhorn Mountain Resort. Continue south and then east on CO 65 another 2.1 miles to the base of the old Mesa Creek Ski Area.

If approaching from the south, take CO 65 north 29 miles to the base of the old Mesa Creek Ski Area. It is about 11.7 miles past the Grand Mesa Lodge near Island Lake, which you'll pass along the way.

Park on the south side of the road at an obvious pullout near the base. You should see a Forest Service information kiosk near Mesa Creek.

THE ROUTE

From the base area, you'll have a good preview of the former ski area. When in doubt, just pick what you want to ski from below, and skin up to get there.

There are two main options for ski lines. First is to ski the northeast-facing terrain on the looker's right that surrounds the obvious old ski lift line. The second is to ski the northwest-facing terrain on the looker's left that tops out at the Grand Mesa

Scenic Byway. The terrain on the left is generally a bit steeper, but shorter, than the terrain on the right.

To access the northeast-facing terrain near the obvious old lift line, called the Tow Line, you'll have to cross Mesa Creek so that you are on its west side. Keep in mind that much of the creek sits in a deep ravine that often does not hold enough snow to cross. But there is one place near the bottom where you can cross more easily. To get there from the base, immediately head toward the bottom of the Tow Line. This will lead you directly to a point around 8850 where you can safely cross the creek. You may even find a primitive bridge there if it is not covered in snow.

Once across the creek, follow south along the west side of Mesa Creek for another one-third to a half mile to an elevation of 9000 feet. Here, begin veering looker's left, away from the creek and up the slopes in a southwest direction. Around an elevation of 9650 feet, you could stop and choose to turn around and ski your ascent route. Or you could head upward and farther right to the top of the Tow Line at 9750 feet.

Descent. You can either reverse your ascent route or descend the Tow Line to the base. Remember that you'll need to cross the creek at the bottom of the Tow Line at 8850 feet.

Alternate Route. To access the northwest-facing terrain, commonly referred to as the Mudslide Runs, follow south along the east side of the Mesa Creek for about a third of a mile to an elevation of 8950 feet. Here, begin leaving the creek and heading in a more southeast or east direction depending on what you want to ski. Around an elevation of 9550, you'll meet up with the Grand Mesa Scenic Byway. Turn around and ski your ascent route, or use the road to traverse over to a different descent option. This alternate route is less than a half mile shorter than the suggested Tow Line route. Reverse your ascent route or traverse over to one of the other nearby ski runs.

Note: Some skiers choose to access the top of the old ski area from the West Bench Trail that leaves from the Jumbo trailhead at Mesa Lakes. This requires a shuttle.

Opposite: View of the Tyndall Gorge from Emerald Lake on a snowy day, with Dragon's Tail and Dragon's Tooth couloirs on the right.

NORTHERN FRONT RANGE

The Gash on South Diamond Peak

DRIVE WEST ACROSS THE EASTERN PLAINS of Colorado, and you'll eventually see them—the Rocky Mountains! More specifically, the Rocky Mountains that greet travelers are those of the Front Range. The Front Range extends from the peaks west of Fort Collins all the way down to Pikes Peak in the south. Given the close proximity to the Denver area, the Front Range is one of the most popular areas for backcountry skiing. Because there is such a wide range of skiing in this range, we have broken the range into two halves.

The northern Front Range includes the Cameron Pass area, Rocky Mountain National Park, and the Indian Peaks. As a general rule, this part of the range saw heavier glaciation than the southern part of the range. Rocky Mountain National Park contains peaks that are as rough and rugged as anywhere in Colorado, while the lesser-known Indian Peaks hold their own for steepness as well. In fact, most of the Indian Peaks weren't even named until 1914, when botany teacher Ellsworth Bethel suggested naming them after Native American tribes. Most unknown of all, at least outside of Fort Collins–area skiers, is the backcountry playground of Cameron Pass.

Access is possible from the west side of the Front Range, but the vast majority of the trailheads are on the eastern side of the range. This means that common base camps for northern Front Range skiing include Estes Park, Nederland, and the cities on the plains.

While the western part of the range can receive snowfall in line with the rest of Colorado, the peaks closer to the plains tend to be in a snow shadow, blocked from moisture by the peaks even farther west. Longs Peak is an excellent example, as it looks more gray than white most of the winter. The one exception to this rule, and it's a big one, is when an upslope storm feeds moisture into the range from the east, at which point the Front Range can receive huge storm totals. The one constant, however, is the fierce winds that rake the high peaks all winter long. There are times when the snow can be seen blowing off the peaks toward Kansas all the way down in Denver. On the bright side, these westerly winds tend to load up the eastern faces so heavily with snow that it remains all summer long, making the Front Range Colorado's best bet for year-round skiing.

We have included wintertime ski zones in this chapter, but springtime is when the northern Front Range really shines. The steep terrain is best skied with a stable springtime snowpack, especially if wet storms have plastered the steeps with snow.

7 North and South Diamond Peaks: East Faces

Starting Elevation	10,275 feet
High Point	11,701 or 11,852 feet
Vertical Gain/Loss	1600+ feet
Ascent Distance	1.5+/- miles
Descent Distance	1.5+ miles
Time	1.5 to 4 hours
Ski Skills	Moderate to difficult
Fitness Level	Not very strenuous to moderately strenuous
Technical Skills	Moderate
Gear	The basics
Best Months	Mid-February through April
USGS Map	Clark Peak

Located just 65 miles west of Fort Collins on Colorado Highway 14, Cameron Pass is the closest backcountry skiing zone to this booming metropolis. This area sees many backcountry travelers and, with their easy access, the Diamond Peaks are one of the more popular zones. Don't let the ease of access fool you though. With a classic Front Range shallow and wind-affected snowpack, North and South Diamond Peaks are also notorious for avalanches. Make sure conditions are safe enough to venture above tree line when attempting these peaks.

Topping out at 10,275 feet, Cameron Pass has its own unique backcountry ski patrol called the Diamond Peak Ski Patrol. Established in 1990 after the closing of Hidden Valley Ski Area in nearby Rocky Mountain National Park, this organization

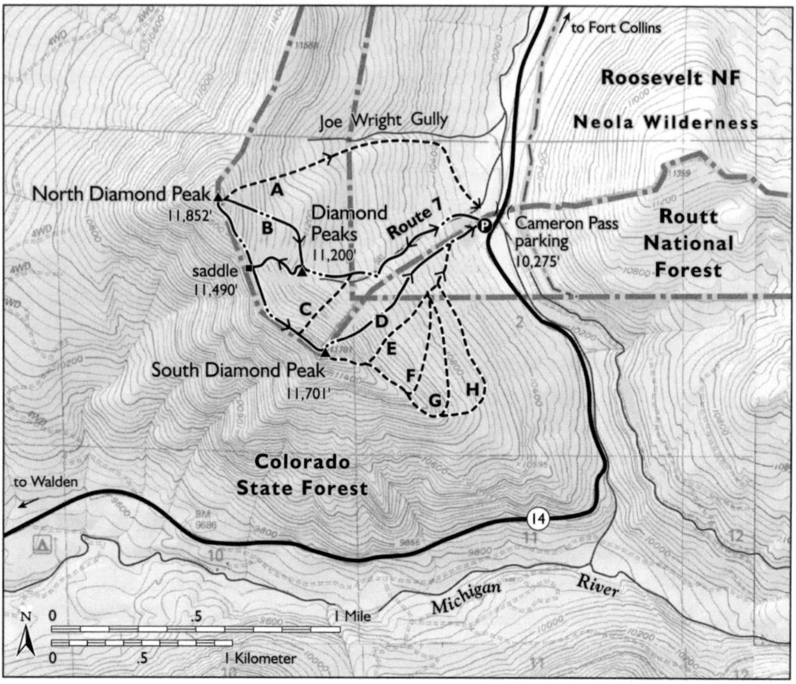

focuses their efforts on search and rescue as well as avalanche education in the Cameron Pass zone.

The Diamond Peaks actually comprise the southernmost end of the Medicine Bow Range, which extends north into south-central Wyoming. Terrain southeast of Cameron Pass is part of the Never Summer Range. The Diamond Peaks are composed of two summits: North Diamond Peak and South Diamond Peak.

GETTING THERE

From Fort Collins, travel west on CO 14 approximately 65 miles to Cameron Pass, roughly 2 miles past Joe Wright Reservoir, which you'll pass on your left. Near the top of the pass, you'll see an established parking area to your right (west). Park here for North and South Diamond Peaks.

If approaching from the west, travel 30 miles east on CO 14 from Walden. Just after the highway takes a large turn from heading east to heading north, you'll reach the top of Cameron Pass. Look for an established parking area on your left (west) near the top of the pass, which is where you'll want to leave your vehicle.

THE ROUTE

Since North and South Diamond Peaks are very popular with backcountry skiers, you will likely find established skin tracks in the area to help guide you. However, do not follow a skin track if you feel that its path of travel is unsafe. When in doubt, create your own safer route of travel.

From the parking lot, you can see the Diamond Peaks to the southwest. Begin traveling southwest, through the forest, following alongside a gully, toward the saddle of these two peaks. Be mindful of the gully as it can be a terrain trap. It is best to travel alongside the gully rather than in it.

As you travel, you will have a good view of South Diamond Peak. If this is the peak you want to ski, you should begin planning your route down the northeast face. Those who frequent the area have names for each of the obvious ski lines down South Diamond Peak. Straight off the summit is the South Diamond Face (D). Looker's right of the summit is a line called Ptarmigan (C). Looker's left of the summit holds runs called the Gash or Avalanche Alley (E) and the Wave (F). The treed area on the far looker's left has two runs called Pap Smear (G) and Taster's Choice (H).

Around 11,000 feet, the trees will begin to thin and the terrain flattens. Head west to reach the saddle between the two peaks at an elevation of 11,490 feet, approximately 1.2 miles from the trailhead. You may find a cornice guarding parts of this saddle and will need to adjust your route of travel accordingly.

At the saddle, you will need to choose whether you want to ski North Diamond Peak or South Diamond Peak. To ascend North Diamond Peak, follow the ridge one-third of a mile north another 350 vertical feet to the summit. To ascend South Diamond Peak, follow the undulating ridge one-third of a mile south to the summit. Although the vertical difference is only about 200 feet to the summit, the actual vertical gain is a bit more due to the undulating nature of the ridge. On both ridges, stay clear of cornices.

Descent. From North Diamond Peak, there are two general zones to descend on the east face. The primary route is just skier's right of center (B) and the alternate is skier's left of center (A). Descending skier's left tends to lead you to the Joe Wright Gully, which you can exit by traversing right (south) at 10,400 feet toward the parking lot. Be wary of the terrain-trap nature of this gully. The safest route of travel is alongside the gully in the forest.

If you choose to descend skier's right of center (B), ski to an elevation of 11,200 feet and then begin traversing right to your skin track. Follow your skin track down. Alternatively, you could also reascend your skin track to the saddle and do another lap on North Diamond Peak or head over to South Diamond Peak.

From the summit of South Diamond Peak, descend your line of choice mentioned above. The primary route is South Diamond Face (D), which leaves directly from the summit, whereas the safest routes are the treed routes (Pap Smear and Taster's Choice) on the far skier's right off the ridge east of the summit. Other possibilities were described in the ascent. As you descend below tree line, try to head north or northeast toward the parking area. Be mindful of the many gullies that you will need to cross in the area. Descending the lines on the center or skier's left of the center put you in a position to return to your skin track around 11,000 feet, allowing you to reascend to the saddle for more laps if you desire.

8 Nokhu Crags: Three Sisters, Grand Central, and Nokhouloir

Starting Elevation	9630 feet
High Point	Approximately 12,300 feet
Vertical Gain/Loss	2800+ feet
Ascent Distance	3.5+/- miles
Descent Distance	3.5+/- miles
Time	4 to 7 hours
Ski Skills	Moderate to difficult
Fitness Level	Not very strenuous to moderately strenuous
Technical Skills	Moderate
Gear	The basics
Best Months	Mid-March to early May
USGS Maps	Mount Richthofen and Clark Peak

Those who travel Colorado Highway 14 likely take note of a very distinctive peak that lies just south of the Cameron Pass summit. This peak is called Nokhu Crags, a morphed translation of the Arapaho words *neaha-no-xhu*, meaning "eagle's nest." Nokhu Crags composes the northern end of the Never Summer Range, which extends 10 miles south, with Rocky Mountain National Park on its east side and the Never Summer Wilderness to the west.

Backcountry skiers typically do not ski Nokhu Crags from the summit, which tops out at 12,485 feet. Instead, they ski one of the many couloirs close to the summit or within the cirque that lies northeast of the peak. This cirque is a ski mountaineer's dream, full of couloir after couloir, at least one for every day of the week!

The cirque faces east to north to west, so you can ski multiple lines in one day and time them according to the sun's position and warming of the snow. While the Nokhu Crags zone is easily accessible within a day, some people choose to set up a base camp in the cirque to allow for multiple days of exploration. Multiday adventurers may want to explore the Snow Lake Basin as well.

GETTING THERE

From Fort Collins, travel west on CO 14 approximately 65 miles to the top of Cameron Pass. Continue descending from the pass as CO 14 travels south and then west. On the left (south), you'll see a small parking area, 2.5 miles from the top of the pass.

If approaching from the west, travel 28 miles east on CO 14 from Walden. Just before the highway takes a large turn from heading east to heading north, you'll see a small parking area on your right (south).

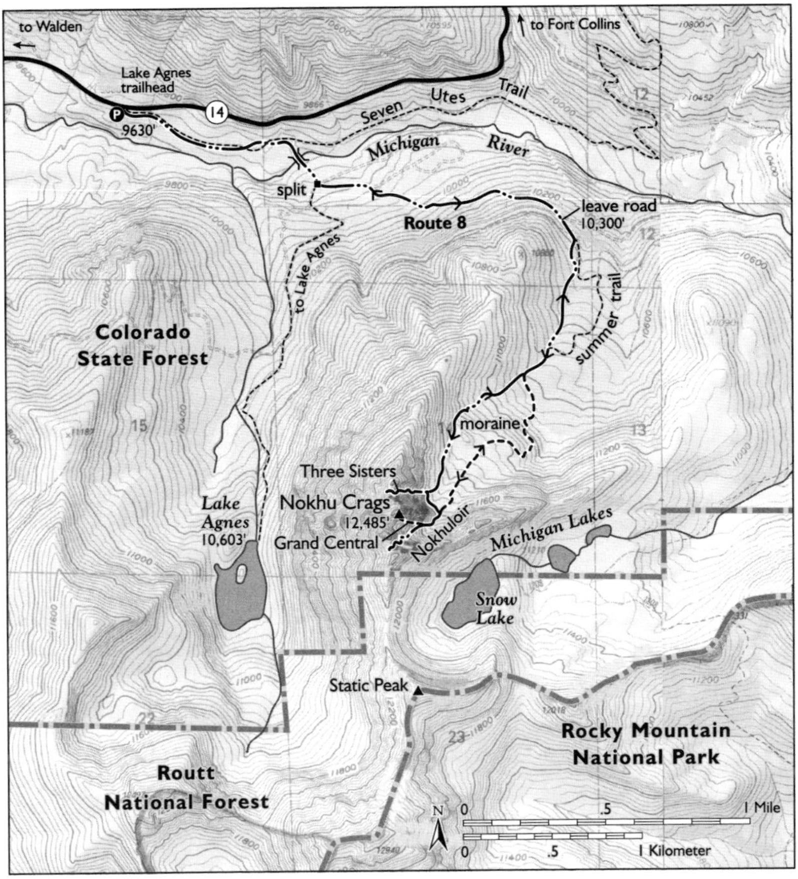

At the parking area, you should see signs indicating you are at the Lake Agnes trailhead. You'll also see a fee station. This area is a state park called Colorado State Forest, and at the time of writing a $7 day-use fee was required.

THE ROUTE

From the Lake Agnes trailhead, head eastward and down to the Michigan River on the Seven Utes Trail. After about 0.75 mile, head right (south) to a bridge to cross the Michigan River. Follow signs for the Nokhu and Lake Agnes cabins. About 0.25 mile after the river crossing, you'll see a split in the trails. The right fork leads to Lake Agnes, but you want to take the left fork that goes toward Crags Campground. Follow along the trail, which is an old road, as it heads east, contouring around the north side of the mountain, parallel with but above the Michigan River.

At approximately 10,300 feet, you'll leave the road and begin heading due south into the cirque that lies northeast of the Nokhu Crags summit. There is a summer trail

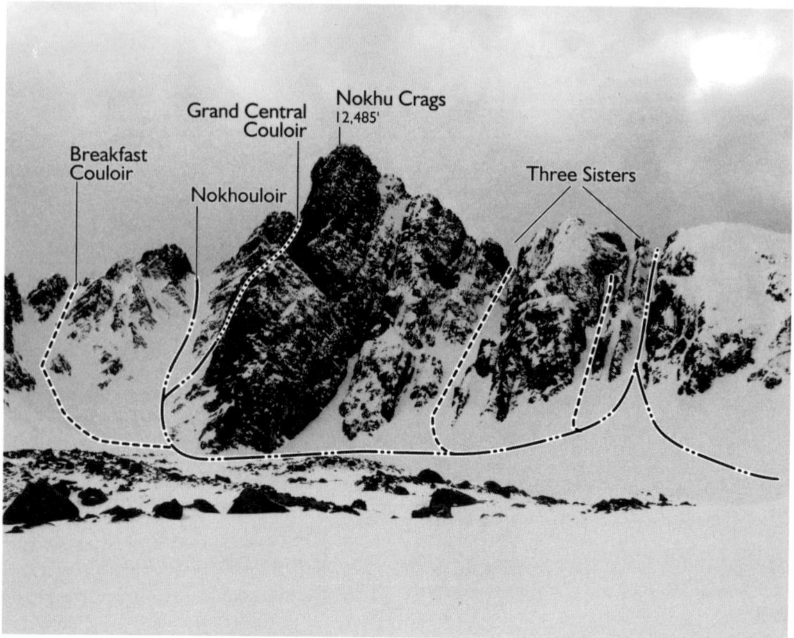

that travels through the area, but you may find it easier to travel along one of the few small drainages that lead up toward the cirque.

By now, you will have noticed some of the many couloirs in the area. But there are more ahead! This guide details access to some of the more popular couloirs known as the Three Sisters, Grand Central Couloir, and Nokhouloir. But there are many other choices for line options. If you see something you like and the conditions and timing are right for the line, go climb it and ski back down! Keep in mind that the cirque faces east to north to west, so you can plan your route choices based on the movement of the sun.

With the approach required and the somewhat short vertical of each couloir, we recommend skiing two or more couloirs in this area to get a better bang for your buck. The primary route described below includes both the Three Sisters and Nokhouloir.

As tree line thins around 11,000 feet, you'll see a mound of glacial moraine ahead. You'll need to decide whether to go looker's left or right of the moraine pile. The primary route to the right provides a more direct approach for Three Sisters, Grand Central Couloir, and Nokhouloir. Alternatively, the left route is less than half a mile longer, but it provides better views of each of those lines.

Around 11,450 feet, you should have a good glimpse of the three chutes that comprise the Three Sisters on the western side of the cirque. Each of these is a nice vertical of about 750 feet or more depending on how far you descend on the apron. These east-facing couloirs make a great way to start off your day before heading up toward the larger lines farther up the cirque. Pick one of the three couloirs to ascend and descend.

After skiing the Three Sisters, continue on to the northeast-facing Grand Central Couloir and Nokhouloir by heading south in the cirque until its end. Slightly to your right, you'll see two wide couloirs coming down from the ridge, south of the summit of Nokhu Crags, separated by a pyramid-shaped rock between them at the top. The one on the looker's right is the Grand Central Couloir, and the one to the left of it is Nokhouloir. Nokhouloir is the primary route suggested. Climb Nokhouloir about 750 feet to the top of its notch around 12,300 feet. Alternatively, ascend Grand Central Couloir or the less obvious Breakfast Couloir to the left of both of these, giving you yet another ski option.

Descent. As a general rule, descend your ascent route. If timing is right after you descend and you are not too tired, ski another couloir—or two or three! To exit the cirque, follow your ascent route back to the Lake Agnes trailhead.

9 Sundance Mountain: North Face

Starting Elevation	12,100 feet (Low point: 10,100 feet)
High Point	Approximately 12,310 feet
Vertical Gain/Loss	2200 feet or less
Ascent Distance	1.2+/- miles
Descent Distance	1.2+/- miles
Time	1 to 3 hours
Ski Skills	Easy to difficult
Fitness Level	Not very strenuous
Technical Skills	Low to moderate
Gear	The basics, plus ice axe and crampons
Best Months	Late May to July
USGS Map	Trail Ridge

In Rocky Mountain National Park, the historic Trail Ridge Road refers to a section of US Highway 34 between Estes Park and Grand Lake, winding through miles of scenic landscape, including 11 miles of alpine tundra. Construction of this road began in 1929 and was not finished until 1938. Currently, the road is closed in winter due to the high amount of snow the area receives. But this scenic byway typically opens around Memorial Day, providing access to lines deep in the park, like Sundance Mountain.

Sundance Mountain has some of the best late-season skiing around. At only 12,486 feet, it's surprising that snow would stay on this mountain well into summer. That is a testament to the prolific snowfall and wind loading of the area. You will find that the steepness of lines on Sundance varies quite a lot, offering something interesting for

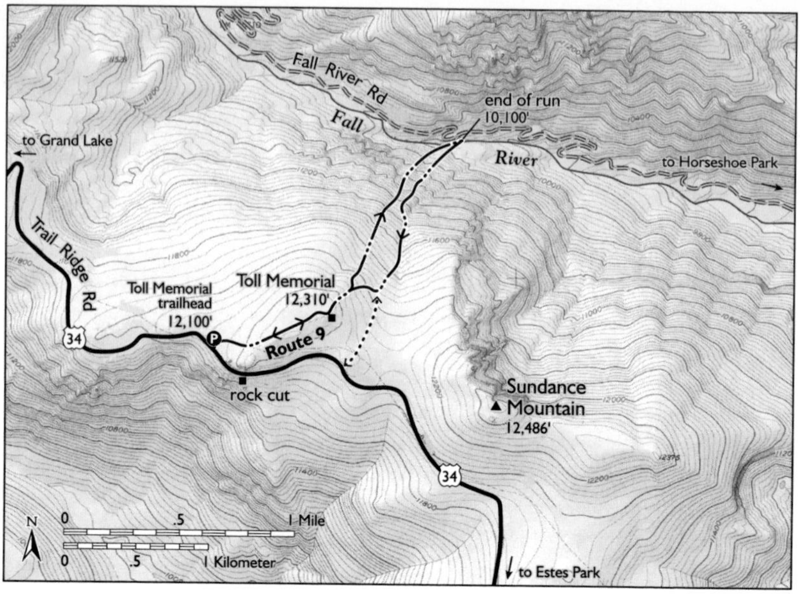

skiers of all abilities. The north face of Sundance is also unique because it's typically done "upside-down," meaning that you first descend and then reascend your route.

GETTING THERE

Rocky Mountain National Park is east of Grand Lake and west of Estes Park. Trail Ridge Road, part of US 34, winds between the two towns located on either side of the park. From the east, follow the signs for US 36 west to the Beaver Meadows Park Entrance for Rocky Mountain National Park. Continue following US 36 west through the park for 4.5 miles until it merges with US 34. Follow US 34 west until you see the parking for the Toll Memorial, located just past the rock cut, approximately 17 miles from the Beaver Meadows Park Entrance.

If you are traveling from the west, follow US 34 east from Grand Lake to the Grand Lake Entrance of Rocky Mountain National Park. Travel another 24.5 miles east to the parking for the Toll Memorial.

Since this mountain is located in a national park, National Park Service fees do apply. At the time of writing, day-use passes were $20.

THE ROUTE

From the parking area, follow the signs for the paved trail that takes you northeast 0.5 mile to the Toll Memorial. The skiing begins down and to the climber's left of the memorial.

Alternatively, you could avoid the Toll Memorial by leaving from various parking areas about 0.5 mile east of the parking lot for the memorial. Head north on flat, likely

Enjoying spring slush as the slopes on Sundance Mountain steepen near the bottom

snow-covered ground, and you'll find yourself just below the rock outcropping where the Toll Memorial is placed.

Descent. The descent of the north face of Sundance is fun in that it keeps getting steeper and steeper along the way. The first turns are in the 15- to 20-degree range, but the line steepens to 45 degrees for the last 1000 to 1200 vertical feet. Descend as much as you want or feel comfortable with, and then reascend your route. The north face ends at the bottom of the valley with Fall River and the corresponding Fall River Road, around 10,100 feet.

Some people choose to exit via Fall River Road instead of reascending. To do this, you will need to leave a vehicle at the seasonal road closure near Horseshoe Park and then use another one to access the Toll Memorial. After descending, walk east on Fall River Road for about 6 miles to your vehicle.

Extra Credit: Those skiers wanting more of a challenge should take a look at the northeast-facing couloirs that drop off closer to the true summit of Sundance Mountain, a bit more to the east of Toll Memorial. These couloirs have sections that go up to 50 degrees of steepness!

10 Flattop Mountain: Dragon's Tail Couloir

Starting Elevation	9460 feet
High Point	Approximately 11,900 feet
Vertical Gain/Loss	2500 feet or less
Ascent Distance	2.5 miles
Descent Distance	2.5 miles
Time	4 to 6 hours
Ski Skills	Very difficult
Fitness Level	Moderately strenuous
Technical Skills	High
Gear	The basics, plus ice axe and crampons
Best Months	March and April
USGS Map	McHenrys Peak

Even with the winter closure of Trail Ridge Road, Rocky Mountain National Park is still a mecca for backcountry skiers. Throughout winter and spring, many lines are accessible off Bear Lake Road. A winter tour to the magical Emerald Lake leaves backcountry skiers feeling enchanted. Skiing the daunting yet popular Dragon's Tail Couloir, which hovers behind it, is even more rewarding.

GETTING THERE

From Estes Park, follow the signs for US Highway 36 west to the Beaver Meadows Park Entrance for Rocky Mountain National Park. Once through the fee station, continue west on US 36 for 0.25 mile and then turn left (south) onto Bear Lake Road. Follow this road approximately 9.4 miles to its end near the Bear Lake Ranger Station.

Since this route is located in a national park, National Park Service fees do apply. At the time of writing, day-use passes were $20.

THE ROUTE

The Bear Lake area is popular year-round. You'll likely find fairly compacted trails that will help guide you. While many of these trails tend to follow the summer routes, others do not. But most will lead you to the right place if you know the general direction you need to go.

From the parking area, head in a westward direction toward Dream Lake. The summer trail will take you by Nymph Lake at 9708 feet along the way. From Dream Lake at 9908 feet, continue west up to the next ledge to reach Emerald Lake (10,110 feet), approximately 1.5 to 1.75 miles from the trailhead.

Take some time to enjoy the fabulous views from enchanting Emerald Lake. Notice the pair of couloirs that are ahead and slightly to your right, facing southeast, separated

by a large rock formation called the Dragon's Tail Buttress. The one on the left is called Dragon's Tooth Couloir (or sometimes called Dead Elk Couloir after the elk carcass that was found by a group of skiers), and the one on the right is your intended Dragon's Tail Couloir.

Work your way around Emerald Lake and begin ascending Dragon's Tail Couloir, which tops out about another 1800 feet above Emerald Lake, at an elevation of 11,900 feet. When the route splits about three-quarters of the way up, stay climber's left, following along beside the Dragon's Tail Buttress. The route to the right, east of a buttress called the Incisor, is not recommended because the smooth rocks that lie under this area make it more susceptible to avalanches. Shortly after the split, the route will constrict and you'll come to a small rock band that can be a crux in the route. The rock band can usually be bypassed to the climber's left. Above the rock band, the couloir steepens to the low 50-degree range, the steepest skiing of the route. Push through this for 100 feet or so, and the couloir will gradually become less steep until you reach the top on the east ridge of Flattop Mountain.

Descent. Reverse your ascent route.

Extra Credit: Dragon's Tooth is another fun route to try. Although a little less steep than Dragon's Tail, this couloir has a rock band about two-thirds of the way up. The rock band can be jumped in some years, and in others it requires a rappel.

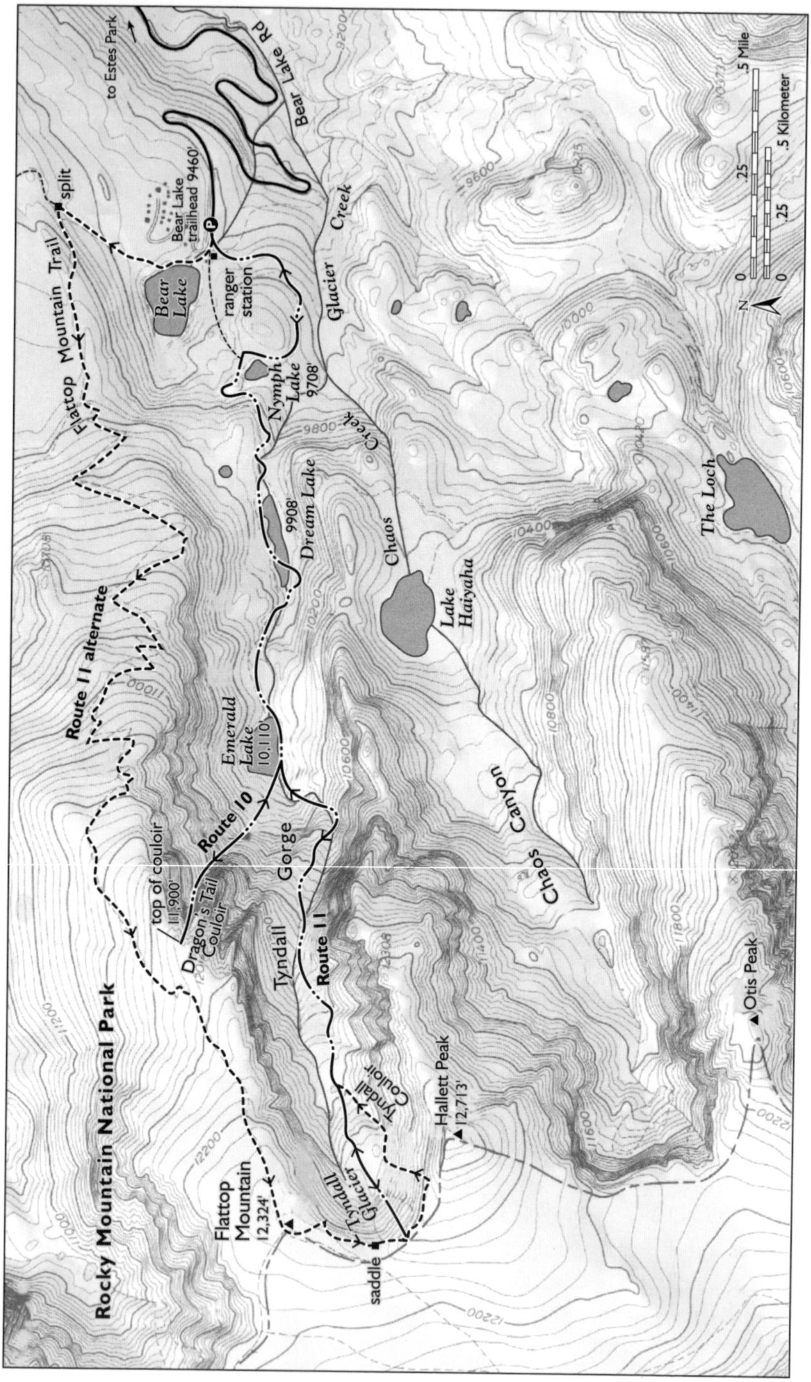
Rocky Mountain National Park
to Estes Park
Bear Lake Rd
split
Flattop Mountain Trail
Bear Lake
Bear Lake trailhead 9460'
ranger station
Glacier Creek
Nymph Lake 9708'
Dream Lake 9908'
Chaos Creek
Lake Haiyaha
The Loch
Route 11 alternate
Emerald Lake 10,110'
Route 10
top of couloir 11,900'
Dragon's Tail Couloir
Tyndall Gorge
Route 11
Chaos Canyon
Flattop Mountain 12,324'
Tyndall Glacier
Tyndall Couloir
Hallett Peak 12,713'
saddle
Otis Peak
0 .25 .5 Mile
0 .25 .5 Kilometer
N

11 Tyndall Gorge: Tyndall Glacier and Couloir

Starting Elevation	9460 feet
High Point	12,324 to 12,440 feet
Vertical Gain/Loss	2900 to 3000 feet
Ascent Distance	4 or 5 miles, depending on route
Descent Distance	4 miles
Time	4 to 6 hours
Ski Skills	Moderate to very difficult
Fitness Level	Strenuous
Technical Skills	Low to moderate
Gear	The basics; ice axe and crampons may be needed depending on ascent route
Best Months	March to June
USGS Map	McHenrys Peak

Farther up the valley from Emerald Lake and Dragon's Tail (Route 10), nestled between Flattop Mountain (12,324 feet) and Hallett Peak (12,713 feet), lies the Tyndall Glacier and its corresponding couloir. While the glacier can offer nice turns during much of the winter and well into the summer, the more challenging Tyndall Couloir is best left for prime spring conditions. A tour of the Tyndall Gorge provides a great overview of the Bear Lake area.

Although the word "glacier" is used to describe the permanent snowfield that caps the end of the Tyndall Gorge, the glacier is not large enough to develop crevasses.

GETTING THERE

From Estes Park, follow the signs for US Highway 36 west to the Beaver Meadows Park Entrance for Rocky Mountain National Park. Once through the fee station, continue west on US 36 for 0.25 mile and then turn left (south) onto Bear Lake Road. Follow this road approximately 9.4 miles to its end near the Bear Lake Ranger Station.

Since this route is located in a national park, National Park Service fees do apply. At the time of writing, day-use passes were $20.

THE ROUTE

To ascend the Tyndall Glacier, you have two options: the first is to climb the direct route; the second is to ascend Flattop Mountain first and then follow the ridge over to the glacier. Climbing the route directly is nice because then you'll have a good idea of what to expect for snow conditions, but this is not recommended late in the spring or summer when snow is not present just above Emerald Lake. Climbing this

area without snow involves a lot of bushwhacking. For this reason, when snow is not present above 10,000 feet, Flattop Mountain makes a much better alternative approach route. Even though it is about a mile longer, the Flattop Mountain Trail allows for faster travel later in the season. An ice axe and crampons are recommended when climbing the route directly.

To climb the route directly, head in a westward direction toward Dream Lake from the parking area. The summer trail will take you by Nymph Lake at 9708 feet along the way. From Dream Lake at 9908 feet, continue west up to the next ledge to reach Emerald Lake (10,110 feet), approximately 1.5 to 1.75 miles from the trailhead.

The best way for you to ascend the headwall past Emerald Lake is to aim for the southwest corner of the lake. An obvious drainage leads into the lake from this area. Ascend this drainage. You will find it begins to level off after about 500 feet, around an elevation of 10,600 feet. Continue west, following the Tyndall Gorge upward. At the end of the valley, due west, you'll see the Tyndall Glacier. Slightly to your left (southwest), you'll see the steeper Tyndall Couloir.

The easiest route out of the Tyndall Gorge is to ascend the Tyndall Glacier to your right, toward the north end. This slope typically falls within the low 30-degree range for steepness. Ascend this to the saddle between Hallett Peak and Flattop Mountain at 12,300 feet.

Alternate Ascent. To approach via Flattop Mountain, head north on Bear Lake Trail from the parking area. You will pass Bear Lake on your left (to the west). About

0.5 mile past the start of the trail and shortly after the lake, there is a fork. Bear right, or straight. At the second fork, turn left onto Flattop Mountain Trail. Continue on Flattop Mountain Trail as it heads west and switchbacks all the way to the summit at 12,324 feet, roughly 4.5 miles from the trailhead.

This peak is aptly named as the summit is indeed very flat. In fact, it is so flat that you will likely have a difficult time telling exactly where the summit is; there is no sign marking the exact high point. From the approximate summit, work your way to the southern edge of the ridge to catch a good glimpse of Tyndall Glacier and Couloir. Here you'll want to plan your descent route.

Follow the ridge west and south past the summit, for approximately 0.5 mile past the summit, to reach the saddle between Hallett Peak and Flattop Peak at 12,300 feet.

Descent. From the saddle, descend directly into Tyndall Glacier. The skier's left side of the glacier will have slopes in the 30-degree range, while the skier's right side can steepen to as much as 50 degrees. Alternatively, if you want to descend Tyndall Couloir, continue following the ridge slightly upward and southeast for another 0.2 mile until you're above the couloir. Descend the couloir.

Both the Tyndall Glacier and Couloir flatten into a bowl around 11,870 feet. If snow is present above 10,000 feet, descend east down the Tyndall Gorge to Emerald Lake. Follow trails eastward to Dream Lake and Nymph Lake and back to the parking area. Later in the season when snow is not present above 10,000 feet, you'll find it's easier to reascend the glacier and then descend Flattop Mountain Trail. Otherwise, be ready for heinous bushwhacking!

12 Bear Lake: Terrain Park

Starting Elevation	9460 feet
High Point	10,600+ feet
Vertical Gain/Loss	2000+ feet
Ascent Distance	2 to 3+ miles, depending on route
Descent Distance	2 to 3+ miles
Time	1.5 to 6 hours
Ski Skills	Easy to difficult
Fitness Level	Not very strenuous to moderately strenuous
Technical Skills	Low
Gear	The basics
Best Months	January to early April
USGS Map	McHenrys Peak

Access to midwinter skiing in Rocky Mountain National Park can be challenging with the closure of Trail Ridge Road. But the Bear Lake zone offers a wealth of options for those wanting to explore the park during this time of year. Terrain Park typically refers to the low-hanging fruit areas accessed out of the Bear Lake

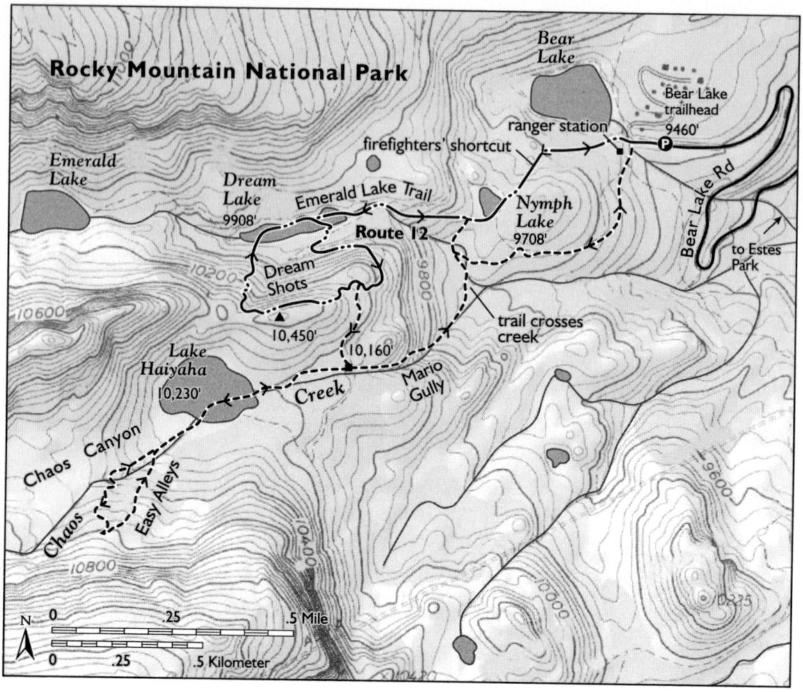

Road area, at the base of Glacier Gorge, Loch Vale, Chaos Canyon, and the Tyndall Gorge. Indeed, there is no established terrain park here. You won't find rail slides or manicured jumps. But Terrain Park is aptly named as it's the perfect play zone for midwinter snow and powder days. From mellow tree runs to pillows and cliffs, this area is bound to keep you entertained.

Terrain Park offers runs that range between 30 degrees and 50 degrees. Plan your routes wisely according to snow and avalanche conditions.

GETTING THERE

From Estes Park, follow the signs for US Highway 36 west to the Beaver Meadows Park Entrance for Rocky Mountain National Park. Once through the fee station, continue west on US 36 for 0.25 mile and then turn left (south) onto Bear Lake Road. Follow this road approximately 9.4 miles to its end near the Bear Lake Ranger Station.

Since this region is located in a national park, National Park Service fees do apply. At the time of writing, day-use passes were $20.

THE ROUTE

The Bear Lake area is popular year-round. You will likely find fairly compacted trails that will help guide you. While many of these trails tend to follow the summer routes, others do not. But most will lead you to the right place if you know the general direction you need to go.

Dropping into the Dream Shots

Terrain Park is a complex zone of short ski lines. Many of them interweave between one another, and it can take years to really get this area dialed in. The suggested route this guidebook presents for this area just scratches the surface with a quick overview of a few of the available options. As a general rule, if you see something you want to ski, go ski it, assuming that the avalanche conditions allow a reasonable descent of that line. Exploration is the key to Terrain Park.

From the parking area you will want to ascend southwest toward Nymph Lake at 9708 feet. There are two main ways to get to this lake. One option is to take the summer trail, which heads south, then west, and then north around a knob for 0.5 mile to reach the lake. But the primary winter route that is best with adequate snow is the "firefighters' shortcut," which bypasses this knob and heads directly southwest to Nymph Lake. The shortcut starts just behind the ranger station. You follow the Bear Lake Trail for roughly 100 feet and then bear left off the trail into a clearing where the shortcut trail begins. Once at Nymph Lake, follow the Emerald Lake Trail west to Dream Lake at 9908 feet.

From Dream Lake, you can catch a glimpse of the Dream Shots directly to the south. There are four main runs that come through this zone, each with its own name according to skiers and snowboarders who frequent the area. Runs range in steepness from mid-30 degrees to the mid-40 degrees. You will want to take a look at these routes from below and plan your descent. To ascend to the top of the Dream Shots, look for a skin track to your left as you face south toward your intended line. Usually the skin track begins at the summer trail that leaves Dream Lake toward Lake Haiyaha. Eventually you will find yourself on a ridge to the looker's left of the Dream Shots. Leave the summer trail, and head west to the top of the knob above the Dream Shots, topping out at an elevation of approximately 10,450 feet.

Descent. Descend north back to Dream Lake, and be wary of cliff bands as you descend. This run can also be skipped as the tour continues from Dream Lake, or you can choose to lap the area as well.

Alternate Routes. Once at Dream Lake again, follow the skin track mentioned above as it heads left and south around a ridge, following the summer trail to Lake Haiyaha, which is your next general destination. Instead of following the ridge west to the top of Dream Shots, continue following the trail as it heads south. The trail will cross Chaos Creek at an approximate elevation of 10,160 feet. Do not cross the creek. Instead, follow west along the creek, remaining on its north side until you reach Lake Haiyaha at 10,230 feet.

From Lake Haiyaha, look at the slopes to the south. These low-angled treed runs are called Easy Alleys. Notice that some of the areas are directly below steeper chutes above. Depending on avalanche conditions, you may want to steer clear of the runouts of these chutes. Pick a route to skin up and ski down. Typically, the starting zone for your descent of the Easy Alleys is around 10,600 feet. Descend back to Lake Haiyaha. Reascend for a second lap or two if you desire!

Once back at Lake Haiyaha, descend east along the north side of Chaos Creek. Instead of retracing your trail back north, continue heading east along the creek another 0.1 mile to where the terrain begins to steepen. This is the start of Mario Gully, named after the Mario video games that were popular in the late 1980s and early 1990s, because you can jump from pillow to pillow as if you were Super Mario himself. The steepness of this gully is typically in the mid-30-degree range. Descend northeast down the Mario Gully to where the terrain becomes considerably less steep around an elevation of 9740 to 9720 feet. From here, begin heading north out of the gully to reach Nymph Lake.

From Nymph Lake, you could return to the Dream Shots or head back to your vehicle at the Bear Lake trailhead.

13 Mount Audubon: Crooked Couloir

Starting Elevation : 10,360 feet
High Point : 13,223 feet
Vertical Gain/Loss : 2900 feet
Ascent Distance : 5+/- miles
Descent Distance : 5 miles
Time : 5 to 7 hours

Ski Skills : Difficult
Fitness Level : Strenuous
Technical Skills : High
Gear : The basics, plus ice axe and crampons
Best Months : April to June
USGS Map : Ward

You would be hard-pressed to find a better view of the majestic Indian Peaks from any other drivable location than Brainard Lake, a very popular recreation area in summer. Towering above the lake, Navajo, Apache, and Shoshoni peaks stand proud. Look to your right and you'll catch a glimpse of Pawnee Peak and the western edges of Mount Audubon.

The Crooked Couloir on Mount Audubon is both a classic and rewarding ski in the Indian Peaks. The peak itself provides excellent views of the magnificent Mount Toll (Route 14).

GETTING THERE

While great skiing exists in the Indian Peaks that lie above Brainard Lake, this area is typically difficult to access due to seasonal road closures. The road is normally closed at the fee station, 2.1 miles from the lake, until early to mid-June. After that, the road is not usually open past Brainard Lake until late June or July.

Access is not too difficult if the road is open to Brainard Lake itself, but you'll be adding another 4 miles round trip if it's closed at the fee station. In late spring, some people choose to use bikes to help ease their access.

Ward is located roughly 11 miles north of Nederland and 30 miles south of Estes Park on Colorado Highway 72. The turn toward Brainard Lake is on CO 72, immediately north of Ward. Turn west onto Brainard Lake Road and drive 2.7 miles to the entrance fee station. If no one is present, use the self-service kiosk to pay your fee. At the time of writing, the day-use fee was $10 per vehicle.

Continue west on Brainard Lake Road 2.1 miles to the parking at the east end of Brainard Lake. If you are lucky, the road will be open 1.1 miles farther to the Mitchell Lake trailhead. To reach this, take the right fork at the lake to head west along the north shore of Brainard Lake. At the end of the lake, follow the road as it heads north, taking a right at the fork with Long Lake Trail, following the signs to Mitchell Lake trailhead.

To inquire about the status of Brainard Lake Road, call the Boulder Ranger District (see Resources).

THE ROUTE

As mentioned above, access changes seasonally. Assuming you parked at Brainard Lake (elevation 10,360 feet), follow the instructions above to the Mitchell Lake trailhead at 10,505 feet. From the trailhead, follow the Blue Lake Trail No. 912 northwest. After 1 mile, you'll pass to the south of Mitchell Lake. From there, the trail begins heading west for a bit before veering northwest again to reach Blue Lake (elevation 11,309 feet), 3 miles past the trailhead. If you have trouble following the summer trail from the southwest end of Mitchell Lake, follow the obvious drainage upward as it heads southwest, west, and then northwest to Blue Lake. The summer trail generally follows just north of this drainage.

Once at Blue Lake, you'll see Mount Toll on your left and Mount Audubon will be on your right. You won't be able to see much of the Crooked Couloir from the lake itself as it is hidden behind the rocks in the mountain. To climb the Crooked Couloir, head west on the north shores of the Blue Lake until you are about half of the way across the lake. The chute will meet the lake here.

Ascend the Crooked Couloir roughly 1600 feet until you reach the ridge at an elevation of 13,000 feet. At the ridge, you'll likely find the snow beginning to trickle out and you'll be traveling over dry or nearly dry talus. If you want to continue on to the summit, follow the ridge east another 223 vertical feet and 0.25 mile to the top. Otherwise, stop at the top of the Crooked Couloir and make your transition there.

Descent. Reverse your ascent route.

Extra Credit: If you have extra time, consider descending the northwest-facing Coney Couloirs from the summit of Audubon toward Coney Lake. There are three couloirs, two of them leaving from the ridge just west of the summit and the third leaving just east of the summit.

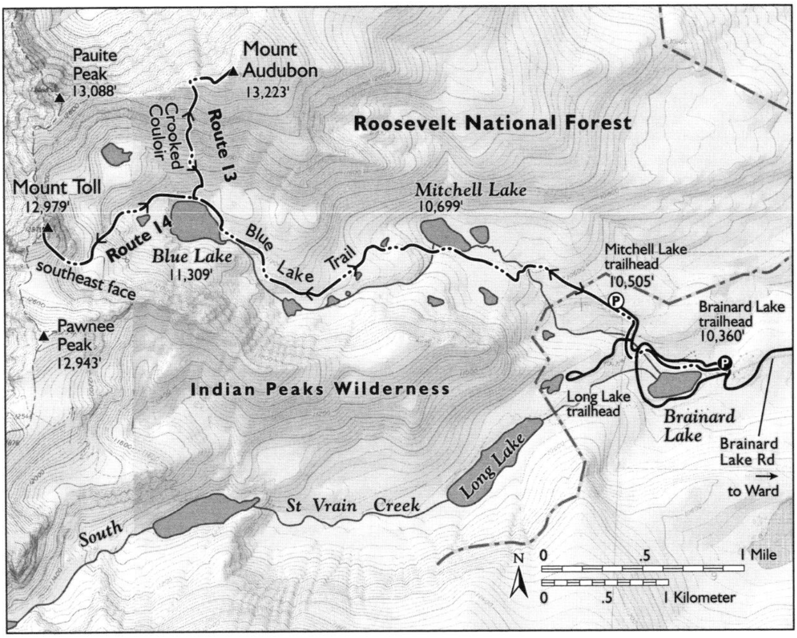

14 Mount Toll: Southeast Face

Starting Elevation : 10,360 feet
High Point : 12,979 feet
Vertical Gain/Loss : 2700 feet
Ascent Distance : 5+/- miles
Descent Distance : 5 miles
Time : 5 to 7 hours
Ski Skills : Moderate to difficult
Fitness Level : Strenuous
Technical Skills : High
Gear : The basics, plus ice axe and crampons
Best Months : April to June
USGS Maps : Ward and Monarch Lake

Standing above the beautiful Blue Lake, Mount Toll is one of the iconic mountains of the Indian Peaks Wilderness. Mount Toll is easily seen from the plains east of Boulder, and Front Range residents can monitor its snowpack from miles away. Despite having an elevation that is under 13,000 feet and a south-facing line, this mountain holds snow well into the summer. Even with the difficulty of access, Mount Toll is a popular and beautiful backcountry ski for locals.

The descent on Mount Toll

GETTING THERE

Mount Toll is accessed through the popular recreation area of Brainard Lake. The road to Brainard Lake has seasonal closures. Please see Route 13 (Mount Audubon) for details.

Ward is located roughly 11 miles north of Nederland and 30 miles south of Estes Park on Colorado Highway 72. The turn toward Brainard Lake is on CO 72, immediately north of Ward. Turn west onto Brainard Lake Road and drive 2.7 miles to the entrance fee station. If no one is present, use the self-service kiosk to pay your fee. At the time of writing, the day-use fee was $10 per vehicle.

Continue west on Brainard Lake Road 2.1 miles to the parking at the east end of Brainard Lake. If you are lucky, the road will be open 1.1 miles farther to the Mitchell Lake trailhead. To reach this, take the right fork at the lake to head west along the north shore of Brainard Lake. At the end of the lake, follow the road as it heads north, taking a right at the fork with Long Lake trailhead, following the signs to Mitchell Lake trailhead.

THE ROUTE

As mentioned above, access changes seasonally. Assuming you parked at Brainard Lake (elevation 10,360 feet), follow the instructions above to the Mitchell Lake trailhead at 10,505 feet. From the trailhead, follow Blue Lake Trail No. 912 northwest. After 1 mile, you'll pass to the south of Mitchell Lake. From there, the trail begins heading west for a bit before veering northwest again to reach Blue Lake (elevation 11,309 feet), 3 miles past the trailhead. If you have trouble following the summer trail from the southwest end of Mitchell Lake, follow the obvious drainage upward as it heads southwest, west, and then northwest to Blue Lake. The summer trail generally follows just north of this drainage.

The summer trail will end at Blue Lake. From the lake, you will see the obvious Mount Toll standing before you. The southeast-facing snow route wraps around behind the rock to the summit. If the lake is not frozen, you will find it best to pass around the lake on its north shore. Cliff areas on the south shore make it difficult to navigate unless you go above the cliffs. Once on the western edge of Blue Lake, head southwest to the apron of Mount Toll's southeast snow route. Climb the snow route as it heads west and then north approximately 1600 feet to the summit. From the summit, you will have fabulous views of Mount Audubon and the Crooked Couloir (Route 13).

Descent. Reverse your ascent route back to Blue Lake. Keep in mind as you descend that you'll find steeper skiing to your left and less steep skiing to your right on the snow route. Once at Blue Lake, follow your ascent route back to Mitchell Lake trailhead or Brainard Lake.

15 Apache Peak: Queen's Way and Apache Couloir

Starting Elevation	10,360 feet
High Point	13,441 feet
Vertical Gain/Loss	3400 feet
Ascent Distance	6.25+/- miles
Descent Distance	6.25 miles
Time	8.5 to 11 hours
Ski Skills	Difficult
Fitness Level	Strenuous
Technical Skills	High
Gear	The basics, plus ice axe and crampons
Best Months	April to June
USGS Maps	Ward and Monarch Lake

If Brainard Lake is the heart of the Indian Peaks, then Apache Peak is the gem of the range. Visitors to Brainard Lake can't help but look at this magnificent mountain in awe. The second highest of the Indian Peaks, with steep slopes on all sides, Apache Peak is a magnet for backcountry skiers willing to go the distance.

GETTING THERE

Apache Peak is accessed through the popular recreation area of Brainard Lake. The road to Brainard Lake has seasonal closures. Please see Route 13 (Mount Audubon) for details.

Ward is located roughly 11 miles north of Nederland and 30 miles south of Estes Park on Colorado Highway 72. The turn toward Brainard Lake is on CO 72, immediately north of Ward. Turn west onto Brainard Lake Road and drive 2.7 miles to the entrance fee station. If no one is present, use the self-service kiosk to pay your fee. At the time of writing, the day-use fee was $10 per vehicle.

Continue west on Brainard Lake Road 2.1 miles to the parking at the east end of Brainard Lake. If you are lucky, the road will be open 1 more mile to the Long Lake trailhead. To reach this, take the right fork at the lake to head west along the north shore of Brainard Lake. At the end of the lake, follow the road as it heads north away from the lake, making a left turn 0.1 mile later (the right goes toward Mitchell Lake). Take this road until it ends at the Long Lake trailhead.

THE ROUTE

As mentioned above, access changes seasonally. Assuming you parked at Brainard Lake (elevation 10,360 feet), follow the instructions above to the Long Lake

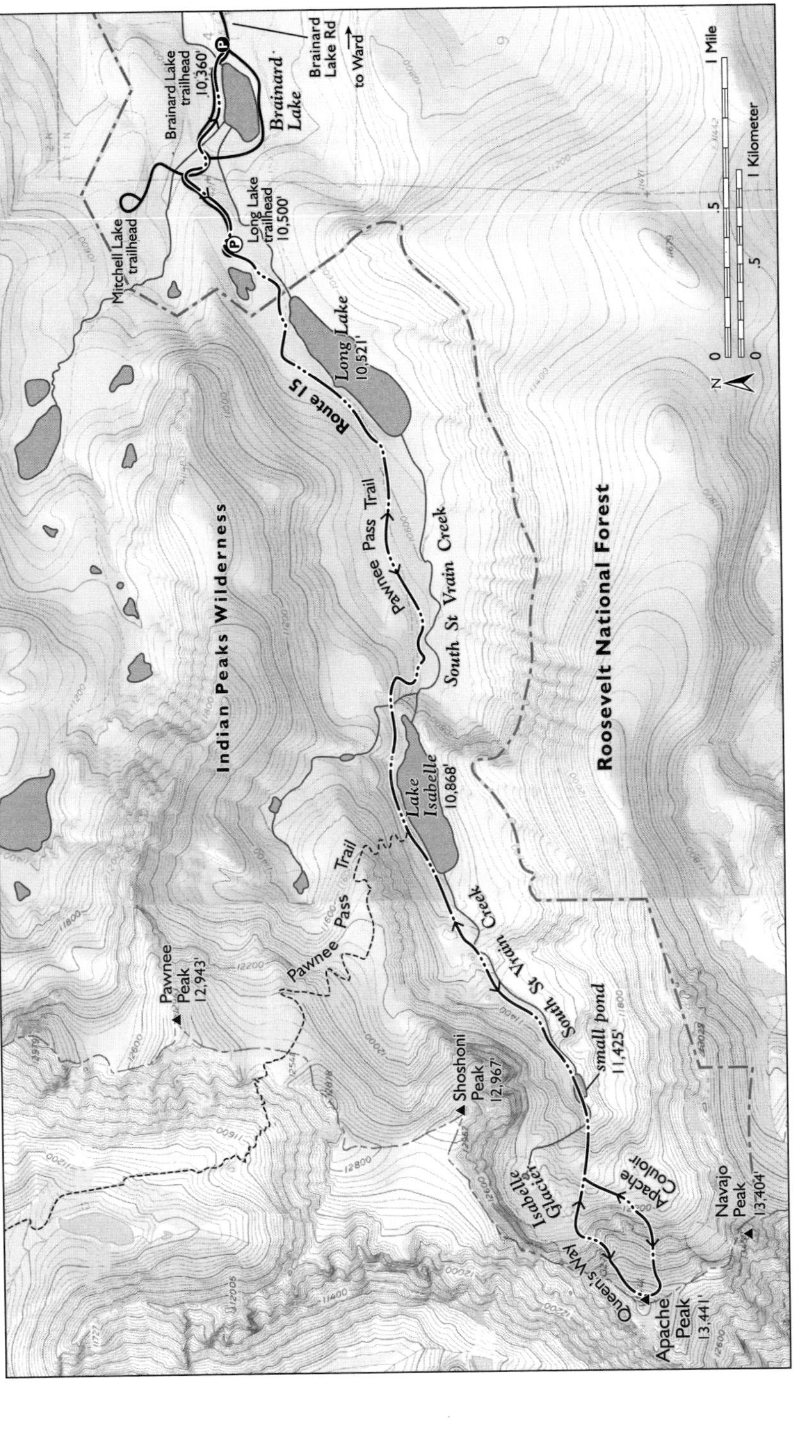
Mitchell Lake trailhead
Brainard Lake trailhead 10,360'
Brainard Lake
Brainard Lake Rd
to Ward
Long Lake trailhead 10,500'
Long Lake 10,521'
Route 15
Pawnee Pass Trail
South St Vrain Creek
Indian Peaks Wilderness
Roosevelt National Forest
Lake Isabelle 10,868'
Pawnee Pass Trail
Pawnee Peak 12,943'
Shoshoni Peak 12,967'
small pond 11,425'
Isabelle Glacier
Apache Couloir
Queen's Way
Apache Peak 13,441'
Navajo Peak 13,404'
1 Mile
1 Kilometer

trailhead at 10,500 feet. From the trailhead, travel west on Pawnee Pass Trail No. 907. After 0.25 mile, you will pass along the north shore of Long Lake (elevation 10,521 feet). Continue west on the trail until you reach Lake Isabelle (elevation 10,868 feet), which is 2 miles from the trailhead.

At Lake Isabelle, you will have a great view of Apache Peak. The east side of the mountain has two primary snow routes that lead to the summit. The one on the looker's left of the summit facing due east is called the Apache Couloir, and the one on the looker's right facing northeast is Queen's Way. Apache Couloir is steeper overall, but it has a more consistent pitch and its steepness lessens near the top. Queen's Way is less steep overall, but it is quite steep for the last 300 vertical feet near the summit. The east-facing Apache Couloir tends to be impacted by the sun earlier in the day. Both offer high-quality descents. Your timing and the condition of the snow may impact which route you choose.

At Lake Isabelle, you may notice that the trail fades if it is snow covered. Continue traveling west along the north shore of the lake. About halfway across the lake, the Pawnee Pass Trail heads up and to the north in the direction of Pawnee Peak. Leave the trail here and continue west along the north shore of Lake Isabelle. At the end of the lake, continue west following along the north side of the South St. Vrain Creek until you reach a small pond at an elevation of 11,425 feet. You will be just below the Isabelle Glacier to the northwest. The route will steepen a little here. Continue west, following along snow paths that make your travel easier.

Around 11,900 feet, a rock outcropping will be in front of you, and you will need to decide whether to head slightly left to ascend Apache Couloir or slightly right to ascend Queen's Way. If you ascend Apache Couloir, climb the chute until you reach the south ridge at approximately 13,300 feet. Follow the ridge north about 150 vertical feet to the summit. If you climb Queen's Way, you will notice that the route steepens at around 13,000 feet and begins to face east here. You may find it safer to ascend directly to the north ridge, which likely does not have snow, and follow the ridge south to the summit. Both routes will likely require a bit of easy class 2 talus for the last 150 feet to reach the summit.

Descent. Descend what you climbed or make a loop out of it using the other route if your timing and snow conditions allow! Enjoy your turns to the small pond at 11,425 feet. Retrace your ascent route back to Lake Isabelle and then continue on to Long Lake trailhead or Brainard Lake.

16 North Arapaho Peak: Northstar Couloir

Starting Elevation	10,120 feet
High Point	13,502 feet
Vertical Gain/Loss	4300 feet
Ascent Distance	5.3 miles
Descent Distance	5.3 miles

Skinning toward the start of the Northstar Couloir

Time	7 to 9 hours
Ski Skills	Difficult
Fitness Level	Strenuous
Technical Skills	High
Gear	The basics, plus ice axe and crampons
Best Months	May and June
USGS Map	Monarch Lake

Hidden on the western side of the Indian Peaks, Northstar Couloir is an unassuming but incredibly enjoyable route to a spectacular peak. The western side of the mountain is quiet, and you'll forget how close you are to a major metro area. What you are not likely to forget is how much fun you had in this nearly 2000-foot couloir.

GETTING THERE

From Colorado Highway 119 in Nederland, head west on Eldora Road toward the Eldora Ski Area. After 1.4 miles, stay right toward the town of Eldora rather than going left toward the ski area. Continue straight on Eldorado Avenue in the town of Eldora. At the end of town, the road becomes a rough 2WD road known as 4th of July Road. Stay on this road for 4.8 miles to the 4th of July trailhead, where you will park. This road is not plowed past Eldora in the winter, and it usually reopens in late May. To inquire about road status, call the Boulder County Road Department (see Resources).

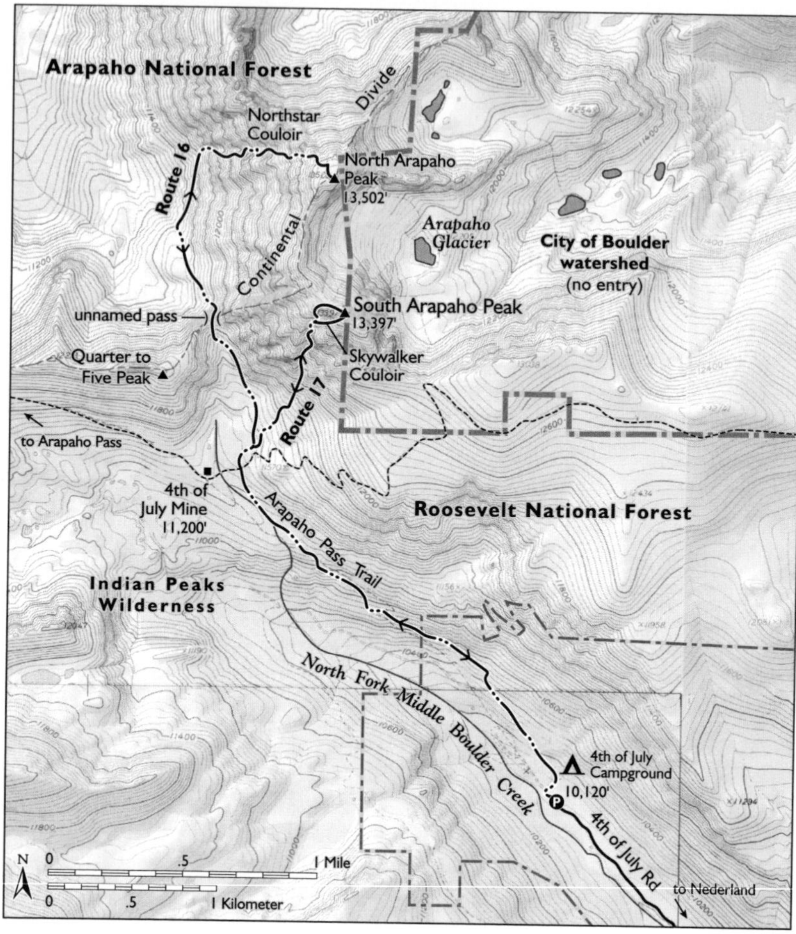

THE ROUTE

From the parking at 4th of July trailhead, follow the well-marked Arapaho Pass Trail toward the 4th of July Mine. The mine is located 2.3 miles from the trailhead at an elevation of 11,200 feet. From the mine, head north toward the small unnamed pass on the Continental Divide between South Arapaho Peak and "Quarter to Five" Peak. From the pass, traverse north, staying as high as possible although you will likely lose at least 500 feet of hard-earned vertical. Identifying Northstar Couloir may be the crux of this route. The easiest way to identify the route is to continue traversing until a vertical cliff band blocks any further traversing. Northstar will be directly above. Climb the couloir through several twists and turns to a saddle at 13,300 feet above the steep north face of North Arapaho. Continue up mellow terrain toward the summit, which is marked by a large cairn.

Descent. The eastern side of this peak is part of the City of Boulder watershed and is posted no trespassing. Descend the west-facing Northstar Couloir for roughly 2000 feet until the terrain opens up into the basin. Either begin your traverse back to the unnamed pass here or milk a few extra turns down the basin before transitioning back to skins. Follow your route back to the trailhead.

17 South Arapaho Peak: Skywalker Couloir

Starting Elevation	10,120 feet
High Point	13,397 feet
Vertical Gain/Loss	3277 feet
Ascent Distance	4 miles
Descent Distance	4 miles
Time	5 to 7 hours
Ski Skills	Extremely difficult
Fitness Level	Moderately strenuous
Technical Skills	High
Gear	The basics, plus ice axe and crampons
Best Months	May and June
USGS Map	Monarch Lake

Long considered a classic steep snow climb, the short springtime approach of the Skywalker Couloir makes it a classic for skiers and snowboarders as well. The Skywalker Couloir steepens considerably as it nears the ridgeline, making it one of the more surprisingly steep routes in this book.

Approaching the Skywalker Couloir

GETTING THERE

From Colorado Highway 119 in Nederland, head west on Eldora road toward the Eldora Ski Area. After 1.4 miles, stay right toward the town of Eldora rather than going left toward the ski area. Continue straight on Eldorado Avenue in the town of Eldora. At the end of town, the road becomes a rough 2WD road known as 4th of July Road. Stay on this road for 4.8 miles to the 4th of July trailhead, where you will park. This road is not plowed past Eldora in the winter, and it usually reopens in late May. To inquire about road status, call the Boulder county road department (see Resources).

THE ROUTE

From the parking area at 4th of July trailhead, follow the well-marked Arapaho Pass Trail toward the 4th of July Mine. The mine is located 2.3 miles from the trailhead at an elevation of 11,200 feet. From the mine, the Skywalker Couloir should be visible directly above. While the couloir faces south/southwest, the high rock walls shield it from sunlight and it stays shaded until later in the day than one might expect. Skywalker gradually ramps up in steepness, and the last moves out of the couloir may be melted and/or icy. From the top of the couloir, it's a short stroll to the summit on easier ground.

Descent. The eastern side of this peak is part of the City of Boulder watershed and is posted no trespassing. The Skywalker Couloir is popular with climbers, so make sure you do not descend on top of anyone heading up. The top of the couloir is often described as being in the mid-50-degree range. Retrace your approach back to the trailhead.

Opposite: Two skiers climb Shit for Brains Couloir on Black Mountain.

SOUTHERN FRONT RANGE

THE SOUTHERN FRONT RANGE incorporates the areas generally surrounding Interstate 70, including the incredibly popular backcountry areas of Berthoud Pass and Loveland Pass. While there is certainly steep skiing to be had, the southern Front Range is gentler than the northern area in a general sense. The aforementioned Berthoud and Loveland passes have probably introduced more backcountry skiers to the sport than any other area in Colorado.

Routes in this chapter can easily be reached from the Denver metro area in a day, making these areas some of the most visited in this book. Other towns that provide easy access to the southern Front Range include Winter Park, Idaho Springs, Georgetown, and the towns of Summit County.

While the western part of the range can receive snowfall in line with the rest of Colorado, the peaks closer to the plains tend to be in a snow shadow, blocked from moisture by the peaks even farther west. The one exception to this rule, and it's a big one, is when an upslope storm feeds moisture into the range from the east, at which point the Front Range can receive huge storm totals. The one constant, however, is the high winds that rake the high peaks all winter long. There are times when the snow can be seen blowing off the peaks toward Kansas all the way down in Denver. On the bright side, these westerly winds tend to load up the eastern faces so heavily with snow that it remains all summer long, making the Front Range Colorado's best bet for year-round skiing.

The southern Front Range contains an amazing variety of skiing. Backcountry skiers can ski powder all winter long at the passes before stepping it up in the spring on the bigger peaks.

18 Skyscraper Peak: Skyscraper Glacier

Starting Elevation: 11,660 feet+/- (Low point: 11,120 feet)
High Point: 12,183 feet
Vertical Gain/Loss: 1450 feet
Ascent Distance: 2.4 miles
Descent Distance: 2.4 miles
Time: 2 to 3 hours
Ski Skills: Moderate to very difficult
Fitness Level: Moderately strenuous
Technical Skills: Low
Gear: The basics
Best Months: June and July
USGS Map: East Portal

East-facing cirques off the Continental Divide hold snow well into the summer due to wind loading from strong west winds. "Skyscraper Peak" and many of the cirques in the area are prime examples of this scenario. Unofficially named, Skyscraper Peak

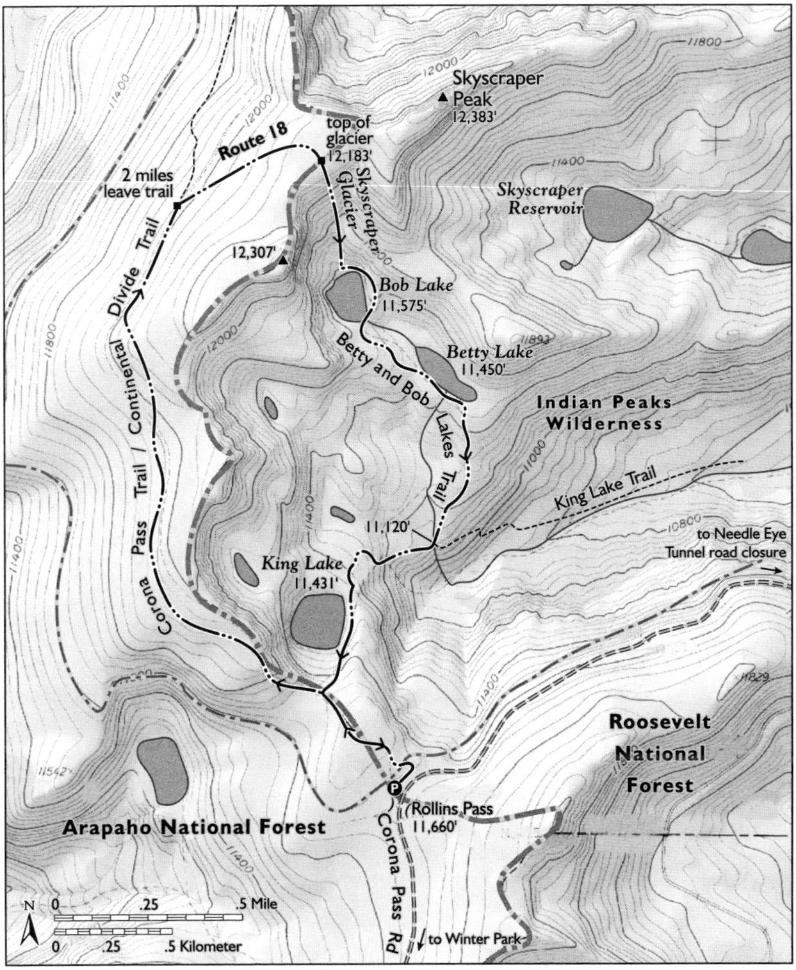

is Point 12,383 on USGS maps just west of Skyscraper Reservoir. Skyscraper Glacier is a permanent snowfield southwest of the peak, just above Bob Lake. This route is popular for those wanting turns in summer or even in fall as there is snow year-round. Although it is commonly referred to as a glacier, the snowfield is not large enough to harbor crevasses.

GETTING THERE

Skyscraper Peak is accessed from the popular Rollins Pass. While Rollins Pass can be reached with a little extra hiking from the east (see Route 19, Getting There), it is best to approach it from the west.

Drive south from the town of Winter Park on US Highway 40. Just north of the typical turnoff to the west for skier parking, you will see a turn to the east onto County

The upper portions of Skyscraper Glacier can be quite steep! (Photo by Kim Ross)

Road 80 (Corona Pass Road [Forest Road 149]). Signs may also indicate that this is the road for Rollins Pass. Follow this road as it heads north and then east, winding through switchbacks to the top of Rollins Pass 14 miles past the intersection with US 40. Corona Pass Road is a dirt road. A 4WD vehicle is not absolutely necessary, but the road is bumpy and it can be rough on cars without strong shocks. This road typically does not open until June 15. To inquire about the status of the Corona Pass Road, call the Sulphur Ranger District (see Resources).

THE ROUTE

From the parking area at Rollins Pass, head north on the Corona Pass Trail (High Lonesome Trail), part of the Continental Divide Trail. Stay left at the junction with the Betty and Bob Lakes Trail. After 2 miles you will notice Point 12,307 on your right. Leave the trail here and head right, veering northeast and then east to a slight depression short of Skyscraper Peak ahead. You'll find the start of the Skyscraper Glacier here around 12,183 feet.

Descent. The condition of Skyscraper Glacier can vary widely from year to year as well as during different times of year. In late spring or early summer, a cornice can be present at the entrance. Later in the summer and fall, as the snow melts it creates a very steep headwall near the top, which can be intimidating to descend. In late spring or early summer, that same headwall is sometimes hardly noticeable. The start of the glacier can also have a gap between the snow and the mountain, technically called a randkluft. All of these things are hazards you should be aware of as you descend. If the headwall is intimidating to you, look for a gentle southwest-facing slope to the skier's left that might help you bypass this steeper portion.

Ski down the glacier until you reach Bob Lake at an elevation of 11,575 feet. From here, continue southeast toward Betty Lake (11,450 feet). If the route is devoid of snow past the lake, look for a faint trail between Bob Lake and the lower Betty Lake, southwest of the creek that connects them. Head southeast along the southwest shore of Bob Lake to find the Betty and Bob Lakes Trail. Follow this trail down and south for 0.4 mile past Betty Lake until it intersects with the King Lake Trail, which will be the low point of your loop at an elevation of 11,120 feet. Turn right (west) onto the King Lake Trail and follow it up for 0.7 mile until it meets with the Corona Pass Trail. You will pass east of King Lake along the way. Head left (south) on the Corona Pass Trail another 0.4 mile back to the Rollins Pass parking area.

Extra Credit: The bowl above King Lake and the south-facing line that leads down from the ridge east of the summit of Skyscraper make other great descents in the area as well.

19 Radiobeacon Mountain: East Cirque

Starting Elevation	11,660 feet from Rollins Pass, 9210 feet from East Portal, 11,040 feet from Forest Lakes
High Point	12,072 feet
Vertical Gain/Loss	1500 feet from Rollins Pass, 2900 feet from East Portal, 1300 feet from Forest Lakes
Ascent Distance	2 miles from Rollins Pass, 5+/- miles from East Portal, 1.5 miles from Forest Lakes
Descent Distance	1.5 miles from Rollins Pass, 4.5 miles from East Portal, 1 mile from Forest Lakes
Time	2 to 3 hours from Rollins Pass, 5.5 to 7.5 from East Portal, 2 to 3 hours from Forest Lakes
Ski Skills	Moderate to very difficult
Fitness Level	Not very strenuous to strenuous
Technical Skills	Moderate to high
Gear	The basics, plus ice axe and crampons
Best Months	May and June
USGS Map	East Portal

USGS maps show a point on the Continental Divide marked at 12,072 and indicate the placement of a radio beacon next to the summit. This peak has no official name according to the USGS, but Ron Haddad and Eileen Faughey, authors of *Front Range Descents*, decided to name this point Radiobeacon Mountain based on the USGS label. The name has mostly stuck, although morphed versions of it exist, such as Radiobeacon Peak or Beacon Peak. While the radio beacon near the summit no longer exists, a concrete slab still remains reminding us of its presence.

Due to high winds that occur along the Continental Divide and the resulting wind loading, the east-facing cirque of this mountain holds a wealth of snow well into the summer. The cirque has many different aspects, which range from north to east to south, and various lines that range in steepness from 30 degrees to 50 degrees or more, providing options for many different levels of skiers.

GETTING THERE

Radiobeacon Mountain is accessed via Corona Pass Road or Moffat Road, part of which was formerly a railway. But the road is no longer fully passable by vehicles from east to west, or vice versa, after a rock fell from the ceiling of the Needle Eye Tunnel just below the east side of Rollins Pass, injuring a firefighter in 1990. Boulder County then sealed the tunnel shut.

You will need to decide if you want to access Radiobeacon Mountain from the west via Winter Park and Rollins Pass or from Rollinsville to the east. The west provides shorter and quicker access, but the road to Rollins Pass does not typically open until mid-June. From the east, you can access Radiobeacon earlier in the season, but the starting point is farther away from the mountain.

If you are accessing from the west, drive south from the town of Winter Park on US Highway 40. Just north of the typical turnoff to the west for skier parking, you will see a turn to the east onto County Road 80 (Corona Pass Road [Forest Road 149]). Signs may also indicate that this is the road for Rollins Pass. Follow this road as it heads north and then east, winding through switchbacks to the top of Rollins Pass 14 miles past the intersection with US 40. Corona Pass Road is a dirt road. A 4WD vehicle is not absolutely necessary, but the road is bumpy and it can be rough on cars without strong shocks. This road typically does not open until June 15. To inquire about the status of the Corona Pass Road, call the Sulphur Ranger District (see Resources).

If you are accessing from the east, drive 5 miles south on Colorado Highway 119. Turn right (west) onto County Road 16 (East Portal Road). Although the road becomes dirt, is it passable by most passenger vehicles. After 7.5 miles, you'll reach an intersection with County Road 117. Stay straight on CR 16, driving another 0.75 mile to a large parking area for the East Portal trailhead. You will see the East Portal of the Moffat Tunnel used for trains from the parking lot. This trailhead is typically accessible year-round. You can park here, or you can take your chances and see how far you can get up the Rollins Pass Road.

If you want to continue, from CR 16 turn east onto CR 117 (Rollins Pass Road). Here the road begins to get a bit rougher. A 4WD vehicle is recommended but not

A skier negotiates one of the steep entrances to a couloir on Radiobeacon Mountain.

always necessary. You may not be able to drive to your desired destination due to snow cover. Follow this road upward, and it will eventually begin bearing west. If possible, drive 11 miles to the other end of the Forest Lakes Trail at an elevation of 11,040 feet. Alternatively, you could park at a switchback 7.7 miles up the road from the intersection with CR 16, at an elevation of 10,435 feet. If you choose this access, you will not have a trail to help you travel to Forest Lakes.

THE ROUTE

From Rollins Pass: Head south, downhill, on Corona Pass Road for 0.7 mile until you reach the start of the Loop Trail on your left. Follow the Loop Trail up and south to the summit of Radiobeacon Mountain. Travel north or south along the ridge from the summit, and find your best path of descent.

From East Portal: Travel southwest on the South Boulder Creek Trail for 1.25 miles. Turn right or northeast onto the Forest Lakes Trail. Follow this trail as it heads north to Forest Lakes. The first lake is approximately 3.25 miles from the trailhead at an elevation of 10,670 feet. The trail will travel to the west of the lake and then begin to turn north and cross a stream. Leave the trail here, remaining south of the

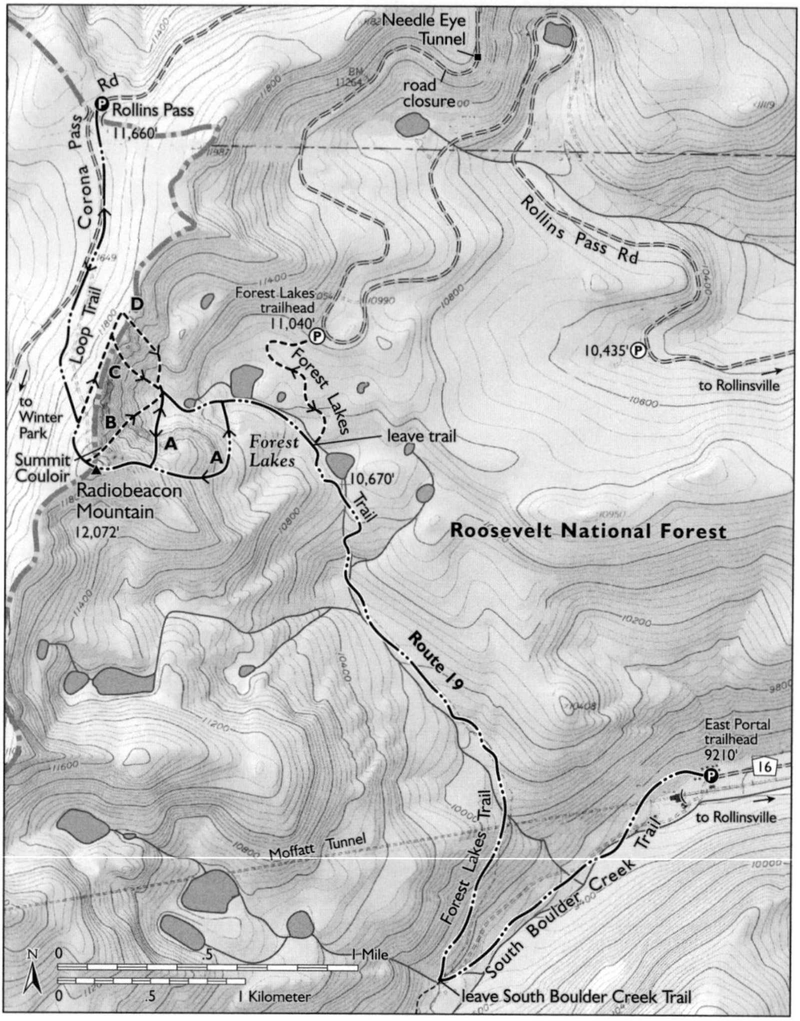

stream, and follow the drainage as it heads northwest to the upper Forest Lakes. Once at Forest Lakes, the easiest ascent option follows the chutes and ridge on the south side of the cirque (option A) 1.5 miles and 1250 vertical feet to the summit. You can also ascend your intended descent route.

From Forest Lakes Trailhead: Follow the trail as it heads southwest toward the Forest Lakes. Around 0.5 mile, the trail will turn and begin to head southeast. You may find it best to leave the trail here and continue traveling southwest to the upper Forest Lakes.

Descent. There are many different lines to descend. As mentioned above, lines in this cirque range from 30 degrees to 50-plus degrees. Their lengths typically vary from 800 to 1250 vertical feet. Take note that some of the lines may be guarded by cornices at the top, making them difficult to enter from above and also posing the additional hazard of potential cornice fall on your ascent. The east ridge on the south end of the cirque and the associated north-facing chutes coming down from it can provide easier descent and ascent options (A) and are considered the primary routes here.

Many of the couloirs in the cirque have names. The Summit Couloir (B) leads down just to the looker's right of the summit. Another noticeable line is a southeast-facing route with a double fall line called Double Fall Line Couloir (C). The wider line to the looker's right of that is the Forest Lake Bowl South (D).

If you are approaching from the east and Forest Lakes, you may want to climb what you skied or descend via the east ridge on the south end of the cirque. Pick a line to descend and ski back to upper Forest Lakes and then go up for another lap or two, or return to the trailhead via your ascent route.

If approaching from Rollins Pass, you may want to reascend what you skied or ascend via the east ridge on the south end of the cirque. Once at the top, either return to Rollins Pass via your ascent route or go back for a second lap.

20 James Peak: North and East Couloirs

Starting Elevation	10,400 feet
High Point	13,294 feet
Vertical Gain/Loss	3650 feet
Ascent Distance	4 miles
Descent Distance	4.75 miles
Time	6 to 8 hours
Ski Skills	Easy to very difficult
Fitness Level	Strenuous
Technical Skills	Low to moderate
Gear	The basics, plus ice axe and crampons if climbing the couloirs directly
Best Months	April and May
USGS Map	Empire

In the heart of the James Peak Wilderness lies the prominent 13,294-foot James Peak, for which it is named. Certainly one of the most aesthetic peaks in the Front Range, James Peak is a great destination for ski mountaineers. The peak itself was named in honor of Dr. Edwin James, who was an explorer, historian, botanist, and one of Colorado's first true mountaineers. In 1820, James was a member of the army expedition led by Stephen H. Long. On that expedition he, along with two companions, became the first people to climb the 14,000-foot peak now known as Pikes Peak.

James Peak offers a range of descent options from under 30 degrees to 60 degrees. The variability, as well as its ease of access, makes James Peak a popular ski-mountaineering destination for Front Range residents.

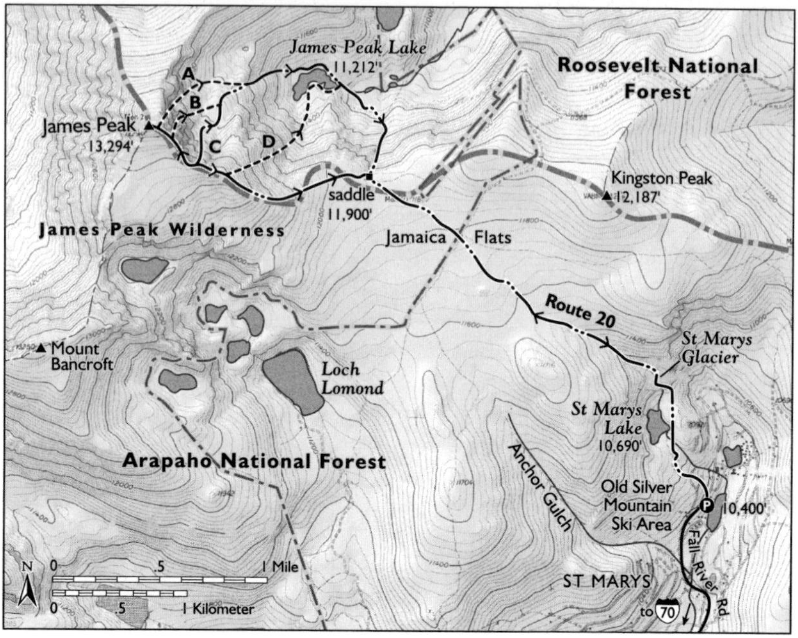

GETTING THERE

From Interstate 70, take exit 238 for Fall River Road, located just west of Idaho Springs. Drive north on Fall River Road for 8.6 miles until you see parking for St. Marys Glacier, passing the small town of Alice along the way. The closest option for parking is the farthest north and holds approximately twenty cars. But there are options back south toward the defunct Silver Mountain/Silver Lake ski area. The parking here is fee-based, and at the time of writing the cost to park one vehicle was $5 per day.

Some people approach this area from the James Lake trailhead, but this access is not usually open until sometime in June due to snow on the road.

THE ROUTE

From the parking area at 10,400 feet, follow the signs for the trail to St. Marys Lake/Glacier, which heads northwest along an old dirt road. Just below the glacier, you'll find the lake at 10,690 feet. Continue northwest and ascend the slopes of the glacier above the lake. Note that St. Marys Glacier is a popular tourist destination and a fun place to get some moderate year-round ski turns that are not too difficult to access, a little under a mile from the parking area.

Near the top of the glacier, the slope begins to flatten and then flattens even more. You've arrived at an area called the Jamaica Flats, around 11,500 feet, approximately 1.5 miles from the trailhead. Continue northwest, and you will eventually be able to see the summit of James Peak beyond and above the flats. After traveling northeast

Descending Starlight Couloir on James Peak on a stormy day (Photo by Chris Miller)

for just over a mile, you will reach the southeast ridge of James Peak. Follow this ridge northwest another 1 to 1.5 miles to the summit.

Descent. The easiest ski route is to descend your ascent route, which is a classic James Peak ski. But the real meat lies in the eight or so descent options that lie on the east-facing cirque of James Peak, a few of which we'll mention. The primary route is Starlight Couloir (C), which typically hovers around a reasonable 40 degrees and is located 0.3 mile east of the summit around 12,900 feet. Alternatively, from the summit, you could drop east into Shooting Star (A), which approaches 60 degrees near the summit and lessens to around 50 degrees. This route typically lacks a cornice. Sky Pilot (B) lies just below the summit about 200 yards to the southeast and is a 50-degree double fall-line chute over exposed cliffs. The easiest descent option leading down to James Peak Lake Basin is a wider line called Bailout (D), and it descends almost due east from the southeast ridge at 12,850 feet, just a little bit down from Starlight, and then curves north part of the way down the line.

No matter your descent option on the northeast face, you will end up at the bottom near James Peak Lake (11,212 feet). If you want to go up for a second lap, you will find it best to climb what you ski. To return to the trailhead, work your way to the east end of the lake, at which point you will want to begin ascending the north slopes to the ridge. Contour southeast to about 12,300 feet, where you will want to ascend an obvious gully south to the saddle, which you will gain around an elevation of 11,900 feet. From here, retrace your ascent route through Jamaica Flats. Be careful not to descend into

Anchor Gulch, which is slightly more skier's right than the drainage that harbors St. Marys Glacier. In general, trend a little more east than south to descend back down St. Marys Glacier. Follow the old road back to the trailhead.

Extra Credit: Two couloirs, Super Star and Starbright, lie north of the summit of James Peak and drop into the same cirque. These also make challenging descents.

21 Mount Eva: Eva Bowl and Southeast Face

Starting Elevation	9550 feet or more
High Point	13,130 feet
Vertical Gain/Loss	3600 feet or less
Ascent Distance	6+/- miles or less
Descent Distance	6 miles or less
Time	4 to 7 hours
Ski Skills	Easy to difficult
Fitness Level	Strenuous
Technical Skills	Low
Gear	The basics; ice axe and crampons may be needed
Best Months	April to June
USGS Maps	Ward and Monarch Lake

While Fall River Reservoir is a popular destination for fishing, not many people venture beyond it to the high peaks near the Continental Divide. Mount Eva is one of those peaks that can sometimes go unnoticed by passersby. But it offers a beautiful tour with fabulous summit views and a range of slopes to suit a variety of ski abilities.

Dr. Charles Parry, who was a botanist in the 1800s, named the peak after his wife, Eva. In fact, he named several of the Front Range mountains after his friends and family. Parry Peak, which the doctor named after himself, lies immediately north of Mount Eva.

Perhaps the most distinguishable feature of Mount Eva is the now-defunct radio tower that lies just southwest of the summit. It was constructed before the establishment of the James Peak Wilderness. When the wilderness legislation passed in 2002, it specifically called for the removal of this tower. However, the tower still remains. Perhaps marmots will help take it down some day!

GETTING THERE

From Interstate 70, take exit 238 for Fall River Road, located just west of Idaho Springs. Head north on Fall River Road for 6.7 miles to a big right-turning switchback. In the middle of the switchback, there is a road on the left. Turn left (northwest) onto Rainbow Road (Forest Road 174.1).

If you don't have a high-clearance 4WD vehicle, it is recommended that you park here near the intersection at an elevation of 9550 feet as the road is dirt and quickly becomes rough. Should you venture higher, be aware that this road travels

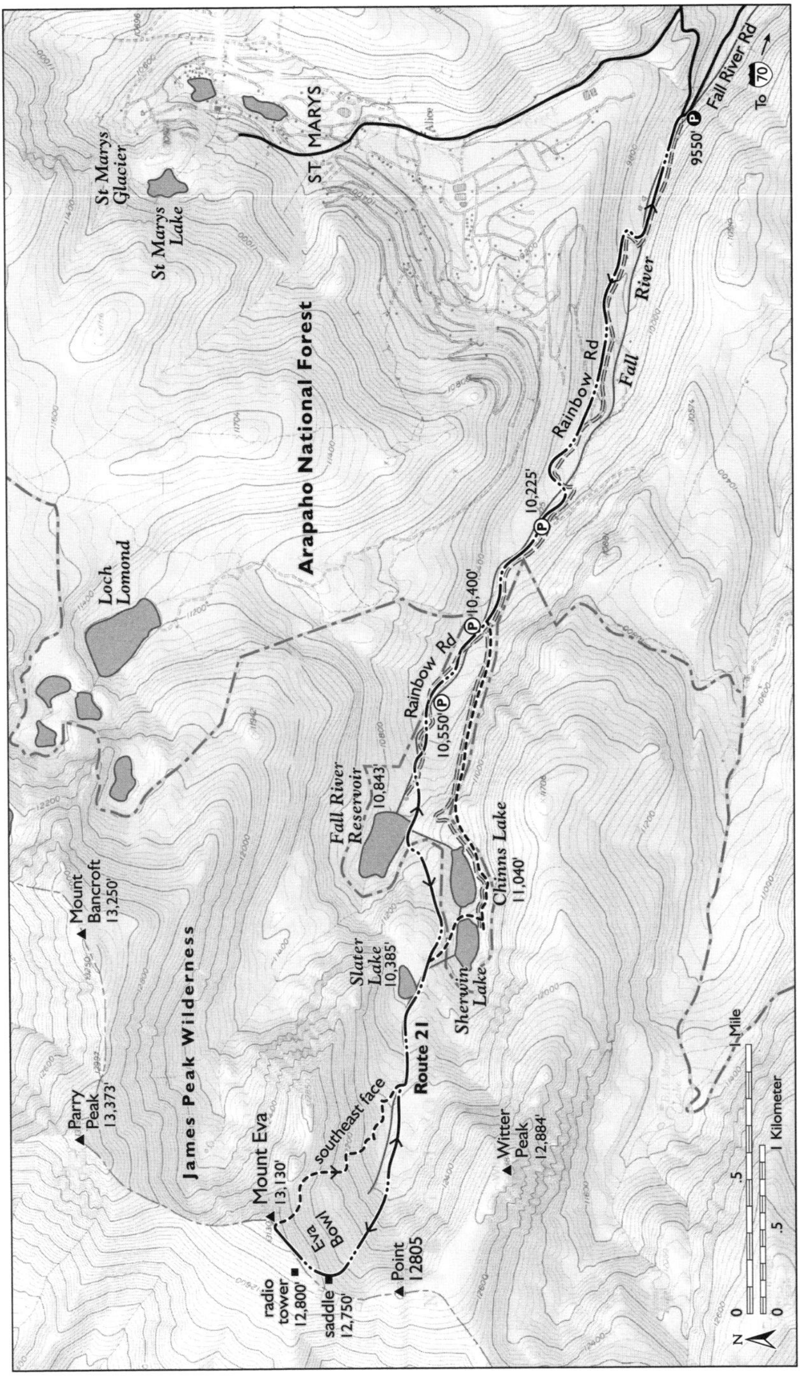
Mount Eva
13,130'
Parry Peak
13,373'
Mount Bancroft
13,250'
James Peak Wilderness
Loch Lomond
Arapaho National Forest
St Marys Glacier
St Marys Lake
ST MARYS
Alice
Fall River Reservoir
10,843'
Chinns Lake
11,040'
Slater Lake
10,385'
Sherwin Lake
Route 21
southeast face
Eva Bowl
radio tower
12,800'
saddle
12,750'
Point
12805
Witter Peak
12,884'
Rainbow Rd
10,550'
10,400'
10,225'
Fall River
9550'
Fall River Rd
To 70
1 Mile
1 Kilometer

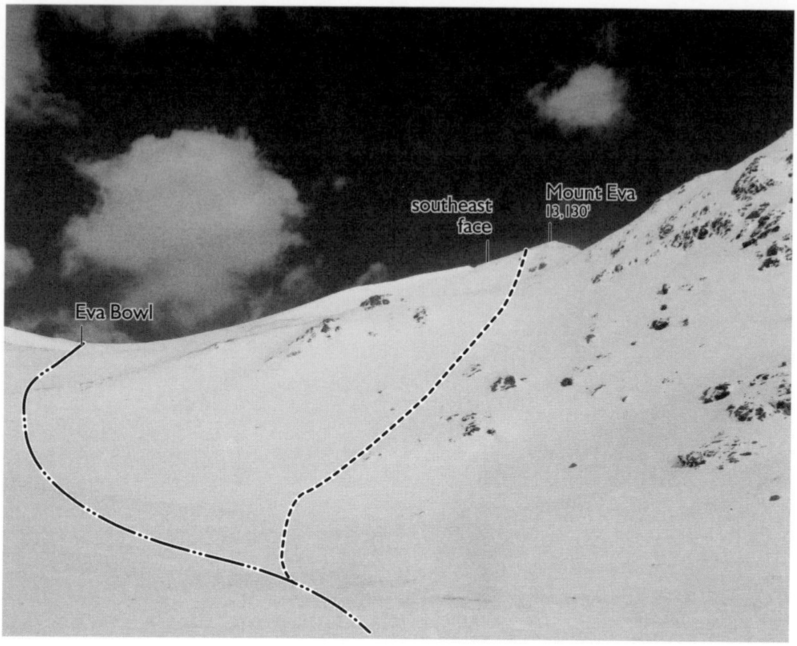

through more than 2 miles of private property at the beginning. Signs near the beginning of the road state that you can only park in designated Forest Service areas, and these can be hard to find during snow cover. Your best bet is to try to make it up to 10,225 feet where the Continental Divide Trail crosses the road. About one-quarter mile after this intersection, the road enters Forest Service land and private property is generally no longer an issue. Even so, if you try to drive past the Continental Divide Trail, it is recommended that you park near the east side of the Fall River Reservoir about 3.5 miles up from Fall River Road, near 10,400 or 10,700 feet.

THE ROUTE

If you parked near the start of Rainbow Road at 9950 feet, follow the road northwest to Fall River Reservoir. At 2.75 miles, you will see a road veering off to the left toward Chinns Lake. If snow is not present from 11,000 feet and below, take this alternate road to Chinns Lake and then west to Sherwin Lake. From here, head north to reach the south side of Slater Lake. If the area is devoid of snow, there is a summer trail that leads from Sherwin Lake to Slater Lake.

If snow is present below 11,000 feet, continue up Rainbow Road to where the road splits to go around the Fall River Reservoir. Take the left fork, which heads west. Just after the road crosses the stream that comes down from Chinns Lake to the west, leave the road and begin contouring along the south side of the slope, heading west. Try to stay high, above Chinns Lake, but remaining below Slater Lake.

Pass along the south shores of Slater Lake (elevation 11,385 feet), continuing to head west up the drainage. At Slater Lake, the trees begin to thin and soon you will find yourself above tree line. Mount Eva will lie to your right, Eva Bowl will be straight ahead, and Witter Peak will be on your left. Ascend Eva Bowl toward the obvious saddle just north of Point 12,805 around 12,750 feet. Follow the ridge northeast to the summit of Mount Eva at 13,130, passing the old radio tower around 12,800 feet.

Descent. The easiest descent option is to ski your ascent route back through the east-facing Eva Bowl and is the primary descent route. A steeper alternative is to ski the southeast face. Dropping into this face directly from the summit can be difficult due to cornices. To work your way around the cornices, head southeast on the ridge for just a bit until you find a place to enter without a cornice. In general, the farther skier's left you go, the steeper the route. Both routes flatten around 11,850 feet. From here, follow your ascent route back to your car.

Extra Credit: On your ascent, you passed beneath a south-facing couloir that drops down from the east ridge of Mount Eva. This can have good skiing after a nice wet spring storm but before the snow warms to cause wet slides.

22 Berthoud Pass

Starting Elevation	11,307 feet (Low point: 10,770 feet)
High Point	11,963 feet
Vertical Gain/Loss	1980 feet
Ascent Distance	1.7 miles
Descent Distance	1.7 miles
Time	2 to 4 hours
Ski Skills	Moderate
Fitness Level	Not very strenuous
Technical Skills	Low
Gear	The basics
Best Months	December to April
USGS Map	Berthoud Pass

Starting in 1937, Berthoud Pass was a ski area, but the lifts stopped turning in 2001 and the area is now a popular backcountry destination. The pass offers a wide variety of terrain, and many skiers are introduced to the backcountry for the first time at Berthoud (including the authors of this book). Berthoud Pass diehards can spend years learning the finer intricacies of routes in the area, while the short tour here gives a good overview for first-timers.

GETTING THERE

Berthoud Pass is located on US Highway 40, 13.5 miles from Winter Park to the north, or 15.1 miles from the Interstate 70 turnoff near Empire. A large parking lot

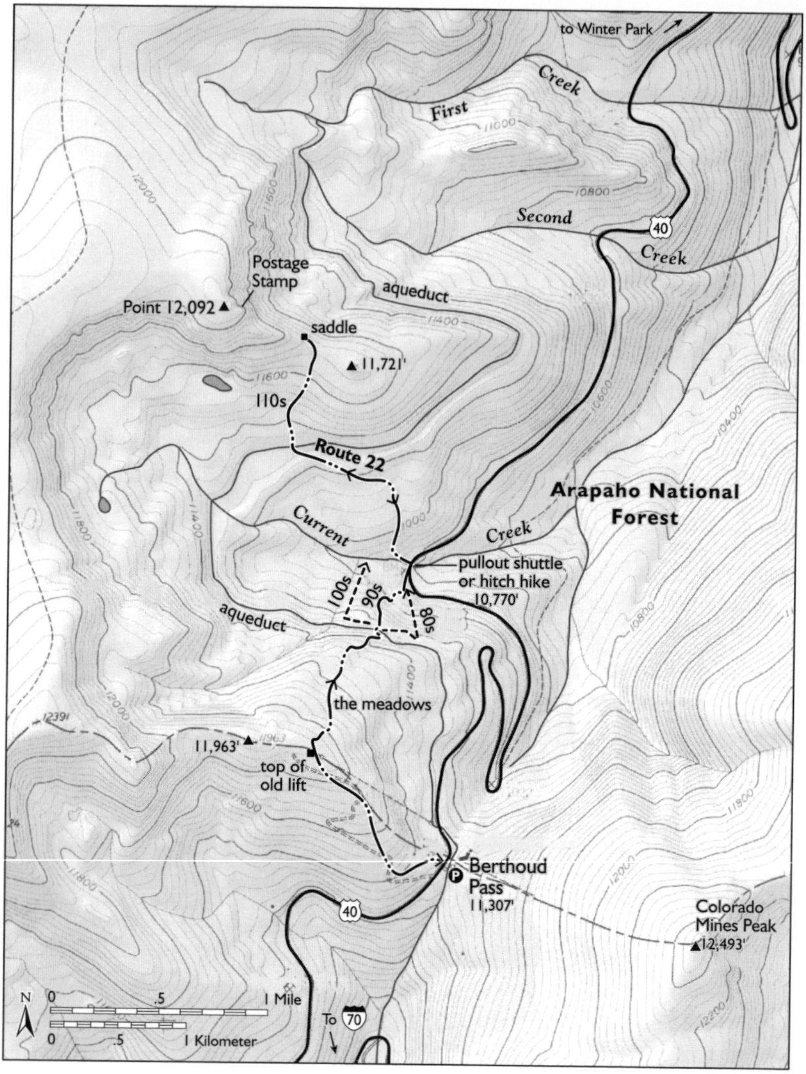

complete with a warming house and bathrooms is located on the east side of the pass. Routes at Berthoud Pass often descend to different points along the highway, so you may want to consider running a car shuttle. For this route, the Current Creek pullout, where you can leave a second car, is 1.9 miles north of the Berthoud Pass trailhead on US 40.

THE ROUTE

Cross the highway to the west side, and begin skinning up an old access road to the west/southwest. Turn northwest when you reach one of the old Berthoud Pass Ski

Finding a powder stash on the pass (Photo by Keith Spargo)

Area runs, and follow this general direction toward a high point just east of Point 11,963. At one time, one of the chairlifts stopped just below this high point.

Descent. Ski an area called the meadows to the north/northeast, through punji-tree-created wind drifts. This run starts off mellow but steepens a bit as it approaches the aqueduct that traverses across the area. The areas below the aqueduct are steeper than the terrain above. To the skier's right are the 80s, the 90s are in the middle, and the 100s are skier's left. Conditions permitting, ski any of these to a pullout on the highway below, but the 90s are considered to be the primary route in this book. From the pullout at 10,770 feet, you can try to hitch a ride back to the pass (assuming you didn't run your own shuttle), or skin up to an area called the 110s for another lap.

To continue on to the 110s, head west/northwest up the Current Creek drainage. Your goal is a small saddle between points 11,721 and 12,092. Chances are high that several different skin tracks will head in this direction, so take whichever one makes the most sense. The southeast face of Point 12,092 is known as the "Postage Stamp," and it's best to give this avalanche-prone area a wide berth. From the saddle, ski back down the southern slopes (the 110s) that you just ascended back to the Current Creek pullout. Given the southern exposure, it's best to ski this area quickly after a storm. From the pullout, return to the Berthoud Pass trailhead by hitchhiking or utilizing a car shuttle.

Though not necessary, the climb to Hagar's summit is a fun one!

23 Hagar Mountain

Starting Elevation	10,700 feet
High Point	13,195 feet
Vertical Gain/Loss	2600 feet
Ascent Distance	4.1 miles
Descent Distance	4.1 miles
Time	5 to 7 hours
Ski Skills	Difficult
Fitness Level	Moderately strenuous
Technical Skills	Moderate
Gear	The basics, plus ice axe and crampons
Best Months	March to early June
USGS Map	Loveland Pass

Visible from Loveland Ski Area and for a very short time while traveling west on Interstate 70, Hagar is a terrific mountain with a number of routes on its south side. Combined with easy access right off I-70, Hagar has long been a favorite of Front Range skiers.

GETTING THERE

The Dry Gulch trailhead can be reached by using exit 216 off I-70. This exit is located just east of the Eisenhower Tunnel, and it is the same exit used for the Loveland Ski Area. Parking is located on the north side of this exit, the opposite side of the highway from the ski area. You will find a small pullout off the road, just west of the dirt (or snow-covered) Dry Gulch Road.

THE ROUTE

Begin the tour by paralleling the interstate to the northeast, on Dry Gulch Road. This road is slightly downhill, so you will want to start off with skins in your pack. Later in the season, you may be able to drive this short section until reaching a gate. Regardless, the road begins heading in a more northerly direction, away from the highway and the din of traffic. Follow the road as it passes a fenced storage area and begins curving to the northwest then west as you near tree line. At tree line, the southeast and east slopes of Hagar are directly above.

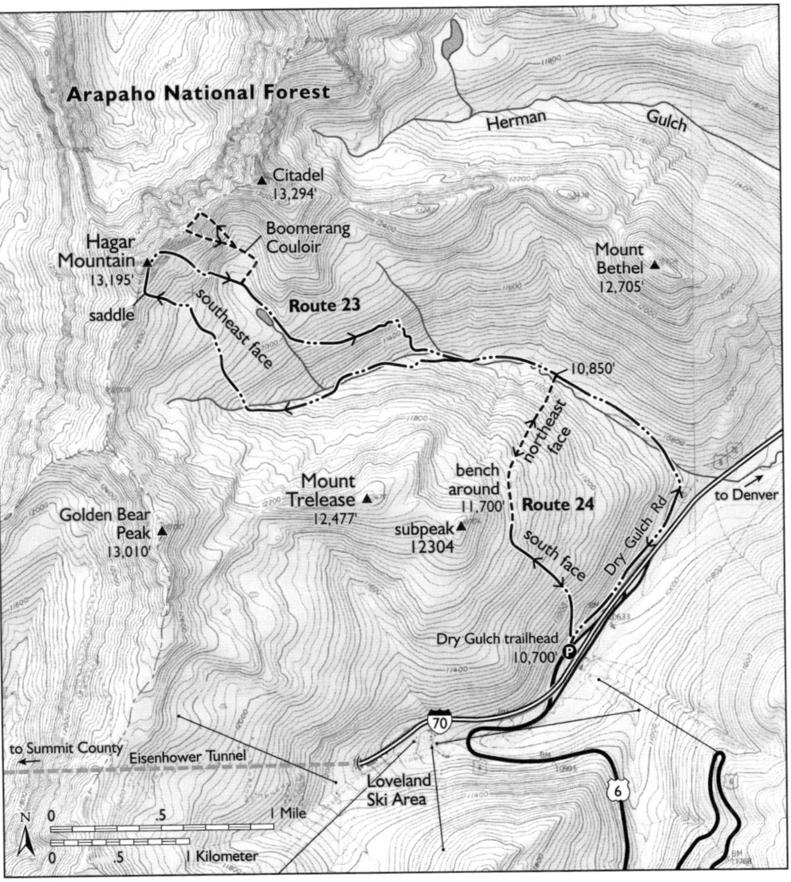

One of the great things about Hagar Mountain is that it gives skiers a number of choices. The southeast face is the easiest and can be reached by climbing it directly or by ascending to the small saddle on the south ridge and following the ridge north toward the summit. An alternative route is the Boomerang Couloir, a dogleg route that is tough to see from top to bottom, located on the looker's right of the face. Looking even farther to the looker's right are more routes that face more easterly. All of these routes can be reached by climbing them directly, and the distance required is the same.

Descent. All of these routes receive early sunlight and should be skied early in the day. You could even ski both routes described in one day. Descend the southeast face or Boomerang Couloir and follow your skin track back to I-70. Remember that you will have a slight climb back to your car on the last part of Dry Gulch Road.

Extra Credit: Nearby Citadel is another option in this area.

24 Mount Trelease: South and Northeast Faces

Starting Elevation	10,700 feet
High Point	11,700 feet
Vertical Gain/Loss	1100 feet or more
Ascent Distance	1 to 2 miles
Descent Distance	1 to 2 miles
Time	1.5 to 5 hours
Ski Skills	Easy to moderate
Fitness Level	Not very strenuous
Technical Skills	Low
Gear	The basics
Best Months	December to April
USGS Map	Loveland Pass

Easily visible from Interstate 70 and Loveland Ski Area, Mount Trelease (see map in Route 23) is a popular destination for backcountry skiers. Its low-angle slopes and evenly spaced trees provide a great playground to enjoy a powder day. But this mountain does contain an element of risk above tree line and near the summit. Here the east-facing aspects are particularly prone to sliding, and avalanches have been known to be triggered remotely from skiers below. For that reason, most tours of Mount Trelease don't involve actually going to the summit. Instead, most stay lower down in the trees. Use caution and make sure you are traveling through this area safely.

GETTING THERE

The Dry Gulch trailhead can be reached by using exit 216 off I-70. This exit is located just east of the Eisenhower Tunnel and is the same exit used for the Loveland

Playing in powder on the northeast side of Mount Trelease

Ski Area. Parking is located on the north side of this exit, the opposite side of the highway from the ski area. You will find a small pullout off the road, just west of the dirt (or snow-covered) Dry Gulch Road.

THE ROUTE

The south face provides the quickest access and can have some great turns as well, provided the snow has not been impacted by solar radiation yet. From the parking lot, look for a gully that comes down from the looker's right. Follow this gully northeast and then due north. Around 11,250 feet, the forest will begin to thin and you will begin following the natural terrain as it bears northwest. As you climb, you will see the 12,304-foot subpeak of Trelease to your left. Note that the eastern face of this peak poses an avalanche hazard, and you should plan your ascent route accordingly to stay away from avalanche paths that descend from this face. A normal stopping point is at a bench around 11,600 or 11,700 feet.

Descent. Turn around at the bench and descend your ascent route back to the parking area.

Alternate Route. The northeast face of Trelease provides another great skiing zone that is more sheltered from the sun, but it is a longer tour. This zone is also more complex than the south face and has some potentially dangerous rollovers and terrain traps that are more prone to sliding during higher avalanche conditions, especially during or after a storm. However, the area is manageable for experienced backcountry skiers.

From the parking area, travel northeast and then northwest for approximately 1.5 miles along Dry Gulch Road and Dry Gulch drainage. Around an elevation of 10,850 feet, observe the northeast slopes of Mount Trelease and look for a good ascent path through the forest. Skiers typically top out just below tree line at a bench around 11,600 or 11,700 feet.

Alternatively, this route can be accessed by ascending the south slopes described above and then traversing north along a bench, remaining just under an elevation of 11,800 feet. This traverse is not recommended unless snow conditions are stable as it will take you beneath east-facing avalanche paths from the subpeak at 12,304 feet.

You can easily connect the main route and the alternative route together by ascending the south slopes first, traversing north along the bench (described above), and then descending the northeast face. Once in the Dry Gulch drainage, put your skins back on and reascend what you skied. Traverse south on the bench until you reach the south face. Descend the south face back to the parking area.

25 Loveland Pass: Hippie Trees

Starting Elevation	10,600 feet
High Point	11,820 feet
Vertical Gain/Loss	1200 feet
Ascent Distance	1 mile
Descent Distance	1 mile
Time	1.5 to 2.5 hours
Ski Skills	Moderate to difficult
Fitness Level	Not very strenuous
Technical Skills	Low
Gear	The basics
Best Months	December to April
USGS Map	Loveland Pass

Between the two popular ski areas of Loveland and Arapahoe Basin lies Loveland Pass, arguably the most treacherous portion of US Highway 6 that spans the country. Still, Loveland Pass remains one of the most popular backcountry ski zones in the state of Colorado. It also is one of the most frequently closed sections of road during the winter. While higher areas of Loveland Pass are certainly worth exploring, you will want to know areas that are outside of the typical closure boundaries. On that storm day when everyone is waiting for Loveland Pass to open, you can be out there enjoying lap after lap in the Hippie Trees.

GETTING THERE

Many people access the Hippie Trees from the top of Loveland Pass. But accessing them from the bottom allows you to enjoy them when they are best—when Loveland

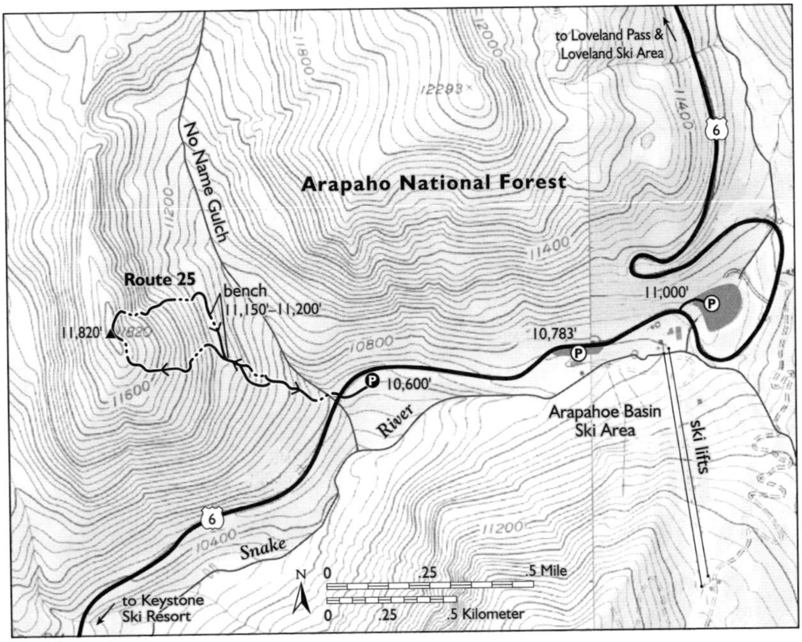

Pass is closed. The Hippie Trees starts at No Name Gulch, on the west side of Loveland Pass (US 6), roughly 0.8 mile west of the turns for the major parking areas for Arapahoe Basin Ski Area. The gulch is a drainage hidden in the trees, but those looking for it will find it. The best places to park are pullouts on either side of US 6 a little east of the gulch.

THE ROUTE

Begin your tour on the north side of US 6 and on the west side of No Name Gulch. Head northwest through a set of dead trees that have been impacted by beetle kill, eventually following a slight ridge as you gain elevation. Around 11,150 feet you will come to a bench. After this, the terrain becomes considerably steeper. If the snow is deep, you may want to just start your first lap from here. If you want to continue upward, one of the easiest routes involves changing course a bit to a more westward direction. Continue up to an obvious ridge whose high point is at 11,820 feet.

Descent. Descend the east and southeast aspects. Keep in mind, the farther you work your way north, the shorter the "good" skiing will be as you will arrive at No Name Gulch farther up in elevation. For a quality descent, descend to the bench, which lies at an elevation of 11,150 to 11,200 feet, and then traverse south on the bench to ski the southeast trees. This area makes a great zone to do multiple laps!

Extra Credit: A little farther west you will find Porcupine Gulch, another zone worth exploring especially when US 6 is closed. When Loveland Pass is open, many lines are accessible off the top of the pass.

Hippie Trees is a perfect playground for a powder day.

26 Black Mountain: Shit for Brains Couloir

Starting Elevation	11,000 feet
High Point	12,900 or 13,193 feet
Vertical Gain/Loss	1900 to 2200 feet
Ascent Distance	1 to 1.3 miles
Descent Distance	1 to 1.3 miles
Time	3 to 5 hours
Ski Skills	Very difficult
Fitness Level	Moderately strenuous (due to steep nature)
Technical Skills	High
Gear	The basics; ice axe and crampons may be needed
Best Months	March to April
USGS Map	Grays Peak

Though technically unranked, this peak is locally known as "Black Mountain" and it's easy to see why. From Interstate 70 and the Frisco area, Black Mountain stands tall and dark, with a big white streak cutting straight down it, dividing the mountain in half. That white streak has become known as the Shit for Brains Couloir, a classic ski mountaineering route. If you've skied at Arapahoe Basin Ski Area, chances are you've stared right up this line as Black Mountain sits adjacent to the ski area boundaries.

Timing for Shit for Brains can be a bit tricky. As a classic ski mountaineering route, typical snowpack and avalanche patterns dictate that the safest time to ski it is in spring. But due to the dark rock that towers above and the west-facing nature of this route, snow can warm very quickly, especially in spring. You can usually see wet slide debris in the couloir by April, if not earlier. This can impact the quality of skiing, especially at the bottom of the route. We recommend that you ski Shit for Brains before significant warming, or look for a small bit of fresh snow to soften up the parts speckled with debris.

GETTING THERE

Black Mountain is best accessed from the Arapahoe Basin parking lots. Arapahoe Basin is about 5 miles east of Keystone Ski Resort on US Highway 6. Arapahoe Basin can be reached from the east by exiting I-70 at the Loveland Ski Area exit, just east of Eisenhower Tunnel. From Loveland Ski Area, follow US 6 westbound about 7.5 miles up and over Loveland Pass to Arapahoe Basin Ski Area. The Colorado Department of Transportation (CDOT) often closes Loveland Pass, and it is your best resource for an updated status (see Resources).

If the ski area is open, you can park in its lots. The uppermost lot is the closest to the starting point. If the ski area is closed, parking in these lots is prohibited. To reach

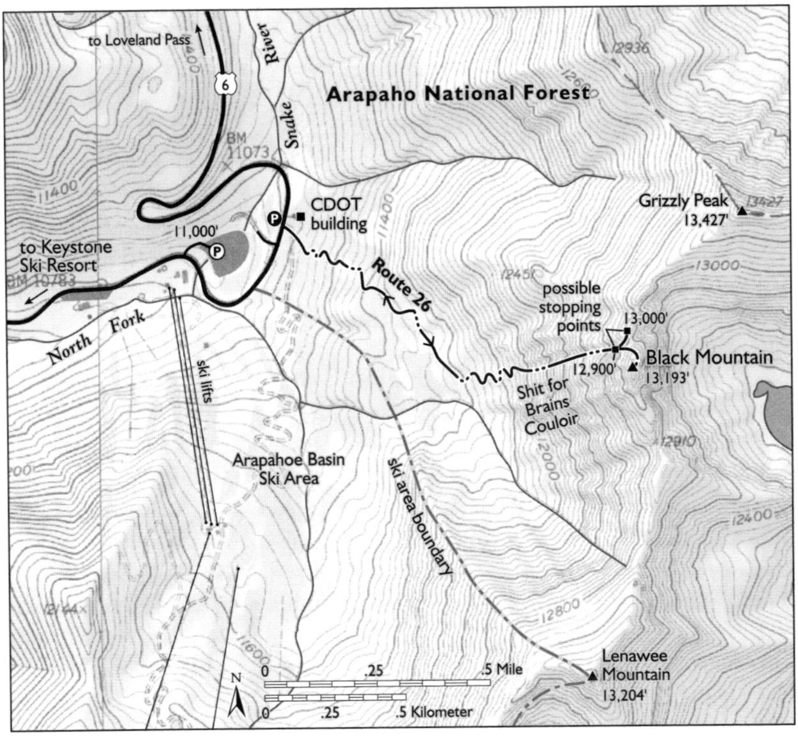

Climbing the upper part of Shit for Brains Couloir on Black Mountain (Photo by Alex Riedman)

the parking area closest to the trailhead, drive 0.1 mile up (eastbound) the road to a parking area near the CDOT building. Please be sure to obey any "No Parking" signs.

THE ROUTE

The start of this route travels very close to Arapahoe Basin's ski area boundaries. When the ski area is in operation, please make sure to avoid ski area land. The route passes by the ski area's northeastern border, which is usually well marked with ski area boundary signs. To avoid the ski area, start on US 6 just north of the Arapahoe Basin Ski Area just south of the CDOT building on the eastern edge of a large horseshoe in the road. There you'll find a small access road heading east and then quickly veering south.

As soon as the access road begins to turn south, start ascending through the forest, trending southeast, avoiding the ski area boundary. The best route switchbacks through the forest between a drainage to the south and another to the north. At 11,000 feet, the trees open up and you will see Black Mountain standing in front of you. Ascend the apron to the base of Shit for Brains Couloir. There are several couloirs on the west face of Black. The one you're looking for is just looker's left of the summit. From the bottom, you should be able to look straight up to a saddle that is just left of the peak.

Most backcountry skiers bootpack beginning somewhere in the apron or bottom of the Shit for Brains Couloir. Rock fall is common in this couloir, so you should ascend early and wear a helmet. The top of the couloir often lacks snow, so many people opt to stop ascending around 12,900 feet. Alternatively, you could climb a steep pitch looker's left of the couloir to a ridge and bench about 100 feet higher (13,000 feet). If you want to reach the summit, stay in the couloir and keep climbing to a saddle at 13,040 feet. From there, follow the ridge south to the summit at 13,193 feet. Due to lack of snow, you may need to downclimb from the summit to 12,900 feet.

Descent. Ski your ascent route, taking care of a narrow choke about one-third of the way down the couloir. The angle remains in the 40-degree range for over 1000 feet, making for a very fun descent!

Extra Credit: On looker's left lie two alternate couloirs, Dog Shit and Dogleg. These can make fun additions to your tour!

27 Grizzly Peak: Grizzly Couloir

Starting Elevation	9800 feet
High Point	12,850 feet
Vertical Gain/Loss	3050 feet
Ascent Distance	4.5 miles
Descent Distance	4.5 miles
Time	7 to 9 hours
Ski Skills	Difficult
Fitness Level	Moderately strenuous
Technical Skills	Moderate
Gear	The basics, plus ice axe and crampons
Best Months	March to early June
USGS Map	Grays Peak

While less famous than the Grizzly Peak near Independence Pass, *this* Grizzly Couloir provides an equally striking line accessed directly off Interstate 70. Guarded by large cornices at the top, Grizzly Couloir is a line that should be taken seriously and can challenge many ski mountaineers. The north face of Grizzly Peak harbors other choices for ski mountaineers looking to extend their day.

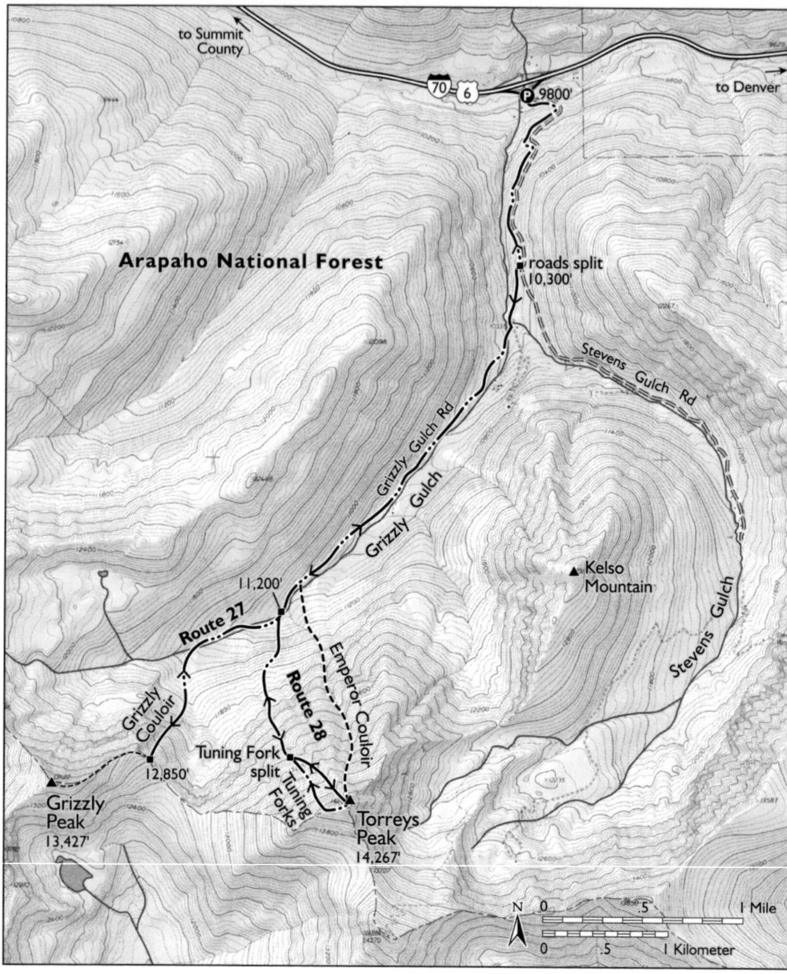

GETTING THERE

Exit I-70 at the Bakerville exit east of the Loveland Ski Area. Park on the south side of the highway at the bottom of Stevens Gulch Road. Later in the season, it may be possible to drive farther up the road. Take care when doing this, and do not attempt to drive over deep-frozen snow. Many a car has become stuck doing this very thing. Don't be "that guy"!

THE ROUTE

Ascend Stevens Gulch Road for 1 mile, and then head right on Grizzly Gulch Road at 10,300 feet. Follow Grizzly Gulch Road toward the couloir, which will be in sight for much of this tour. Later in the season, following this road may entail stream crossings. It is also possible to drive up this rough 4WD road by early summer.

Finding the pow stashes on Grizzly

At an elevation of 11,200 feet, you will pass beneath the runout of the Tuning Forks (Route 28). Continue heading southwest up the valley to approximately 11,300 feet where you will need to bear more south to reach the couloir.

From the base of the couloir around 11,700 feet, take note of the giant cornice that droops above the couloir. Climb quickly and stay to the sides of the couloir whenever possible. Most skiers will stop below the cornice, although it is possible to bypass the cornice with some exposed moves. From the top of the couloir, it is an additional 0.5 mile and 600 vertical feet to the summit.

Descent. Descend the northeast-facing couloir for roughly 1000 feet, and follow your approach route back to the trailhead.

Extra Credit: This route can easily be combined with the Tuning Forks (Route 28) to make for a long day. Due to the aspect of each route, it is usually better to ski the Grizzly Couloir first.

28 Torreys Peak: Tuning Forks

Starting Elevation	9800 feet
High Point	14,267 feet
Vertical Gain/Loss	4467 feet
Ascent Distance	4.6 miles
Descent Distance	4.6 miles
Time	7 to 9 hours
Ski Skills	Difficult
Fitness Level	Strenuous
Technical Skills	Moderate
Gear	The basics, plus ice axe and crampons
Best Months	March to early June
USGS Map	Grays Peak

Racing the evening sun down the Tuning Forks

Torreys Peak is one of Colorado's most popular fourteeners due to its close proximity to Denver and its ease of access. Many backcountry ski routes are possible on this iconic peak, but the Tuning Forks offer one of the longest descent options. Rising 3000 feet from the valley floor, this line provides a long and consistent descent. If you're seeking a line that feels like it goes on forever, the Tuning Forks should be at the top of your list.

GETTING THERE

Exit Interstate 70 at the Bakerville exit east of the Loveland Ski Area. Park on the south side of the highway at the bottom of Stevens Gulch Road. Later in the season, it may be possible to drive farther up the road. Take care when doing this, and do not attempt to drive over deep-frozen snow. Many a car has become stuck doing this very thing. Don't be "that guy"!

THE ROUTE

Ascend Stevens Gulch Road for 1 mile, and then head right on Grizzly Gulch Road at 10,300 feet. Follow Grizzly Gulch Road up the valley. Later in the season, following this road may entail stream crossings. It is also possible to drive up this rough 4WD road by early summer. At 11,000 feet, you will pass the avalanche runout zone of the Emperor Couloir, which is another great line. Continue up Grizzly Gulch to the bottom of the Tuning Forks at 11,200 feet. Climb the broad couloir to the split of the Tuning Forks around 13,000 feet, and then choose right or left depending on

conditions. Either way, the top of the lines may be blown free of snow, but some easy scrambling will take you to the west ridge and the summit.

Descent. Descend the northwest-facing couloir, and follow your approach route back to the trailhead.

Extra Credit: The Emperor Couloir or the east-facing Dead Dog Couloir, which drops into Stevens Gulch, also make for fun descent options.

29 Square Top Mountain: East Bowl

Starting Elevation: 10,800 or 11,669 feet
High Point: 13,794 feet
Vertical Gain/Loss: 3000 feet or less
Ascent Distance: 3.6 miles or more
Descent Distance: 3 miles or more
Time: 4 to 6 hours
Ski Skills: Moderate to difficult
Fitness Level: Moderately strenuous
Technical Skills: Moderate
Gear: The basics; ice axe and crampons may be needed
Best Months: March through May
USGS Maps: Montezuma and Mount Evans

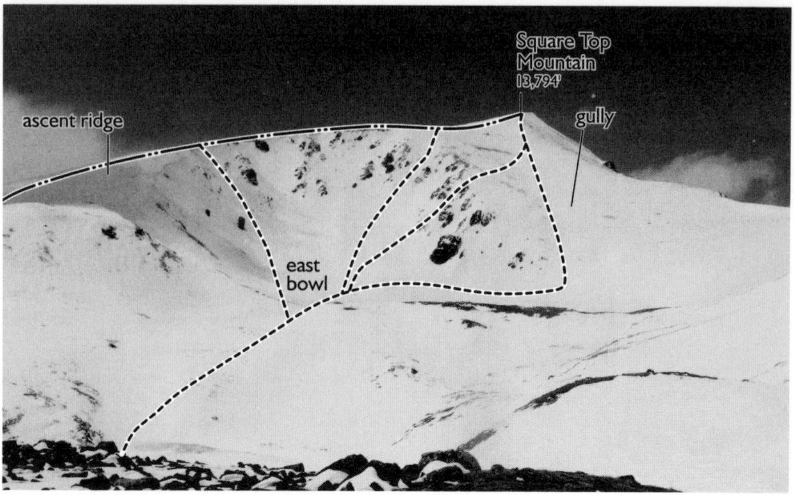

In the shadows of loftier fourteeners like neighboring Mount Evans and Mount Bierstadt, Square Top can sometimes be overlooked. Ranked as the 111th highest summit in Colorado, this peak appears to have a square-shaped top when viewed from the north or west. But the views from the summit are beautiful, and the east bowl provides a quality descent for varying levels of skiers. Square Top is a great ski-mountaineering destination!

GETTING THERE

From Interstate 70, take exit 228 for Georgetown, which is 45 miles west of Denver. Follow the signs for Guanella Pass, which will take you right through the center of Georgetown. As you leave town, you will begin going up a steep hill on Guanella Pass Road (County Road 381). Continue south on this road for 9 miles to a parking area at a big left switchback, immediately past Guanella Pass Campground. Just above, the road is typically closed in winter. But if the road is open, you may opt to continue another 1.8 miles to the summit of Guanella Pass and begin your tour from there.

THE ROUTE

If you start at the top of Guanella Pass (11,669 feet), you will have a good view of your destination. Find the Square Top Mountain summer trail on the west side of the pass and follow it west toward Square Top Lakes until you reach snow. When the trail becomes snow covered, continue traveling west toward the obvious east bowl. Square Top Lakes sit at the foot of the cirque.

If you start at the winter parking at the Silver Dollar trailhead (10,800 feet), you have two approach options to reach Square Top Lakes. The first is to follow Guanella Pass Road to the top of Guanella Pass where you can find the summer trailhead. Or you could head west on Naylor Lake Road for a few hundred feet and then turn south, ascending the north-facing slopes to the far end of the east ridge of Square Top. You

The top turns on Argentine's Waldorf bowl are steep! (Photo by Scott Edlin)

should round the ridge and head west toward Square Top Lakes. If there is ample snow, you may find it better to stay above the location of the summer trail.

Once at lower Square Top Lake, follow the east-facing ridge on your left up to the top of the bowl, approximately 13,300 feet. From here, you could descend the bowl or continue west on the ridge to the summit at 13,794 feet. As you ascend, pay attention to potential descent routes.

Descent. From the summit, descend the ridge east back to the top of the east bowl. Follow your ascent route back to the parking area.

Alternate Descent. Another easy descent is a slight gully, which tends to hold snow late into the year, just north of the east bowl. Steeper descent options lie in the many chutes that make up the bowl itself. However, some of these are guarded by cornices at the top. You may find it best to travel a little down on either side of the bowl to find routes that are less impacted by cornices. Once at Square Top Lakes, go up for another lap, or follow your ascent route back to your vehicle.

Extra Credit: On the other side of Guanella Pass, the west face of 14,060-foot Mount Bierstadt is a fun moderate ski.

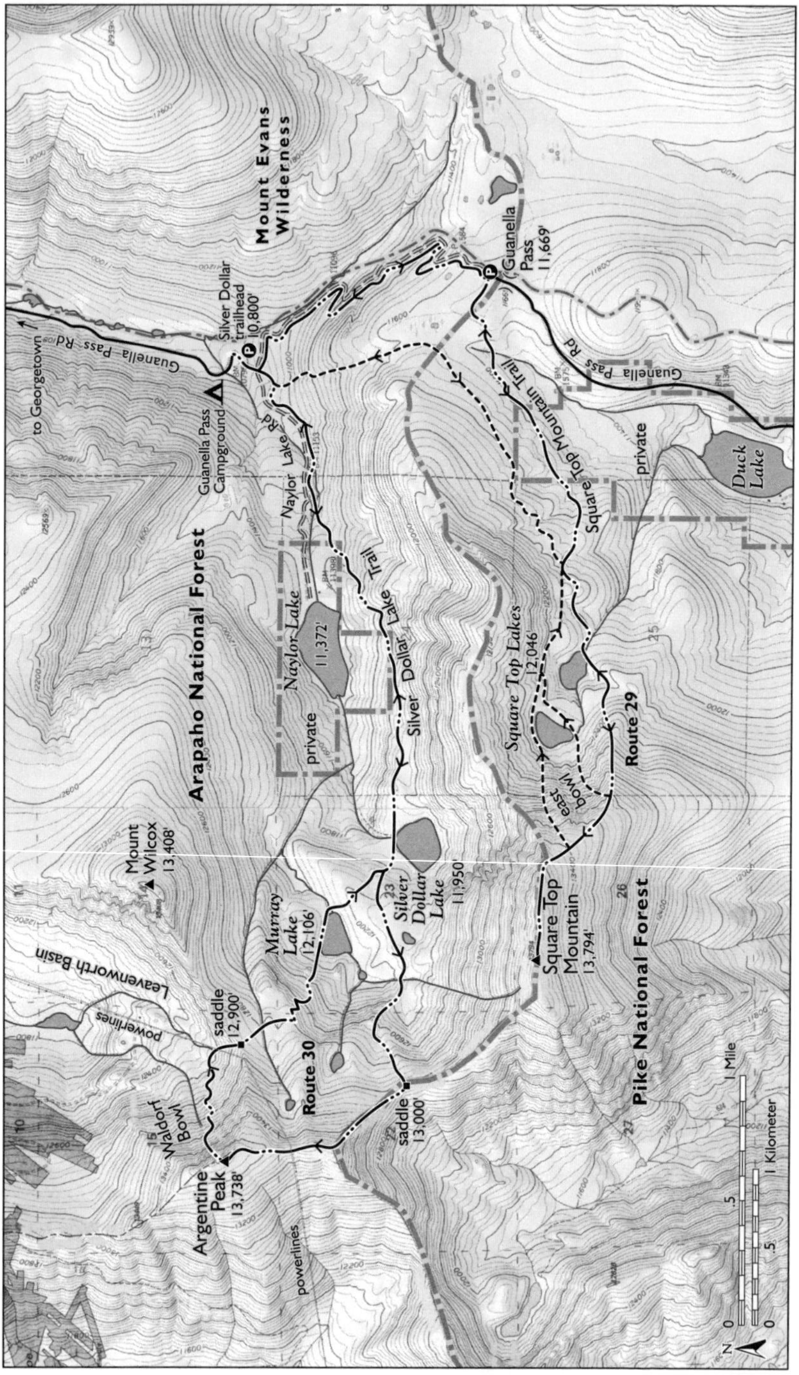
Arapaho National Forest
Mount Evans Wilderness
Pike National Forest
to Georgetown
Guanella Pass Rd
Silver Dollar trailhead 10,800'
Guanella Pass Campground
Guanella Pass 11,669'
Naylor Lake Rd
Naylor Lake 11,372'
private
Silver Dollar Lake Trail
Square Top Lakes 12,046'
Square Top Mountain Trail
Duck Lake
Route 29
east bowl
Mount Wilcox 13,408'
Murray Lake 12,106'
Silver Dollar Lake 11,950'
Square Top Mountain 13,794'
saddle 12,900'
saddle 13,000'
Leavenworth Basin
powerlines
Waldorf Bowl
Route 30
Argentine Peak 13,738'
0 .5 1 Mile
0 .5 1 Kilometer
N

30 Argentine Peak: Waldorf Bowl

Starting Elevation	10,800 feet
High Point	13,738 feet
Vertical Gain/Loss	3500 feet
Ascent Distance	5 miles
Descent Distance	4.5 miles
Time	4 to 6 hours
Ski Skills	Difficult to very difficult
Fitness Level	Moderately strenuous
Technical Skills	Moderate
Gear	The basics; ice axe and crampons may be needed
Best Months	April and May
USGS Maps	Montezuma and Mount Evans

A somewhat obscure mountain, Argentine Peak's northeast-facing bowl holds some fairly steep skiing and tends to hold snow late into the year. The bowl is named after the ghost town of Waldorf that sits below it at 11,666 feet, just north of the peak. From 1906 to 1918, the Argentine Central Railway ran a train regularly from Silver Plume, which was 6 miles away and very popular with tourists. Today, not much remains of this once mighty mining area. But Argentine Peak stands watching quietly above the ghost town, waiting to be visited.

GETTING THERE

From Interstate 70, take exit 228 for Georgetown, which is 45 miles west of Denver. Follow the signs for Guanella Pass, which will take you right through the center of Georgetown. As you leave town, you will begin going up a steep hill on Guanella Pass Road (County Road 381). Continue south on this road for 9 miles to a parking area at a big left switchback, immediately past Guanella Pass Campground.

THE ROUTE

From the parking area, head west on Naylor Lake Road for about a half mile. Here you'll find the start of the Silver Dollar Lake Trail. While you may be tempted to proceed on the road toward Naylor Lake, that area is private property. Please respect private property, and use the established trail, which allows public access through the area.

Continue west on the Silver Dollar Lake Trail, passing above and to the south of Naylor Lake. After 2.5 miles, you will arrive on the north shore of Silver Dollar Lake at 11,950 feet. You will see Square Top Mountain on your left and Argentine on your right. From here, leave the Silver Dollar Lake Trail. The easiest ascent option is to continue heading west, between Silver Dollar and Murray lakes, to arrive at a saddle (elevation 13,000 feet) between Square Top Mountain and Argentine Peak. Follow the ridge north another 700 vertical feet to the summit, passing under powerlines along the way.

Descent. You will find many entrances into the northeast bowl; some are steeper than others. Cornices can exist as well. Choose one that you like and enter the bowl. Once in the bowl, you will enjoy some high 40- to 50-degree turns near the top, becoming less steep as you descend. Ski for roughly 1200 vertical feet, stopping at an elevation between 12,500 and 12,600 feet, at which point the bowl begins to flatten.

You now are in the Leavenworth Basin, and you need to get back over to the Silver Dollar Lake Basin. To do this, head south and ascend the slopes roughly 300 to 400 vertical feet to a saddle that tops out at 12,900 feet. Descend southeast to Murray Lake (12,106 feet) and Silver Dollar Lake (11,950 feet), where you may also find some fun skiing. Follow the Silver Dollar Lake Trail back to the trailhead, again remaining clear of private property around Naylor Lake

Opposite: North Chute C of Pacific Peak, as seen from nearby Crystal Peak

MOSQUITO AND TENMILE RANGES

STARTING AT FRISCO and ending near Buena Vista, the Mosquito and Tenmile ranges are frequently lumped together because they are the same, geologically speaking. The Continental Divide crosses the range east to west, splitting the range into north and south. North of the Divide is the Tenmile Range, and south of the Divide is the Mosquito. With North Star Mountain lying exactly on the Divide, technically this peak is half in the Tenmile Range and half in the Mosquito. Some of Colorado's most intensive mining took place in these ranges, with Leadville on the west side and the mining camps surrounding Fairplay on the east. Combine the mining history with the generally benign topography of these mountains, and you're left with easy access and high trailheads.

The spine of the Mosquito/Tenmile Range covers 40 miles, yet at its widest only measures a few miles. Most high peaks in the range can be spotted from the Arkansas Valley on the west as easily as South Park on the east. While many of the peaks in the range can be most accurately described as giant hills, several of the peaks on the northern end of the range are genuinely steep and rugged.

When it comes to weather in the Mosquito/Tenmile, the first word that comes to mind is wind. This narrow and high range is battered by winds from the west, seemingly nonstop. What should be classic lines on west faces are commonly scoured by the wind, and only a heavy dose of wet springtime snow fills them in every few years.

The Mosquito and Tenmile ranges offer surprises for backcountry skiers who take the time to know them. For a small range so close to the Denver metro area, it offers untapped opportunities.

31 Mount Victoria: Victoria Trees and J Chute

Starting Elevation	9100 feet
High Point	11,300 to 11,785 feet
Vertical Gain/Loss	2200 to 2700 feet
Ascent Distance	2 miles
Descent Distance	2 miles
Time	2 to 3.5 hours
Ski Skills	Moderate to difficult
Fitness Level	Not very strenuous
Technical Skills	Low
Gear	The basics
Best Months	January to March
USGS Map	Frisco

If you're in need of some sheltered trees and moderate terrain for an easier tour or a good powder day, then "Mount Victoria" is a great choice. J Chute stands noticeably

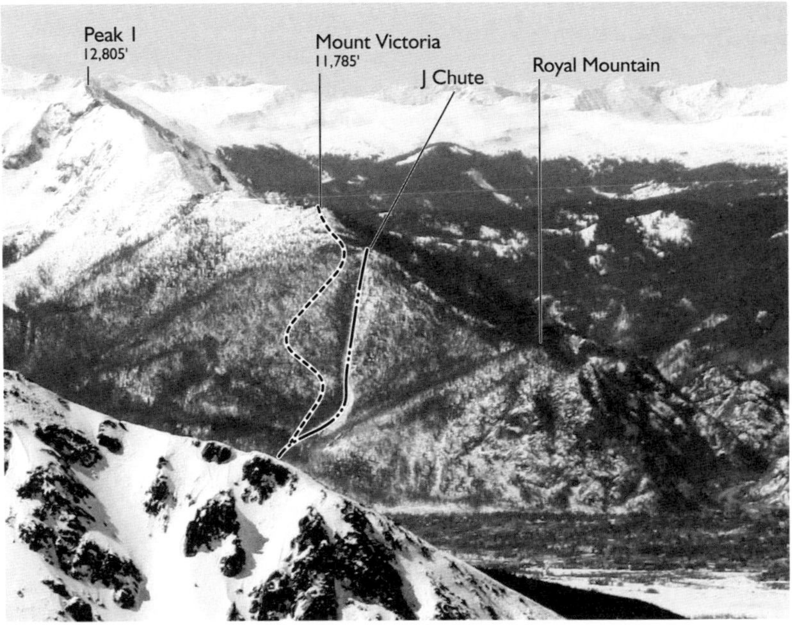

to the west above Frisco and is an avalanche chute that cuts through the trees creating a J shape. The trees on either side harbor some fantastic skiing as well, especially on a powder day. With its ease of access, Mount Victoria is also a great option for those looking for a short tour.

Beneath the J Chute, at roughly 9600 feet, sits the site of the historic Victoria Mine and Masontown. The mine was founded in 1872 and boomed in the early 1900s, but it was precariously placed at the bottom of J Chute, an obvious avalanche path. Perhaps it was inevitable that an avalanche would strike the town in 1912 as the mine was waning. Another avalanche in 1926 obliterated what was left. Now all that remains of the mine and the town is the foundation and fireplace structure of an old cabin. Let the lessons be learned from this history of avalanches.

GETTING THERE

There are two areas to access Mount Victoria. The first is the lot just southeast of Interstate 70, which also is used to access the Coin Slot on Royal Mountain (Route 32). To park here, take exit 201 off I-70 for Frisco's main street. Head east toward Frisco on Main Street a few hundred feet. Turn right and park in the public parking area just south of Main Street and east of I-70.

The second option provides better access for your return, but possibly less room for parking. Take exit 201 off I-70 for Frisco's Main Street. Head east toward Frisco on Main Street for 0.6 mile and then turn right (south) onto 2nd Avenue. Follow 2nd Avenue for about 0.4 mile until it dead-ends at a parking area.

THE ROUTE

If you are parking at the I-70 lot, head southeast on the paved Temple Trail, skirting the edge of condos and homes in Frisco. This trail is not typically plowed, but it does see a lot of traffic in the form of dog walkers, snowshoers, and hikers. After a half mile on this trail, you will see the marked trail to Royal Mountain on your right.

If you are parking at the area off 2nd Avenue, head southwest and cross over the well-used (paved if no snow cover) Temple Trail. Immediately after, look for a trail that goes right. Take this trail northwest for about one-third of a mile until it intersects with the Mount Royal Trail. Turn left onto the Mount Royal Trail, heading southeast.

The Mount Royal Trail is popular year-round, and user compaction usually makes a straightforward ascent route, contouring southeast, then south, along the side of Royal Mountain, passing just above the historic Masontown. Shortly after, the trail begins

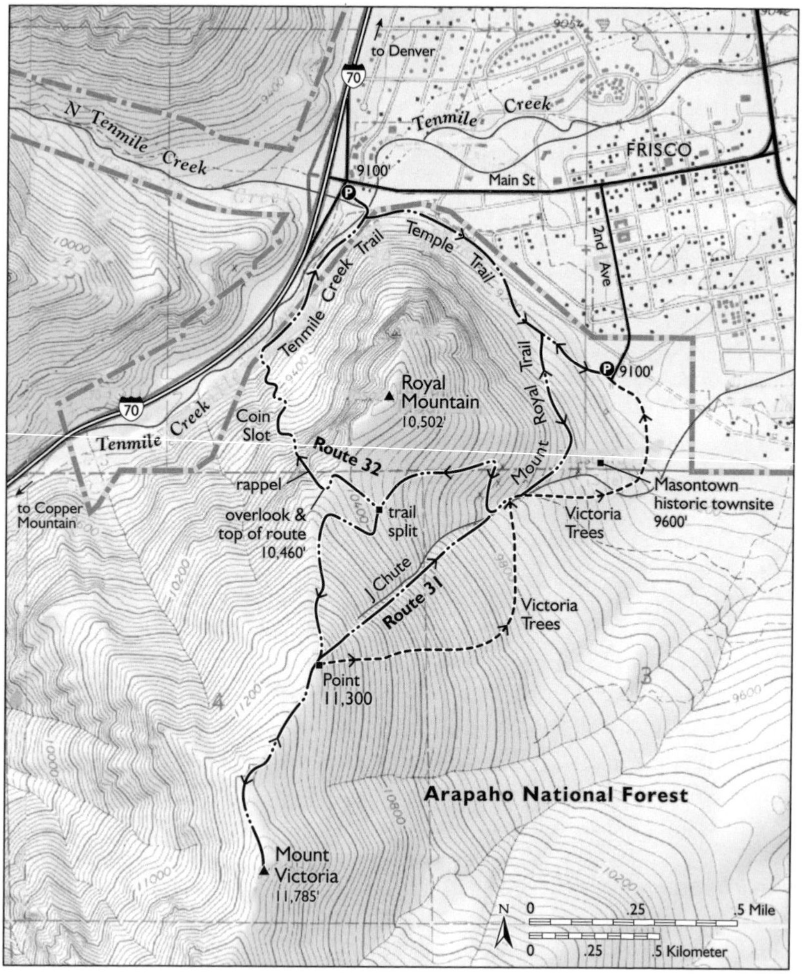

to head more westward. As you ascend, you will have good views of the J Chute. At about 1.5 miles, the trail splits. The right side heads up to Mount Royal and the Coin Slot (Route 32). Instead, take the left fork, which continues straight. Here, the trail may begin to become less traveled and be a little more difficult to follow, especially shortly after new snowfall. The trail will head southwest for a few hundred yards before switchbacking to the west to eventually gain the northeast ridge of Mount Victoria. If you have difficulty finding the trail, gain the ridge and then follow it southwest to the summit.

As you travel along the ridge, the trees will begin to open up around 11,300 feet. This point lies directly above the J Chute and is the stopping point for many skiers and snowboarders. If you want to continue to the summit of Mount Victoria, follow the ridge another half mile southwest to the summit at 11,785 feet and then return down the ridge to the point at 11,300 feet.

Descent. From the point at 11,300 feet, descent options are plentiful. The J Chute drops straight down to the northeast. Keep in mind that this is an avalanche path and it is prone to sliding. Assess avalanche conditions before you drop in. You may find a safer option and better snow conditions in the trees just skier's right of the J Chute, called Victoria Trees. If you choose this option, you will want to begin contouring left back toward the J Chute around 9,800 feet or you may have difficulty exiting on the given terrain. The J Chute avalanche path eventually meets up with the Mount Royal Trail. Follow your ascent route back to your vehicle or find some fun paths through the east-facing trees to the Temple Trail.

32 Royal Mountain: Coin Slot Couloir

Starting Elevation	9100 feet
High Point	10,460 feet
Vertical Gain/Loss	1360 feet
Ascent Distance	1.9 miles
Descent Distance	0.9 miles
Time	3.5 to 4.5 hours
Ski Skills	Difficult to very difficult
Fitness Level	Not very strenuous
Technical Skills	Very high
Gear	The basics, 50-meter rope, harness, rappel device, webbing, and other anchor material
Best Months	February to March
USGS Map	Frisco

Despite its location directly above Interstate 70, motorists speeding by below often overlook the narrow Coin Slot Couloir. Just a ski-length wide at its narrowest, with a taste of mountaineering thanks to a short rappel into the couloir, this unique route

has gained popularity among Summit County skiers. Best of all, once you ski it, you will gaze up at the route and remember the experience each and every time you pass by along the interstate.

GETTING THERE

This is one of the easiest trailheads to reach in this book. Take exit 201 off I-70 for Frisco's main street. Head east toward Frisco on Main Street for a few hundred feet. Turn right and park in the public parking area just south of Main Street and east of I-70.

THE ROUTE

From the trailhead, head southeast on the paved Temple Trail, skirting the edge of condos and homes in Frisco. This trail is not typically plowed, but it does see a lot of traffic in the form of dog walkers, snowshoers, and hikers. After a half mile on this trail, you will see the marked trail to Royal Mountain on your right. This is a popular trail year-round and user compaction usually makes a straightforward ascent route, contouring southeast and then to the south side of Royal Mountain, passing just above the historic Masontown. Shortly after, the trail begins to head more westward. At mile 1.5, the trail splits. Stay right and continue up the southern forested slopes of Royal Mountain to a saddle at mile 1.8 (roughly 10,400 feet). This is not the top of the route. Veer southwest a couple hundred feet around a small knob to another overlook about 50 feet higher with some big, picturesque old trees.

Descent. At the overlook, take a break and ready yourself for the exciting skiing to come. Put your harness on here, strap your skis to your pack, and make sure your rope and other gear are easily accessible. Most years, the top of the route will not have enough snow to ski down to the rappel. Instead, carefully downclimb the north-facing terrain over scree, talus, and shrubs for roughly 50 vertical feet to the top of the line. If you've come to the correct place, you will be above and slightly skier's right of the Coin Slot, at a tree that is the rappel station to enter the couloir. Inspect the old webbing and other gear and replace it with your own if it seems prudent to do so. A 50-meter rope or two 30-meter rando ropes should be plenty for the short, slabby rappel.

If you're the first one down, start making a platform for yourself and transition to skis. The route will be obvious below you, dropping straight toward I-70, visible below. Once all members of the party have finished the rappel and you've stowed the rope, it's time to ski.

Ski the route one at a time, and take advantage of the occasional pull-off to either side of the couloir. The skinny couloir is only a ski-length wide at certain points along the way, with some steeper rolls and slight twists and turns.

After exiting the couloir, choose your path toward the valley below. You may find yourself traversing to find better snow or heading toward one of the many fun pillow lines that highlight the bottom of the route. You will then find yourself in the valley, on the paved but unplowed Tenmile Creek Trail. Head right (northeast) back to your car, roughly half a mile away. Depending on conditions, it may be easier to put your skins back on for this short section.

33 Crystal Peak: North Face

Starting Elevation	10,950 feet
High Point	13,852 feet
Vertical Gain/Loss	3500 feet/3700 feet
Ascent Distance	4.6+/- miles
Descent Distance	4 miles

Time	4.5 to 6.5 hours
Ski Skills	Difficult
Fitness Level	Strenuous
Technical Skills	Moderate
Gear	The basics; ice axe and crampons may be needed
Best Months	April to mid- to late May
USGS Maps	Breckenridge and Copper Mountain

As you exit Interstate 70 near Copper Mountain and head south on to Colorado Highway 91, a peak stands prominent and proud in the distance—a peak that backcountry skiers can't help but gaze at with eyes of lust. Although a bit more remote than some nearby lines, the north face of Crystal Peak makes a fantastic descent.

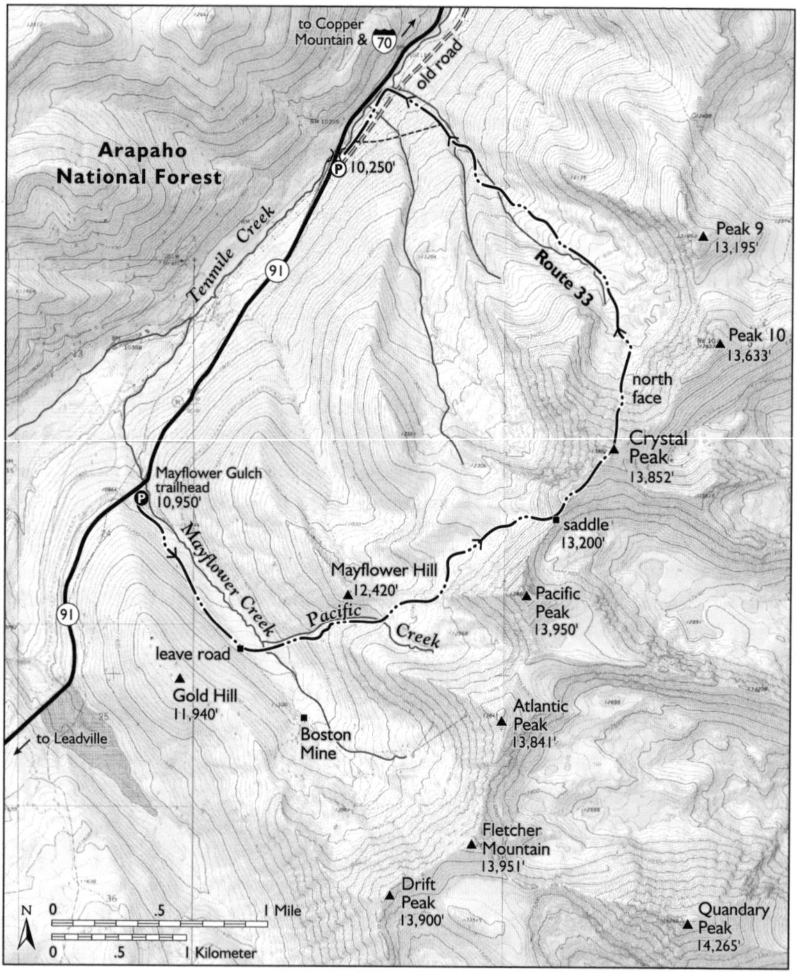

Descending the north face of Crystal Peak (Photo by Scott Edlin)

This route is best done using a shuttle, leaving one vehicle for pick up where CO 91 crosses Tenmile Creek, and then continuing another 2.6 miles on the highway to your starting point at Mayflower Gulch. As the exit requires skiing through some rather tight and steep trees, it is recommended that you ski this line when there is still snow down to 10,750 feet.

GETTING THERE

From the north: From I-70, take exit 195 for CO 91 toward Copper Mountain/Leadville. Beginning at the intersection of Copper Road and CO 91 (the main entrance to the Copper Mountain Ski Area), drive south 3.5 miles to where the highway crosses over the Tenmile Creek using a bridge. Just after the bridge, there's a pull-off to your left. Leave one vehicle here as this will be where you finish your route (10,250 feet). With another vehicle, continue driving 2.6 miles up CO 91 to the Mayflower Gulch parking lot on your left.

From the south: Set your odometer at the intersection of CO 91 and US Highway 24, just north of Leadville. From there, drive north on CO 91 over Fremont Pass, and notice the Mayflower Gulch trailhead on your right at mile 15.9. From there, go another 2.6 miles to where CO 91 crosses the Tenmile Creek using a bridge. Just before crossing the bridge, there will be a pull-off to your right. Leave one vehicle there for your return (10,250 feet). With another vehicle, reverse your tracks and drive south on CO 91 2.6 miles back to the Mayflower Gulch parking lot.

THE ROUTE

From the trailhead, head southeast on an old mining road. Obey any "No Trespassing" or "Private Property" signs should you find any in this area. At the time of writing, we are unaware of any private-property issues in this area. Depending on snow cover, it may be easier to leave the road and continue skinning up the valley floor.

While traveling, notice a steep gully to the east. This is the Pacific Creek Gully. After traveling for about 1.3 miles on the road, veer left off the road to make your way to the base of the Pacific Creek Gully. Follow along the ascender's right side of the gully until an elevation of about 12,200 feet, where the terrain begins to flatten.

Work your way northeast following along a flatter bench below the west slopes of Pacific Peak. Once rounding the corner of Pacific's west ridge, you'll start to notice Crystal Peak to the northeast. Around 12,800 feet, begin heading in a more easterly direction with the goal of climbing toward the saddle between Pacific Peak and Crystal Peak (elevation 13,200 feet). From there, continue traveling northeast, following along Crystal Peak's southwest ridge another 650 vertical feet to the summit.

Descent. The north face of Crystal Peak usually contains an interesting wind-drift formation just below the summit. Usually this feature is harmless and can actually help to provide some shelter on a breezy day. But be sure to take caution if you venture near it. The wind drift is also avoidable on the skier's right side.

You'll find many choices for lines to descend down Crystal Peak's north face. But be aware that there are numerous cliff bands on this face, especially toward the bottom. Most skiers choose to ski an obvious gully or couloir that is just a little skier's right of the summit. To reach this couloir, you'll need to descend a few hundred feet down on the face first before reaching the couloir's entrance, slightly skier's right off the summit. Depending on how the snow developed through the season, this entrance could require a couple of turns that are around 50 degrees in steepness. Otherwise, the majority of the face is in the low to mid-40-degree range.

Once you've enjoyed the 1550-foot descent down the north face, you'll find yourself in a valley. Descend north and then northeast, following the natural course of the drainage. Once below tree line, continue following along the obvious drainages, keeping an eye out for terrain traps. Around 11,000 feet, you may find that the drainage steepens quite a bit, in which case it is often better for you to follow to the skier's left of the gully.

Descend along the gully until you reach an old road around 10,300 feet. Alternatively, you may opt to "cut the corner" by veering a hard left (west) at 10,550 feet, continuing to descend through the trees, and eventually reaching the road. Follow the road southwest and sometimes slightly upward to the intersection of CO 91 where you left your second vehicle (10,250 feet).

34 Pacific Peak: North Chutes

Starting Elevation	10,380 feet
High Point	13,950 feet
Vertical Gain/Loss	3600 feet
Ascent Distance	5.4 miles
Descent Distance	5.4 miles
Time	6 to 8 hours
Ski Skills	Difficult to extremely difficult
Fitness Level	Strenuous
Technical Skills	Moderate
Gear	The basics, plus ice axe and crampons
Best Months	April and May
USGS Map	Breckenridge

Only 50 feet short of "fourteener" status, Pacific Peak is a centennial summit, ranking 61st in the order of Colorado's highest peaks. Many aspects of this peak are quite worthy of skiing, but the north chutes have some of the greatest status. Crystal Peak (Route 33) provides fantastic views of the north side of Pacific Peak, if you're questioning conditions. But if you make the trek in to Mohawk Lakes Basin, you're likely to reap some rewards!

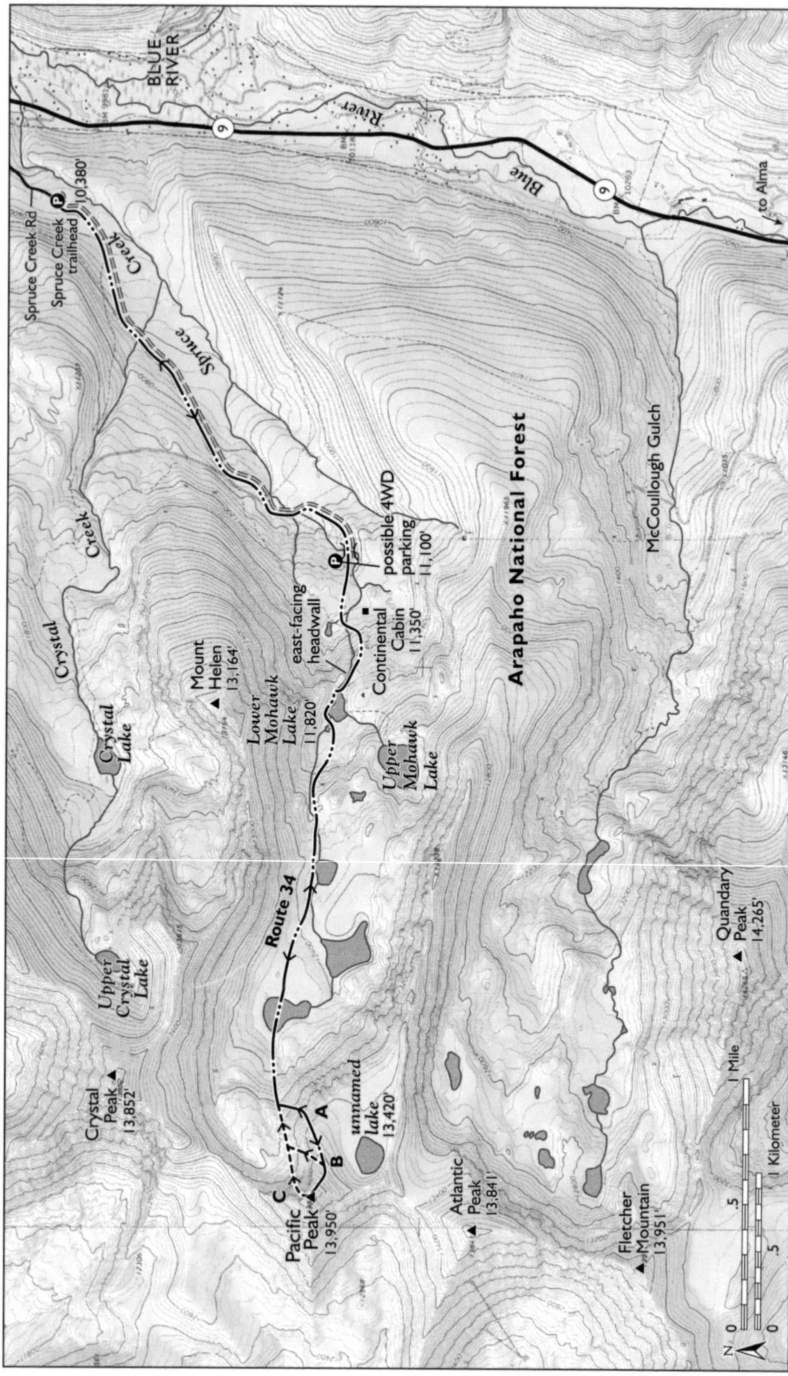

Spruce Creek Rd
Spruce Creek trailhead
10,380'
BLUE RIVER
Blue River
to Alma
Spruce Creek
Crystal Creek
Crystal Lake
Upper Crystal Lake
Crystal Peak 13,852'
Mount Helen 13,164'
Lower Mohawk Lake 11,820'
Upper Mohawk Lake
east-facing headwall
possible 4WD parking 11,100'
Continental Cabin 11,350'
Arapaho National Forest
McCoullough Gulch
Route 34
A
B
C
unnamed lake 13,420'
Pacific Peak 13,950'
Atlantic Peak 13,841'
Fletcher Mountain 13,951'
Quandary Peak 14,265'
N
0 .5 1 Mile
0 .5 1 Kilometer

GETTING THERE

The north side of Pacific Peak is best accessed from the Spruce Creek trailhead. From the intersection of South Main Street and Broken Lance Drive on the south side of Breckenridge, follow Colorado Highway 9 south for about 2.5 miles. Turn right (west) onto Spruce Creek Road.

If you're coming from Alma just northwest of Fairplay, travel north on CO 9 for 13.3 miles and then turn left (west) onto Spruce Creek Road.

Spruce Creek is a dirt road and will travel through a residential neighborhood and eventually onto forest land. After 1.2 miles, Spruce Creek Road ends at a parking area (elevation 10,380 feet), which is the winter trailhead. Most passenger cars have no trouble accessing this trailhead. Late in spring or early summer, you may find that the road continues past this area for another 1.8 miles, but it requires 4WD.

THE ROUTE

From the winter parking area at 10,380 feet, follow along Spruce Creek Road for about 1.8 miles. Here, you will cross Spruce Creek using a bridge and then the road will end (elevation 11,100 feet).

From the crossing, there is a summer trail that works its way up to Lower Mohawk Lake. You may find evidence of this trail and be able to follow it. Otherwise, generally follow westward up through the trees. If you're on trail, you'll likely pass by the Continental Cabin (elevation 11,350 feet), an old miner's cabin built around 1883. At the time of writing, this primitive cabin was open to the public and could provide viable shelter, although it was in a bit of disrepair.

Beyond the cabin, the route begins to steepen to a difficult east-facing headwall. This area can pose great risk to backcountry travelers as it is fairly steep and devoid of trees, with cliff bands scattered in between. Take care to choose a safe path through this area. In general, you'll want to stay south of the gully that leads down from Lower Mohawk Lake to avoid even steeper terrain. Veering ascenders left can often lead to safer and less steep options. Keep in mind you'll be passing through this east-facing terrain on your descent, and wet slides could be possible.

Once at Lower Mohawk Lake (11,820 feet), you'll leave the summer trail if it's melted out and follow westward up the valley another 2 miles, passing by three other lakes, until you're below the northeast slopes of Pacific Peak at an approximate elevation of 12,850 feet. From there, you'll have to decide whether you want to ascend your ski line or choose a different route.

For the easiest ascent route, ascend the northeast-facing slopes (Option A recommended) of Pacific Peak to gain the east ridge, and then follow the ridge westward to the summit, passing by North Chute B along the way. Otherwise, continue west up the valley to ascend North Chute B or North Chute C. If you ascend North Chute B, you'll need to follow the ridge west to reach the summit. Both of these options allow you to catch a glimpse of the high, unnamed lake at 13,420 feet, one of the highest lakes in North America. The extra adventurous could choose to ascend North Chute

C, which steepens to 55 degrees or more. Once at the top of this chute, you'll need to follow the west ridge east to reach the summit.

Descent. Pacific Peak is not always skiable from the summit. Often, a summit ski requires a few turns on Pacific's easy south slopes, which can sometimes be melted. Wet spring snowstorms can help to keep decent coverage on this aspect.

Option A. Descend the recommended ascent route, which is also the easiest. Travel east on the ridge past North Chute B to about 13,500 feet. Descend the north slopes from there back down into the valley.

North Chute B. To access this descent route, descend along the east ridge using snow slopes that may connect on the upper southeast slopes. This route is the first line along the ridge that is an obvious descent. The entrance lies at an elevation of approximately 13,560 feet.

North Chute C. This is the king of descents on Pacific Peak. A classic couloir, North Chute C steepens to 55 degrees or more and is not to be underestimated despite how short it is (about 600 vertical feet). As it steepens, it also becomes narrow, possibly less than 180 centimeters wide. If you have long skis, this route may not be for you. While the top part of this couloir faces north, the bottom part swings slightly east. Keep this in mind as you plan your timing. This route is also prone to conditions. It needs some strong wet spring storms to adequately cover the terrain for a descent. Additionally, northern wind patterns can blow all the snow out of this line and make it impossible to ski. To access this route, you'll need to follow the ridge west, downclimbing class 3 terrain that usually does not have enough coverage to ski. Follow the ridge for a few hundred feet before coming to an obvious notch that marks the top of the couloir.

Once back in the valley, descend your general ascent route, bearing in mind that the east-facing headwall below Lower Mohawk Lake could be prone to wet slides. In this area, it may be better to work the skier's right side of the valley, keeping along north-facing aspects as much as possible.

35 Mayflower Gulch: Mayflower Hill

Starting Elevation	10,950 feet
High Point	11,950 to 12,420 feet
Vertical Gain/Loss	1000 to 1450 feet
Ascent Distance	1.5 to 2.5 miles
Descent Distance	1 to 2 miles
Time	1.5 to 3 hours
Ski Skills	Easy to moderate
Fitness Level	Not very strenuous
Technical Skills	Low
Gear	The basics
Best Months	December to February
USGS Map	Copper Mountain

Enjoying powder turns on Mayflower Hill with Fletcher Mountain and Drift Peak in the distance (Photo by Susan Mol)

Some days you're just looking for a safe place to make good midwinter powder turns. With relatively low-angle slopes and a southwest aspect, Mayflower Hill is one of those go-to spots. This hill is also a great place for backcountry beginners because of its short vertical and easy skiing.

But the southwest nature of the slope also presents some problems. This aspect of Mayflower Hill can also warm quickly when the sun comes out after a good powder storm has ended. So make your turns early, before the snow gets too heavy or crusty.

GETTING THERE

From the north, take exit 195 off Interstate 70 for Colorado Highway 91 toward Copper Mountain/Leadville. Beginning at the intersection of Copper Road and CO 91 (the main entrance to the Copper Mountain Ski Area), drive south 6.1 miles and reach the trailhead parking lot on your left.

If traveling from the south, set your odometer at the intersection of CO 91 and US Highway 24, just north of Leadville. From there, drive north on CO 91 over Fremont Pass, and reach the trailhead on your right at mile 15.9.

THE ROUTE

From the parking lot, head southeast on an old mining road (used to access the Boston Mine farther up valley) that will likely be covered in snow. About a half mile into the tour, veer left off the road and cross Mayflower Creek. Begin skinning up the southwestern slopes of Mayflower Hill, staying in the trees for as long as possible if you want to minimize avalanche danger usually associated with powder days.

Around 11,500 feet, you will emerge above tree line and crest on to a slight ridge. Follow the ridge southeast and onto the summit, or a few hundred feet below it. There are many skiing options from the ridge.

Descent. While skinning on the ridge, many people choose to stop around 11,950 to 12,000 feet and descend the less treed southwest-facing slopes just below them. Others continue another half mile and 500 vertical feet to the summit, or somewhere in between, and ski the southwest slopes from there. Either way, the skiing possibilities are nearly endless.

Avalanche danger is often fairly low on these slopes since they tend to have an angle of less than 25 degrees. But be wary of rollovers that can be in the 30-degree range and more prone to sliding. These are easy to avoid if you pay attention to your ski route.

Ski the southwest slope to the bottom of the valley. Follow along the Mayflower Creek northwest to exit back to the parking lot. If you ended in the valley around 11,200 feet or higher, you may find it easier to exit on the skier's left side of the gulch (southwest of the creek). Otherwise, follow the right side of the gulch (northeast of the creek) until you find a good place to cross Mayflower Creek, which may be where you crossed it early in your tour. Follow the snow-covered road back to the parking lot.

Extra Credit: To the southwest of Mayflower Hill on the other side of Mayflower Gulch lies Gold Hill, whose northeast-facing slopes can also be a fun place to explore on a powder day.

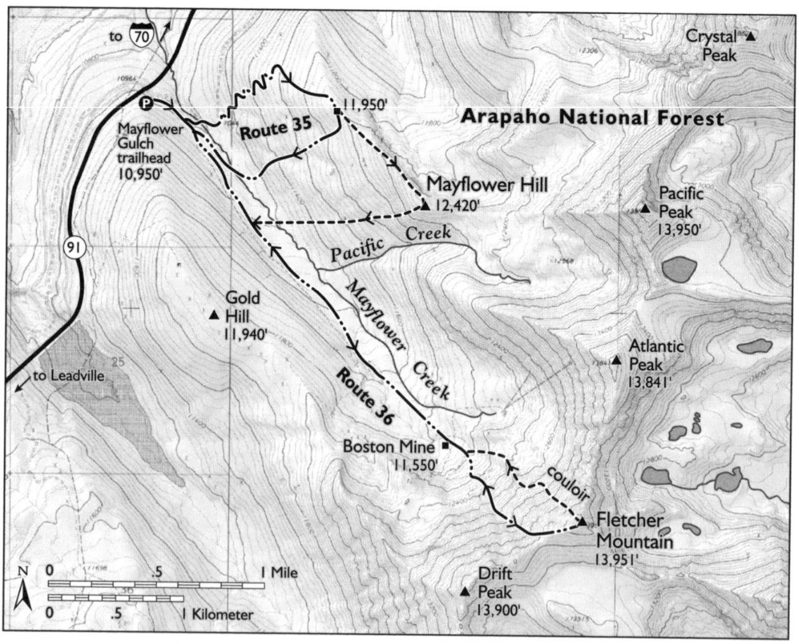

36 Fletcher Mountain: Northwest Face

Starting Elevation	10,950 feet
High Point	13,951 feet
Vertical Gain/Loss	3001 feet
Ascent Distance	3 miles
Descent Distance	3 miles
Time	4.5 to 5.5 hours
Ski Skills	Difficult to very difficult, depending on line choice
Fitness Level	Moderately strenuous
Technical Skills	Moderate
Gear	The basics, plus ice axe and crampons
Best Months	March to May
USGS Map	Copper Mountain

Falling roughly 50 feet shy of the magical 14,000-foot elevation, Fletcher Mountain is one of the most striking mountains of the Tenmile Range. Access via Mayflower Gulch is quick and easy, and with a number of other high-quality descents on neighboring peaks, such as "Drift Peak," this is an area that should be high on every Colorado skier's list.

GETTING THERE

From the north, take exit 195 off Interstate 70 for Colorado Highway 91 toward Copper Mountain/Leadville. Beginning at the intersection of Copper Road and CO 91 (the main entrance to the Copper Mountain Ski Area), drive south 6.1 miles and reach the trailhead parking lot on your left.

If traveling from the south, set your odometer at the intersection of CO 91 and US Highway 24, just north of Leadville. From there, drive north on CO 91 over Fremont Pass, and reach the trailhead on your right at mile 15.9.

THE ROUTE

From the trailhead, head southeast on an old mining road that leads to the abandoned Boston Mine (elevation 11,550 feet), located roughly 1.5 miles from the trailhead. This mining area was a bustling town in the early 1900s. Obey any "No Trespassing" or "Private Property" signs should you find any in this area. At the time of writing, we are unaware of any private-property issues in this area. Depending on snow cover, it may be easier to leave the road and continue skinning up the valley floor. Fletcher Mountain and other ski objectives in Mayflower Gulch will quickly come into view. Survey your ascent and descent options as you continue up the flat terrain.

One ascent option is to climb the broad gully to the 13,650-foot saddle southwest of the summit, on a ridge that connects Fletcher Mountain with Drift Peak. From the

saddle, turn left (northeast) and ascend the technically easy ridge for another 300 vertical feet to the summit.

The north and northwest faces of Fletcher offer a number of descent options, some of which may be difficult to identify from the summit. For that reason, you may choose to climb your intended descent route to the summit or to the top of your intended line.

Descent. As previously mentioned, Fletcher Mountain is a skier's mountain offering several descent options. The easiest route is also the most straightforward ascent route. Ski down the southwest ridge to the aforementioned saddle between Fletcher and Drift, and then descend the ascent gully.

The skier's left of the face has at least three different routes to choose from. All of these routes are similar in nature, so pick whichever route has the most appeal and is in the best condition. These routes do tilt slightly east and will therefore begin thawing not long after sunrise. Staying on the skier's right side of these shallow couloirs will provide more shade. To access the top of these routes, once again ski down the southwest ridge until locating the top of your intended line.

The final option is on the more shaded skier's right side of the face, just north of the summit. This route forms an aesthetic double-dogleg couloir. Depending on snow cover, this route may be difficult to enter from the top. Descend the north ridge a short distance and then assess your options. In a good snow year, a short, exposed traverse may be all that is necessary to gain access to the couloir. In a bad snow year, a small downclimb may be necessary. If this appears to be the case from the valley, it may be wise to ascend this couloir and descend from the top of the snow cover, although this may also mean skipping the summit.

From the bottom of any of these routes, glide, ski, skate, and pole your way back down Mayflower Gulch to your vehicle.

Extra Credit: The northwest face of Drift Peak also makes a fabulous descent. Additionally, Fletcher Mountain has some great skiing on its northeast side, accessed by McCullough Gulch (see Route 38 map).

37 Mount Tweto: Northeast Face

Starting Elevation	11,050 feet
High Point	13,672 feet
Vertical Gain/Loss	2620 feet
Ascent Distance	4 miles
Descent Distance	3.5 to 4 miles, depending on route
Time	4 to 6 hours
Ski Skills	Very difficult
Fitness Level	Moderately strenuous
Technical Skills	Moderate
Gear	The basics, plus skins; ice axe and crampons may be needed
Best Months	March to May
USGS Map	Climax

Tucked away at the head of a basin that marks the headwaters of the Arkansas River, and largely hidden from view, stands Mount Tweto. Often overshadowed by neighboring peaks such as Mount Democrat and Mount Arkansas, this peak holds its own, and its intricate and steep northeast face offers a fantastic backcountry descent!

GETTING THERE

The north side of Mount Tweto is best accessed from Climax Corner, a big hairpin turn on Colorado Highway 91 between Leadville and Fremont Pass, near the headquarters of the Climax Mine.

From the north: From Interstate 70, take exit 195 for CO 91 toward Copper Mountain/Leadville. Beginning at the intersection of Copper Road and CO 91 (the main entrance to the Copper Mountain Ski Area), drive south 11.7 miles to Climax Corner.

From the south: Set your odometer at the intersection of CO 91 and US Highway 24 just north of Leadville. From there, drive north for 10.4 miles to Climax Corner.

On the southern side of Climax Corner, look for a road that heads south. This is Trail Road (Forest Road 135). During most of ski season, this road will remain snow covered and you'll have to park at the start of the road. Otherwise, continue up the 4WD FR 135 until you reach snow or an appropriate parking place.

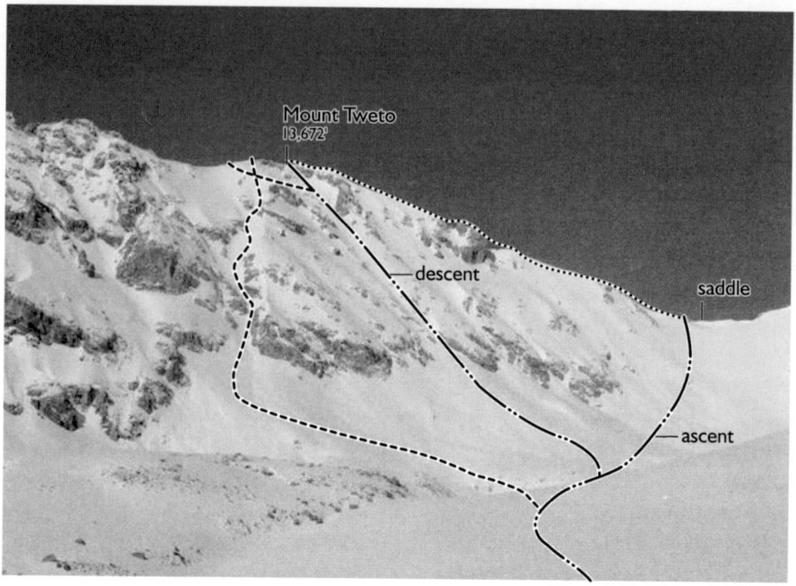

Climax Corner and the beginning of FR 135 are within the property boundaries of the operational Climax Mine. At the time of writing, there was an easement in place allowing access to this valley. To confirm access still exists, call the Leadville Ranger District (see Resources). To respect private property, please stay on FR 135 for approximately 1.75 miles.

THE ROUTE

Assuming your vehicle is parked at Climax Corner, begin on foot by following FR 135 in a southeast direction. After about 800 feet, there is a fork in the road. Take the right fork, heading west. The road will then begin to switchback and climb upward, eventually traveling southeast. At about 1.3 miles, there is another fork in the road. The right fork climbs higher while the left fork stays low in the valley. Either road is okay to follow as they both head up valley. But please stay on the roads until you have traveled about 1.75 miles to respect private property.

Continue up the East Fork Arkansas River valley, passing along Mount Arkansas to your right and Mount Democrat to your left, and the valley will eventually head south. After traveling about 3 miles, the valley will veer slightly west and you will likely have a good view of the northeast face of Mount Tweto. From below, it is important to plan your descent route, as not all lines are skiable every season.

To ascend Mount Tweto, you may choose to ascend your descent route. Alternatively, you can head to a saddle that sits just northwest of the peak (to the looker's right) to an elevation of 13,225 feet, and then follow the northwest ridge another 450 vertical feet to the summit.

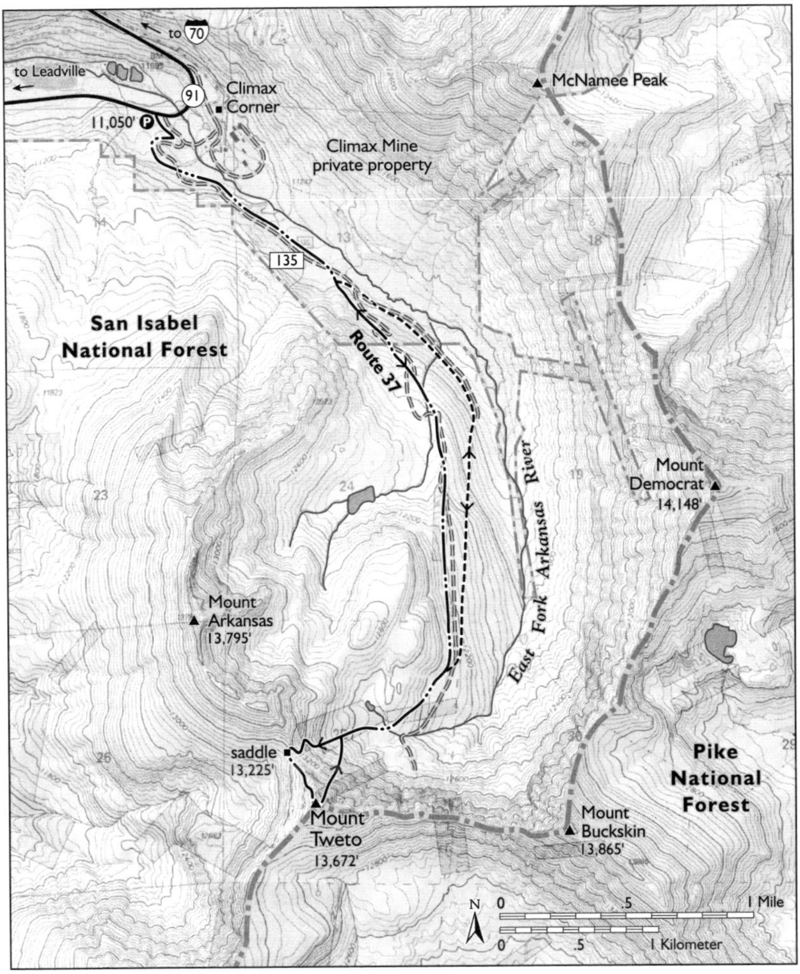

Descent. The most obvious ski route on the northeast face of Mount Tweto is straight off the summit and down. In some years, however, it might not be possible to ski right into this line off the summit as there may not be enough snow cover. But it is possible to get into it by heading a few feet down on the eastern ridge and then skirting skier's left back into the line.

Another possible route is an almost due-east line that cuts across the face sideways. The crux of this route, which is a rock band that is low in the line, may melt out early in the season. So make sure that you observe the viability of this line on your ascent.

Generally, each line provides a solid 1,200 vertical feet of skiing before you reach the valley floor. Follow your ascent route to descend through the valley and back to Climax Corner.

38 Quandary Peak: Cristo Couloir

Starting Elevation	10,900 feet
High Point	14,265 feet
Vertical Gain/Loss	3400 feet
Ascent Distance	3.75 miles
Descent Distance	3.8 miles
Time	4 to 5.5 hours
Ski Skills	Difficult
Fitness Level	Moderately strenuous
Technical Skills	Moderate
Gear	The basics; ice axe and crampons may be needed
Best Months	March to May
USGS Map	Breckenridge

In a tie along with Castle Peak in the Elk Range, Quandary Peak stands as the 12th highest peak in Colorado. For many avid backcountry skiers and snowboarders, this proud peak becomes their first official fourteener to descend. On most good-weather days through the winter and spring, Quandary sees a fair number of people on its eastern ascent. A lesser number venture into the south-facing Cristo Couloir, which is actually more of a wind-loaded gully as opposed to a couloir protected by rock features. Nonetheless, the Cristo Couloir is a classic Colorado descent and is certainly a must-do for backcountry snow riders.

GETTING THERE

From the intersection of South Main Street and Broken Lance Drive on the south end of Breckenridge, travel south on Colorado Highway 9 for 7.3 miles. Turn west (right) on to Forest Road 850 (Blue Lakes Road).

From Alma just northwest of Fairplay, travel north on CO 9 for 8 miles. After a very large switchback, turn west (left) on to FR 850 (Blue Lakes Road).

Once on Blue Lakes Road, look for a well-marked parking lot on your right, on the north side of FR 850. This parking lot will be only a few hundred yards past the intersection with CO 9.

THE ROUTE

From the parking lot, follow the trail signs northwest through the trees until you meet up with Forest Road 851 (McCullough Gulch Road). You should follow this road north about one-quarter mile to an obvious trail that leaves the road and heads northwest and upward through the forest. Usually the trail is heavily compacted from year-round backcountry use. However, if a trail is not obvious, continue northwest and upward through the trees.

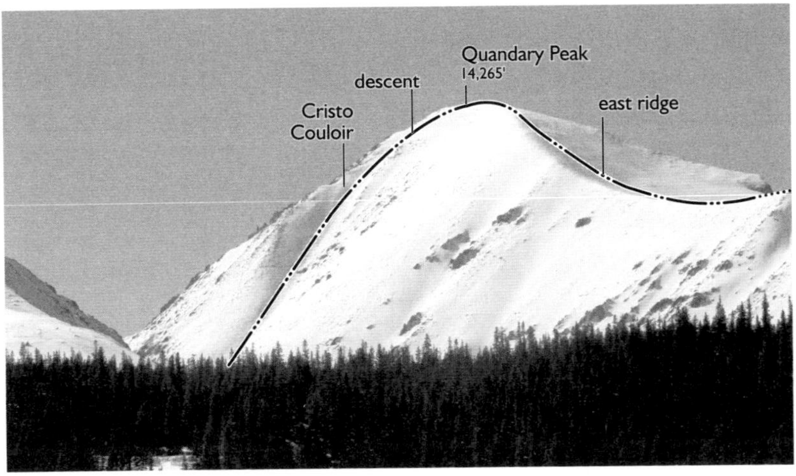

After you emerge above tree line around 11,800 feet, the route becomes more obvious. Simply follow westward along the east-facing snow slopes and ridge until you reach the summit at 14,265 feet. A flat area around 13,100 feet makes a good resting spot before the final 1100-foot push along the ridge to the summit.

Descent. Finding the Cristo Couloir from the summit may actually be the trickiest part about skiing it. From the summit, many skiers see an obvious and inviting couloir that drops to the south and slightly west. This is not the Cristo Couloir, and in fact, this couloir is usually not continuous. Do not be drawn here!

Instead, backtrack east a few hundred feet down the ridge to an open snowfield. Begin descending south on that slope, eventually cutting across on snow to your right to a more obvious but very wide gully. The gully drops straight down toward the east end of Upper Blue Lake, a good marker to indicate that you're on the right route. Remember, the Cristo Couloir is more of a wide gully. If you find yourself in a tight, rock-walled couloir, you are in the wrong place.

Sometimes the last few hundred vertical feet may require navigating around cliff bands. Take caution as the cliff bands are avoidable. Usually bearing to your left will lead to a clearer route. Upon reaching Upper Blue Lake, follow the obvious road (FR 850 [Blue Lakes Road]) east to the parking lot. This road usually has adequate snow cover to descend into May. After about 2.3 miles, you will likely reach a plowed section of road, often used as the Blue Lakes winter trailhead. This trailhead is roughly one-third of a mile away from the parking lot where you started. Continue traveling east along FR 850 until you reach the parking lot. By mid-May you may find that the Blue Lakes Road is plowed higher than the winter trailhead.

Alternate Descent. If you're worried about warming or avalanche danger, or looking for an easier descent route, follow your general ascent route along the east ridge as a descent. You may choose to descend paths close to the ridge, but not exactly on the ridge, for better snow conditions if avalanche conditions allow.

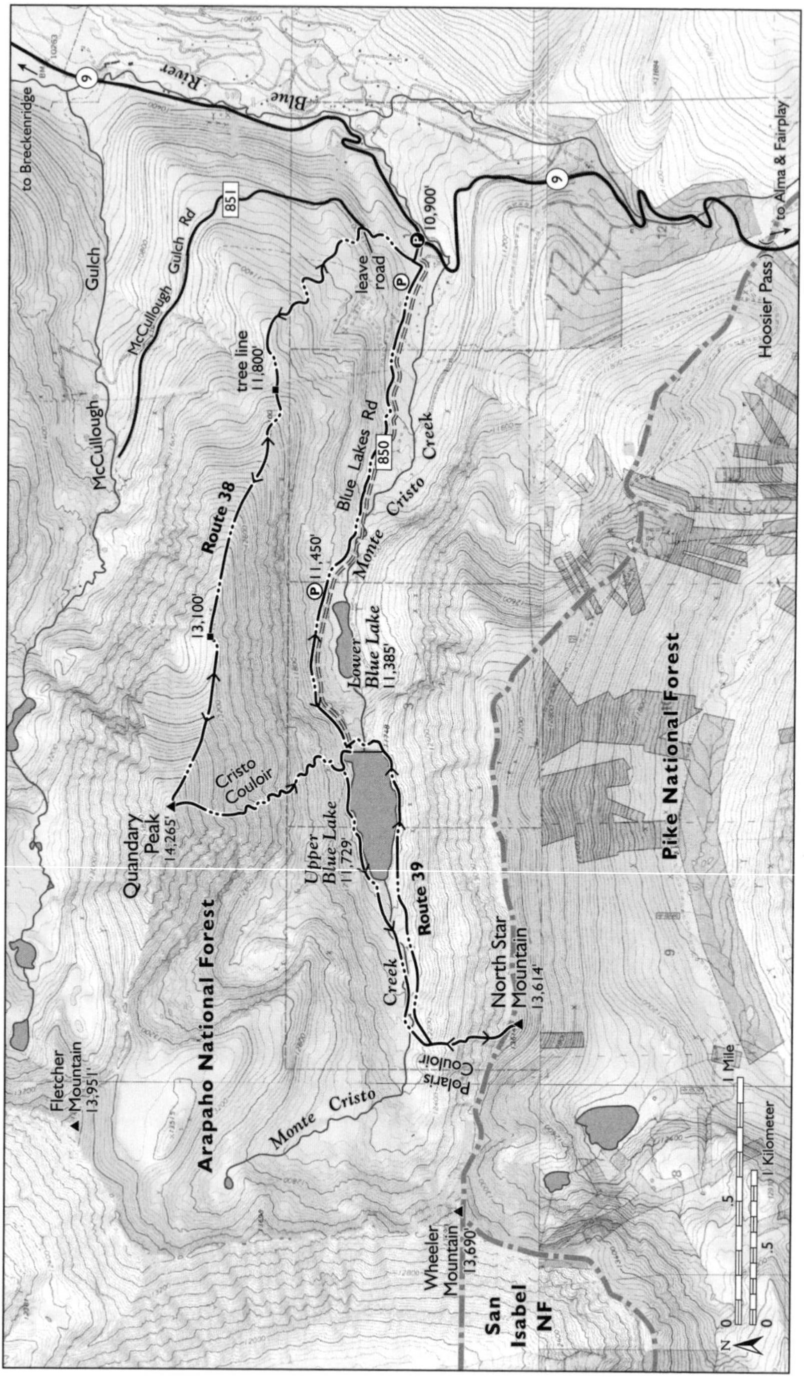
to Breckenridge
to Alma & Fairplay
Blue River
9
851
McCullough Gulch Rd
McCullough Gulch
10,900'
leave road
tree line 11,800'
Route 38
13,100'
Quandary Peak 14,265'
Cristo Couloir
850
Blue Lakes Rd
11,450'
Monte Cristo Creek
Lower Blue Lake 11,385'
Upper Blue Lake 11,729'
Route 39
Hoosier Pass
Pike National Forest
Arapaho National Forest
North Star Mountain 13,614'
Polaris Couloir
Fletcher Mountain 13,951'
Monte Cristo
Wheeler Mountain 13,690'
San Isabel NF
N
0 .5 1 Mile
0 .5 1 Kilometer

39 North Star Mountain: Polaris Couloir

Starting Elevation	10,900 feet or higher
High Point	13,614 feet
Vertical Gain/Loss	2200 to 2750 feet depending on location of trailhead
Ascent Distance	5.4 miles or less
Descent Distance	5.4 miles or less
Time	4 to 7 hours depending on location of trailhead
Ski Skills	Very difficult to extremely difficult
Fitness Level	Moderately strenuous
Technical Skills	High
Gear	The basics, plus ice axe and crampons
Best Months	April and May
USGS Map	Breckenridge

Although the actual summit of North Star Mountain is not obvious, the ridge along which it lies is very noticeable and often taunts backcountry skiers and snowboarders who find themselves atop the neighboring Quandary Peak. The Polaris Couloir on North Star is easy to access and provides steep skiing that ranges from the mid-40-degree range and into the low 50-degree range. For those looking for a more challenging line in the Blue Lakes area, Polaris Couloir fits the bill.

GETTING THERE

From the intersection of South Main Street and Broken Lance Drive on the south end of Breckenridge, travel south on Colorado Highway 9 for 7.3 miles. Turn west (right) on to Forest Road 850 (Blue Lakes Road).

From Alma just northwest of Fairplay, travel north on CO 9 for 8 miles. After a very large switchback, turn west (left) on to FR 850 (Blue Lakes Road).

Once on Blue Lakes Road, look for a well-marked parking lot on your right, on the north side of FR 850. This parking lot will be only a few hundred yards past the intersection with CO 9. If the road is open, continue west. The winter closure is usually about a half mile past the intersection with CO 9. However, later in the season as the snow melts and the road is plowed, it may be possible to drive up farther. Often by mid- to late May, you can drive to a closure gate near Lower Blue Lake at about 11,450 feet.

THE ROUTE

From the trailhead on Blue Lakes Road (FR 850), continue west along the road until it ends shortly after the dam on the east side of Upper Blue Lake. From here, follow along the north side of the shores of Upper Blue Lake. You'll pass beneath the Cristo Couloir on Quandary Peak (Route 38) to your right. After reaching the western edge of Upper Blue Lake, travel approximately another 0.8 to 1 mile up valley before veering slightly south to the base of the Polaris Couloir.

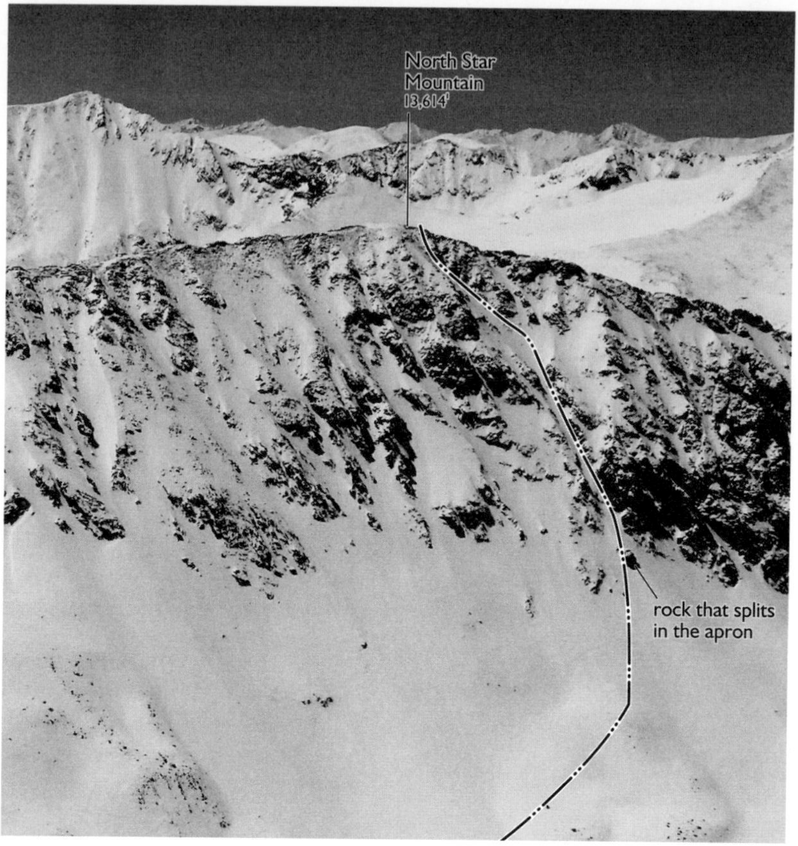

The Polaris Couloir may be difficult for you to spot as you will likely notice many couloirs coming off the north-facing slopes that comprise North Star Mountain. The couloir is fairly narrow in the middle and contains a rock outcropping that splits the line in the apron. You may need this information to identify the correct line.

Since the location of the actual Polaris Couloir can be difficult to find, it is essential that you climb what you ski. Many routes go from the ridge along North Star Mountain, but not all of the routes go continuously.

As you ascend the couloir, it will be narrow and steep through the middle. Around 13,200 feet, the route will begin to widen and become a little less steep. If you choose to reach the summit, it is best to veer slightly climber's left to a branch that is slightly more west-facing. After ascending a few more hundred feet, you may find that the snow ends and meets a pile of talus. Follow the class 2 or class 3 climb over rock another 150 or 200 vertical feet to the summit if you desire.

Polaris Couloir is rarely skiable from the summit as the last 100 to 200 vertical feet are often wind scoured and devoid of snow.

Descent. Reverse your ascent route down the Polaris Couloir. Once in the valley, you may find it easier to ski along the south shores of Upper Blue Lake rather than the north shores as it tends to hold snow later in the year. If this is the case, follow the south shores to the dam. From there, use the dam to cross back over to Blue Lakes Road (FR 850). Follow the road back to your vehicle.

40 Mount Democrat: North Face

Starting Elevation	10,960 feet or higher depending on location of trailhead
High Point	14,148 feet
Vertical Gain/Loss	3250 feet or less
Ascent Distance	4.6 miles or less
Descent Distance	4.6 miles or less
Time	4 to 7 hours depending on location of trailhead
Ski Skills	Difficult to very difficult
Fitness Level	Strenuous to moderately strenuous
Technical Skills	High
Gear	The basics, plus ice axe and crampons
Best Months	April and May
USGS Maps	Climax and Alma

Similar to Quandary Peak (Route 38), this 14,000-foot gem is another popular peak in the Mosquito/Tenmile Range and holds some of the best fourteener skiing in the area. While most hikers tend to access Mount Democrat from Kite Lake to the south, the best skiing lies on the north side of this peak. Because some lines on the north face can end in cliffs, it is highly recommended that you climb what you ski. For this purpose, the classic north face of Mount Democrat is best accessed from the Montgomery Reservoir trailhead.

Montgomery Reservoir actually has an interesting story. In the 1860s, the nearby Magnolia Mill was bustling and the town of Montgomery housed around 1000 people below. But by the end of the decade, the town was practically abandoned. Colorado Springs purchased the land in the 1890s and built Montgomery Reservoir, which now submerges much of the original townsite. But the Magnolia Mill still stands, and you'll even pass by it on this tour.

GETTING THERE

If driving from the north, take Colorado Highway 9 south over Hoosier Pass. About 0.9 mile past the crest of the pass, turn right (west) on to County Road 4.

If driving from the south, from Alma just northwest of Fairplay, travel north on CO 9 for 4.8 miles. Turn left (west) on to CR 4.

Once on CR 4, begin measuring your mileage. Stay straight at the intersections around 0.3 and 0.6 mile. After 1 mile, veer right at the fork near the Montgomery

to Breckenridge
Arapaho National Forest
9
Hoosier Pass
4
to Alma & Fairplay
Montgomery Reservoir
P
10,960'
South Platte
Middle Fork
408
mine
mine
mine
mine
Pike National Forest
Mount Lincoln 14,286'
Mount Cameron 14,238'
leave road 11,680'
Wheeler Lake
Wheeler Mountain 13,690'
Platte Gulch
Route 40
12,850'
1
2
3
Mount Democrat 14,148'
San Isabel National Forest
Clinton Peak 13,857'
McNamee Peak 13,780'
Traver Peak 13,862'
0 .5 1 Mile
0 .5 1 Kilometer
N

A skier descends the classic north face of Mount Democrat.

Reservoir, taking the higher road (Forest Road 408). Do not take the road that goes down toward the spillway of the dam. Follow FR 408 a little less than a mile as it follows along the north side of the reservoir and onto its east side. The typical winter closure is on the southwest end of the Montgomery Reservoir.

If snow has melted and you have a 4WD vehicle, you may choose to continue up FR 408 for another 2.4 miles (elevation 11,680 feet) or as far as you feel comfortable. The road will become increasingly rough.

THE ROUTE

From the southwest side of Montgomery Reservoir, follow FR 408 westward and up the valley about 2.4 miles, traveling parallel with the Middle Fork of the South Platte. Around 11,680 feet, the road will begin heading northwest, heading toward Wheeler Lake. At this point, leave this forest road and continue southwest along Platte Gulch. If snow has melted, you will find that working your way through the willows in the area can be a serious challenge. Look for a faint 4WD road to help you navigate more easily.

Follow along Platte Gulch as it begins to curve to the south to the head of the basin at 12,250 feet. Here you will need to pick your line. You will likely see that there are three main routes on the north face of Mount Democrat. The first leads from the looker's left of the summit and is the easiest route. The second cuts straight down the center of the face from the summit and you can have an interesting exit when descending through a cliff area. The third leads downward just looker's right of the summit, and it has an exit even farther to the looker's right through a rock band. Since not all lines are in condition during all seasons, it is recommended that you ascend your intended descent route. Based on conditions, pick your line and ascend it another 1900 feet to the summit.

Descent. Reverse your ascent route.

Opposite: Climbing one of the couloirs on West Skiers Point, with Little Skiers Point in the background

GORE RANGE

THOUGH THE GORE RANGE is within an hour or two of the Denver area, it remains one of the less explored areas of Colorado. Ignored by miners, no roads pierce the steep mountains here. Meanwhile, with no fourteeners or other big attractions, climbers have long pursued other areas of the state. Access to the range is generally difficult, with poor trails when there is even a trail at all. Undulating terrain clogged with trees and deadfall makes most Gore approaches an exercise in patience and routefinding.

To add to the routefinding difficulties, many of the peaks do not have official names on USGS maps. By the early 1930s, only a few of the Gore Range peaks had names. As a result, Carl Erickson and Edmund Cooper developed a system of naming the peaks with letters of the alphabet. Eagles Nest at the north end of the range was called Peak A, Mount Powell became Peak B, and Peak C didn't have a name, so it became known as Peak C. The system continued on down the range, all the way to the letter Z. As a result, many peaks have two names—an official or unofficial name and an "alphabet" name. This book has stuck with the "non-alphabet" names where possible.

The Gore Range is small and compact, measuring only 20 miles long by 5 miles wide. What the range lacks in size it makes up for in ruggedness, with most of the peaks jutting straight up from the valley below. Amazingly, however, the peaks and ridges often seem tailor-made for skiers, with line after line enticing hardy skiers to continue exploring the range.

Lying in a heavy snowfall zone, the high peaks of the Gore often receive double what the nearby ski resorts of Copper Mountain and Vail may receive. Similar to other northern ranges of Colorado, the Gore Range will often hold snow far longer than the higher peaks of other ranges, even with their typically lower elevations. Access into the Gore is typically begun from the Vail area or off Colorado Highway 9 between Silverthorne and Kremmling.

Those who ski the Gore Range will usually fall into one of two categories. Skiers who find enjoyment and satisfaction with long, difficult approaches will typically become true Gore aficionados. Others, who prefer more straightforward ski tours with less effort, will probably turn their attentions elsewhere. This dichotomy is exactly what makes the Gore so unique in Colorado.

41 Peak C: CC Rider Couloir

Starting Elevation	9350 feet
High Point	13,220 feet
Vertical Gain/Loss	4000+/- feet
Ascent Distance	5.5 miles
Descent Distance	5.75 miles
Time	8 to 10 hours
Ski Skills	Difficult
Fitness Level	Very strenuous
Technical Skills	High

Peak C as seen from the distance on Red Sandstone Road

Gear : The basics, plus ice axe and crampons
Best Month : June
USGS Maps : Vail East, Vail West, Mount Powell

Tucked deep in the Gore, just south of Mount Powell, lies "Peak C." From the beautiful and popular tourist area at Piney Lake, CC Rider Couloir looks like a nearly vertical strip that cuts the mountain in half. For as intimidating as the couloir appears from afar, its looks can be deceiving. CC Rider's slopes measure in the low 40-degree range, and the couloir itself is just under 1000 vertical feet. Nonetheless, CC Rider ranks high in both aesthetic and ski quality and is certainly one of the top picks of the Gore Range. If you venture to Piney Lake during June, you're bound to be bombarded with questions from tourists about where you skied that day. All you'll need to do is point to the line you skied and they'll have quite the story to tell!

GETTING THERE

The trailhead at Piney Lake is accessed through Red Sandstone Road. This road is typically closed in winter. During mid- to late winter, snowmobiles can be used to access the area. But as the lower part of the road melts out in early spring, the use of snowmobiles is usually no longer possible. Many online sources say that Red Sandstone Road is not open until June 21; however, oftentimes this road is open in early June or possibly even late May. To inquire about the closure, call the Holy Cross Office of the Eagle–Holy Cross Ranger District (see Resources).

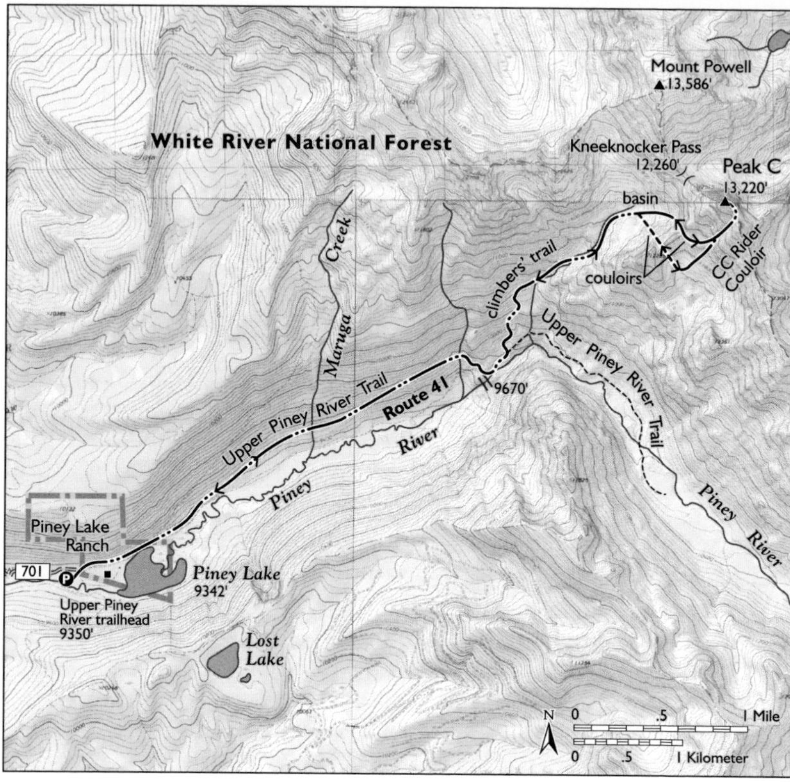

From either direction on Interstate 70, take exit 176 at Vail. If you are coming from the west, you'll want to head north at the end of the exit ramp to cross under I-70. Once on the north side of I-70, you'll find a roundabout that you will use to head west on North Frontage Road for about 0.5 mile. Turn right onto Red Sandstone Road (Forest Road 700). Follow this road as it winds through a residential area. After 0.7 mile, there is a sharp curve to the right. Go straight onto a dirt road where you should see a Forest Service sign indicating that you are on Red Sandstone Road. Reset your odometer here to track mileage. Although the road is dirt, it is usually passable by most passenger vehicles.

Continue traveling northwest on Red Sandstone Road for 2.7 miles, where you will reach the intersection with Lost Lake Road. Continue left on FR 700. Around mile 6.5, you will pass Red and White Mountain Road (FR 734), which forks to the left. Continue straight to remain on FR 700. At 0.2 mile later, you'll pass another fork to the left for Muddy Pass/Moniger Road. Take the right fork. Some maps indicate that the road changes names here to Piney Lake or Piney River Road (FR 701). Continue on this road until mile 10.7, where you'll see a Forest Service parking lot just before the Piney Lake Ranch. Park here as the ranch is private.

THE ROUTE

From the parking lot east of the Piney Lake Ranch, look for a trail sign on the northeast corner of the road. Take the Upper Piney River Trail No. 1885 as it heads east and then northeast above but parallel to Piney River. After 2.8 miles (elevation 9670 feet), the trail gets very close to the river and you'll likely see (or at least hear) the nearby waterfalls.

Here you'll need to veer left and look for a climbers' trail that heads up and to the northeast. If there is no snowcover, you must find this trail, especially at the beginning, to avoid possible episodes of bushwhacking. Although this trail is not maintained, it is fairly well used in the summer. But it can be faint at times. Try your best to stay on the trail as it does have the best route to tree line. At about 10,400 feet, the trail begins to follow along the drainage that leads down from the basin below Kneeknocker Pass (12,260 feet). Continue following this trail or drainage until you reach this basin.

From this basin, you'll have a fantastic view of the southwest face of Mount Powell (13,586 feet), the highest peak in the Gore Range. You may even scope out some lines that you could come back for another time! To looker's right of Mount Powell, you'll see an obvious saddle that straddles between Mount Powell and Peak C. This saddle is Kneeknocker Pass. Continue heading northeast up the drainage and toward this saddle, but do not go all the way to the pass.

As you travel up the drainage, you'll notice two couloirs to your right. Around 11,250 feet, you'll want to begin veering right, or southeast, toward one of these couloirs. You can climb either of them. The one to the right is steeper, but it allows better views of CC Rider from the top. However, you'll have to descend about 300 feet to access CC Rider. The one on the left is less steep, and once at the top, you can traverse over to CC Rider without descending very much. However, only the lower portions of CC Rider are visible from the top.

Ascend either of these couloirs, but the one on the left is the primary route marked on the map in this guidebook. At the top (approximately 11,900 or 11,990 feet), you'll notice another basin to the southeast that sits south below Peak C. Depending on the couloir you ascended, traverse or descend and then traverse over to the base of CC Rider on the southwest-facing slopes of Peak C. Ascend CC Rider Couloir as it climbs up Peak C for about 1000 feet.

The couloir tops out at an obvious notch around 12,940 feet, about 300 feet short of the summit. Getting to the summit from here involves some class 3 scrambling and can sometimes be difficult. Many skiers opt to skip the summit and descend from here.

Alternatively, if conditions allow, you could look for a different snow-ramp route to the summit as you ascend CC Rider. The best snow ramp veers off to the left from the main CC Rider line at 12,750 feet. This line does not tend to hold snow as well as CC Rider. But with adequate snow, it can allow for a nice climb directly to the summit and a summit ski descent as well.

Descent. Descend your ascent route down CC Rider Couloir and into the basin below around 11,000 feet. Ascend about 300 feet up to one of the notches to the north that forms the twin couloirs you climbed earlier in the day. Descend down either of them into the basin below Kneeknocker Pass. The one on skier's left will allow for a few more turns beneath CC Rider and is the recommended route for descent. From there, follow your ascent route back to the falls and the Upper Piney River Trail back to the trailhead.

42 Outpost Peak: South Side

Starting Elevation	8440 feet
High Point	12,362 feet
Vertical Gain/Loss	4200 feet
Ascent Distance	4 miles plus 0.25- to 0.5-mile ascent on descent
Descent Distance	4 miles
Time	5.5 to 7 hours
Ski Skills	Moderate to difficult
Fitness Level	Strenuous
Technical Skills	Moderate
Gear	The basics
Best Months	February and March
USGS Map	Vail East

On the west side of Pitkin Creek drainage lies "Outpost Peak" (see map in Route 43) along with a zone often called "Little Skiers Point." Carefully working the south aspects and ridgelines of these zones can allow skiers to have some great skiing earlier in the season when conditions haven't yet transformed to more stable spring snow. The ridgeline also offers fabulous views of the Birthday Chute (Route 43) and "West Skiers Point" Chutes (Route 44) across the valley.

GETTING THERE

The Pitkin Lake trailhead is the primary access used for the Pitkin Creek drainage. Traveling east or west on Interstate 70, take exit 180 at Vail. If traveling from the east, turn right immediately off the exit and head north. Take the first right onto Fall Line Drive. If coming from the west, at the end of the exit ramp, turn left, heading north on Big Horn Road. Cross under I-70 and then take a right onto Fall Line Drive.

Once on Fall Line Drive, head east about 0.2 mile until the road ends in a residential area. Look for public parking for the trailhead just before the condominium buildings.

THE ROUTE

From the public parking area, look for the trail signs for Pitkin Lake. Begin following this trail upward and to the northeast over steep terrain, switchbacks, and stairs. You will start on the east side of Pitkin Creek and very shortly you will use a bridge to cross over to the west side. Due to the relatively low elevation and southwest-facing

Skiing the south slopes of Outpost Peak (Photo by Dave Bourassa)

aspect at the start, this trail is often fairly dry for the first 0.5 to 0.75 mile. Around 8900 to 9000 feet, the trail begins to flatten a bit, and with the change in steepness, it tends to hold more snow. With snow, the trail will likely fade. You should follow the drainage up the valley, remaining on the west side of Pitkin Creek.

Approximately 1 mile from the start of the trail and at an elevation of 9250 to 9300, you will notice that the space between trees on your left side begins to widen. Ascend north through these trees, which you'll find are largely aspens. Eventually the slope will become more gradual and will lead to the south ridge of Outpost Peak. Continue traveling north along this ridge.

The ridge will lead directly to Point 11,637, also called Little Skiers Point or Little Skiers Peak. Some skiers may choose to stop here and descend their ascent route or descend the southeast-facing slopes off Little Skiers Point into the Pitkin Creek drainage (described in the descent). If you want to continue on to Outpost Peak, keep following the ridge north about another 0.8 mile and 700 vertical feet to the summit.

Descent. Descend your ascent route.

Alternate Descent. From the summit of Outpost Peak you should have a clear view of most of the south slopes. You will have the best skiing by descending these slopes for a bit and then reascending back to the ridge to Little Skiers Point. Be sure to plan out possible ascent routes from the top.

For this option, descend these south slopes about 1000 feet to an approximate elevation of 11,250 feet. As you descend, gradually contour to your left. Eventually, you will need to put your skins back on to ascend to the ridge and return to Little Skiers Point.

Once on Little Skiers Point, you have two options. The safest option is to descend your skin track following the ridge and south slopes. You will likely find great skiing in the aspen trees on the south slopes that you ascended. Once you've reached Pitkin Creek, continue following your ascent route back to the Pitkin Lake trailhead.

If conditions allow, a little steeper skiing can be found by following either of the two gullies leading to the southeast from Little Skiers Point. Keep in mind that these are avalanche chutes, so you should assess the safety of the snow conditions before dropping into either of these lines.

Descend the gullies about 1800 vertical feet. At an elevation of 9800 feet, you should begin contouring to your right, heading south along the Pitkin Creek drainage and remaining on the west side of Pitkin Creek. You may find indications of the Pitkin Lake summer trail as you navigate your way through this undulating terrain.

Around 9450 feet, you may run into tracks from those who crossed over to the east side of Pitkin Creek to access lines like the Birthday Chute (Route 43) and West Skiers Point (Route 44). Remain on the west side of the creek, traveling another half mile until you meet up with the tracks from your ascent around 9300 feet. Follow your ascent route on the Pitkin Lake Trail back to the trailhead.

Extra Credit: From the summit of Outpost Peak, you can enjoy a much steeper alternative descent down the east-facing bowl. Many descent options are possible here, all leading back to the Pitkin Creek drainage.

43 Pitkin Creek Drainage: Birthday Chute

Starting Elevation	8440 feet
High Point	12,167 feet
Vertical Gain/Loss	3900 feet
Ascent Distance	4 miles
Descent Distance	4 miles
Time	5 to 7 hours
Ski Skills	Moderate to difficult
Fitness Level	Strenuous
Technical Skills	Moderate
Gear	The basics; ice axe and crampons may be needed
Best Months	March and April
USGS Map	Vail East

Sitting just north of widely traveled Interstate 70, the Pitkin Creek drainage is one of the jewels of the Gore Range for backcountry skiers. Those who venture into the area quickly realize the endless possibilities of lines and exploration that exists in the area. Descending from unranked Point 12,167 for well over 2000 feet, the Birthday Chute is a moderate line that allows visitors to get an overview of the drainage and enjoy some great skiing along the way.

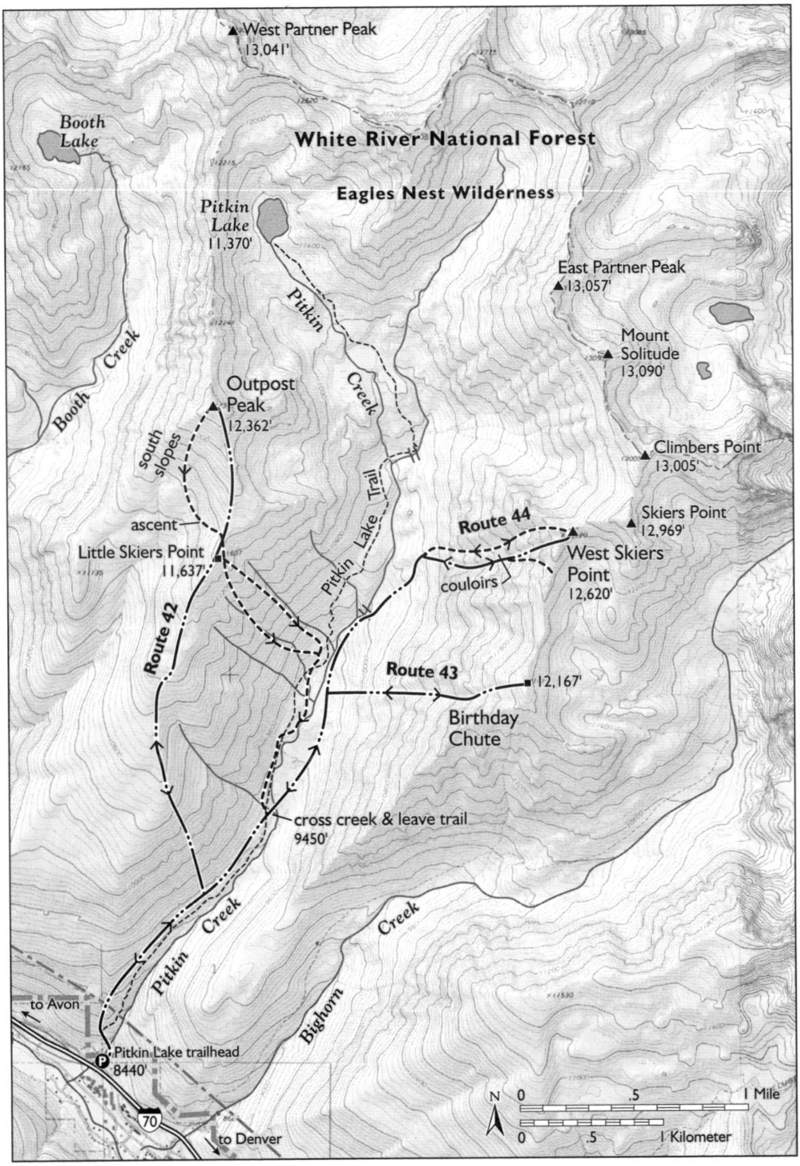

GETTING THERE

The Pitkin Lake trailhead is the primary access used for the Pitkin Creek drainage. Traveling east or west on I-70, take exit 180 at Vail. If traveling from the east, turn right immediately off the exit and head north. Take the first right onto Fall Line Drive. If coming from the west, at the end of the exit ramp, turn left, heading north on Big Horn Road. Cross under I-70 and then take a right onto Fall Line Drive.

Once on Fall Line Drive, head east about 0.2 mile until the road ends in a residential area. Look for public parking for the trailhead just before the condominium buildings.

THE ROUTE

From the public parking area, look for the trail signs for Pitkin Lake. Begin following this trail upward and to the northeast over steep terrain, switchbacks, and stairs. You will start on the east side of Pitkin Creek and very shortly you will use a bridge to cross over to the west side. Due to the relatively low elevation and southwest-facing aspect at the start, this trail is often fairly dry for the first 0.5 to 0.75 mile. Around 8900 to 9000 feet, the trail begins to flatten a bit, and with the change in steepness, it tends to hold more snow. With snow, the trail will likely fade. Follow the drainage up the valley, remaining on the west side of Pitkin Creek.

After about 1.5 miles and at an elevation of about 9450 to 9500 feet, you will cross an unnamed creek that comes down from the west. A few hundred feet later, you should cross over Pitkin Creek itself, leaving the typical summer trail, and travel up the valley on its east side. After this point, the terrain becomes easier to travel on the east side of the drainage. Continue traveling north up the Pitkin Creek drainage, through undulating terrain, passing many great ski lines along the way.

At about 9700 feet and after traveling about 2.5 to 3 miles, you should notice an obvious ski line to your right (east). You may only see the bottom part, after it narrows through a rock band and widens again for the bottom apron. You may choose to ascend the line directly, but it is safer to ascend the looker's right side through the trees. Eventually, the terrain becomes difficult to navigate, and you will likely find yourself working your way back into the chute itself around an elevation of 11,000 feet. For another 500 feet, the line narrows a bit but begins to widen again around an elevation of 11,500 feet. After this elevation, you may find safer terrain by working small ridgelines that lie to the looker's left or right of the main chute. Within the line, you will find slight changes in aspect ranging from southwest to northwest. Keep this in mind as you plan your ascent route and make sure to plan for warming snow, especially on more south-facing aspects.

As you ascend, look for possible wind-loaded zones near the top that could be potential avalanche hazards. The last 100 feet of the route may not be skiable due to wind scouring.

Descent. Enjoy about 2300 feet of turns down the Birthday Chute. Once at the valley floor around 9700 feet, follow your ascent route back to the Pitkin Lake trailhead.

Extra Credit: This route can easily be combined with the southeast-facing gullies on Little Skiers Point (see Route 42).

44 Pitkin Creek Drainage: West Skiers Point

Starting Elevation	8440 feet
High Point	12,620 feet
Vertical Gain/Loss	4300 feet
Ascent Distance	5.5 miles
Descent Distance	5.5 miles
Time	8 to 10 hours
Ski Skills	Difficult to very difficult
Fitness Level	Strenuous
Technical Skills	Moderate to high
Gear	The basics, plus ice axe and crampons
Best Months	March and April
USGS Map	Vail East

Miles up the Pitkin Creek drainage lies an unofficial peak at 12,620 feet that harbors many chutes that go for over 2000 vertical feet on its west-facing slopes. These chutes are excellent ski routes and are very worth traveling the long approach to access them. Despite their west-facing aspect, these chutes are often little impacted by the winds, and some fantastic skiing can be found here.

Many people refer to this peak as "Skiers Point," but names in the Gore Range are often confused as many maps of the area are devoid of names. The true Skiers Point lies to the east of 12,620 feet, at an approximate elevation of 12,969 feet. Thus 12,620 feet is better referred to as "West Skiers Point" (see map in Route 43).

GETTING THERE

The Pitkin Lake trailhead is the primary access used for the Pitkin Creek drainage. Traveling east or west on Interstate 70, take exit 180 at Vail. If traveling from the east, turn right immediately off the exit and head north. Take the first right onto Fall Line Drive. If coming from the west, at the end of the exit ramp, turn left, heading north on Big Horn Road. Cross under I-70 and then take a right onto Fall Line Drive.

Once on Fall Line Drive, head east about 0.2 mile until the road ends in a residential area. Look for public parking for the trailhead just before the condominium buildings.

THE ROUTE

From the public parking area, look for the trail signs for Pitkin Lake. Begin following this trail upward and to the northeast over steep terrain, switchbacks, and stairs. You will start on the east side of Pitkin Creek and very shortly you will use a bridge to cross over to the west side. Due to the relatively low elevation and southwest-facing aspect at the start, this trail is often fairly dry for the first 0.5 to 0.75 of a mile. Around 8900 to 9000 feet, the trail begins to flatten a bit, and with the change in steepness, it tends to hold more snow. With snow, the trail will likely fade. Follow the drainage up the valley, remaining on the west side of the Pitkin Creek.

After about 1.5 miles and at an elevation of 9450 to 9500 feet, you will cross an unnamed creek that comes down from the west. A few hundred feet later, you should cross over Pitkin Creek itself, leaving the typical summer trail, and travel up the valley on its east side. After this point, the terrain becomes easier to travel on the east side of the drainage. Continue traveling north up the Pitkin Creek drainage, through undulating terrain, passing many great ski lines along the way.

At about 9700 feet and after traveling about 2.5 to 3 miles, you will notice the Birthday Chute (Route 43) ski line descending from your right (east). Continue traveling north up the valley along the east side of Pitkin Creek. Around 9800 feet, you will need to navigate around cliffs that become waterfalls during summer runoff. You may find it easier to ascend the actual drainage itself or remain on the east side of the drainage.

A little less than a mile past the Birthday Chute and at about 10,300 feet, you will find yourself at a flatter area below the West Skiers Point Chutes. At the bottom, you will find two main entrances up the chutes. As you ascend, you will notice that each of these branches off into a maze of branches as well. Ascend the couloir of your choice about 2000 to 2300 feet. Depending on your line choice and conditions, you may not reach the high point at 12,620 feet, but you may end up gaining the ridgeline instead. Class 4 terrain can exist on the ridgelines, making it difficult to reach the actual high point using the ridge.

Descent. Descend your ascent route down the chute on West Skiers Point. Once at the bottom of the chutes at 10,300 feet, follow your ascent route back to the Pitkin Lake trailhead.

45 Uneva Peak: West & Southwest Aspects

Starting Elevation	10,580 feet
High Point	12,522 feet
Vertical Gain/Loss	1950+/- feet
Ascent Distance	3+/- miles
Descent Distance	3+/- miles
Time	2 to 5 hours
Ski Skills	Easy to moderate
Fitness Level	Moderately strenuous
Technical Skills	Low
Gear	The basics
Best Months	December to February
USGS Map	Vail Pass

Accessed from the top of Vail Pass, Uneva Peak's gentle slopes are a stark contrast to the surrounding peaks of the Gore Range. But these same gentle slopes make this peak a great gateway into the range. Although you'll find a variety of terrain on Uneva Peak for all levels of backcountry skiers and snowboarders, the majority of terrain is most suited for storm days and those needing more entry-level topography.

GETTING THERE

Vail Pass is located on Interstate 70, about 5.2 miles west of Copper Mountain and 14.5 miles east of East Vail. Take exit 190, toward Shrine Mountain Pass Road. Vail Pass has a rest area, and although you may want to use these facilities, you cannot park here long term. Instead, park in one of the two recreation area lots. The upper lot, located northwest of the bridge crossing I-70, is intended primarily for recreation users with snowmobiles. The lower recreation lot is just southwest of the I-70 bridge. Even lower and farther to the south is the parking for the rest area.

The Vail Pass Winter Recreation Area is a fee area for all users. At the time of writing, the fee is $6 per person, although children thirteen and under are free. Frequent visitors to the area can pay $40 for a season pass. A few self-serve fee stations exist in the area, but you'll need to look for them. An obvious one remains in the snowmobile recreation lot. These funds are used by the Forest Service for many things, including snow removal at the recreation lots. These lots are actively patrolled so be sure to pay the fee.

THE ROUTE

From the recreation lot, you get a good view of Uneva Peak to the northeast on a clear day. Routes are plentiful there, so you should begin planning your route here.

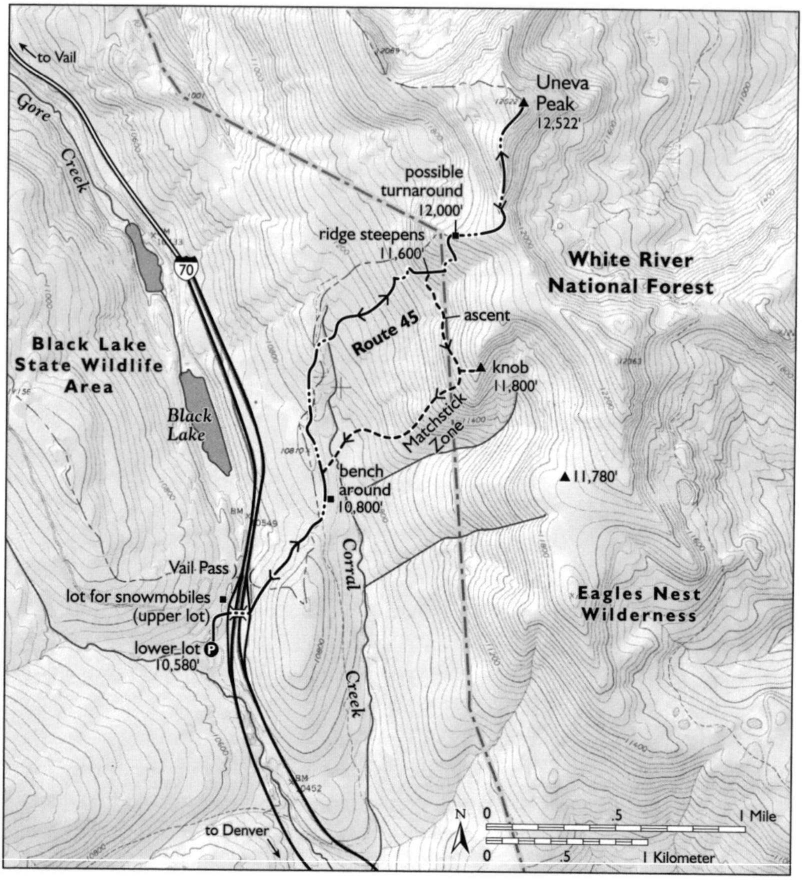

From the parking area, walk on the road and head east across the bridge that crosses I-70. Just on the other side of the bridge you'll see a Vail Pass Winter Recreation Area sign. This is the typical start of the skin track.

Through the forest, travel northeast, contouring terrain until reaching an obvious bench around 10,750 to 10,800 feet. From this bench, many routes are possible, not all of them leading from the summit. If you want to reach the summit, continue north, following the bench until it fades. Continue ascending north, and then northeast, following a gentle ridgeline.

At approximately 11,600 feet, the ridge steepens and you'll want to veer looker's right, staying on some gentle slopes that are to the south of the ridge. Eventually, you will meet back up with the ridgeline around 12,000 feet, just above tree line. Many people opt to ski from here, as skiing off the summit from this approach is not always possible due to lack of snow. But if you want to reach the summit, continue following the obvious ridge east, and then north another 0.7 mile and 900 vertical feet to the summit.

Descent. Descend your ascent route back to the road.

Ascending the slopes of Uneva Peak with the high peaks of the Tenmile and Mosquito Ranges in the distance

Alternate Descent. Begin by descending your ascent route to about 11,500 feet. Then put the skins back on for a quick ascent. Head south and slightly east, contouring upward toward a knob with many dead trees. This is called the Matchsticks Zone. Skin up to a knob around 11,800 feet, right above tree line. Most opt to descend the west-facing slopes through the burn zone from here.

Extra Credit: For another fun line that does not reach the summit, leave the bench previously mentioned (elevation 10,750 to 10,800 feet) about 0.4 to 0.5 mile after starting on the skin track at the Vail Pass Winter Recreation Area sign. Ascend upward and to the east to where the terrain flattens around 11,780 feet. From there, descend your ascent route.

WINTER TRAVEL AT VAIL PASS

Today, Vail Pass winter travel is simple: motorized travel is allowed to the west of Interstate 70 and nonmotorized is east. Within the motorized area, there are parts that are nonmotorized, with the intention of preserving it for skiers. That means, for those wanting, sled laps are plentiful. And across the highway, users still get their area of peace and quiet—if there is such a thing close to a major highway.

But winter travel in the Vail Pass area wasn't always so simple. In the 1980s, various user groups seemed to be at each other's throats. Vicious stories have been passed down—of instances like people putting up fishing line between trees. According to Chuck Ogilby, owner of the Shrine Pass Hut (see Rescources), "The area at the time was being overrun with snow machines with no areas reserved for quiet use. A helicopter operated a heli-ski operation, a snow-cat operator was there, several private snow-cat clubs, and of course the Shrine Mountain Inn, the Jackal, Janet's, and the Fowler-Hilliard huts. This intense use was chaos. But the use then was a fraction of what it has become today." Something had to change.

Enter the Vail Pass Task Force. Conversations first began around 1989 or 1990 and evolved through the years. The group is made up of eight individuals representing various users and interests in the area. Compromises have been made, including the motorized versus nonmotorized divisions. But the task force also initiated a fee.

The thought process was, if you implement a fee, people would be more likely to follow the designated rules, especially since some of those fees could go to signage and education of user groups. And that seems to actually be working.

Where do the fees go? Ninety-five percent of the fees collected remain at the Vail Pass Winter Recreation Area site. The other 5 percent is distributed among other fee sites and used for administrative purposes. Here's what the fees are used for (taken from Vail Pass Winter Recreation Area map, 2015–16):

Managed parking and snow removal. Signage and maintenance of motorized and nonmotorized trails, including grooming.

Visitor information services. Trail and backcountry monitoring by the US Forest Service.

Maps. Production of Vail Pass Winter Recreation Area maps to hand out to the public.

46 Buffalo Mountain: Silver Couloir

Starting Elevation	9760 feet
High Point	12,777 feet
Vertical Gain/Loss	3100 feet
Ascent Distance	3 miles
Descent Distance	4 miles
Time	4 to 6 hours
Ski Skills	Moderate
Fitness Level	Moderately strenuous
Technical Skills	Moderate
Gear	The basics
Best Months	March to May
USGS Maps	Vail Pass, Frisco, Willow Lakes, Dillon

As travelers head west on Interstate 70 from the Eisenhower Tunnel, numerous peaks in front of them simply cannot go unnoticed. One of the most dramatic is Buffalo Mountain. I-70 is one of the best places to view the Silver Couloir as it drops off the northeast aspect of this mountain. Buffalo is a striking mountain, rising 4000

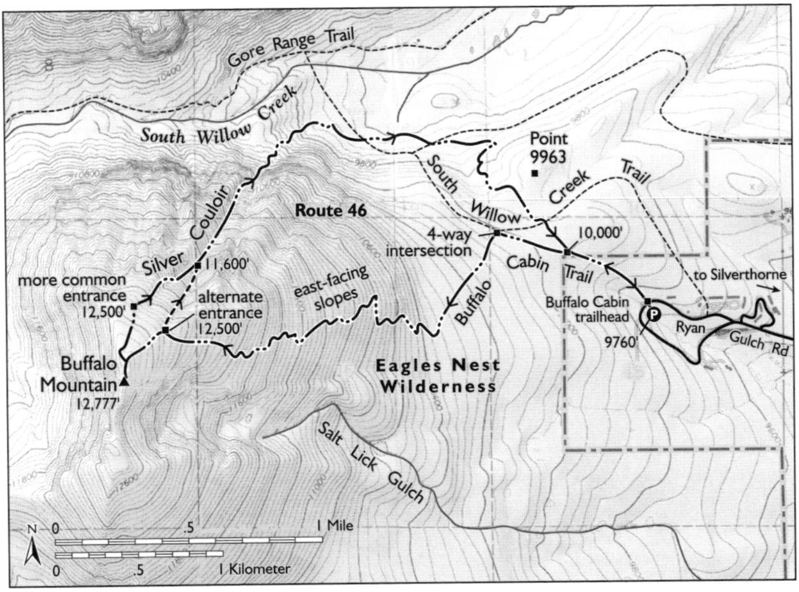

vertical feet above the town of Silverthorne. Over recent years, the Silver Couloir has become one of the classic skis of Summit County. In reality, it's just one of many potential lines on this summit.

Although the Silver Couloir is only a moderate ski, there have been quite a few skier fatalities and avalanches on this route. Should an avalanche occur on this line, it typically slides fairly large. Be certain about avalanche conditions before attempting this line.

GETTING THERE

From either direction on I-70, take exit 205 at Silverthorne. Travel north on Colorado 9 (Blue River Parkway) to the first stoplight. Turn left (west) onto Wildernest Road, which will become Ryan Gulch Road. Follow this road about 3.2 miles as it switchbacks and winds up the hillside, passing many condominium complexes along the way. The road will begin to crest on the top of a hill, where you'll find the start of the trailhead on the right (northwest). On the left (southwest), you'll find a parking area for the Buffalo Cabin. Park here. Make sure to not confuse this with the Lily Pad Lake trailhead, which is about 50 yards south of this parking area, on the west side of the road.

THE ROUTE

The easiest route to the top of the Silver Couloir follows the summer route along the east-facing slopes of Buffalo Mountain. However, going this way does not allow you to preview the conditions of the snow, nor does it allow you to be familiar with the correct couloir entrance or your exit route out of the South Willow Creek drainage,

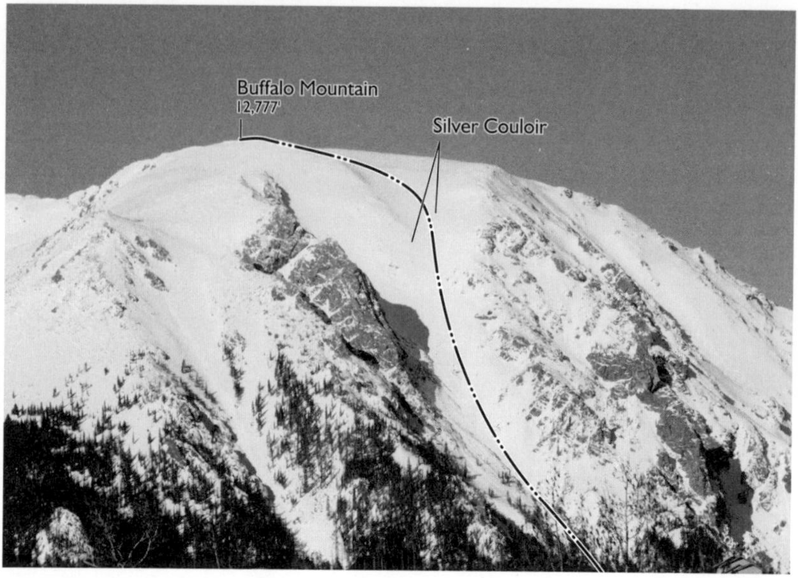

both of which can be tricky. Based on the popularity of the Silver Couloir, climbing the couloir itself might not be the best option as you may end up with skiers descending above you. If you want to ascend what you will ski, follow the description below in reverse. The route description will assume you want to approach the Silver Couloir using the summer trail.

Many of the trails in this area see significant use even during the winter. Thus, at lower elevations, the trails can be easy to follow as they are often compacted.

From the parking area, head northwest on the Buffalo Cabin Trail (Buffalo Mountain Trail), following the signs for Buffalo Cabin. After approximately 0.7 mile and at an elevation of 10,000 feet, you'll likely come to a four-way junction with the South Willow Creek Trail. Note that if you want to ascend the Silver Couloir directly, you should continue straight, following the South Willow Creek Trail and eventually contouring west to the bottom of the line.

To follow the summer route, at this junction turn left, heading southwest through the forest. If you're on route and there's not too much snow cover, you may pass by cabin remains at 10,350 feet. Continue traveling up the trail as it switchbacks to head more directly west. If the trail fades, make your own ascent route through the forest on the east-facing slopes of Buffalo Mountain.

Around 11,000 feet, you'll notice that the trees begin to thin as you approach terrain that will be above tree line. An obvious gully (Salt Lick Gulch) splits the west side of Buffalo Mountain into a north and a south side. Remain on the north side, eventually working your way up to the ridge to the east of the summit. Continue traveling west on the ridge. Around 12,500 feet, you'll pass one of your descent options into the Silver Couloir. Most skiers enter using a line that is slightly farther to the west, also at an elevation of approximately 12,500 feet. The two lines eventually meet at an elevation of 11,600 feet.

At 12,500 feet, you have not yet reached the summit. If weather and timing allow, continue onward for another quarter mile and 277 vertical feet to the summit.

Descent. From the summit of Buffalo Mountain, head north and very slightly east to find the wide entrance for the Silver Couloir around 12,500 feet. Be careful not to head directly north or slightly west. This can lead to lines that are more difficult, some of which may not be a continuous ski. Bear in mind that Buffalo Mountain is a popular ski zone and following other ski or snowboard tracks may not necessarily lead you into the correct line. The start of the Silver Couloir is very open, but it eventually rolls over and narrows a bit as you descend.

Descend the Silver Couloir about 3000 vertical feet to an elevation just below 9800 feet. You will be in the South Willow Creek drainage. Do not follow this drainage all the way out, as you will end up miles away from where you started. Instead, without losing much elevation, traverse to your right, heading east along the upper part of the drainage. After traversing east for about a half mile, you'll want to begin ascending the gentle slopes to your southeast, climbing out of the South Willow Creek drainage. As you ascend, remain looker's right of Point 9963. Eventually, you'll intersect with the Buffalo Cabin Trail around 10,000 feet. Descend this trail southeast back to the trailhead.

A word of caution: This area has several different trails, which can be very confusing, especially in winter. If you intersect a trail, it may not be the actual Buffalo Mountain Trail that you want to be on. Use of a GPS device or compass in this area can help ensure that you're on the right trail and make your travels more efficient.

47 Red Peak: Big Bad Wolf

Starting Elevation	8975 feet
High Point	13,189 feet
Vertical Gain/Loss	4400 feet
Ascent Distance	6+/- miles
Descent Distance	6 miles
Time	9 to 11 hours
Ski Skills	Very difficult
Fitness Level	Very strenuous
Technical Skills	High
Gear	The basics, plus ice axe and crampons
Best Months	April to early June
USGS Maps	Willow Lakes and Dillon

The Gore Range is known for its long approaches. But visitors are rewarded with amazing scenery and fabulous ski descents. Red Peak upholds this reputation. Scenes from the Willow Lakes are difficult to top, and the descent options on Red Peak are

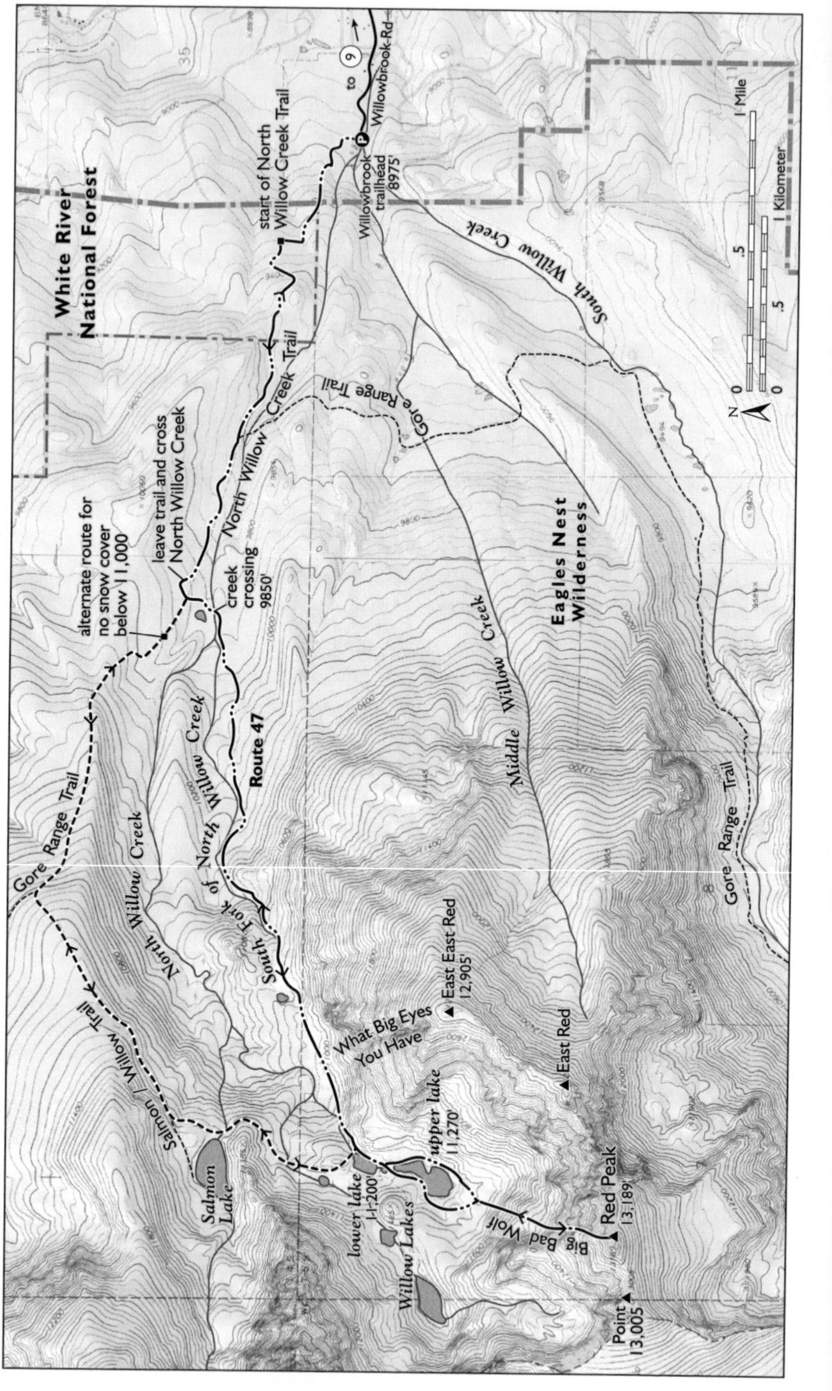
White River National Forest
Eagles Nest Wilderness
Route 47
start of North Willow Creek Trail
Willowbrook trailhead 8975'
Willowbrook Rd
to 9
leave trail and cross North Willow Creek
alternate route for no snow cover below 11,000
creek crossing 9850'
North Willow Creek Trail
Gore Range Trail
South Willow Creek
Middle Willow Creek
North Willow Creek
South Fork of North Willow Creek
Salmon / Willow Trail
Salmon Lake
Willow Lakes
lower lake 11,200'
upper lake 11,270'
What Big Eyes You Have
East East Red 12,905'
East Red
Red Peak 13,189'
Big Bad Wolf
Point 13,005
1 Mile
1 Kilometer

worth the lengthy approach. The Big Bad Wolf is one of many ski options in the Willow Lake Basin. From Willow Lakes alone you could count at least a dozen other ski lines in the area, and you'll pass a few more while going up the valley. If you have the time, this zone is a great place to haul in a tent and set up a base camp to allow ample opportunity to explore and enjoy what the Willow Lakes area has to offer.

GETTING THERE

From either direction on Interstate 70, take exit 205 at Silverthorne. Travel north on Colorado Highway 9 (Blue River Parkway) 1.9 miles and then turn left (west) onto Willowbrook Road. After driving about 1.1 miles through a residential neighborhood on Willowbrook Road, you'll see a small parking area on your left and trail signs indicating the Willowbrook trailhead. Keep in mind that this trailhead does not allow overnight parking so you'll need to make other arrangements if you're camping.

THE ROUTE

The start of this route can be a bit confusing as there are several trails and intersections in this general area, many of which do not appear on USGS maps. These trails tend to see consistent use through the winter and spring and, thus, will likely be compacted and relatively easy to follow at lower elevations.

From the trailhead, your goal is to follow the Willow Creek Trail. However, at the time of writing, signage for this trail was unclear at the start. There is an immediate split at the start of the trail. If the sign does not indicate which trail is the Willow Creek Trail, follow the right fork, which is Ditches Trail No. 9156. This trail will head northwest adjacent to some houses. After about 0.6 mile, take the left fork onto North Willow Creek Trail No. 9157. You will eventually be following parallel to North Willow Creek, on its north side. If you have trouble following this trail system, look for the North Willow Creek drainage and follow along its north side.

After traveling about 2 miles from the start of the trailhead, you'll reach the intersection with the Gore Range Trail. Continue straight, or northwest, onto the Gore Range Trail for approximately 0.6 mile. By then you should be at an elevation of approximately 9850 or 9900, and you will notice that the trail begins heading uphill and slightly north, leaving the drainage. If there is adequate snow cover, you'll want to leave the trail, veering left and descending into the North Willow Creek drainage.

If you are pretty certain that you will not have adequate snow cover until about 11,000 feet, continue following the Gore Range Trail for a total of 1.9 miles to about 11,850 feet, turn left (southwest) onto the Salmon/Willow Trail for 1.1 miles, and then head left (south) onto the Willow Lakes Trail. Follow this trail another mile to Willow Lakes.

Assuming you have adequate snow cover, following along the North Willow Creek drainage is the more efficient option. Once in the North Willow Creek drainage, you'll want to cross the creek immediately before it splits into two separate creeks a little farther up. You will now be on the south side of North Willow Creek. Head west, up the valley, continuing to follow along the drainage. At 9880 feet, you'll notice that

the creek splits. Remain on the south side of the South Fork of North Willow Creek. Continue following this drainage west and up the valley.

Around 11,000 feet, you should end up in a clearing at the base of "East East Red Peak," where you will notice a distinct, and popular, couloir to your left (south) called What Big Eyes You Have. Continue following up the valley at the base of this mountain, remaining largely in the clearing, all the way to Willow Lakes at 11,200 feet.

Once at Willow Lakes, you'll have a good view of Red Peak before you. You'll also have a great view of dozens of potential ski lines that surround the basin. Turn the corner, and you'll find even more options. You'll probably find lines you'll want to come back for.

From the lower lake, make your way to the upper lake at 11,270 feet. From there, you'll have about 1900 vertical feet of climbing to the summit. The couloir that forms the Big Bad Wolf descends directly from the obvious summit of Red Peak. The couloir itself is fairly wide and splits into three branches at the very top. The one on the looker's left is the least steep, the middle is fairly steep, and the right is the steepest, potentially ramping up into the 50-degree range. Ascend the couloir and choose the branch of your choice. You will end up on a ridge and will need to follow it about 100 to 150 vertical feet to the summit.

Descent. Descend Red Peak via your ascent route. You may find it necessary to downclimb for the first 100 feet due to the rocky terrain on the ridge. Be aware that the Big Bad Wolf is northeast facing, and the side that faces east the most may be more impacted by the sun. Make your turns down the Big Bad Wolf couloir all the way back to Willow Lakes. Once at Willow Lakes, continue following your ascent route back to the Willowbrook trailhead.

Opposite: Ascending the southwest face of Maroon Peak

ELK MOUNTAINS

IF EXPERIENCED COLORADO SKIERS were polled about their favorite range in Colorado, the Elk Mountains would be mentioned frequently, possibly even ending up on top. And why wouldn't it? Blessed with highly aesthetic peaks and prodigious snowfall, the Elks can keep skiers entertained for a lifetime.

Much of the range consists of very loose red sedimentary rock, such as the iconic Maroon Bells. These peaks are often far more enjoyable climbs when they are covered with snow, as the rock fall danger is minimized. They're a lot more fun on the way back down too. Other areas of the range are igneous intrusions that tend to have more solid rock.

Perhaps no other range in Colorado fits so prominently in the history of North American ski mountaineering than the Elks. Two of the most groundbreaking historical descents include the north face of North Maroon by Fritz Stammberger in 1971, and Chris Landry's descent of the east couloir of Pyramid Peak in 1978, now called the Landry Line. Even the seemingly impossible Capitol Peak now has multiple ski lines on it, most of which were probably first skied only recently.

The Elk Mountains are generally accessed from the Aspen area from the north or Crested Butte from the south. Both of these towns offer a wide range of services and accommodations. The tiny town of Marble makes up for its lack of services with natural beauty, and it's not far from the fun town of Carbondale.

The Kebler Pass area to the west of Crested Butte and the Marble area regularly receive the most snowfall in Colorado. Skiers accustomed to the high winds near the Continental Divide will also be surprised at the comparative lack of wind in the Elk Mountains. Even in midwinter, many peaks will have a solid coating of snow at every aspect and every elevation.

Despite being a temptress of avid mountaineers, the Elk Mountains aren't limited to steep skiing. Beginners can find their place in the Elks as well, with gladed powder skiing available for those who seek it.

48 Huntsman Ridge

Starting Elevation	8700 feet
High Point	10,100 feet
Vertical Gain/Loss	2300+/- feet
Ascent Distance	3.2+/- miles
Descent Distance	3+/- miles
Time	3+ hours
Ski Skills	Moderate to difficult
Fitness Level	Moderately strenuous
Technical Skills	Low
Gear	The basics
Best Months	December to March
USGS Map	Placita

McClure Pass is the low-lying and seldom-traveled pass that separates the Crystal River valley from the North Fork of the Gunnison. Not far from the small town of Marble, the area receives surprisingly heavy snowfall, hence its inclusion in this book. Huntsman Ridge is the most popular area off McClure Pass, and it provides fantastic midwinter skiing usually starting in late December. As an added bonus, the views of the Elk Mountains surrounding Marble are as good as it gets.

GETTING THERE

McClure Pass is 25.8 miles south on Colorado Highway 133 from the intersection with CO 82 near Carbondale. From the southwest, McClure Pass is 33.1 miles from downtown Paonia. Park on the north side of the highway at a pullout located slightly east of the pass.

THE ROUTE

From the pullout, head slightly east until you reach a narrow road, which you follow north as it winds through scrub oak and aspens from the pass. After about a mile, near a small flattish area at 9400 feet, trend slightly northeast to reach the ridge near 9900 feet. The route up to the ridge is nearly free from avalanche danger, and skiing the southern slopes back to your vehicle is a great run for aspiring backcountry skiers. The southern exposure, however, means that these slopes will often be icy or crusty.

Descent. The steeper northern slopes of Huntsman Ridge spread out below once you've reached the ridge crest. To the northwest is the high point known as "Hayes

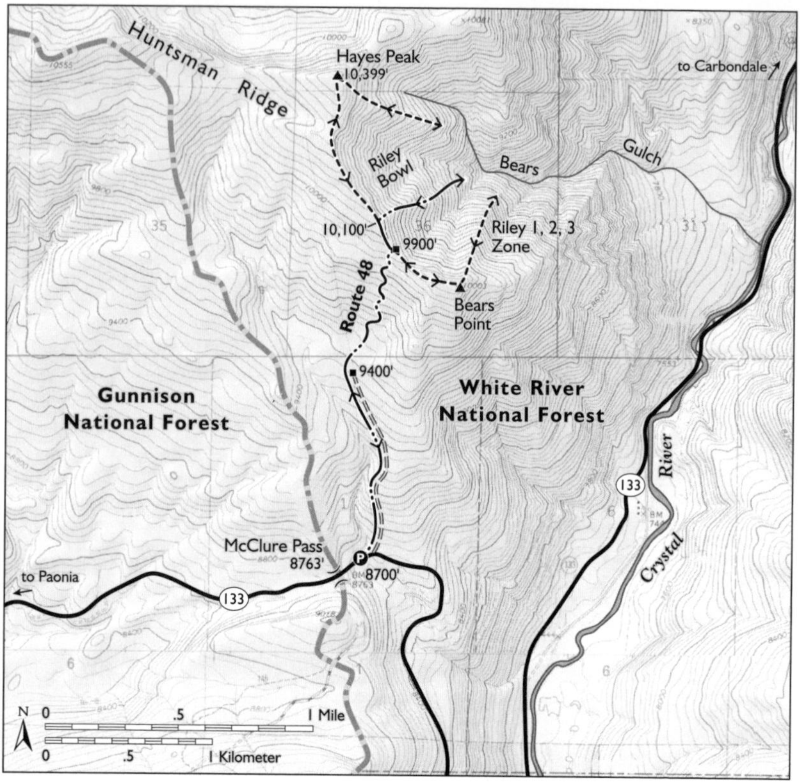

Peak," while the high point directly southeast is "Bears Point." Runs starting at Hayes Peak will face somewhat east, while Bears Point offers more northerly exposures. Experienced skiers will quickly recognize that many of these open slopes head straight into deadly terrain-trap gullies. Therefore, skiers tend to work the higher ribs and stop well short of the gullies. The most common descent may be the open bowl known as Riley Bowl, which is the primary route in this book. But the glades known as Riley 1, 2, and 3 off Bears Point are another great option. These glades look thick with trees but are surprisingly open once you drop in.

Before descending any of these routes, plan your route back to Huntsman Ridge. For Riley Bowl, this will likely mean heading back up one of the ribs, while the Riley glades can be reclimbed back through the trees. Be sure to stop well short of Bears Gulch gully as it is a terrain trap. While the elevation of this gully varies, it generally results in descents of 800 to 1200 feet. Ideally, do several laps reusing an established skin track.

The stats for this route assume one lap before heading back down the southern slopes to the trailhead. Do not attempt to descend to the highway using any route other than the southern slopes from the ridge back to the trailhead.

49 Marble Peak

Starting Elevation	8900 feet
High Point	11,314 feet
Vertical Gain/Loss	2414 feet
Ascent Distance	1.6 miles
Descent Distance	1.6 miles
Time	3 to 4 hours
Ski Skills	Moderate
Fitness Level	Not very strenuous
Technical Skills	Low
Gear	The basics
Best Months	December to April
USGS Map	Marble

The tiny town of Marble on the western side of the Elk Mountains has been a skiing destination for years. For a few years in the early '70s, there was a ski resort, and in the early '80s there was even a heli-skiing operation. It only makes sense that commercial skiing gained a foothold here, given the terrific terrain, jaw-dropping scenery, and most of all the heavy snowfall in the area. Rising quickly from the lower-elevation terrain to the west, the mountains surrounding Marble eke out every last drop of moisture from passing storms. Today, the area is popular with backcountry skiers intent on earning their turns.

GETTING THERE

Drive to the well-marked Marble turnoff on Colorado Highway 133. This turnoff is 21 miles south of Carbondale and 36 miles north of Paonia over McClure Pass. From the turnoff, it's another 6 miles to Marble. In Marble, turn right at the fire station on 3rd Street toward the Yule quarry. You are now on Yule Quarry Road, and you should reset your odometer here. This road is a narrow shelf road threatened by numerous avalanche paths. Plowing is minimal, and 4WD is recommended, along with chains at times. This is a wild road.

Parking for this route is located 2.6 miles from the turnoff in Marble, at a small pullout that fits only a vehicle or two. Numerous other small parking areas exist along the road, although parking is limited at best. If you are meeting other skiers, it is highly recommended that you carpool from town. It is extremely important to remember that the quarry farther up the road is a working mine, and work vehicles have the right of way. If you encounter a truck on the road, you will need to find a pullout and get out of the way. When parking, be absolutely sure that your vehicle leaves plenty of room for the large work trucks. If you don't leave room, you may be ticketed and/or towed,

The Marble area is known for deep snow, and this day was no exception.

not to mention the fact that you could jeopardize access for skiers in the future. If the quarry ever ceases operation, the road would no longer be plowed, and access would begin in the town of Marble.

THE ROUTE

For the east bowl of Marble Peak, begin skinning slightly south of the Mud Gulch drainage. The correct track will climb a steep hillside in a northwest direction before heading south after only 50 vertical feet. Continue south, or slightly southwest, until you reach the edge of a slide path. Follow the edge of this slide path in a more westerly direction. As you approach the summit, you'll be on a more defined ridge; heading southwest and steep skinning will take you to the top.

Descent. The east face of Marble Peak is the most commonly skied run in the area, although a quick look around should give you more ideas for future exploration. Assuming conditions are favorable, ski the avalanche path you followed alongside as you ascended. The best skiing is often near the top, and it may be worth lapping short runs before heading down to the road. Near the bottom of the run, at 9500 feet, you may find it easier to avoid a terrain-trap gully by heading skier's right and following a path through heavy brush to the road. Many of the runs in the Marble area contain large gullies, all of which should be avoided as terrain traps. Follow the road back to your vehicle.

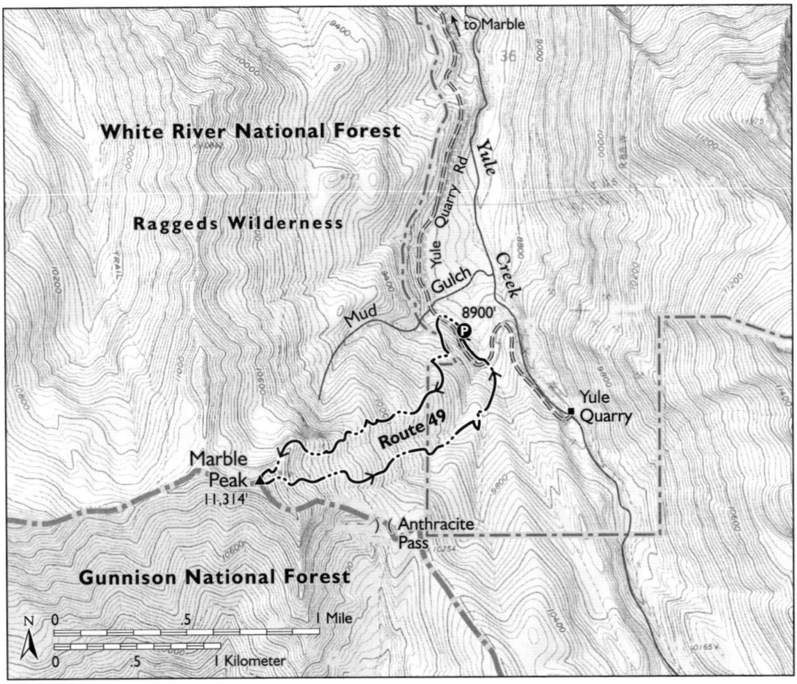

50 Mount Sopris: The Elbow

Starting Elevation	8635 feet
High Point	12,953 feet
Vertical Gain/Loss	4600 feet
Ascent Distance	7 miles
Descent Distance	6.5 miles
Time	8 to 10 hours
Ski Skills	Difficult
Fitness Level	Very strenuous
Technical Skills	Moderate
Gear	The basics, plus ice axe and crampons
Best Months	April and May
USGS Map	Mount Sopris

Rising nearly 6000 feet above the valley below, with the town of Carbondale at its feet, Mount Sopris is more reminiscent of a Cascade volcano than a peak of the Rocky Mountains. Although the actual elevation of this peak is under 13,000 feet, Mount Sopris makes up for it in stature and grandeur. It is certainly the most distinguishable feature of the Roaring Fork Valley. Named after Richard Sopris, a surveyor

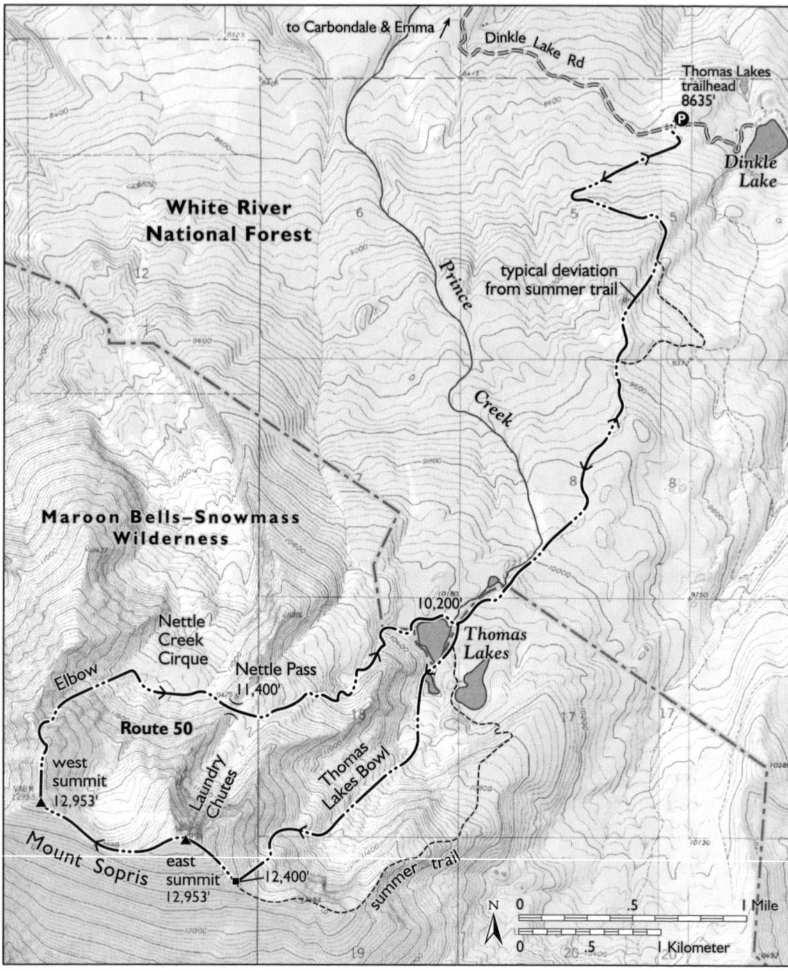

who led an expedition near the area in the 1860s, this twin-peak mountain seems like it has been built for backcountry skiing, as it has a variety of routes to quench your desires.

GETTING THERE

From the townsite of Emma, which is located just off of Colorado Highway 82, 22 miles southeast of Glenwood Springs or 18 miles northwest of Aspen, turn south onto Emma Road and then make an immediate left turn (east), again onto Emma Road. This road heads east for 0.1 mile and then turns right (south) at which point it will become Sopris Creek Road (County Road 7). After 1 mile you will come to a T intersection. Turn right (west) onto West Sopris Creek Road (County Road 6), which

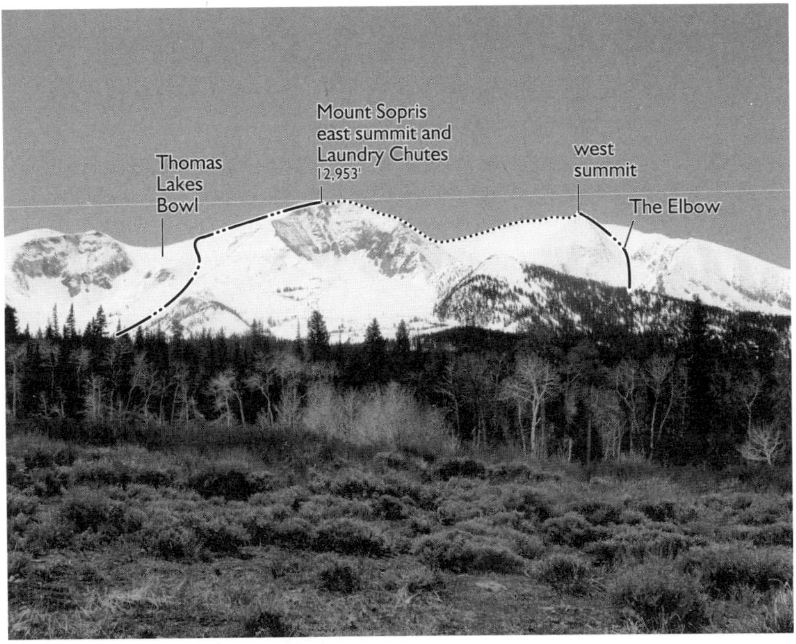

becomes a passenger-car-friendly dirt road. Drive 5.5 miles to where the road crests. During the winter, the typical road closure is here at Prince Creek Divide (8110 feet).

If the road is open, take the left (south) on to Dinkle Lake Road (County Road 6A) and drive for 2 miles to a crest in the road and the parking for Thomas Lakes trailhead (8635 feet).

Typically beginning in late April or early May, this area can be accessed from Carbondale via Prince Creek Road. Carbondale is located just off of CO 82, roughly 30 miles northwest of Aspen and 12 miles south of Glenwood Springs. From the intersection of CO 82 and CO 133, travel south on CO 133 for 2.7 miles, just past the south edge of town. Turn left (east) onto Prince Creek Road (County Road 5), which becomes a dirt road passable by most passenger vehicles. Travel 6 miles on this road until the Prince Creek Divide. Turn right (south) onto Dinkle Lake Road and drive 2 miles to the Thomas Lakes trailhead and park.

THE ROUTE

From the Thomas Lakes trailhead, begin by following the summer trail southwest 3.8 miles to Thomas Lakes (10,200 feet). This trail does see signifigant use through the winter, so it will likely be compacted and easy for you to follow. You may notice areas where the winter trail deviates from the summer trail. If you lose the trail, head in a general southwest direction to meet up with Prince Creek around 9950 feet. Follow the creek to Thomas Lakes.

Once at Thomas Lakes, you have a good view of the Thomas Lakes Bowl ahead. Leave the trail and continue southwest up the bowl to gain the southeast ridge of Mount Sopris around an elevation of 12,400 feet. Follow the ridge northwest another 550 vertical feet to the east summit of Mount Sopris.

To reach the Elbow, continue northwest along the ridge to reach the West Sopris summit. From the summit, continue north on the nearly flat ridge until it opens up to a north/northeast-facing slope.

Descent. From the east summit, you can return via your ascent route through Thomas Lakes Bowl. This is the most common descent, but this route assumes you continue heading north.

From the west summit, drop north toward the Elbow. The first 200 feet of this line may have a thin snowpack. But a little lower you can really open it up and enjoy about 1400 feet of fantastic 35- to 40-degree turns. Descend the Elbow into Nettle Creek Cirque until the route flattens in a bowl around 11,300 feet. From here, you will see a notch in the ridge to your right (east), which is Nettle Pass. Traverse west across the cirque and ascend to the top of this pass, which tops out around 11,400 feet. From the pass you will have excellent views of the famed Laundry Chutes to your right. Descend into the Laundry Chutes Cirque and follow the natural course of the gullies in a northeast direction back to Thomas Lakes. From there, retrace your ascent route back to the trailhead.

Extra Credit: Those wanting a very challenging ski can descend into one of the Laundry Chutes, which drop northeast from the east summit. These lines are notoriously difficult due to cornices near the top and/or rock bands near the bottom that often require a skier to jump or rappel. The easiest one is on the skier's right of the summit. A steep entrance avoids a cornice, but you will need to negotiate the cliff band at the bottom. In some good snow years, this cliff band is hardly noticeable. Other years, it can require a rappel.

51 Ski Hayden Peak

Starting Elevation	9040 feet
High Point	13,316 feet
Vertical Gain/Loss	4375 feet
Ascent Distance	3.8 miles
Descent Distance	3.8 miles
Time	5 to 7 hours
Ski Skills	Difficult
Fitness Level	Strenuous
Technical Skills	Moderate
Gear	The basics
Best Months	February to April
USGS Map	Hayden Peak

Looking up at the Stammberger Face; the ascent route heads climber's right.

"Ski Hayden" is the popular unofficial subpeak of Hayden Peak, and it can be seen from Castle Creek. This area is so enticing for skiing that developers in the 1930s considered it the prime location for a ski area in Aspen, but it was never developed. Lucky for us backcountry skiers! This moderate descent can be made during periods of low avalanche danger in wintertime, yet it also has a steeper variation known as the Stammberger Face, which is usually safe by springtime, for fans of steep skiing.

GETTING THERE

From the big traffic circle on Colorado Highway 82 on the west end of Aspen, follow Castle Creek Road south for 7.7 miles. A small parking lot marks the trailhead on the right.

THE ROUTE

From the trailhead, follow the signs that mark the easement for skiers through private property. The route descends slightly to Castle Creek, and then heads downstream until crossing Castle Creek via logs or a snow bridge. After the creek crossing, the easement continues on a southwest heading through an aspen forest toward Sawyer Creek and an old road. Follow this road, which ends at 9600 feet, and then continue

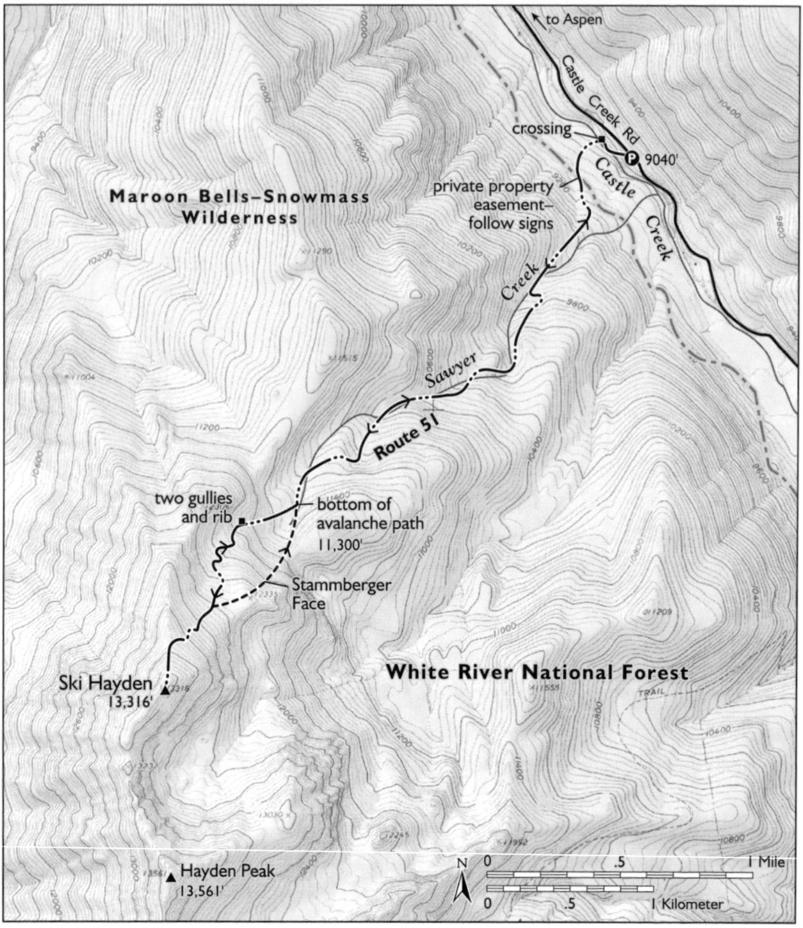

southwest up Sawyer Creek. Several areas of this trail are susceptible to avalanches and have gullies that are bad terrain traps, so choose your path carefully.

At 11,300 feet, you will reach the bottom of an avalanche path. The Stammberger Face is the steep face ahead—make a mental note if you have plans to ski it. Ascend the bowl to the skier's right of the Stammberger Face, utilizing a small rib between two gullies. At the top of the rib/gully feature, the upper face of Ski Hayden is above. Ascend the face, either to the north ridge or the summit depending on conditions.

Descent. The views from Ski Hayden are some of the best in the area, particularly for skiers keen on observing the Landry Line on Pyramid Peak, which is due east. The top of the Stammberger Face is the flat area toward the skier's right if steeper skiing is in your immediate future. Otherwise, ski the route you just ascended. The route through the trees follows your skin track back to the trailhead, which may turn into an icy bobsled run in the springtime.

52 Greg Mace Peak

Starting Elevation	9450 feet or more
High Point	12,580 feet
Vertical Gain/Loss	3130 feet
Ascent Distance	6.1 miles
Descent Distance	5.1 miles
Time	6 to 8 hours
Ski Skills	Difficult
Fitness Level	Strenuous
Technical Skills	Moderate
Gear	The basics
Best Months	March to early May
USGS Maps	Pearl Pass and Hayden Peak

"Greg Mace Peak" (see map in Route 53) is named for a Mountain Rescue Aspen member who died during a training exercise in 1985. The peak itself stands like an island in the midst of the highest Elk Mountains near Pearl Pass. With the Green-Wilson and Tagert huts nearby, Greg Mace Peak is a logical choice during springtime and is an excellent reconnaissance ski for the east face of Castle Peak and other nearby mountains. With good timing, the northwest face of Greg Mace Peak can often be skied in springtime powder conditions.

GETTING THERE

From the Aspen area, take the well-signed Castle Creek Road, which originates at the traffic circle on Colorado Highway 82 on the west side of town. From the circle, it is 11.1 paved miles to the former mining town of Ashcroft (now a ghost town), which marks the winter closure. Later in the year, you may be able to drive farther up the road, which becomes dirt past Ashcroft. The road becomes progressively worse, and crossing Castle Creek near 10,200 feet definitely requires 4WD.

THE ROUTE

Follow Castle Creek Road from the winter closure toward Pearl Pass. After 1.9 miles, stay right at Cooper Creek. Observe the various northwest-facing lines of Greg Mace Peak as the road passes underneath them. Just before reaching the switchbacks toward Montezuma Basin, at mile 4.1, begin skinning up an obvious avalanche path to the southeast, near the 10,900-foot level. The route up until this point is used by snowmobiles, which may aid in your approach. At 11,600 feet, begin heading slightly south toward a shallow gully and flatter terrain on Greg Mace's west side. Gain the southwest ridge of Greg Mace Peak from the flat area, and follow it toward the summit. The summit is a rocky block with difficult climbing, but it is not necessary to reach it for any ski route.

Descent. The southeast face of Greg Mace Peak is a short route that may be skied if you have the time and energy. If you do this, reclimb your descent route back to the summit ridge of Greg Mace. From the summit ridge, several northwest-facing couloirs drop away to the Castle Creek valley below. Descend any of these, depending on conditions. These sheltered routes often hold powder after springtime storms. Retrace your approach back to Ashcroft.

53 Castle Peak: East Face

Starting Elevation	9450 feet or more
High Point	14,265 feet
Vertical Gain/Loss	4815 feet or less
Ascent Distance	8 miles or less
Descent Distance	6.5 miles or less
Time	10 to 12 hours
Ski Skills	Very difficult
Fitness Level	Moderately strenuous to very strenuous
Technical Skills	High
Gear	The basics, plus ice axe and crampons
Best Months	April to May
USGS Map	Hayden Peak

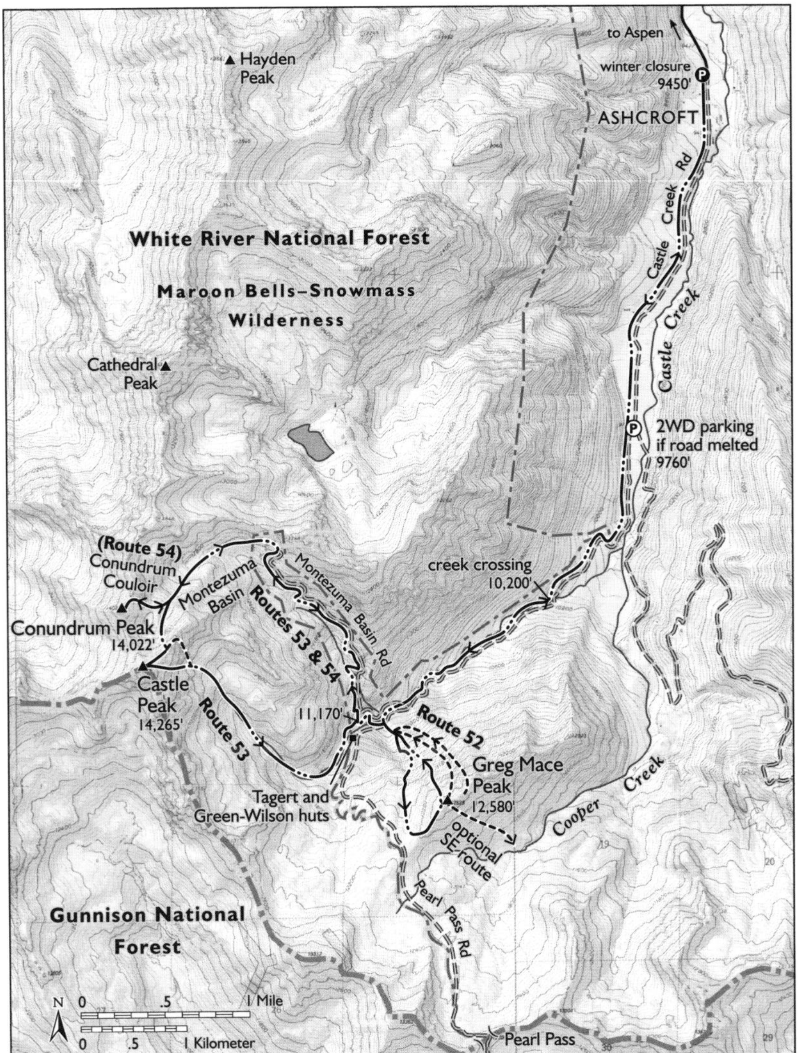

The Elk Range is known for its aesthetic summits, and Castle Peak is no exception. The Ridge of Gendarmes leads south from the summit and can be viewed from atop many of the highest peaks in Colorado. The highest peak in the Elk Mountains, Castle Peak offers skiing in every direction off its summit. The most classic line is perhaps the steep and intimidating-looking east face.

GETTING THERE

From the Aspen area, take the well-signed Castle Creek Road, which originates at the traffic circle on Colorado Highway 82 on the west side of town. From the circle, it

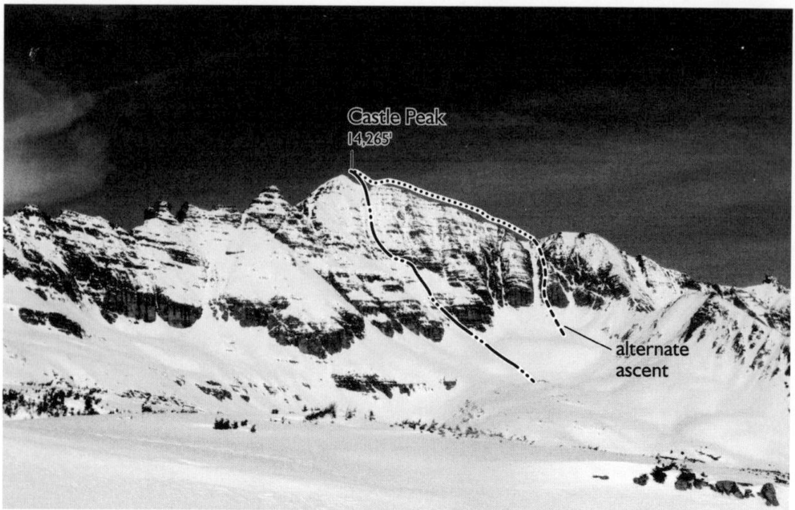

is 11.1 paved miles to the former mining town of Ashcroft (now a ghost town), which marks the winter closure. Later in the year, you may be able to drive farther up the road, which becomes dirt past Ashcroft. Two-wheel-drive parking is typically located about 1.8 miles past the town of Ashcroft, at 9760 feet, once the lower part of the road is melted out. The road becomes progressively worse, and crossing Castle Creek near 10,200 feet definitely requires 4WD.

To aid your access, you may plan to stay at either Tagert or Green-Wilson huts, located off Pearl Pass Road, just past the intersection with Montezuma Basin Road. These are both part of the 10th Mountain Division Hut system (see Resources.)

THE ROUTE

Follow the Castle Creek/Pearl Pass Road toward Montezuma Basin Road. This turn is located at 11,170 feet, roughly 5 miles from Ashcroft. Typically, skiers will be able to begin their tour somewhere between Ashcroft and Montezuma Basin, depending on snowmelt. This route assumes that you will start at the winter closure at Ashcroft, while starting higher will significantly shorten this tour.

At the split, take the right fork and follow the road north into Montezuma Basin. Montezuma Basin will slowly curve toward the west. With solid snow cover, it may not be necessary to follow the road. Once past a steep headwall, you will have great views of Castle Peak from the upper basin. With good snow cover, climbing the north couloir to the northeast ridge may be the most straightforward route to the summit. Later in the season, or with questionable avalanche conditions, the summer route may be a better choice. The summer trail switchbacks up from Montezuma Basin on a talus face to a small saddle on the northeast ridge, at 13,750 feet. The northeast ridge from here to the summit is tedious as it passes several obstacles, but it stays at class 2 with careful routefinding.

If you do not feel confident about conditions or your ability to find the route on your descent, it may be advisable to climb the east face before skiing it. A smaller couloir on the climber's right side of the east face may also be used to gain the northeast ridge and follow the route described above, while simultaneously letting you observe the face up close. From the summit of Castle Peak you will have excellent views of Conundrum Couloir (Route 54) to the north.

Descent. Castle's east face warms quickly, so if you've taken too long to reach the summit consider the north couloir back to Montezuma Basin instead. The east face ski route drops directly off the summit down the middle of the face. While there are several microvariations on the face, conscientious routefinding will keep you on track. Halfway down the face, near 13,600 feet, the route bends slightly to the skier's left. The difficulties of the face end near 13,000 feet. After the thrilling turns of the east face, the easier skiing in the valley will feel anticlimactic as you descend toward Pearl Pass Road. Reach the road approximately a quarter mile above the turnoff to Montezuma Basin. Follow the road down valley toward the trailhead.

54 Conundrum Peak: Conundrum Couloir

Starting Elevation	9760 feet or more
High Point	14,022 feet
Vertical Gain/Loss	8750 feet or less
Ascent Distance	6 miles or less
Descent Distance	6 miles or less
Time	8 to 10 hours
Ski Skills	Very difficult
Fitness Level	Moderately strenuous to strenuous
Technical Skills	High
Gear	The basics, plus ice axe and crampons
Best Months	May and June
USGS Map	Hayden Peak

In the shadows of Castle Peak stands Conundrum (see map in Route 53). Known more for the popular hot springs that lie just a few hiking miles west of the summit, Conundrum Peak has a steep couloir on its east face that holds snow well into summer. A pleasure to ski, Conundrum Couloir is another classic line in the Elk Range.

GETTING THERE

From the Aspen area, take the well-signed Castle Creek Road, which originates at the traffic circle on Colorado Highway 82 on the west side of town. From the circle, it is 11.1 paved miles to the former mining town of Ashcroft (now a ghost town), which marks the winter closure. Later in the year, you may be able to drive farther up the road, which becomes dirt past Ashcroft. Two-wheel-drive parking is typically located about 1.8 miles

Climbing the upper pitches of Conundrum Couloir (Photo by Larry Fontaine)

past the town of Ashcroft, at 9760 feet, once the lower part of the road is melted out. This tour assumes you've been able to park at the 2WD parking at 9760 feet.

For those wanting to venture higher in their vehicles if the road is melted, the road becomes progressively worse, and crossing Castle Creek near 10,200 feet definitely requires 4WD.

THE ROUTE

Follow the Castle Creek/Pearl Pass Road toward the Montezuma Basin Road to a turn that is located at 11,170 feet, roughly 3 miles from the 2WD parking at 9760 feet and 5 miles past Ashcroft.

At the split, take the right fork and follow the road north into Montezuma Basin. Montezuma Basin will slowly curve toward the west. With solid snow cover, it may not be necessary to follow the road. Once past a steep headwall that flattens around 13,300 feet, you will have great views of Castle Peak (Route 53) from the upper basin. Conundrum lies just ahead to your right. The east-facing couloir is not distinguishable until you are almost beneath it. Ascend the apron and couloir, which ends at the north ridge at approximately 13,970 feet. Near the top, you may encounter a cornice. Usually the easiest way around this cornice is to the climber's right.

From the ridge, oftentimes the route to the summit is devoid of enough snow to make a worthy ski descent. But if you want to summit anyway, follow the ridge south for a quarter mile to the top.

Descent. Return via your ascent route. In late spring or early summer, you could encounter very icy conditions. Despite its east-facing aspect, Conundrum Couloir can remain shaded for a good part of the morning even in early summer. Nonetheless, it's always better to get an earlier start in the day and wait for the necessary warming to occur than to be late on your timing of the line.

55 Pyramid Peak: The Landry Line

Starting Elevation: 8750+/- feet
High Point: 14,018 feet
Vertical Gain/Loss: 5268+/- feet
Ascent Distance: 6+/- miles
Descent Distance: 6+/- miles
Time: 9 to 12+/- hours
Ski Skills: Extremely difficult
Fitness Level: Very strenuous
Technical Skills: Very high
Gear: The basics, plus ice axe and crampons. Some parties may want a rope, especially in a low snow year.
Best Months: April to early May
USGS Map: Maroon Bells

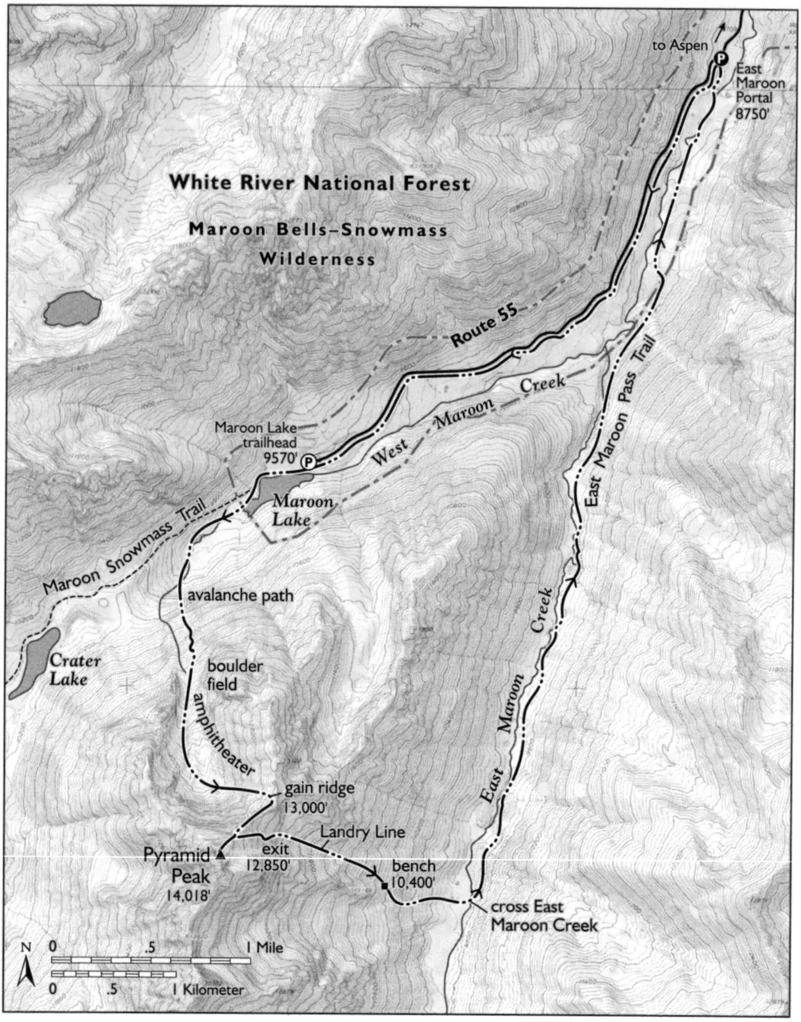

Pyramid's Landry Line needs no introduction. It is one of Colorado's steepest, longest, and most aesthetic lines. First skied in 1978 by Chris Landry, it wasn't skied again until 2006. Not only does this line require stamina, climbing skills, and steep skiing skills, most of all it requires impeccable timing. The short ski window on the Landry Line, which may last only a few days per season, may be the crux of the route.

GETTING THERE

From the Aspen area, take the well-signed Maroon Creek Road, which originates at the traffic circle on Colorado Highway 82 on the west side of town. Starting at the traffic circle, it is 3.1 miles to the winter closure at the T-Lazy-7 Guest Ranch (8236

feet). From the closure, it's 3.3 additional miles to the East Maroon Portal (8750 feet) and 6.3 miles to the Maroon Lake trailhead (9570 feet). From mid-June through September, this road is restricted and closed to vehicles during the day unless you are an overnight hiker. Generally speaking, the Landry Line will no longer be in skiable shape by the time the restrictions begin, however.

The winter closure of Maroon Lake Road has long been an annoyance for ski mountaineers. Early in the year, it will be snow packed, and you can make good time skinning the road or utilizing a snowmobile. Later on, however, the paved road will be plowed yet the gate will remain closed. Under these circumstances, your best option may be riding a bicycle up the road. A bike trailer will make this experience far more enjoyable. Otherwise, it's a long walk with a heavy pack to Maroon Lake.

Maroon Creek Road is operated by the Forest Service. To inquire about the status of the road, call the Aspen Ranger District (see Resources).

THE ROUTE

This tour assumes that you have been able to start at the East Maroon Portal trailhead. Depending on circumstances, you may be more likely to start at Maroon Lake or all the way down at T-Lazy-7. If possible, running a shuttle between the East Maroon Portal trailhead and Maroon Lake will save 3 miles and 850 feet of vertical gain.

Head up valley from Maroon Lake for 1 mile, to 9800 feet. Begin climbing a small, comma-shaped avalanche path toward Pyramid's north face. This route is slightly down valley from the standard summer route on Pyramid, and it may be difficult to find in the dark if you've gotten an early start. Continue up this avalanche path, which will open up into a steep slope before reaching a flatter boulder field at the bottom of what's known as the amphitheater. Continue up this amphitheater toward Pyramid's imposing north face before climbing left up a couloir toward the northeast ridge. Reach the ridge near 13,000 feet, and then begin the ridge climb to the summit. Stay near the exposed ridge crest while paying attention to cornices until reaching a small flat area at 13,600 feet, which is your last chance to take a breather before the summit. The route switches over to the east face a short distance past the flat area, climbing through small cliff bands, which may be buried in a big snow year. From the summit, take a deep breath as the difficulties are only half over on this route.

Descent. The steepest turns, which are exposed and in the 55-degree range, are right off the summit. Stay slightly to the skier's right of your ascent route to avoid the small cliff bands, eventually resting near the small flat area. From here, the route is more straightforward, though still steep. The skier's right side tilts ever so slightly to the north, and you may find powder turns here. At 12,850 feet, find the obvious exit to the skier's right (the main couloir dead-ends in a cliff). This exit is traditionally seen as the crux of the route, and it involves tight hop turns from rock to rock. If this area is melted out, as it was on the first descent by Chris Landry, it will require a downclimb, and some parties choose to rope up here. Below the crux, the angle remains steep before finally starting to ease as you reach the larger bowl below. Reach a bench at 10,400 feet. From this bench, you may need to angle either right or left to navigate a final cliff band before reaching the East Maroon Creek valley. Cross East Maroon Creek, and then follow the East Maroon Pass Trail to the East Maroon Portal. If you started at Maroon Lake, you will need to climb Maroon Creek Road for 3 miles to end your day.

56 Maroon Peak: East Face to the Bell Cord

Starting Elevation	9570 feet
High Point	14,156 feet
Vertical Gain/Loss	4700 feet
Ascent Distance	4 miles
Descent Distance	4 miles
Time	7.5 to 10 hours
Ski Skills	Extremely difficult
Fitness Level	Strenuous
Technical Skills	High
Gear	The basics, plus ice axe and crampons
Best Months	April to early June
USGS Map	Maroon Bells

Connected by a ridge, North Maroon and the higher Maroon Peak together make the Maroon Bells. The "Bells," as they are often called, are said to be the most

The turns down the east face of Maroon Peak are steep and airy. (Photo by Pam Rice)

photographed natural place in Colorado, and when you first lay eyes on these snow-capped wonders, you too will want to snap your own picture—or twenty. Don't let the peaceful name of these peaks fool you. The Maroon Bells are also said to be among the most deadly mountains in Colorado, due both to their popularity as Colorado fourteeners and their horribly loose rock. But the Bells can also be rewarding for experienced ski mountaineers looking for a challenge.

Maroon Peak is often called "South Maroon," in contrast to its northern sister. The peaks are split by an obvious couloir, called the Bell Cord, that holds snow well into the summer. Timing for best ski conditions in the Bell Cord can be tricky. You need stable snow to descend the exposed east face above it, but later in the spring the Bell Cord can be laden with wet slide debris and runnels. However, in the right conditions, the east face and the Bell Cord of Maroon Peak can make a fabulous descent.

GETTING THERE

From the Aspen area, take the well-signed Maroon Creek Road, which originates at the traffic circle on Colorado Highway 82 on the west side of town. Starting at the traffic circle, drive 3.1 miles southwest to the winter closure at the T-Lazy-7 Guest Ranch (8236 feet). From the closure, continue southwest to the entrance station at mile 4.7. From mid-June through September, this road is restricted and closed to vehicles during the day unless you are an overnight hiker, but this does not apply during the time period

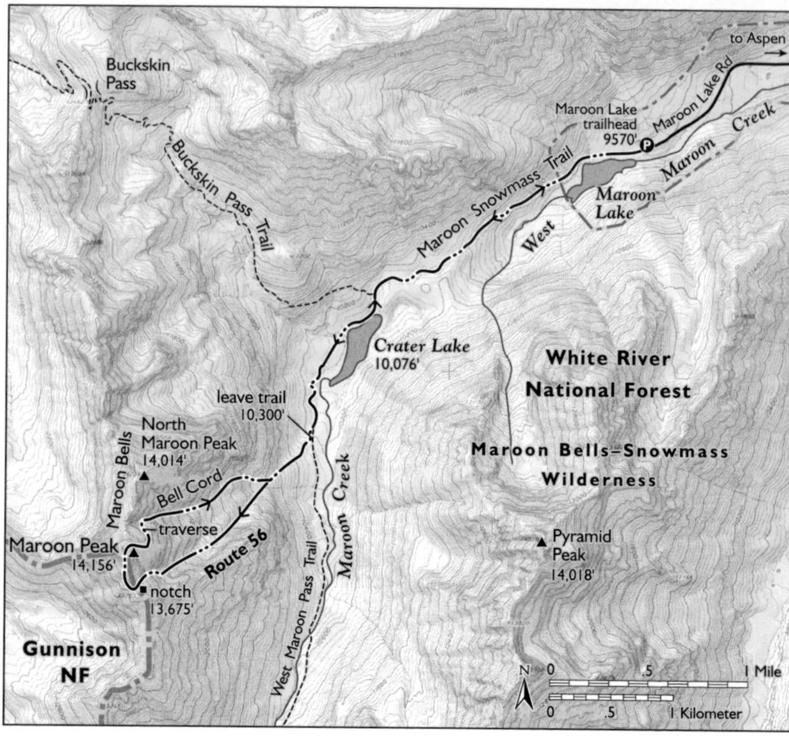

of the winter closure or for alpine starts. The road ends at the Maroon Lake trailhead, 9 miles from the traffic circle and 6.3 miles from the winter closure.

The winter closure of Maroon Lake Road has long been an annoyance for ski mountaineers. Early in the year, it will be snow packed, and you can make good time skinning the road or utilizing a snowmobile. Later in spring, however, the paved road will be plowed yet the gate will remain closed. Under these circumstances, your best option may be riding a bicycle up the road. A bike trailer will make this experience far more enjoyable. Otherwise, it's a long walk with a heavy pack to Maroon Lake.

Maroon Creek Road is operated by the Forest Service. To inquire about the status of the road, call the Aspen Ranger District (see Resources).

THE ROUTE

This tour assumes that you have been able to start at the Maroon Lake trailhead (9570 feet). Begin by following the Maroon Snowmass Trail as it heads southwest toward Crater Lake, passing along the north shore of Maroon Lake. If the trail is snow covered, you may find it easier to skin across the lake and follow the natural course of the drainage. If you are following the trail, you will see an intersection at 1.7 miles. Heading right leads up to Buckskin Pass. Take the left fork, and shortly after you will arrive at Crater Lake (10,076 feet).

Pass on the west side of Crater Lake if it is not adequately frozen. From here, the trail and the drainage change course and you should be heading southwest. After approximately 2.7 miles and at an elevation of 10,300 feet, you will notice some larger snowfields to your right that appear to break through the large cliff bands that make up the east face of the Maroon Bells. As you face these snowfields, you will see a tight couloir to the left, or south side, of these snowfields. Leave the trail and ascend the east-facing slopes, aiming for this couloir, whose base is near 11,050 feet. Climb through this couloir to a more open chute.

At an elevation of 12,950 you will notice a split in the couloir, commonly called the Y couloirs. Take the climber's right chute, closer to the summit of Maroon Peak. This chute leads to an obvious notch at 13,675 feet. Some people choose to descend from this notch. To continue to the summit from the notch, you will need to cross over to the southwest face of the mountain. Here you will begin following the class 3 summer route, which will likely have intermittent snow. On this face, you will be following parallel with the south ridge, but below it on the southwest face. You will be ascending north to gain the summit. Be aware that the rock can be very loose on this face, and on this peak in general. Once on the summit, take time to enjoy the views of the many magnificent mountains that surround you.

Descent. From the summit, head east on the ridge until you reach the east face. The east face is wide and airy. You will have your steepest turns of the day on this face, which falls into the low 50-degree range. Keep in mind as you descend that you are skiing on a hanging snowfield above cliffs. In order to avoid these cliffs, you will need to traverse skier's left (north) over toward the Bell Cord around 13,650 feet to 13,500 feet, roughly 500 to 600 feet below the summit. You will need to work your way through cliffs and benches to reach the Bell Cord Couloir.

Once in the Bell Cord, descend roughly 2000 feet, working your way around potential debris and runnels. At 11,600 feet, you may encounter another cliff band, which you may find is best to avoid by going around to the left. Descend to the Maroon Creek valley at 10,300 feet, and follow your ascent route back to the Maroon Lake trailhead.

57 Unnamed 13,253: White Widow Couloir

Starting Elevation	9600 feet
High Point	13,253 feet
Vertical Gain/Loss	3653 feet
Ascent Distance	5 miles
Descent Distance	5 miles
Time	6 to 8 hours
Ski Skills	Very difficult
Fitness Level	Strenuous
Technical Skills	High
Gear	The basics, plus ice axe and crampons

Best Months : April to May
USGS Map : Gothic

When viewed from the Copper Creek valley near the former mining town of Gothic, the White Widow Couloir appears as an impossibly narrow and steep couloir. While narrow, the couloir is still slightly wider than a pair of skis, and the high rock walls provide a memorable skiing experience. This is one of the Elk Mountain's finest couloir descents.

GETTING THERE

From downtown Crested Butte, head north on Gothic Road (County Road 317) toward Crested Butte Mountain Resort. The winter closure is at the Snodgrass trailhead (elevation 9511 feet) in Mount Crested Butte. The dirt road past the Snodgrass trailhead usually opens in May. Stay on Gothic Road past the town of Gothic until the marked trailhead for Judd Falls/Copper Creek/East Maroon Pass (9600 feet), approximately 4.2 miles past the Snodgrass trailhead.

THE ROUTE

If you're skiing this route in April, chances are you will need to start at the Snodgrass trailhead, which will add 4.2 miles each way to the Judd Falls trailhead. From the Judd Falls trailhead parking, head up the rough 2WD road to the upper trailhead (9850 feet), where the Judd Falls Trail begins. Follow this trail southeast as it winds

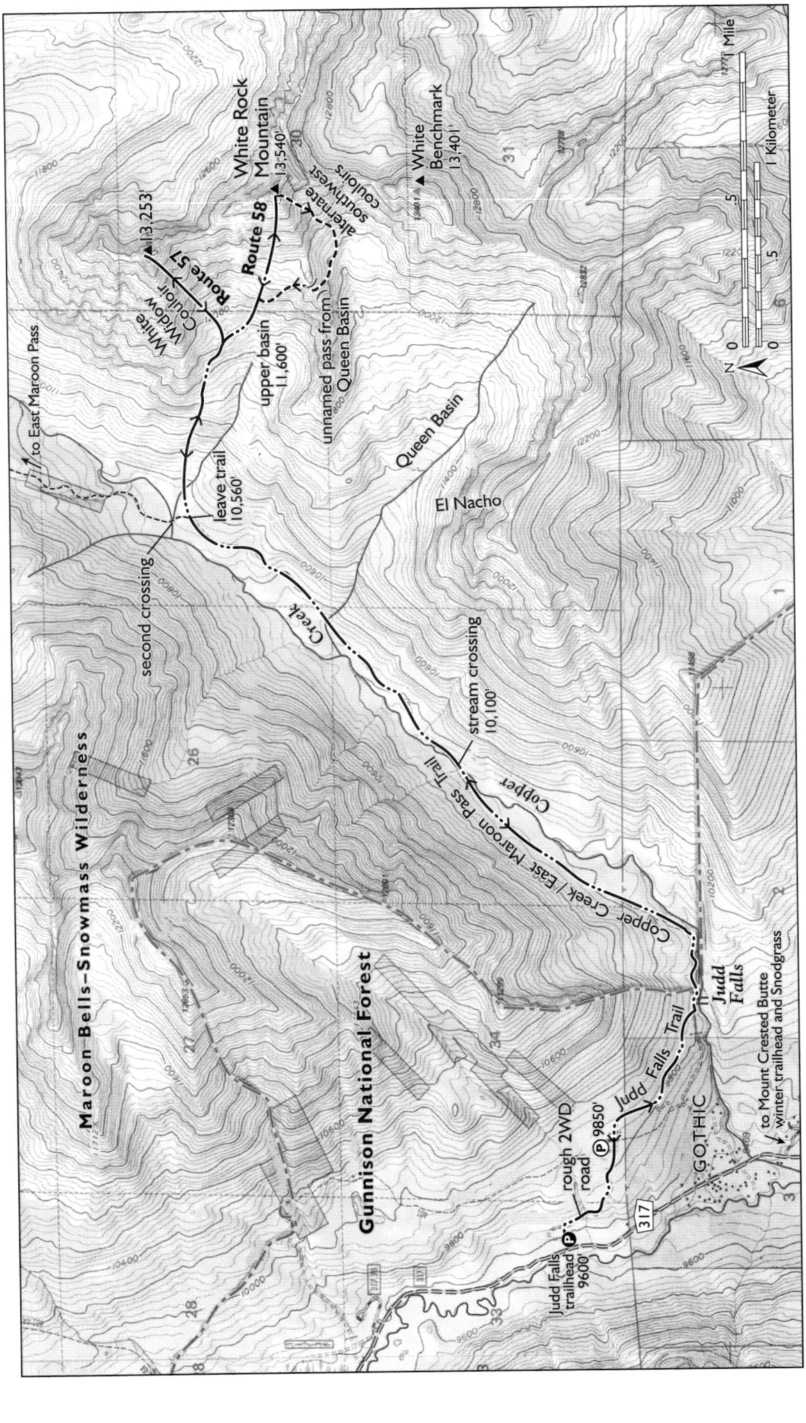
to East Maroon Pass
White Widow Couloir
Route 57
13,253'
White Rock Mountain
13,540'
Route 58
alternate southwest couloirs
White Benchmark
13,401'
upper basin
11,600'
unnamed pass from Queen Basin
Queen Basin
leave trail
10,560'
El Nacho
second crossing
Creek
stream crossing
10,100'
Copper
Copper Creek / East Maroon Pass Trail
Maroon-Bells-Snowmass Wilderness
Gunnison National Forest
Judd Falls
Judd Falls Trail
rough 2WD road
9850'
Judd Falls trailhead
9600'
GOTHIC
317
to Mount Crested Butte winter trailhead and Snodgrass
1 Mile
1 Kilometer

up and down until hitting the wider Copper Creek/East Maroon Pass pack trail at 9800 feet. Follow the trail northeast up the valley. At 10,100 feet, the trail crosses Copper Creek, which you may need to wade across if you are unable to find a snow bridge. You will reach a large avalanche runout zone at 10,560 feet before the trail crosses Copper Creek once again. Head up this avalanche path into the upper basin (elevation 11,600 feet). The White Widow Couloir will be above you in this basin, although from certain angles the entire couloir may not be visible due to a dogleg in the couloir. Climb the couloir to the 13,253-foot subpeak. The upper 100 vertical feet may be bare during windy seasons.

Descent. Transition to ski mode at the summit, and then enjoy the tight couloir and Copper Creek valley back to your vehicle.

58 White Rock Mountain: West Face

Starting Elevation	9600 feet
High Point	13,540 feet
Vertical Gain/Loss	3940 feet
Ascent Distance	5.2 miles
Descent Distance	5.2 miles
Time	7 to 9 hours
Ski Skills	Difficult
Fitness Level	Strenuous
Technical Skills	Moderate
Gear	The basics, plus ice axe and crampons
Best Months	April to May
USGS Map	Gothic

The west face of White Rock Mountain (see map in Route 57) provides one of the longest continuous runs in the area, dropping 3000 feet from the summit to the valley below. From the summit of White Rock, the Elk Mountains unfold before your eyes, particularly giants like the Maroon Bells and Pyramid Peak. The entire Copper Creek valley contains great ski potential, and you will likely find yourself returning for other routes that you spot from White Rock.

GETTING THERE

From downtown Crested Butte, head north on Gothic Road (County Road 317) toward Crested Butte Mountain Resort. The winter closure is at the Snodgrass trailhead (elevation 9511 feet) in Mount Crested Butte. The dirt road past the Snodgrass trailhead usually opens in May. Stay on Gothic Road past the town of Gothic until the marked trailhead for Judd Falls/Copper Creek/East Maroon Pass (9600 feet), approximately 4.2 miles past the Snodgrass trailhead.

THE ROUTE

If you're skiing this route in April, chances are you will need to start at the Snodgrass trailhead, which will add 4.2 miles each way to the Judd Falls trailhead. From the Judd Falls trailhead, head up the rough 2WD road to the upper trailhead (9850 feet), where the Judd Falls Trail begins. This trail winds up and down until hitting the wider Copper Creek/East Maroon Pass pack trail at 9800 feet. Follow the trail northeast up the valley. At 10,100 feet, the trail crosses Copper Creek, which you may need to wade across if you are unable to find a snow bridge. You will reach a large avalanche runout zone at 10,560 feet before the trail crosses Copper Creek once again. Head up this avalanche path into the upper basin (elevation 11,600 feet). A rocky headwall in the upper basin can be climbed on either side. The most continuous route to the summit appears as a diagonal strip from climber's upper left to lower right. Climb these west slopes to the 13,540-foot summit.

Descent. Descend your ascent route. If the southwest couloirs look appealing from the summit, they also make a great descent into Queen Basin. While Queen Basin is a magical place, the best descent will involve a short climb back to a small unnamed pass to rejoin your ascent route in the unnamed basin that lies north of Queen Basin. Additionally, Queen Basin is choked with trees and is therefore not recommended.

Extra Credit: The north-facing El Nacho Couloir in Queen Basin is hard to miss. This route makes a fine objective of its own, or combined with a summit descent of White Rock Mountain.

59 Gothic Mountain: Gothic Spoon and West Chutes

Starting Elevation	9470 feet
High Point	12,631 feet
Vertical Gain/Loss	3518 feet
Ascent Distance	3.4 miles
Descent Distance	3.5+ miles
Time	5 to 6 hours
Ski Skills	Difficult
Fitness Level	Moderately strenuous
Technical Skills	Moderate
Gear	The basics, plus skins; ice axe and crampons may be needed
Best Months	March to May
USGS Map	Oh-Be-Joyful

One of the most impressive and aesthetically pleasing peaks in the Crested Butte area, Gothic Mountain offers easy access and prime skiing during much of the spring.

Gothic is a fun climb and ski and is also a great peak for lesser-experienced ski mountaineers to gain some basic skills. But even experienced ski mountaineers will enjoy the iconic peak.

GETTING THERE

From the town of Crested Butte, head north on 6th Street, which becomes Gothic Road (County Road 317) as it exits town. Travel approximately 2.5 miles on this road until the intersection with Washington Gulch Road. Turn left onto Washington Gulch Road (CR 811) and drive until the obvious winter closure about 2.6 miles after turning off Gothic Road.

THE ROUTE

From the winter closure, begin your tour by heading northwest on Washington Gulch Road. The road is usually easily identifiable as it has continuous cross-country ski and snowmobile travel through the winter and spring. Skins are usually necessary on this part of the tour, but some backcountry users prefer to skate-ski, as the terrain is fairly flat.

You can see the south side of Gothic Mountain from this part of the road. As you travel, take note of the easily identifiable feature that looks like a spoon—a ski descent line called the Gothic Spoon. The ascent route, sometimes called the Ladle, is two ridges to the looker's left of the Spoon.

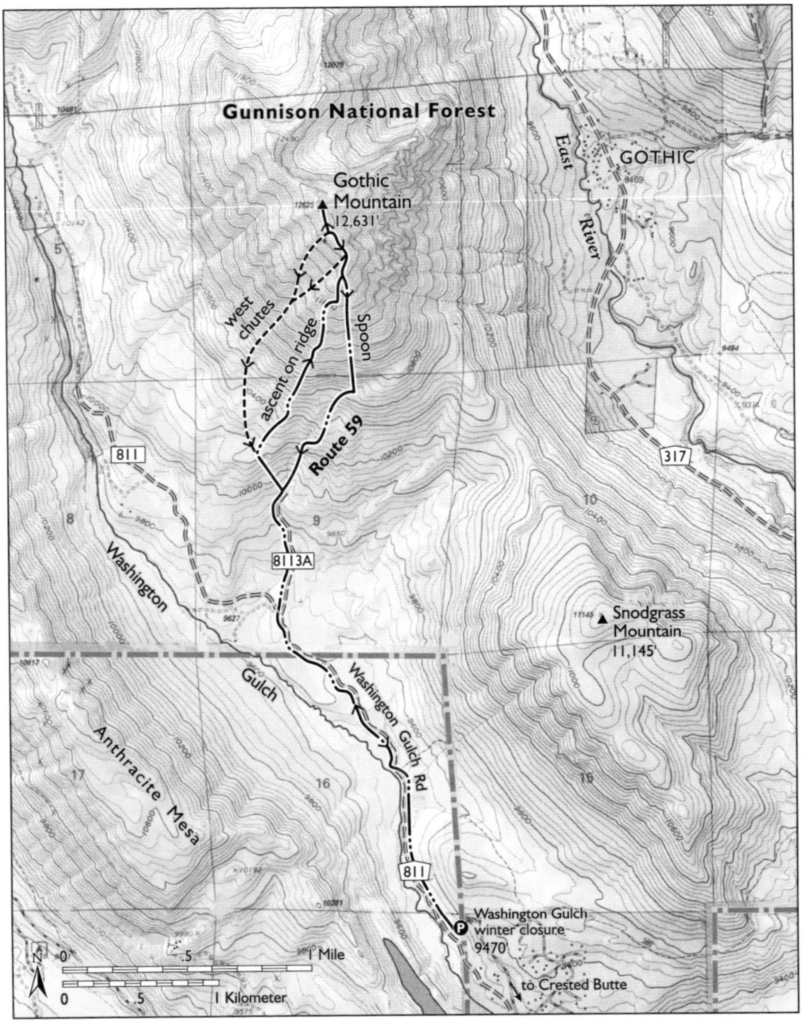

After about 1.6 miles of travel, veer right onto a lesser-traveled, possibly unmarked, road (Forest Road 8113A) that begins to ascend toward the lower slopes of Gothic Mountain. This road will end after another half mile, at an approximate elevation of 9945 feet. Continue through the trees, trending slightly left, until the terrain opens up and you reach an obvious ridge. Most backcountry skiers boot along this ridge, although in some conditions you may be able to skin. As you reach the end of the snowfield (the Ladle) on the initial ascent ridge, head climber's right to another ridge that makes up the left side of the Spoon. Continue following the ridge all the way to the top of the Spoon and then to the summit. Be aware that the ridge past the top of the Spoon is heavily corniced. Stay as far left as possible, on rock, to avoid the cornice edge and the gaps created by the calving cornice.

Descent. You have many options for descents on Gothic Mountain, but the ones that lead you back to Washington Gulch are the west chutes and the south-facing Spoon.

To access the primary route, which is the south-facing Spoon, descend the ridge farther until the south-facing snowfield appears. The Spoon begins at an approximate elevation of 12,200 feet, so you can skip the summit of Gothic Mountain if you are tired or pressed for time. The Spoon begins wide and then narrows. As the line steepens, there is a cliff band you can easily avoid but that is difficult to spot from above. *A fall or an avalanche in the Spoon can take a skier over this cliff, so proceed with caution.* To avoid the cliff band, look for the small snow patch just above it and to the left that you can use to traverse across to a larger area of snow about 100 feet away. Several options exist from here through the trees back to Washington Gulch Road and the trailhead.

Alternate Descent. The west chutes are fairly straightforward. Simply retrace the ascent ridge until you find continuous snow to descend. Sometimes you may need to downclimb 50 or 100 feet to reach the snow on the west side. Once the chutes begin to open up, trend hard left to avoid some road skiing at the end of the line. At the bottom, you will easily spot Washington Gulch Road. Return to the trailhead via this road.

Extra Credit: The east face of Gothic is one of Colorado's most aesthetic, steep ski lines and can easily be viewed from Crested Butte Mountain Resort; however, timing this route is difficult.

60 Teocalli Mountain

Starting Elevation	8950 feet
High Point	13,208 feet
Vertical Gain/Loss	4258 feet
Ascent Distance	8.8 miles
Descent Distance	8.2 miles
Time	10 to 12 hours
Ski Skills	Difficult
Fitness Level	Very strenuous
Technical Skills	Moderate
Gear	The basics, plus ice axe and crampons
Best Months	March to May
USGS Map	Gothic

If you've driven the highway between the towns of Crested Butte and Gunnison, chances are high that you've taken note of Teocalli Mountain, which lies north of Colorado Highway 135. Named after Aztec pyramids, this striking mountain is a skier's dream, with routes leading off the summit in every direction. The south face, visible from the highway, is the most classic line, and also the one described here.

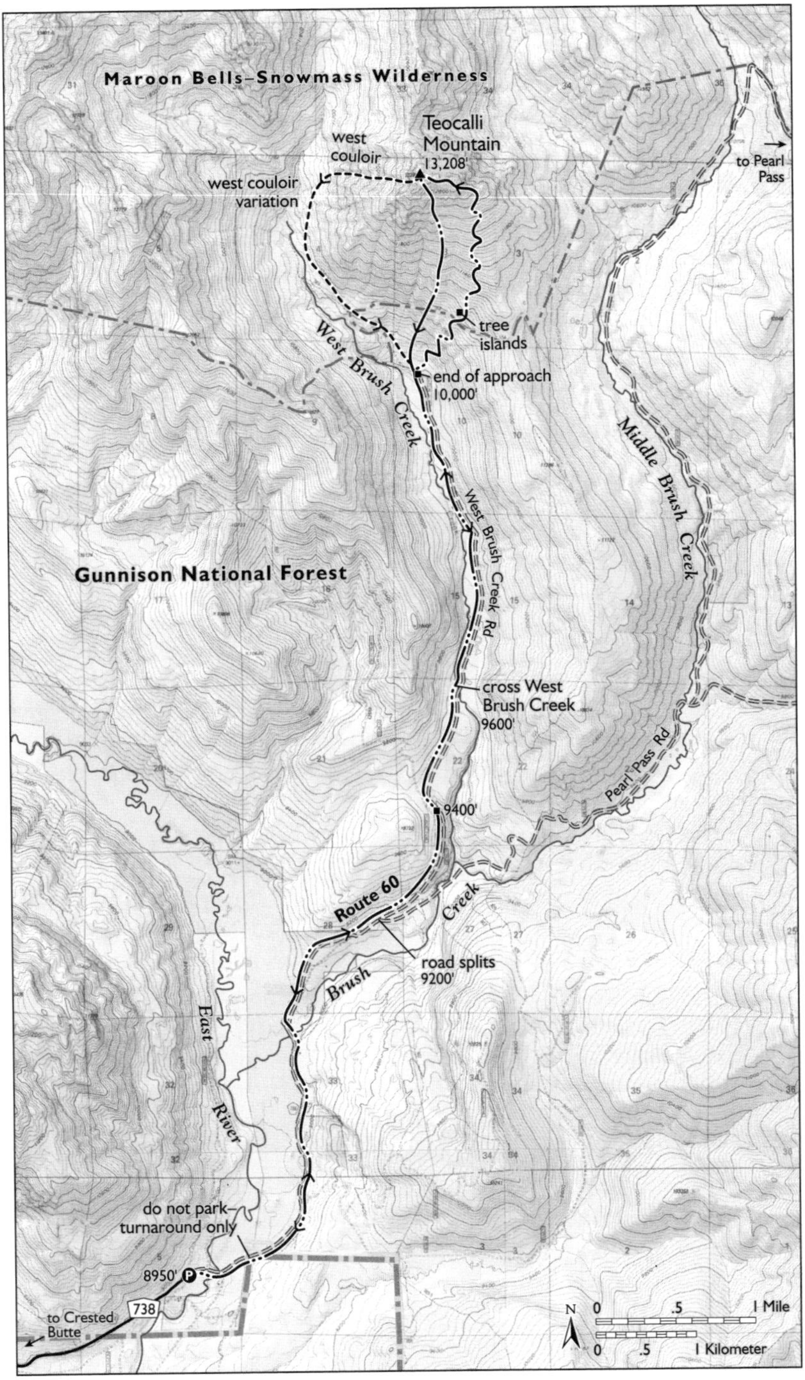
Maroon Bells–Snowmass Wilderness
Teocalli Mountain 13,208'
west couloir
west couloir variation
to Pearl Pass
tree islands
West Brush Creek
end of approach 10,000'
Middle Brush Creek
West Brush Creek Rd
Gunnison National Forest
cross West Brush Creek 9600'
Pearl Pass Rd
9400'
Route 60
Creek
road splits 9200'
Brush
East
River
do not park–turnaround only
8950'
738
to Crested Butte
N
0 .5 1 Mile
0 .5 1 Kilometer

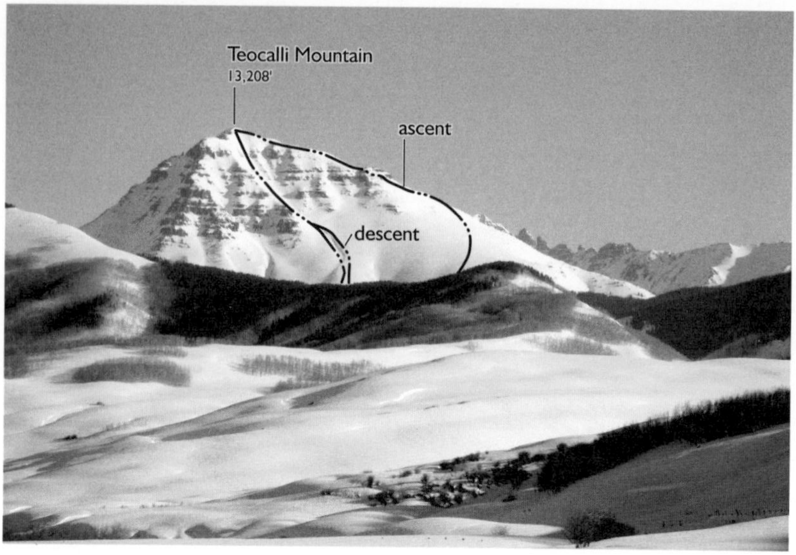

GETTING THERE

Starting in Crested Butte, travel south on Colorado Highway 135 for 2 miles, and then turn left (north) onto Brush Creek Road (County Road 738). Drive Brush Creek Road for 2.5 miles and park in the well-marked Brush Creek trailhead parking lot. The road remains plowed for an additional half mile to a few ranch outbuildings, but this area is marked "No Parking." At best, you could quickly unload gear here before parking in the designated parking lot.

THE ROUTE

Skin or skate north up the flat Brush Creek valley for 3.1 miles to the intersection (9200 feet) of West Brush Creek Road and Pearl Pass Road (Middle Brush Creek). Take the left fork, following West Brush Creek Road as it traverses across a low-lying southeast-facing hillside. The road flattens at the top of this small hillside at 9400 feet. Follow the road up the West Brush Creek valley, which is again quite flat or even slightly downhill at times. Five miles from the trailhead, near 9600 feet, keep your eyes peeled for any feasible river crossing on a snow bridge or beaver dam. Continue up the valley, now on the east side of West Brush Creek. Near the 10,000-foot level, the approach is finally over, and you can begin ascending Teocalli Mountain. The entire approach is lightly traveled by snowmobiles, which may aid in your approach.

From the 10,000-foot level, veer east through a steep aspen grove to reach the open, west-facing terrain leading toward Teocalli's south ridge. The most common route will pass near two small tree islands on the way to the ridge. Once on the ridge, continue toward the small cliff bands that dot Teocalli's south ridge. All of these cliff bands can be easily bypassed. While Teocalli's summit can be reached completely on skins, it's more likely that you will bootpack a few sections, and possibly even want crampons if conditions are icy. Take time to note the steep northeast couloirs that drop down from the ridge as you approach the summit.

Descent. The classic line is the south face "swoosh." Descend this line straight toward the valley, making slight adjustments for any small cliff bands that are easily bypassed. It is better to stay out of the terrain-trap gullies on the bottom half of the route; instead, staying on the more planar faces to either side. Regain your ascent track in the valley, and follow it back to the trailhead.

Alternate Descent. The west face may contain Teocalli's best line—a 2000-foot couloir. To reach this line, ski the skier's right side of the south face for a short distance to a small depression.

Extra Credit: From the summit, the north face falls to the valley below. Like the northeast couloirs, the north face ends in a different valley than the one you ascended.

61 Coneys

Starting Elevation	9470 feet
High Point	10,850 feet
Vertical Gain/Loss	1500 feet
Ascent Distance	3 miles
Descent Distance	3 miles
Time	2 to 4 hours
Ski Skills	Moderate
Fitness Level	Not very strenuous
Technical Skills	Low
Gear	The basics
Best Months	November to April
USGS Map	Oh-Be-Joyful

Coneys makes a wonderful introduction to backcountry skiing in the Crested Butte area. Despite being a fairly easy ski, Coneys is a slide-prone area and should not be underestimated, although it is skied throughout the winter season.

GETTING THERE

From the town of Crested Butte, head north on 6th Street, which becomes Gothic Road (County Road 317) as it exits town. Travel approximately 2.5 miles on this road until the intersection with Washington Gulch Road. Turn left onto Washington Gulch Road (CR 811) and drive until the obvious winter closure about 2.6 miles after turning off Gothic Road. Coney's is the open area visible up valley and on the left.

THE ROUTE

Skin up Washington Gulch Road, which is popular with multiple user groups in winter months. After a half mile, you may see a skin track veer left. Stay on the road

because the shortcut skin track trespasses through marked private property. At 1.6 miles, the road bends to the west, and the wide open slopes of Coneys will be nearly in front of you. Leave the road and cross Washington Gulch to ascend the trees just to the climber's left of the more wide-open Coney's area. Near the ridge, the terrain becomes steeper and more open, so use caution.

Descent. From the ridge, choose your descent route back to the valley—there are many places to drop in off the ridge. Traverse to your right near the valley floor to

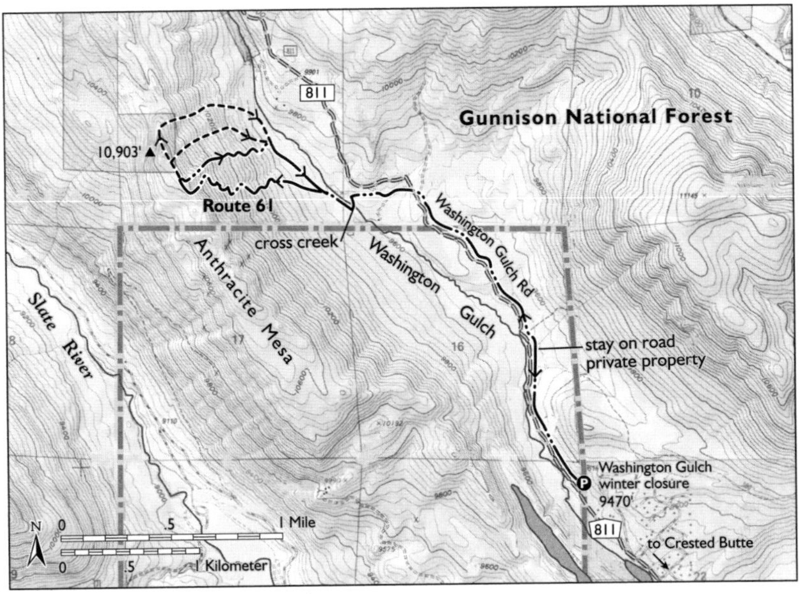

rejoin your ascent route. Many skiers will choose to do multiple laps on Coneys, so either head back up the skin track or retrace your approach route back to your car.

62 Mount Emmons: Red Lady Bowl

Starting Elevation	9200 feet
High Point	12,392 feet
Vertical Gain/Loss	3200 feet
Ascent Distance	3 miles
Descent Distance	2.5 miles
Time	3 to 4 hours
Ski Skills	Moderate
Fitness Level	Moderately strenuous
Technical Skills	Low
Gear	The basics
Best Months	December to March
USGS Maps	Oh-Be-Joyful and Mount Axtell

Lovingly referred to as "Red Lady" by locals, Mount Emmons stands tall to the west of the town of Crested Butte. Red Lady Bowl (see map in Route 63) faces southeast on Mount Emmons and maintains a good reputation as a fun and popular backcountry ski zone. As a bonus, the views of surrounding peaks from the summit cannot be beat.

Red Lady Bowl is a popular dawn patrol ski. Here, a skier works her way to the summit of Mount Emmons on a beautiful morning.

GETTING THERE

From the intersection of 1st Street and White Rock Avenue on the western end of the town of Crested Butte, head west on County Road 12 toward Kebler Pass. Travel 1.8 miles on this road until you reach the winter closure and a parking area.

The typical access route for Red Lady Bowl travels along the ridge just south of Red Lady Basin. This brings you close to the Keystone Mine at the start. At the time of writing this book, the Keystone Mine was not active, but parts of it are still being maintained. In recent years, additional acreage was designated for molybdenum mining. However, actual mining has yet to take place as the price of molybdenum makes mining here uneconomical, and locals continue to fight to prevent the mine from opening. In later years, a mine could open, blocking all or some access to Red Lady Bowl. But for now, it remains one of the most popular backcountry skiing zones in Crested Butte.

To avoid private property issues, obey all signage that pertains to mining closures. To check on public access issues, call the Gunnison Ranger District or the Gunnison–Crested Butte Tourism Association (see Resources).

THE ROUTE

Begin by climbing directly upward from the parking lot on the south-facing slopes of Mount Emmons. After a couple of minutes of skinning, you will cross a dirt road that accesses the Keystone Mine. This road is not meant for public access and is used for mine maintenance, so do not follow the road. Instead, cross it to begin ascending from the other side.

As you ascend the lower slopes, observe the south-facing slopes of Mount Emmons. An obvious drainage descends from the peak. This will be your descent route. The ascent route stays in the trees to the climber's left (south) of this drainage. When crossing the Keystone Mine access road, veer left of this drainage to begin ascending in the trees.

The skin track ascends through the forest, generally following the ridge, and it can be steep in places. At about 11,050 feet, the route will begin crossing through property owned by the inactive Keystone Mine and will continue within this mining claim for another 500 vertical feet. Avoiding this property via this route is difficult due to the steepness of the terrain to the climber's right. At the time of writing, this was the most common route for backcountry users.

Around 11,300 feet, the trees will begin thinning out. Here, the Red Lady Bowl is highly visible to the climber's right. Keep climbing along the obvious ridge just left of the bowl, passing through another inactive mining claim, all the way to the summit.

Descent. From the summit ridge of Mount Emmons, drop into the southeast-facing Red Lady Bowl. The bowl is wide, and there are many choices for lines, although dead center is the most popular. At the bottom of the bowl, the steepness of the route lessens. From there, follow the obvious drainage downward. Better skiing is usually found by hugging the sides of the drainage rather than in the true center. Descend this drainage all the way back to the Keystone Mine access road crossing. Then follow your ascent route back to the parking lot.

Extra Credit: If you want to spend more time skiing, you could return to the summit and ski the upper half of this route again, which is typically its best skiing. From the summit, ski the Red Lady Bowl down to where it begins to flatten out at 11,100 feet. From there, look to the skier's right, toward the ascent ridge. There is an obvious road cut that ascends back to the ridge. Traverse right to gain the road cut and then climb to the ridge. Follow your original ascent route back to the summit.

63 Mount Emmons: Redwell Basin

Starting Elevation	9200 feet
High Point	12,392 feet
Vertical Gain/Loss	3,300 feet
Ascent Distance	3 miles
Descent Distance	4.5 miles
Time	4 to 5 hours
Ski Skills	Moderate
Fitness Level	Moderately strenuous
Technical Skills	Low
Gear	The basics
Best Months	December to March
USGS Maps	Oh-Be-Joyful and Mount Axtell

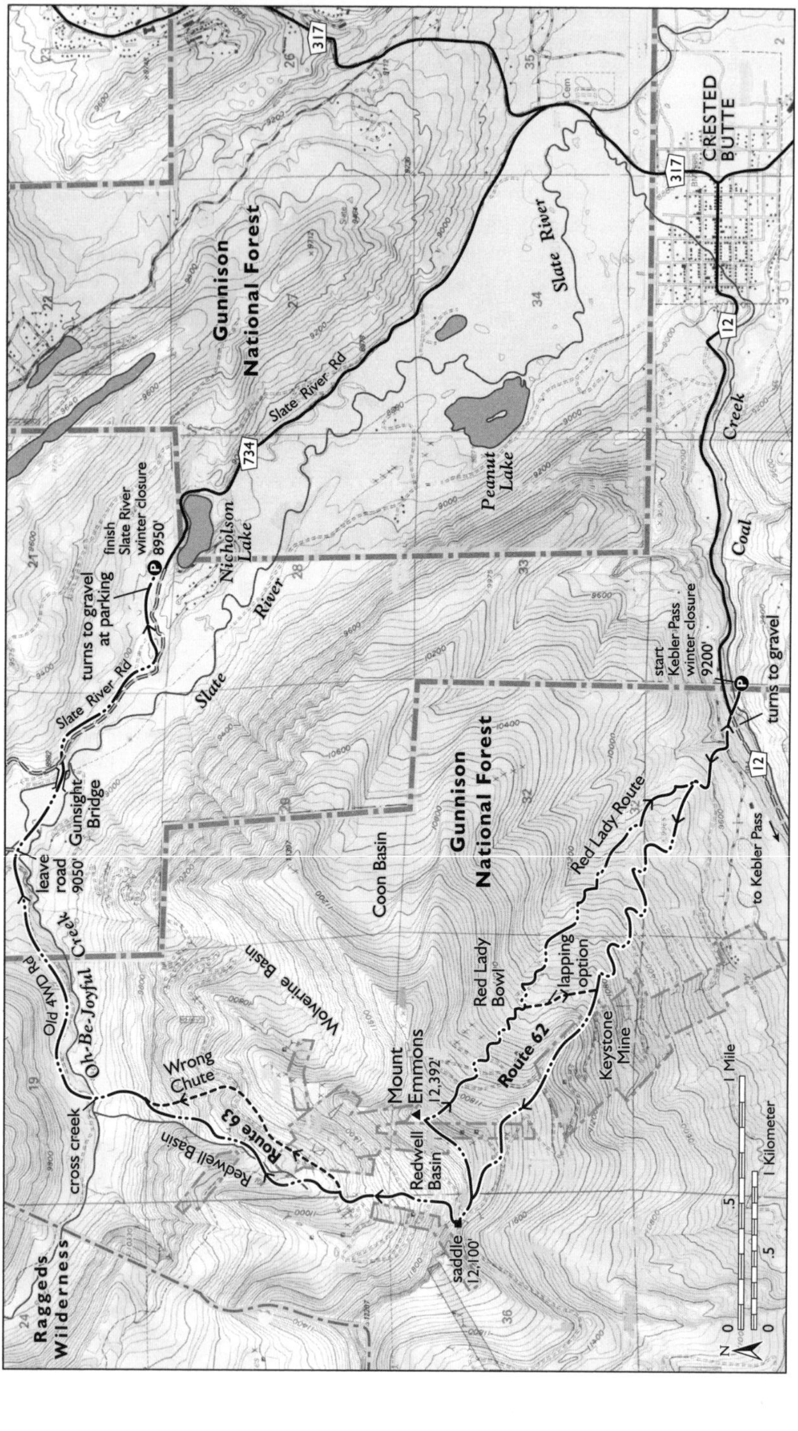
Gunnison National Forest
Slate River Rd
734
317
CRESTED BUTTE
Slate River
Peanut Lake
Nicholson Lake
finish Slate River winter closure 8950'
turns to gravel at parking
Slate River Rd
Gunsight Bridge
leave road 9050'
Old 4WD Rd
Oh-Be-Joyful Creek
Coon Basin
Wolverine Basin
Wrong Chute
cross creek
Redwell Basin
Route 63
Mount Emmons 12,392'
Redwell Basin
saddle 12,100'
Raggeds Wilderness
Red Lady Bowl
lapping option
Route 62
Keystone Mine
Red Lady Route
Gunnison National Forest
start Kebler Pass winter closure 9200'
turns to gravel
Coal Creek
12
to Kebler Pass
1 Mile
1 Kilometer

While Red Lady Bowl is the most popular ski route on Mount Emmons, the north-facing Redwell Basin provides a fun alternative ski descent. Logistically, this route is a bit more difficult than Red Lady proper because it requires a shuttle. However, Redwell Basin offers a wonderfully scenic tour descending into the beautiful Slate River valley.

GETTING THERE

This route is best accessed with a shuttle. You will need to leave one vehicle at the Slate River winter closure and another at the Kebler Pass winter closure.

First, leave a vehicle at the Slate River winter closure, the ending trailhead. From the town of Crested Butte, head north on 6th Street, which becomes Gothic Road (County Road 317) as it exits town. Travel approximately 0.6 mile on this road until the intersection with Slate River Road. Turn left onto Slate River Road (CR 734) and drive until the obvious winter closure about 2 miles after turning off Gothic Road. Leave one vehicle at this trailhead. Don't forget to leave shoes in this car so you don't have to drive in ski boots.

The starting trailhead is located at the Kebler Pass Road winter closure and is the same trailhead used for Red Lady Bowl (Route 62). Retrace your original driving route back to the town of Crested Butte. Continue on 6th Avenue for a few blocks, and turn right onto White Rock Avenue. Follow White Rock Avenue about a half mile west through town. After 1st Street, it becomes County Road 12 (Kebler Pass Road). Travel another 1.8 miles on this road until the winter closure and an obvious parking area.

Be sure to read the Red Lady Bowl route description (Route 62) for details about possible public access issues due to mining activity.

THE ROUTE

Follow the ascent route for Red Lady Bowl to the ridge just west of the summit. Going to the summit is optional. If you do, retrace your steps back to where you gained the west ridge around 12,200 feet. From there, continue westward and down to a low point around 12,100 feet.

Descent. From the saddle at 12,100 feet, drop into the north-facing line below. The entrance to the line at the saddle can sometimes have thin snow. Never fear, the snow will get better after about 50 or 100 feet. Descend the bowl downward to about 10,900 feet. From here, you will need to decide if you want to continue down the obvious drainage below or traverse skier's right to descend via Wrong Chute.

If you decide to descend the drainage, continue downward. An inactive mining claim can be avoided by working the left side of the drainage to about 10,600 feet. Early in the season or in low snow years, the drainage can have some small frozen waterfalls in a gully. If you find ice, just head right or left to ski around it. Around an elevation of 10,350 feet, it's best to head to the right or east side of the drainage to begin planning your exit. Follow the drainage down toward the Oh-Be-Joyful Creek valley, bearing right as you go.

From 10,900 feet, if you decide to take the alternative Wrong Chute, you will need to traverse right and possibly upward a few hundred feet, traveling in a northeast

direction. Your traverse will take you through an inactive mining claim for less than a quarter mile. After traversing and climbing for about a half mile, you will see a north-facing avalanche chute that opens up through the trees below you. Ski this chute down toward the Oh-Be-Joyful Creek valley below.

Both descent options will meet back up around 9500 or 9600 feet. Continue skiing to the valley, and then cross Oh-Be-Joyful Creek via a snow or log bridge. A quick sidestep will bring you to an old 4WD road on the north side of Oh-Be-Joyful Creek.

Follow the old 4WD road until it makes a large turn to the skier's left near 9050 feet. Leave the road to the right through a forest here and ski a short distance to a small meadow. Shortly after, re-cross Oh-Be-Joyful Creek to its south side near its confluence with the Slate River. Early in the season, you can cross the frozen Slate River and head directly to Slate River Road, located northeast. Later in the season when the river has melted, you will need to follow the valley down the Slate River until reaching the Gunsight Bridge, which you can use to cross the Slate River. Follow the Slate River Road for 1 mile back to the Slate River winter closure at 8950 feet.

Opposite: Steep, skinny, and straight as—well—a needle (Photo by Pete Sowar)

SANGRE DE CRISTO MOUNTAINS

THE SANGRE DE CRISTO MOUNTAINS jut up into the sky between the Wet Mountain valley on the east and the San Luis valley on the west. Unique among Colorado mountain ranges for several reasons, the Sangres, as they are often called, may very well be the least often skied of Colorado's major ranges.

Much of the range is characterized by a fault block geologic structure, the same mechanism that created the Tetons in Wyoming. Indeed, both the Tetons and Sangres are steep, narrow mountain ranges. This geologic process is also less favorable to mineral formation than what is found in Colorado's mineral belt, and the result is that the Sangres saw far less mining activity than other ranges.

That does not mean that the Sangre de Cristos lack history; in fact, it's quite the contrary. Colorado's oldest town, San Luis, is located on the west side of the range near the New Mexico border. More than any other range, the influence of Mexico can be felt in the Sangres. On the plus side, that means great Mexican food after a long hard day in the mountains. The downside is difficult or even impossible access to wide swaths of the range as a result of massive Spanish land grants. If there are peaks in Colorado that have never been skied, chances are high they are in one of the large ranches that exist today due to the Spanish land grants.

Access to the Sangre de Cristo Range is difficult for all the factors discussed above. The rugged terrain and minimal mining activity meant that few roads were ever built into the range. Add in the private property, and Sangres skiers will quickly realize there are no "roadside attractions" in the range. Most peaks are accessed from the small towns of Westcliffe to the east and Crestone to the west.

The Sangres lie due east of the massive San Juan Range, which means that the prevailing west-to-east storm track hits the San Juans first. The snow falls in the San Juans hard and heavy, and by the time the storms hit the Sangres, there isn't much precipitation left. Some of the routes in this book may not even be skiable during a dry year in the Sangres. The classic snowfall-producing storm for the range will track through northern New Mexico and eventually center on the east side of the range, resulting in the same upslope conditions that can lead to big storms for the Front Range cities of Colorado. While ski areas have previously operated in the Colorado Sangres, today there are none in operation, at least in part due to the unreliable snowfall. Few skiers base themselves out of the towns surrounding the range—yet another reason skiers who tackle the peaks of the Sangres are likely to find solitude.

The Sangres skier is a hardy breed, one who is willing to begin their ski tour in the dry desert terrain that surrounds the range. Skiers in this range possess the stamina needed to reach the high peaks, the technical skills to climb and ascend them, and a good feel for snowfall trends in the area. Trails in the range are often primitive and rough, and skiers will find difficult travel before they even reach alpine terrain. But in a good snow year, once that alpine terrain has been gained, the Sangres skier will feel like a kid in a candy store—with Mom and Dad's credit card in hand.

64 Eureka Mountain: Eureka Couloir

Starting Elevation	9500+/- feet
High Point	13,507 feet
Vertical Gain/Loss	4007+/- feet
Ascent Distance	6.8+/- miles
Descent Distance	4.8+/- miles
Time	9 to 11 hours
Ski Skills	Difficult
Fitness Level	Strenuous
Technical Skills	High
Gear	The basics, plus ice axe and crampons
Best Months	March to early May
USGS Maps	Rito Alto Peak and Horn Peak

Hermit Pass Road offers great access to this part of the Sangre de Cristo Range, and the northeast couloir of Eureka Mountain will capture your imagination the second that you see it. Although it is a lesser-known peak in the Sangres, the steep skiing offered on Eureka Mountain is certainly worth your while.

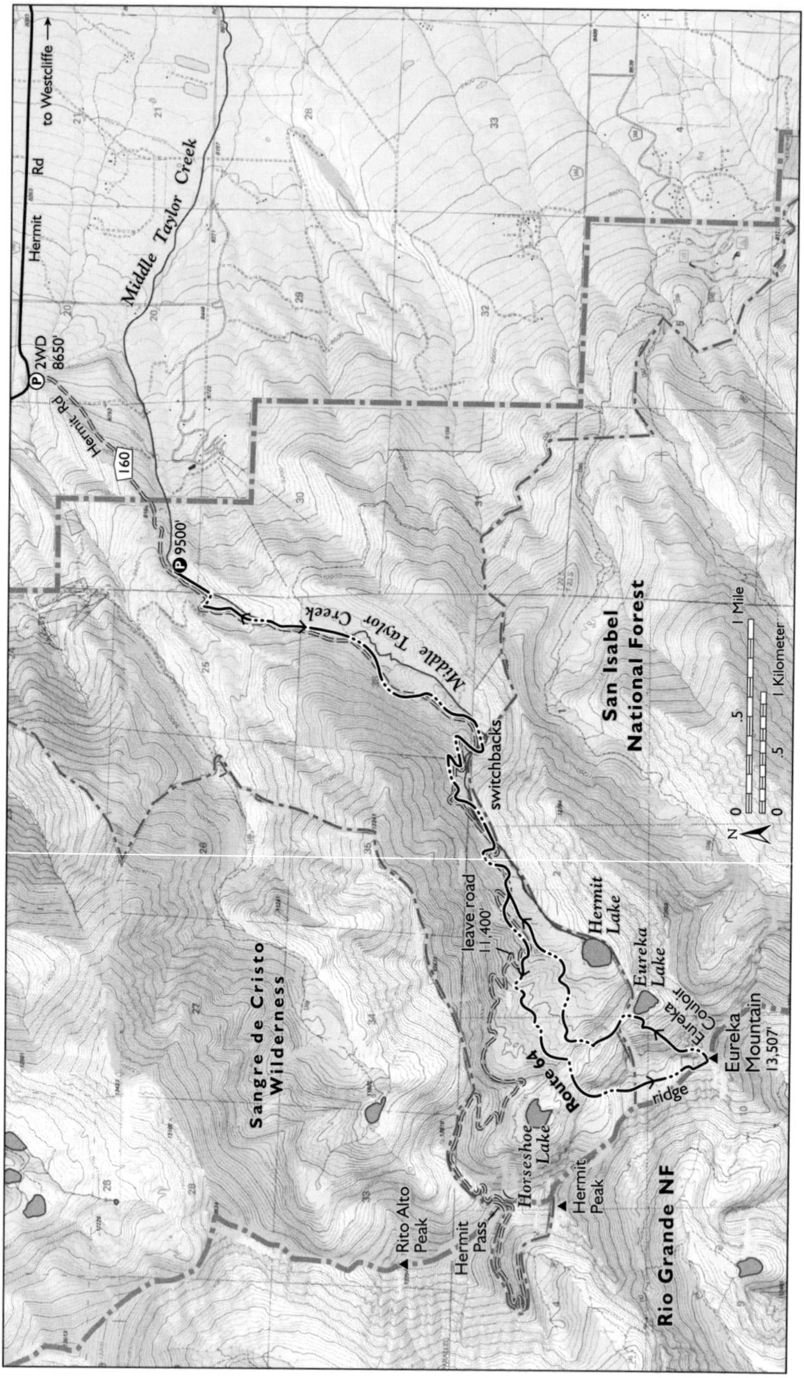
Hermit Rd
to Westcliffe →
Middle Taylor Creek
P 2WD 8650'
Hermit Rd
160
P 9500'
Middle Taylor Creek
switchbacks
San Isabel National Forest
0 .5 1 Mile
0 .5 1 Kilometer
N
Sangre de Cristo Wilderness
leave road 11,400'
Hermit Lake
Eureka Lake
Eureka Couloir
Route 64
ridge
Eureka Mountain 13,507'
Horseshoe Lake
Hermit Peak
Hermit Pass
Rito Alto Peak
Rio Grande NF

GETTING THERE

Start your odometer at the junction of Colorado Highway 69 and CO 96 in downtown Westcliffe, and head south on CO 69. After 0.3 mile, turn right onto Hermit Road (County Road 160). At mile 6, stay left on the well-marked road. The road will begin transitioning from 2WD to 4WD at this point, while it ascends above the old Conquistador Ski Area. Depending on snow cover and your vehicle, you may need to park near the valley floor or be able to continue for several miles. Our starting point at 9500 feet is probably average for springtime.

THE ROUTE

The approach to Eureka Mountain is straightforward, as you simply follow Hermit Road as it slowly gains elevation. Beginning at 10,400 feet, it may make sense to skip a few obvious switchbacks. Near 11,400 feet, leave the road and head toward the climber's right of the steep headwall that separates Hermit Lake and Eureka Lake. The terrain in this area is tedious, and you may need to drop elevation on a few occasions. From the bench above the headwall, you have two choices: either head directly for the couloir and climb it nearly to the summit or ascend a short, steep pitch to the north ridge and follow that to the summit.

Descent. The Eureka Couloir begins just 40 vertical feet from the summit off of the north ridge. The couloir itself makes a couple of slight doglegs as it descends 1500 feet to Eureka Lake. From Eureka Lake, head northwest along the bench toward your ascent route. The first continuous snow off the bench is fun and steep, but be aware that the snow on this eastern exposure may be dangerously thawed, in which case you will want to continue northwest toward more moderate terrain. A high traverse will get you back onto the road, where you can skate and pole your way back to your vehicle.

65 Broken Hand Peak: Broken Dogleg Couloir

Starting Elevation	9950 feet
High Point	13,573 feet
Vertical Gain/Loss	3623 feet
Ascent Distance	4.7 miles
Descent Distance	4.7 miles
Time	10 to 12 hours
Ski Skills	Very difficult
Fitness Level	Strenuous
Technical Skills	High
Gear	The basics, plus ice axe and crampons
Best Months	March to early May
USGS Map	Crestone Peak

While overshadowed by nearby fourteeners like Crestone Needle and Humboldt Peak, the north face of Broken Hand Peak contains a terrific route of its own. Steep and aesthetic, with jaw-dropping views of Crestone Needle, this is a route that you won't want to overlook.

GETTING THERE

Start your odometer at the junction of Colorado Highway 69 and CO 96 in downtown Westcliffe, and head south on CO 69. After 4.5 miles, turn right onto Colfax Lane. At 10 miles, turn right onto south Colony Lakes Road (County Road 120). Drive on south Colony Lakes Road until mile 11.5, where 2WD and midwinter parking is located (elevation 8800 feet). If the road is dry and you have 4WD, continue on until the gate at the 4WD parking at mile 13.8 (elevation 9950 feet).

THE ROUTE

This tour starts at the 4WD parking lot. Hike or skin up the road to reach this point if you need to start lower. At 11,150 feet, leave the road and head southwest then northwest through trees to reach South Colony Lakes at 11,690 feet. South Colony Lakes is a great spot to set up a base camp to spend some time exploring the area.

From the lake, you can see the Broken Hand rock formation that gives the mountain its name. The bottom of the Broken Dogleg Couloir is also visible from here. Put your

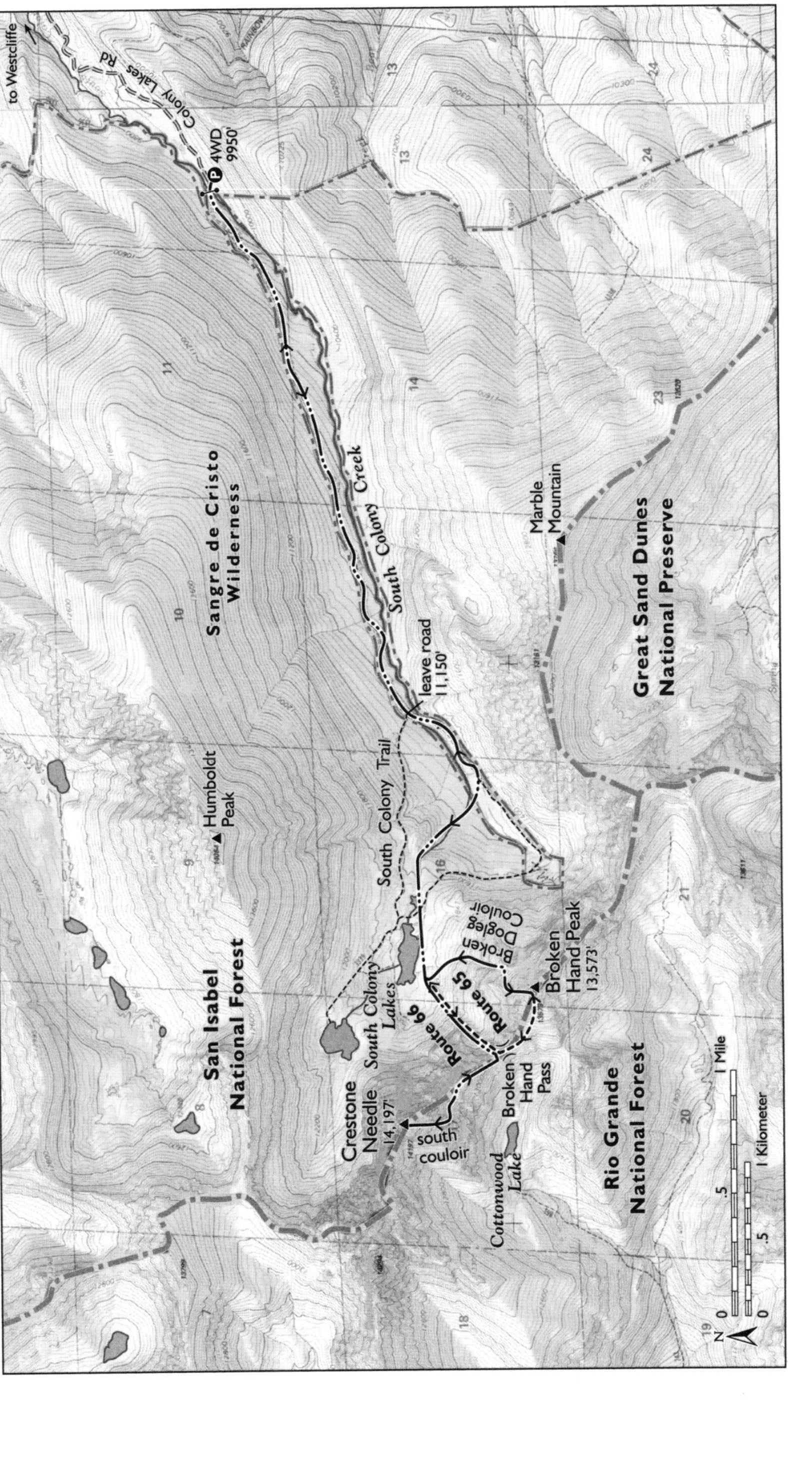
to Westcliffe
Colony Lakes Rd
4WD
9950'
Sangre de Cristo
Wilderness
South Colony Creek
leave road
11,150'
Marble
Mountain
Great Sand Dunes
National Preserve
South Colony Trail
Humboldt
Peak
San Isabel
National Forest
South Colony
Lakes
Broken
Dogleg
Couloir
Route 65
Route 66
Broken
Hand Peak
13,573'
Broken
Hand
Pass
Crestone
Needle
14,197'
south
couloir
Cottonwood
Lake
Rio Grande
National Forest
1 Mile
1 Kilometer

crampons on here and begin your bootpack directly up the Broken Dogleg Couloir. You will probably need to bypass an initial rock band on the west before entering the couloir proper. The first dogleg occurs around 12,800 feet, and the route becomes less confined and more ramplike. The final dogleg is at 13,200 feet, and the terrain gets steeper and leads straight to the summit. Alternatively, you can reach the summit from Broken Hand Pass (see Route 66, Crestone Needle), if there is already a bootpack or you're combining Broken Hand with Crestone Needle or another peak.

Descent. From the summit, your ski tips will be hanging over the edge of a steep 2000-foot ski descent. Assuming you've already climbed the route, your descent will be straightforward—just try not to take too many photos of Crestone Needle on your way down. Retrace your approach back to your vehicle.

66 Crestone Needle: South Couloir

Starting Elevation	9950 feet
High Point	14,197 feet
Vertical Gain/Loss	4247 feet
Ascent Distance	6 miles
Descent Distance	6 miles
Time	10 to 12 hours
Ski Skills	Very difficult
Fitness Level	Strenuous
Technical Skills	Very high
Gear	The basics, plus ice axe and crampons. Some parties may want a rope during low snow years.
Best Months	March to early May
USGS Map	Crestone Peak

The steep and rocky pinnacle of Crestone Needle (see map in Route 65) may not look very skiable from most vantage points, but in truth it harbors one of the best routes in the state. The south couloir is straight, steep, and narrow and descends almost directly from Crestone Needle's summit. Time this one right, and it's sure to be one of your favorite steep ski descents of all time.

GETTING THERE

Start your odometer at the junction of Colorado Highway 69 and CO 96 in downtown Westcliffe, and head south on CO 69. After 4.5 miles, turn right onto Colfax Lane. At 10 miles, turn right onto south Colony Lakes Road (County Road 120). Drive on south Colony Lakes Road until mile 11.5, where 2WD and midwinter parking is located (8800 feet). If the road is dry and you have 4WD, continue on until the gate at the 4WD parking at mile 13.8 (elevation 9950 feet).

Downclimbing one of the rocky sections between Broken Hand Pass and the South Couloir (Photo by Pete Sowar)

THE ROUTE

Begin the tour from the 4WD parking by continuing up the road. At 11,150 feet, leave the road and head southwest then northwest through trees to reach the southern South Colony Lake at 11,690 feet. South Colony Lakes is a great spot to set up a base camp to spend some time exploring the area.

From the lake, begin your ascent toward Broken Hand Pass to the southwest, which is looker's right of Broken Hand Peak—that looks like a broken hand. From the pass, do an ascending traverse to the northwest, following cairns if visible, over broken ground toward the south couloir of Crestone Needle. There is a small, 15-foot downclimb on rock before reaching the couloir proper. Thankfully the Crestone conglomerate yields many hand- and footholds. Ascend the couloir straight to the summit. In low snow years, you may need to climb one or two short sections of water ice or climb through rocks to the climber's right. Some parties have been known to use a rope while descending these water bulges.

Descent. Follow your ascent route back down the couloir, making sure to exit the couloir at the same elevation that you entered it. Depending on snow cover, you may need to traverse dry ground before you can once again ski from Broken Hand Pass to the southern South Colony Lake. Retrace your approach back to your vehicle.

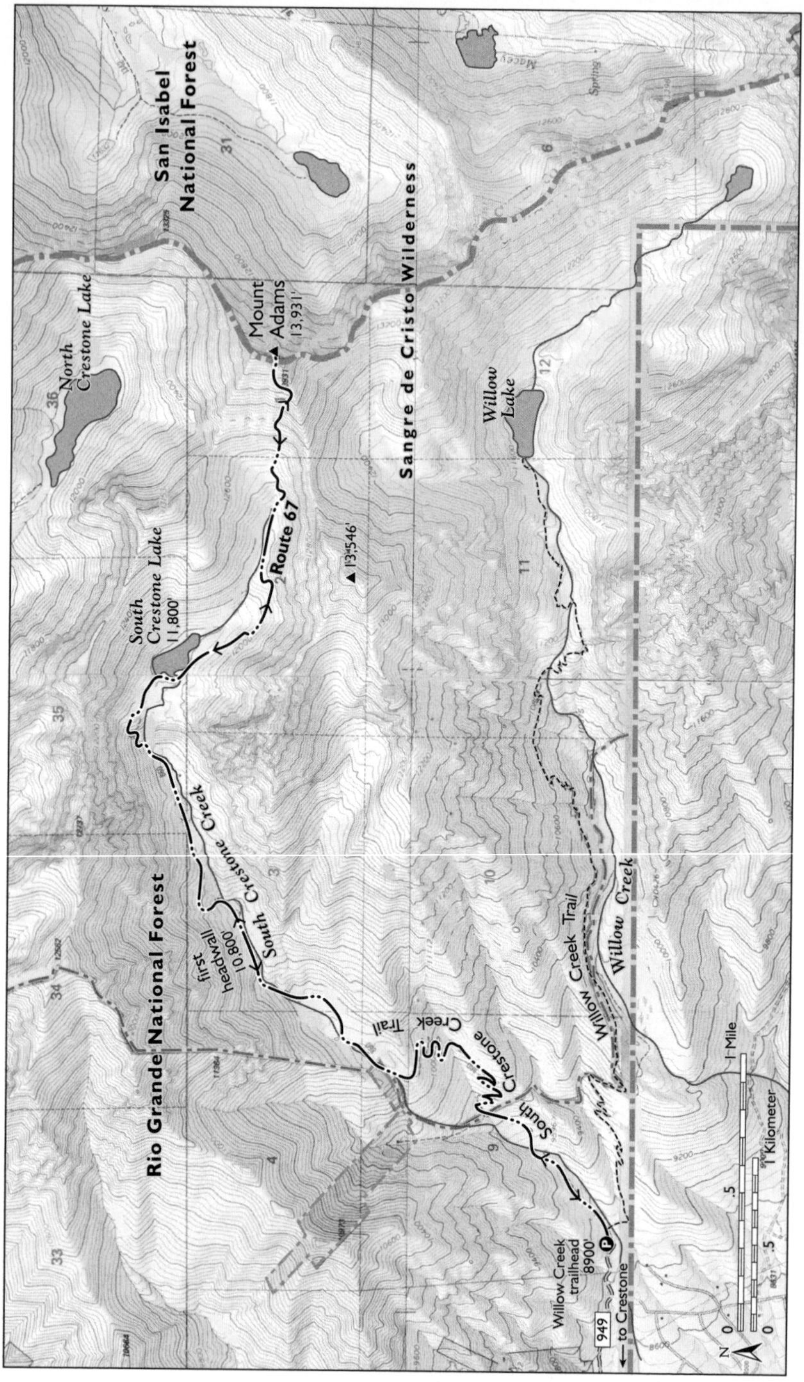
San Isabel
National Forest
North
Crestone Lake
Mount
Adams
13,931'
Sangre de Cristo Wilderness
Willow
Lake
South
Crestone Lake
11,800'
Route 67
13,546'
Rio Grande National Forest
first
headwall
10,800'
South Crestone Creek
South Crestone Creek Trail
Willow Creek Trail
Willow Creek
Willow Creek
trailhead
8900'
949
to Crestone
1 Mile
1 Kilometer
N

67 Mount Adams: West Face

Starting Elevation	8900 feet
High Point	13,931 feet
Vertical Gain/Loss	5031 feet
Ascent Distance	6.5 miles
Descent Distance	6.5 miles
Time	11 to 12 hours
Ski Skills	Difficult
Fitness Level	Very strenuous
Technical Skills	High
Gear	The basics, plus ice axe and crampons
Best Months	March to April
USGS Map	Horn Peak

If you're looking for a Teton-like experience in Colorado, put this route at the top of your list. Skiers who tackle this long approach will be rewarded with one of the most impressive high alpine cirques in the state. Mount Adams is one of Colorado's 100 highest peaks, and the striking west face is a highly aesthetic place to make some turns. Adventurous skiers will want to return and explore other nearby lines in this special place.

A skier takes it all in after a successful run on the west face. The South Cottonwood Creek valley lies below.

GETTING THERE

Start your odometer in the small town of Moffat, located in the San Luis valley. Moffat can be reached from the north or south via Colorado Highway 17. From Moffat, follow the signs to Crestone on County Road T. At 11.8 miles, turn left toward the town of Crestone on CR 71. Veer right at mile 12.8 onto Golden Avenue in Crestone. After another 0.2 mile (mile 13), turn left onto Alder Street. Head north another 0.1 mile, and then turn right onto Galena Avenue. Follow this road and signs to the Willow Creek trailhead, located at mile 15.4.

THE ROUTE

Given the low elevation of Willow Creek trailhead (8900 feet) and that the ideal ski conditions are in the springtime, most skiers will arrive at the trailhead in dry conditions. This trailhead serves two trails, Willow Creek and South Crestone Creek. South Crestone Creek is the trail that leads to Mount Adams and heads left less than 0.1 mile from the shared trailhead. This well-built trail is an enjoyable hike through pines and aspens, mercifully switchbacking up steeper terrain.

Like many approaches in the Sangre de Cristo Range, the easy miles eventually end and the tough ones begin. Around 10,800 feet, the first headwall is encountered. The best route will trend north on the north side of South Crestone Creek. Older maps, of both the paper and GPS variety, may incorrectly state that the trail shifts to the south side of the creek. Stay north. Past the first headwall, easier meadow terrain will lead toward another steep headwall, which blocks easy access to the alpine terrain above. Once again, stay north around these cliff bands, and reach the beautiful South Crestone Lake at 11,800 feet. A week's worth of steep alpine ski terrain surrounds the lake, and this would be a great area to set up a base camp.

Even from the lake, Mount Adams's west face remains hidden. Continue up the valley, and the objective will slowly come into view. This huge face is straightforward to climb. The climber's left side of the face is less steep, and much of it can be skinned. Otherwise, simply climb straight up the center of the face, hitting the northwest ridge just below a small cliff band below the summit. If the summit is your goal, a few short class 3 moves will gain the summit. Otherwise, you can transition to ski mode right at this notch.

Descent. The wide west face can be skied via a number of different routes. You will probably find yourself seeking out micro-terrain variations to find the best snow and most aesthetic descent. The bottom of the face has a number of cliff bands, and while most routes go through these cliff bands, some do not. Therefore, you should take care and be certain that your intended line choice skis through cleanly.

From the bottom of the face, a few more good turns await on the headwalls below tree line, but the major difficulties are past. Follow your ascent route back to the trailhead.

68 Unnamed 13,020: Juice Box Couloir

Starting Elevation	8400 feet
High Point	13,020 feet
Vertical Gain/Loss	4620 feet
Ascent Distance	5.7 miles
Descent Distance	5.3 miles
Time	11 to 12 hours
Ski Skills	Very difficult
Fitness Level	Very strenuous
Technical Skills	High
Gear	The basics, plus ice axe and crampons
Best Months	March to April
USGS Map	Crestone Peak

Anyone who has ever used the Cottonwood Creek approach to the nearby fourteener Crestone Peak has probably taken note of this highly aesthetic line dropping straight from the summit of Unnamed 13,020. Friends of ours skied this line and dubbed it the Juice Box. Not knowing any other name, we'll stick with theirs. Like most lines in the Sangre de Cristo Range, the Juice Box requires strong skills, plenty of stamina, and

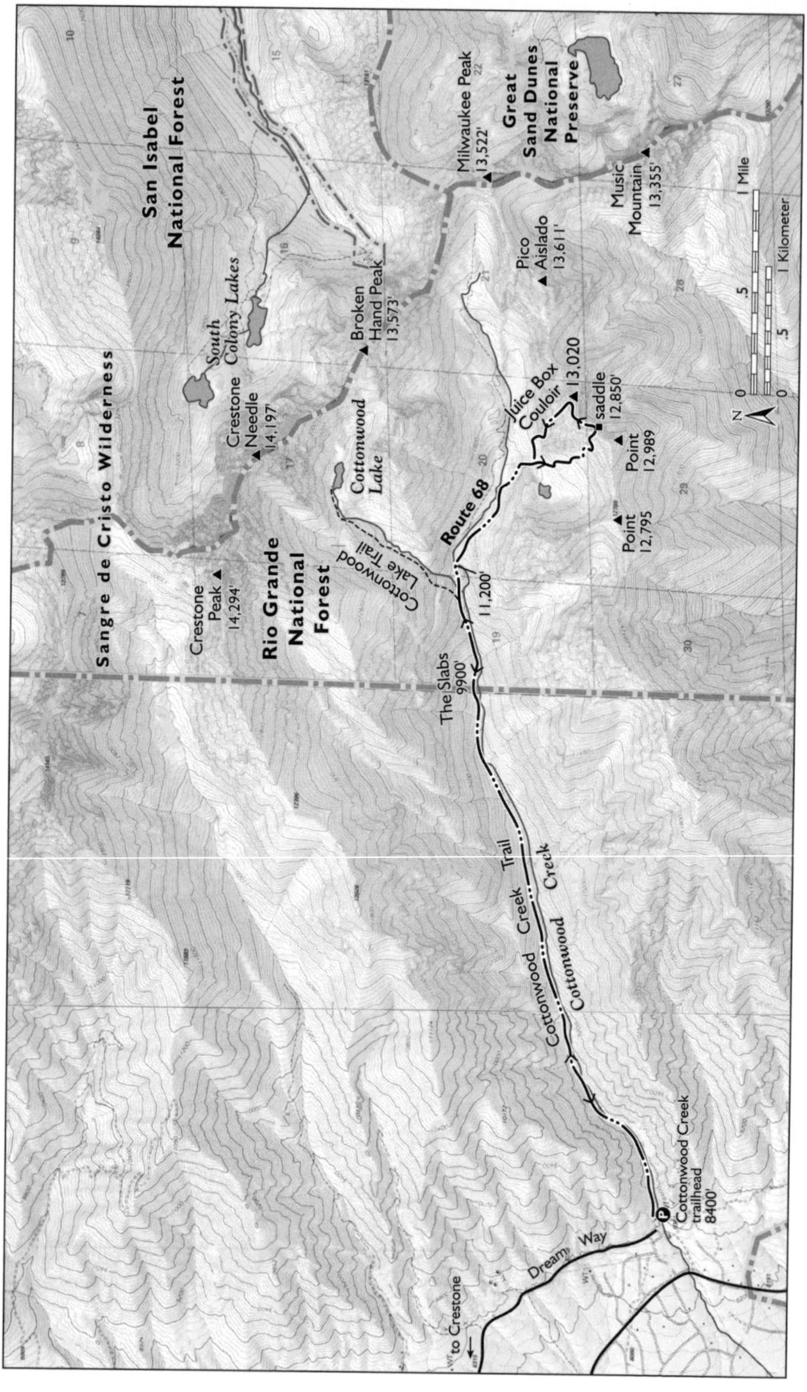
San Isabel National Forest
Sangre de Cristo Wilderness
Rio Grande National Forest
Great Sand Dunes National Preserve
South Colony Lakes
Crestone Needle 14,197'
Crestone Peak 14,294'
Broken Hand Peak 13,573'
Milwaukee Peak 13,522'
Pico Aislado 13,611'
Music Mountain 13,355'
Cottonwood Lake
Cottonwood Lake Trail
Route 68
Juice Box Couloir
13,020
saddle 12,850'
Point 12,989
Point 12,795
11,200'
The Slabs 9900'
Cottonwood Creek Trail
Cottonwood Creek
Cottonwood Creek trailhead 8400'
Dream Way
to Crestone
0 .5 1 Mile
0 .5 1 Kilometer
N

good timing. In a low snow year, this route may not be skiable. When conditions are good, however, the effort required to ski the Juice Box is more than worth it.

GETTING THERE

In the past, private property issues plagued the Cottonwood Creek trailhead used to access this route. But today there is a legal trailhead and access to Cottonwood Lake. Start your odometer in the small town of Moffat, located in the San Luis valley. Moffat can be reached from the north or south via Colorado Highway 17. From Moffat, follow the signs to Crestone on County Road T. At 11.8 miles, just before reaching Crestone, turn right on Camino Baca Grande. Stay on Camino Baca Grande until you reach Dream Way at 15.5 miles. Go left on Dream Way and stay on this road as it winds through private property, past a Buddhist center, and reach the marked Cottonwood Creek trailhead at mile 17.1 (elevation 8400 feet).

THE ROUTE

Given the low elevation of the trailhead, and the fact that ideal ski conditions are in the springtime, most skiers will arrive at the trailhead in dry conditions. The start of this trail goes through private property, and there are plans to reroute the start of the trail in the future. Strap your skis to your backpack, and begin following the Cottonwood Creek Trail. The trail starts off in good shape, but the farther you go, the more difficult and faint it becomes.

The real fun begins around mile 2.5 (9900 feet), when the infamous slab section of the trail begins. Look for cairns marking the route as it weaves through a number of cliff bands, sometimes going directly over class 3 slabs. The trail/best route stays on the north side of Cottonwood Creek, so if the cairns are snow covered, use your best judgment and stay on this side of the valley. The difficulties relent around 11,200 feet, when the Juice Box and other lines come into view. Upper Cottonwood Creek harbors a number of quality routes in addition to the Juice Box, so it may be worth taking a break to soak in all the possibilities.

Enjoy easy skinning up the valley, and survey the route before you. Skiers who prefer to climb what they ski can simply climb the Juice Box straight to the summit of Unnamed 13,020. Because the bottom of this route is exposed to a large cliff, you may choose a less exposed route. For this route, leave the valley around 11,500 feet and head south, up the cirque that lies west of Unnamed 13,020. Make your way toward the 12,850-foot saddle between Unnamed 13,020 and Point 12,989. The views of the Crestones from here are breathtaking. From the saddle, it's an easy ridge walk to the 13,020-foot summit and the top of the Juice Box Couloir.

Descent. The route starts off easily enough, with a wide snowfield that quickly funnels into the more defined couloir below. The route features several rolls and constrictions as it drops down the steep northwest face. Near the bottom, be sure to veer skier's left, as continuing down the fall line will take skiers to a large cliff band. For this reason, this entire route should be considered a no-fall zone. The exit couloir is the tightest and steepest part of the route. From the bottom of the couloir, retrace your ascent route through the slabs and back to the trailhead.

Opposite: A glorious late spring run on Independence Pass (Photo by Jordan White)

SAWATCH RANGE

THE SAWATCH RANGE forms the backbone of Colorado, running north to south in the central part of the state. Colorado's highest peaks are found in this range, and many of them can be easily seen from the Arkansas River valley and Colorado Highway 24.

Sawatch Range mountains are generally large in area and gentle in nature. The rounded summits of the Sawatch will never be mistaken for the craggy peaks of the Sangre de Cristos or the San Juans. Still, pockets of steeper mountainsides exist, especially in the area surrounding Mount of the Holy Cross.

Access to the range can be difficult, often with long approaches and big vertical from the Arkansas River valley. Later in the season, access eases with snowmelt. The opening of Independence Pass typically on Memorial Day weekend quenches the thirst of backcountry skiers looking for easy turns. On the west side of the range, Taylor Park is a common gateway.

Despite its height, the Sawatch Range is less blessed with snow than other ranges in Colorado. Both the Elk Mountains and the San Juans often take the brunt of winter storms, leaving the Sawatch Range high and dry. Add in the typical high winds on the Continental Divide, and the Sawatch can appear very dry indeed. The mountains south of Buena Vista can be particularly dry. Yet, this range can flourish in some spring seasons when strong upslope storms unload high-moisture snow.

Backcountry skiing in the Sawatch is all about finding the sweet spots. Find those, and it's a range that keeps on giving.

69 Mount Oklahoma: Northeast Face

Starting Elevation	10,500 feet (4WD parking)
High Point	13,845 feet
Vertical Gain/Loss	3350 feet
Ascent Distance	4 miles
Descent Distance	4 miles
Time	7 to 9 hours
Ski Skills	Difficult
Fitness Level	Moderately strenuous
Technical Skills	Moderate to high
Gear	The basics; ice axe and crampons may be needed
Best Months	April through June
USGS Map	Mount Champion

Though hidden deep in the heart of the northern Sawatch, Mount Oklahoma stands out when you're on top of other nearby Sawatch peaks. Ranking as a centennial summit, this conspicuous peak typically holds snow late into the spring or summer and has some fun lines for backcountry skiers to enjoy.

The east and north faces of Mount Oklahoma viewed from Mount Massive (Photo by Natalia Moran)

GETTING THERE

From Leadville, travel south on US Highway 24. Just south of Leadville, turn right (west) onto Colorado Highway 300 and immediately cross railroad tracks, starting the mileage on your odometer here. Drive 0.8 mile and turn left (south) onto County Road 11 (Forest Service Road 160 and Halfmoon Road). After traveling 2 miles from the railroad tracks, the road splits again. Instead of going straight, veer right (west) onto FR 110 (Halfmoon Road). The road becomes dirt but is passable by most passenger cars until the North Mount Elbert trailhead at mile 7.5. This trailhead is large, clearly marked, and has bathrooms.

A high-clearance vehicle is recommended to continue beyond the North Mount Elbert trailhead. From there, you'll need to travel another 2 miles (9.5 miles total from original railroad crossing) to the intersection with FR 110.3A at 10,250 feet, the trailhead for Mount Elbert's northwest gullies (Route 70). You can choose to park there, or if you have a good 4WD vehicle, continue 0.5 mile and 250 vertical feet up the road to the North Halfmoon Lakes trailhead.

Please note that during winter months, Halfmoon Road has a winter closure with a placement that varies, but it is usually about 10 miles away from this trailhead. Some people choose to travel via snowmobile on the road to access the desired trailhead when enough snow cover makes this possible. As snow melts in the spring, the location of the trailhead will move farther up valley. But you may not be able to drive to

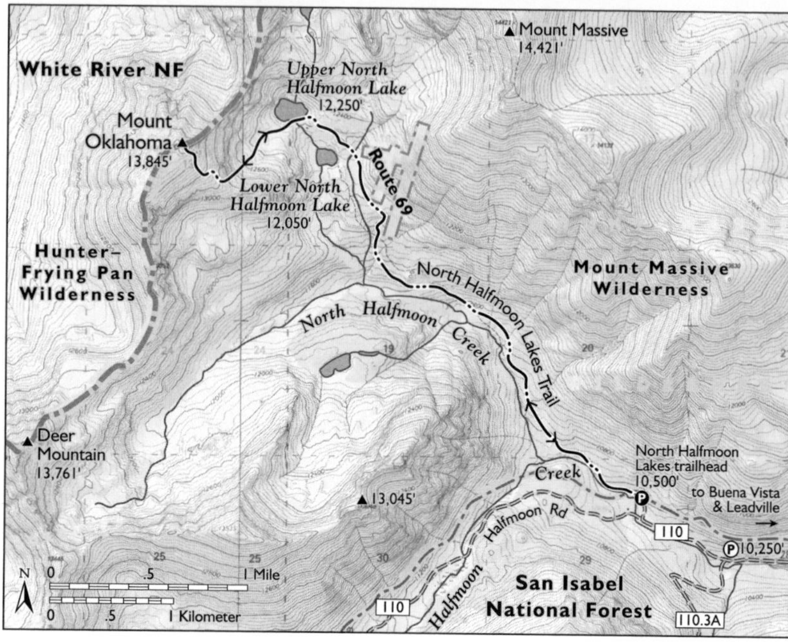

FR 110.3A or the North Halfmoon Lakes trailhead until May or June depending on snowmelt. To inquire about road status, call the Pike and San Isabel National Forests (see Resources).

THE ROUTE

Begin your tour by following the North Halfmoon Lakes Trail as it heads northwest, following along the north side of Halfmoon Creek. As you wind through the forest, be sure to stay on trail or else you can end up having to bushwhack or navigate through cliff bands. A GPS device may be needed to stay on trail during snow cover.

Above tree line, continue heading northwest toward Lower North Halfmoon Lake. Here you may find that the trail fades in and out. Also, be aware that some climbers' trails may lead east toward Mount Massive, and you don't want to follow those.

From Lower North Halfmoon Lake at 12,050 feet, continue 0.5 mile northwest to Upper North Halfmoon Lake at 12,250 feet. You can also bypass Lower North Halfmoon Lake by contouring to the northeast of the lake on an obvious bench. Follow this bench northwest to Upper North Halfmoon Lake.

From Upper North Halfmoon Lake, you will be able to see your ascent and descent route. The summit of Mount Oklahoma lies to the west, but your ascent route is to the southwest, through one of the northeast-facing couloirs. Ascend these couloirs to reach the southeast ridge of Mount Oklahoma, at 13,200 feet. Follow the ridge northwest another third of a mile and 600 vertical feet to the summit of Mount Oklahoma.

Descent. Reverse your ascent route.

70 Mount Elbert: Northwest Gullies

Starting Elevation: 10,250 feet
High Point: 14,433 feet
Vertical Gain/Loss: 4200 feet
Ascent Distance: 4 miles
Descent Distance: 4 miles
Time: 6 to 8 hours
Ski Skills: Difficult
Fitness Level: Strenuous
Technical Skills: Moderate
Gear: The basics; ice axe and crampons may be needed
Best Months: April to June
USGS Map: Mount Elbert

Mount Elbert is the tallest peak in Colorado and the second highest in the Lower 48. However, just because Mount Elbert is tall does not mean that it's extremely difficult to climb and ski. Indeed, skiing options on Mount Elbert are abundant, and all of them are fun.

The northwest gullies on Mount Elbert are often forgotten, being less visible from major highways compared to other routes. But with more than 3000 vertical feet of sustained pitch all the way to the valley floor, these gullies are a Sawatch treasure for backcountry skiers.

GETTING THERE

From Leadville, travel south on US Highway 24. Just south of Leadville, turn right (west) onto Colorado Highway 300 and immediately cross railroad tracks, starting the mileage on your odometer here. Drive 0.8 mile and turn left (south) onto County Road 11, (Forest Service Road 160, Halfmoon Road). After traveling 2 miles from the railroad tracks, the road splits again. Instead of going straight, veer right (west) onto FR 110 (Halfmoon Road). The road becomes dirt but is passable by most passenger cars until the North Mount Elbert trailhead at mile 7.5. This trailhead is large, clearly marked, and has bathrooms.

A high-clearance vehicle is recommended to continue beyond the North Mount Elbert trailhead. From there, you'll need to travel another 2 miles (9.5 miles total from original railroad crossing) to the intersection with FR 110.3A, where you'll turn left. You will start going down toward Halfmoon Creek. This very difficult 4WD road crosses Halfmoon Creek, which will likely be flowing fast. We recommend you park just before the creek crossing.

Please note that during winter, Halfmoon Road usually closes about 10 miles away from this trailhead. Some people choose to travel via snowmobile on the road to access the desired trailhead when enough snow cover makes this possible. As snow melts in

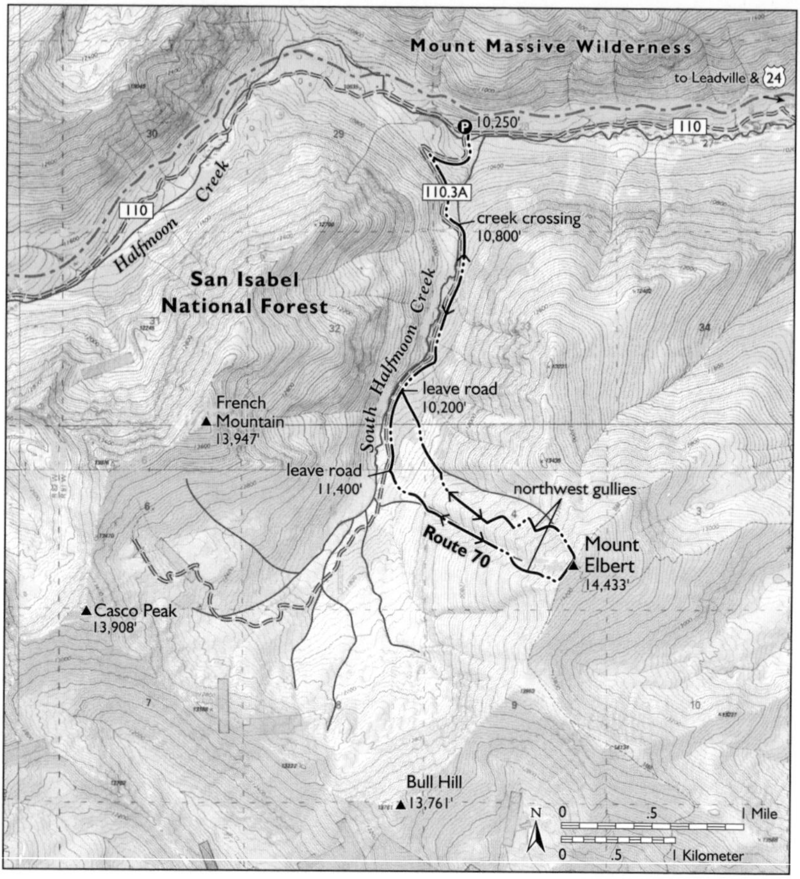

the spring, the location of the trailhead will move farther up valley. But you may not be able to drive to FR 110.3A until May or June depending on snowmelt. To inquire about road status, call the Pike and San Isabel National Forests (see Resources).

THE ROUTE

From the parking area, you will need to immediately cross Halfmoon Creek on foot. During the months we've recommended for this route, this creek will likely be flowing high and fast. Come prepared to get your feet wet. Water shoes or sandals are highly recommended.

After crossing Halfmoon Creek, continue following FR 110.3A upward as it ascends along the South Halfmoon Creek drainage. After traveling close to a mile, you'll reach two consecutive creek crossings, the second one over South Halfmoon Creek (approximate elevation of 10,800 feet). Again, the creeks will be flowing high and fast, so be prepared to get your feet wet. After approximately another mile, looking southeast, you can see the gullies to your left.

The two northwest gullies lie parallel to one another. The closer, more northern gully is steeper than the one that is just a bit farther south. Most people climb the easier southern gully. To do this, you'll need to follow FR 110.3A until mile 2.5 at an elevation of 11,400 feet. From here, follow the obvious gully southeast and up. This gully ends on Elbert's south ridge. Follow the ridge northeast another hundred vertical feet to the summit.

If you opt to climb the steeper northern gully of the pair, follow along FR 110.3A until 10,200 feet, a little over 2 miles from the recommended parking area. Follow the gully southeast and up. For this route, you will top out onto a ridge just north of the summit. You will need to travel south and about 50 vertical feet to reach the summit of Mount Elbert.

Descent. Your descent options mirror the same choices as the ascent. You can ski the northwest-facing gully to the south of the summit, which is less steep, or you can ski the northwest-facing gully to the north of the summit, which is more steep.

To ski the gully north of the summit, simply follow the ridge a few hundred feet to the north. You will see an obvious gully facing northwest and heading down to the South Halfmoon Creek valley. Typically, the skier's left side (more north facing) of the gully is more wind loaded and holds better snow than the skier's right side. If you work the left side of the gully as you descend you will likely have steeper skiing.

To ski the gully south of the summit, head south on the ridge about 0.1 mile from the summit. Head northwest and descend into the gully that drops into the South Halfmoon Creek valley.

For either route, you should descend over 3000 vertical feet until you meet back up with FR 110.3A. Follow FR 110.3A as it descends the South Halfmoon Creek valley, and find your vehicle at the confluence with Halfmoon Creek.

71 Twining Peak: Southeast Face

Starting Elevation	12,095 feet
Finishing Elevation	10,800 feet
High Point	13,711 feet
Vertical Gain/Loss	1650 feet/2900 feet
Ascent Distance	2 miles
Descent Distance	2.5 miles depending on route
Time	2 to 3 hours
Ski Skills	Difficult to very difficult
Fitness Level	Not very strenuous
Technical Skills	Low
Gear	The basics
Best Months	End of May to June
USGS Map	Mount Champion

Independence Pass is a late-season backcountry skiing mecca. Though closed in winter, Independence Pass typically opens for vehicles for thru-traffic around Memorial Day weekend, allowing for easy access to many great backcountry skiing routes.

Twining Peak, also called Blue Peak, is one of those great routes with easy access, great skiing, and more vertical drop than gain. A classic of the Independence Pass area, this peak should not be missed.

GETTING THERE

From the east: From Leadville, head south on US Highway 24 East for 14.5 miles. Turn right (west) onto Colorado Highway 82. If beginning from Buena Vista, head 19 miles north on US 24 West. Turn left (west) onto CO 82, heading toward the town of Twin Peaks and Independence Pass. Once on CO 82, travel west for 23.5 miles to the top of Independence Pass.

From the west: From Aspen, begin at the intersection of East Cooper Street and South Original Street. Head east on East Cooper Street, which is also CO 82. Follow East Cooper/CO 82 as it exits Aspen. Travel 19.3 miles east to the summit of Independence Pass.

The start of the tour is at the top of Independence Pass, but the end is about 4.5 miles down on the east side of the pass at the North Fork Lake Creek trailhead at 10,800 feet. You can leave a vehicle at both trailheads and shuttle between them. Hitchhiking is also common for skiers on this pass, so you could choose to hitch from the end of the tour back to the top of Independence Pass.

Note that Independence Pass is closed during the winter months, typically until around Memorial Day. The winter closure on the west side is about 10 miles east of Aspen, approximately 9 miles from the summit of Independence Pass. The winter closure on the east side is a little over 16 miles west of the intersection of CO 82 and US 24, about 7 miles from the summit of the pass. For the status of Independence Pass, check with the Colorado Department of Transportation (see Resources).

THE ROUTE

Twining Peak lies on the north side of the summit of Independence Pass, but it is obscured by "Blarney Peak" (Point 13,520) to its south. To begin your tour, head north and slightly west to contour below the west side of Blarney Peak. Stay beneath the cliff area seen on the west side of Blarney Peak, periodically linking a series of benches together.

Continue heading north to gain the ridge north of Blarney Peak and south of Twining Peak at a saddle with an elevation of 13,150 feet. From this saddle and ridge, you'll get a good view of several potentially skiable lines off of the east or southeast side of Twining Peak.

Follow the ridge northwest another 0.5 mile and just over 550 vertical feet to the summit of Twining Peak.

Descent. Skiing options on the east aspect of Twining Peak are plentiful. One of the best routes is a face that heads east-southeast directly from the summit.

For a steeper option, consider a set of two southeast-facing chutes to the skier's right of that face (just west of the summit) that merge together to form a Y. Be sure

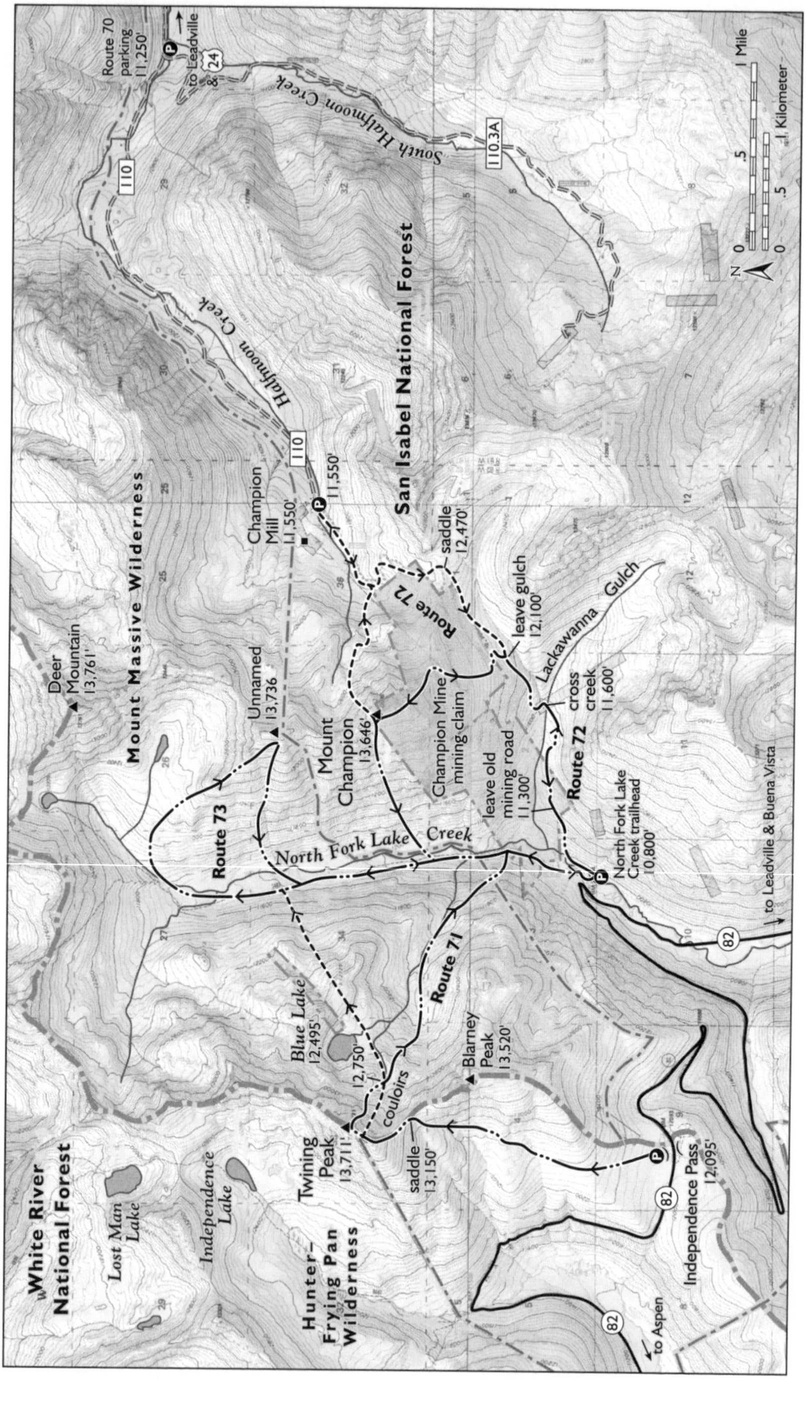

White River National Forest
Hunter–Frying Pan Wilderness
Mount Massive Wilderness
San Isabel National Forest
Lost Man Lake
Independence Lake
Twining Peak 13,711'
saddle 13,150'
couloirs
12,750'
Blue Lake 12,495'
Blarney Peak 13,520'
Independence Pass 12,095'
to Aspen
82
Route 71
Route 73
North Fork Lake Creek
North Fork Lake Creek trailhead 10,800'
to Leadville & Buena Vista
leave old mining road 11,300'
Route 72
cross creek 11,600'
Lackawanna Gulch
leave gulch 12,100'
saddle 12,470'
Champion Mine mining claim
Mount Champion 13,646'
Unnamed 13,736
Deer Mountain 13,761'
Champion Mill 11,550'
11,550'
110
110.3A
Halfmoon Creek
South Halfmoon Creek
Route 70 parking 11,250'
to Leadville
24
N
0 .5 1 Mile
0 .5 1 Kilometer

to get a good look at these chutes as you ascend the southern ridge as they are not always skiable due to a rock band and potential water ice. Cornices can also make the entrance into these chutes a bit tricky.

Enjoy turns down either of the lines southeast to the basin below to an obvious flat spot at 12,750 feet. From there, follow along an east-facing drainage as it descends to the North Fork Lake Creek valley below. Due to potential snowmelt, you should stay skier's right (south) of the drainage. As you enter tree line around 11,650 feet, you may find it best to contour to the skier's right, heading southeast, to position yourself to end up a bit farther down the North Fork Lake Creek valley. Once in the valley, head south to the North Fork Lake Creek trailhead at 10,800 feet.

Alternate Route. This route can also be accessed from the North Fork Lake Creek trailhead. Simply reverse the described descent route. This will add 0.5 mile and approximately 1300 vertical feet to your tour.

Extra Credit: If you're looking for more out of your tour, you can also easily ski Blarney Peak. From either Blarney Peak or Twining Peak, Unnamed 13,736 can also be accessed. See Route 73 for more details.

72 Mount Champion: West Face and Northeast Chutes

ACCESS FROM NORTH FORK LAKE CREEK TRAILHEAD

Starting Elevation	10,800 feet
High Point	13,646 feet
Vertical Gain/Loss	2850 to 3500 feet depending on route
Ascent Distance	3 miles
Descent Distance	2 to 4.5 miles
Time	3 to 7 hours
Ski Skills	Difficult
Fitness Level	Moderately strenuous
Technical Skills	Moderate
Gear	The basics; ice axe and crampons may be needed
Best Months	End of May and June
USGS Map	Mount Champion

Easily visible from Independence Pass and much of the northern Sawatch Range, Mount Champion stands proud just northwest of "Lackawanna Peak" and shares a distinct ridgeline with neighboring Unnamed 13,736. Mount Champion holds an abundance of good skiing options for those willing to explore.

The routes described in this section will take you near the Champion Mill and Mine, which were operated between approximately 1907 and 1919. Gold, silver, galena, and pyrite were mined and milled in this area. The property is most known for its magnificent 6100-foot-long tramline, which once reached a high point of 13,600 feet and parts of which are visible today.

Note that all options of this route travel through several miles of mining claims, most of them belonging to the inactive Champion Mine. Please remember to respect all "Private Property" and "No Trespassing" signs should you see any. Additionally, you should not disturb any mining ruins as they are a significant part of Colorado's history. Last, we recommend that you do not come close to any buildings associated with the inactive mine as they could be structurally unsound and pose safety risks.

GETTING THERE

From the east: From Leadville, head south on US Highway 24 East for 14.5 miles. Turn right (west) onto Colorado Highway 82. If beginning from Buena Vista, head 19 miles north on US 24 West. Turn left (west) onto CO 82, heading toward the town of Twin Peaks and Independence Pass. Once on CO 82, travel west for 19 miles to the North Fork Lake Creek trailhead, about 4.5 miles east of the summit of Independence Pass.

From the west: From Aspen, begin at the intersection of East Cooper Street and South Original Street. Head east on East Cooper Street, which is also CO 82. Follow East Cooper/CO 82 as it exits Aspen. Travel 19.3 miles east to the summit of Independence Pass and then down on the east side of the pass for 4.5 miles to the North Fork Lake Creek trailhead.

Note that Independence Pass is closed during the winter months, typically until around Memorial Day. The winter closure on the west side is about 10 miles east of Aspen, approximately 9 miles from the summit of Independence Pass. The winter closure on the east side is a little over 16 miles west of the intersection of CO 82 and US 24, about 2.5 miles from this trailhead. If you want to access this route from the east, it is possible during the seasonal road closure, but you will need to add 5 miles on to your tour. For the status of Independence Pass, check with the Colorado Department of Transportation (see Resources).

THE ROUTE

From the North Fork Lake Creek trailhead parking lot (elevation 10,800 feet), immediately cross North Fork Lake Creek. If snow bridges are lacking, a good place to cross is via an old roadbed (not marked on most maps) just southeast of the parking lot. Flow can be high on this creek, so cross where it is wide. Without a snow bridge, you should prepare to get wet!

Once on the east side of the North Fork Lake Creek, follow the old mining road as it heads north, parallel with North Fork Lake Creek. After about a half mile, you'll come to where Lackawanna Gulch emerges from the east. Do not cross the stream that

comes down from the gulch. Bear east here, staying to the south side of the gulch, and you should eventually meet up with another old mining road that switchbacks upward.

Follow this road until about 11,300 feet, and then leave this road to head east along the south side of Lackawanna Gulch. Without snow cover, you'll likely see a climbers' trail heading east through the forest. Follow this trail to an old miner's cabin that appears at a meadow between a willow thicket and the forest at about 11,450 feet. Continue eastward, following the gulch.

Without snow cover, you will encounter a very dense willow thicket. Your best bet is to head a little farther to the south to gain higher ground, crossing above the willows over a talus field.

You will likely have trouble crossing Lackawanna Gulch as the stream can flow high and fast in spring. Look for a snow bridge if snow cover is adequate. Otherwise, cross around 11,600 feet, where the stream splits into three segments, making it easier to cross.

Continue northeast, remaining on the north side of the drainage. Around 12,000 or 12,100 feet, leave the gulch to begin ascending up the south slopes of Mount Champion to gain the southeast ridge. You will likely pass mining ruins along the way, remnants of the inactive Champion Mine.

Follow the southeast ridge to reach the summit of Mount Champion.

Descent. You have two choices for your descent. The primary route is the west face, which descends back into the North Fork Lake Creek valley. Alternatively, the northeast chutes hold snow much later in the season than the west face on Mount Champion and have been known to hold snow into the summer but require much more work to return to the trailhead.

For the primary descent, you should look for a gully that faces northwest, slightly to the north of the summit. Lower down, the gully will change aspects to face directly west. Have fun descending this gully over 2500 vertical feet down to the North Fork Lake Creek valley (approximately 11,100 feet). Continue down valley, heading south, eventually retracing your ascent route back to the North Fork Lake Creek trailhead. From the location where you reach the valley floor, you will travel close to a mile back to the North Fork Lake Creek trailhead.

Alternate Descent. To descend the northeast chutes, descend the north ridge about 50 to 100 vertical feet from the summit. Here, you'll see the top of a chute that drops to the northeast into the Halfmoon Creek valley. Ski down toward the valley in the direction of the old Champion Mill, whose ruins should be visible.

Around 12,700 feet, begin veering skier's right, heading east and south at times. Work your way up to reach the old Champion Mining Road at about 11,900 or 12,000 feet. Here you will need to transition to head back uphill. Follow the Champion Mining Road as it heads mainly south to gain a saddle (elevation 12,470 feet) to the southeast of Mount Champion.

Once at the saddle, you should leave the road and head southwest, following the drainage that will eventually feed into the larger Lackawanna Gulch. Cross Lackawanna Gulch where you crossed it during your ascent. Then reverse your ascent route to return to the North Fork Lake Creek trailhead.

ALTERNATE ACCESS FROM HALFMOON ROAD

Starting Elevation	11,550+ feet
High Point	13,646 feet
Vertical Gain/Loss	2100+ feet
Ascent Distance	2.5+ miles
Descent Distance	2 miles
Time	3 to 4 hours or more
Ski Skills	Difficult
Fitness Level	Not very strenuous to moderately strenuous
Technical Skills	Moderate
Gear	The basics; ice axe and crampons may be needed
Best Months	End of April to June
USGS Map	Mount Champion

Mount Champion can also be accessed via Halfmoon Road. This might be a better option when Independence Pass is not yet open for the summer or you are already accessing other routes via this road. Overall, this route is more straightforward and direct than the access from the North Fork Lake Creek trailhead near Independence Pass and is a better way to access the northeast chutes. With a good 4WD vehicle and adequate snow-clearing, you can get far up the Halfmoon Creek valley by car, allowing for some very close access.

GETTING THERE

From Leadville, travel south on US Highway 24. Just south of Leadville, turn right (west) onto Colorado Highway 300 and immediately cross railroad tracks, starting the mileage on your odometer here. Drive 0.8 mile and turn left (south) onto County Road 11 (Forest Service Road 160, Halfmoon Road). After traveling 2 miles from the railroad tracks, the road splits again. Instead of going straight, veer right (west) onto FR 110 (Halfmoon Road). The road becomes dirt but is passable by most passenger cars until the North Mount Elbert trailhead at mile 7.5. This trailhead is large, clearly marked, and has bathrooms.

A high-clearance vehicle is recommended to continue beyond the North Mount Elbert trailhead. From there, you'll need to travel another 2 miles (9.5 miles total from original railroad crossing) to the intersection with FR 110.3A at 10,250 feet, the trailhead for Mount Elbert's northwest gullies (Route 70). You can choose to park there, or if you have a good 4WD vehicle, continue on Halfmoon Road. The road becomes increasingly rough, and you may encounter difficulty crossing some streams that go across the road. Drive until you feel that it is not viable for your vehicle to go farther or until you reach the Champion Mill 3 miles up the road (elevation 11,550 feet).

Please note that during winter months, Halfmoon Road has a winter closure with a placement that varies, but it is usually about 10 miles away from this trailhead. Some people choose to travel via snowmobile on the road to access the desired trailhead when enough snow cover makes this possible. As snow melts in the spring, the location of the trailhead will move farther up valley. But you may not be able to drive to FR 110.3A or the North Halfmoon Lakes trailhead until May or June depending on snowmelt. To inquire about road status, call the Pike and San Isabel National Forests (see Resources).

THE ROUTE

From the Champion Mill, begin by following the mining access road southwest to the saddle southeast of the summit of Mount Champion (elevation 12,470 feet). From there, continue following the mining access road for a bit as it turns northwest. About a quarter mile from the saddle and around an elevation of 12,550 feet, you should leave the mining access road and follow along the southeast ridge. Head northwest along this ridge, traveling another mile and another 1100 vertical feet to the summit.

Descent. From the summit, descend the north ridge about 50 to 100 vertical feet. Here, you'll see the top of a chute that drops to the northeast into the Halfmoon Creek valley. Ski down toward the valley in the direction of the old Champion Mill, whose ruins should be visible. Around 12,700 feet, begin veering skier's right, heading east and south at times. Work your way up to reach the old Champion Mining Road at about 11,900 or 12,000 feet. Continue down valley on the road to where your vehicle is parked by the Champion Mill or beyond.

73 Unnamed 13,736: West Face

Starting Elevation	10,800 feet
High Point	13,736 feet
Vertical Gain/Loss	2950 feet
Ascent Distance	3.5 to 4 miles
Descent Distance	2.75 miles
Time	4 to 6 hours
Ski Skills	Difficult
Fitness Level	Moderately strenuous
Technical Skills	Moderate
Gear	The basics
Best Months	End of May and June
USGS Map	Mount Champion

If you want over 2300 vertical feet of open 40-degree range skiing in a beautiful but relatively easy-to-access zone, then Unnamed 13,736 (see map in Route 71) is the peak for you! Sharing a ridge with the more popular Mount Champion, this peak is somewhat obscured from the highway. But it beckons you from across the valley while you are standing on the summit of Twining or "Blarney Peak."

GETTING THERE

From the east: From Leadville, head south on US Highway 24 East for 14.5 miles. Turn right (west) onto Colorado Highway 82. If beginning from Buena Vista, head 19 miles north on US 24 West. Turn left (west) onto CO 82, heading toward the town of Twin Peaks and Independence Pass. Once on CO 82, travel west for 19 miles to the North Fork Lake Creek trailhead, about 4.5 miles east of the summit of Independence Pass.

From the west: From Aspen, begin at the intersection of East Cooper Street and South Original Street. Head east on East Cooper Street, which is also CO 82. Follow East Cooper/CO 82 as it exits Aspen. Travel 19.3 miles east to the summit of Independence Pass and then down on the east side of the pass for 4.5 miles to the North Fork Lake Creek trailhead.

Note that Independence Pass is closed during the winter months, typically until around Memorial Day. The winter closure on the west side is about 10 miles east of Aspen, approximately 9 miles from the summit of Independence Pass. The winter closure on the east side is a little over 16 miles west of the intersection of CO 82 and US 24, about 2.5 miles from this trailhead. If you want to access this route from the east, it is possible during the seasonal road closure, but you will need to add 5 miles on to your tour. For the status of Independence Pass, check with the Colorado Department of Transportation (see Resources).

THE ROUTE

From the North Fork Lake Creek trailhead (10,800 feet), begin by following the trail north up the valley, staying on the west side of North Fork Lake Creek. You will pass below both Mount Champion and Unnamed 13,736 to your right (east).

After traveling just over 2 miles up the valley, you'll want to veer off the trail around 11,500 feet. Begin heading northeast up the valley, slightly toward Deer Mountain. You'll cross several creeks along the way. Around 11,800 feet, you should begin bearing more directly east to reach the southern side of the basin below Deer Mountain. At 12,000 feet, head southeast to reach a flattened zone around 12,300 feet. From here, you will see the northwest ridge on Unnamed 13,736.

Gain the northwest ridge and follow it in a southeast direction to about 13,100 feet. Here, you can continue following the ridge, but it may be easier to stay just below the ridge on the climber's right side (southwest of the ridge proper) for a bit. You will likely end up on a high point just to the north of the summit. Follow the ridge south 0.1 mile to the true summit of Unnamed 13,736.

Descent. With such an open face to the west, the skiing options are bountiful on Unnamed 13,736. One of the best ski routes is to descend off the summit into an obvious drainage that leads down to the North Fork Lake Creek valley. Below 12,400 feet, you may find that the quality of skiing can deteriorate in the drainage because rocks in the face restrict the width of the drainage, making it prone to wet slides. In this case, simply veer skier's right (a bit more north) to an open slope.

Descend to the North Fork Lake Creek valley. Cross the North Fork Lake Creek, and follow your ascent path through the valley back to the North Fork Lake Creek trailhead.

Alternate Approach: This route can also be accessed from the east side of Twining Peak or "Blarney Peak." Ski the east face of Twining and/or Blarney Peak to approximately 12,750 feet. Then head northeast down to the North Fork Lake Creek valley, working the terrain to end up as far up valley as you can. From where you end up in the North Fork Lake Creek valley, follow the directions described in the Unnamed 13,736 tour description. You will need to hitchhike or set up a shuttle between the top of Independence Pass and the North Fork Lake Creek trailhead.

74 Lackawanna Peak: South Gully and West Face

Starting Elevation	10,400 feet
High Point	13,823 feet
Vertical Gain/Loss	3400 feet
Ascent Distance	2 miles
Descent Distance	2 to 3 miles depending on route
Time	5 to 7 hours
Ski Skills	Moderate to difficult
Fitness Level	Moderately strenuous
Technical Skills	Low
Gear	The basics; crampons or ski crampons may be needed in spring
Best Months	February to mid-May
USGS Maps	Independence Pass and Mount Elbert

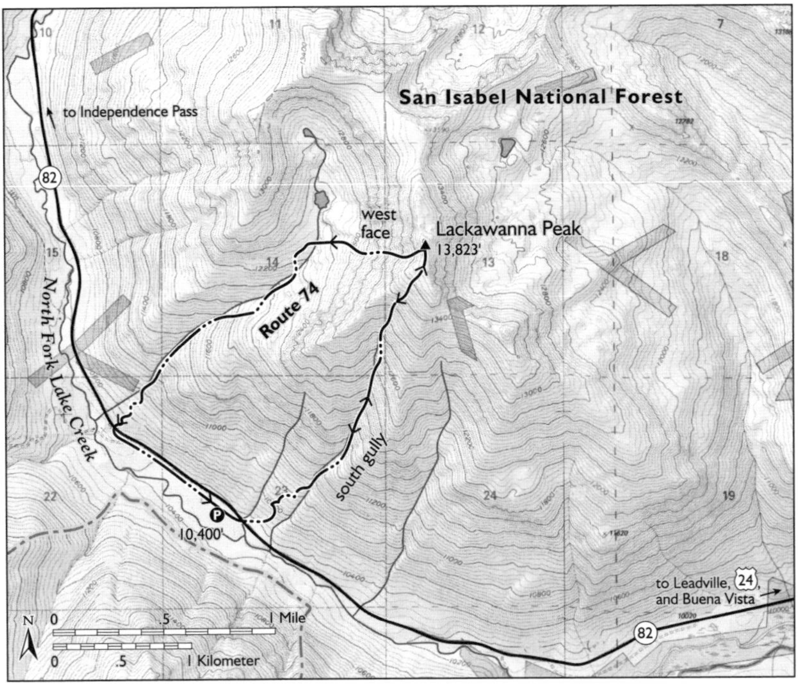

Officially called Unnamed 13,823, "Lackawanna Peak" sits within the realm of Colorado's 100 highest peaks, which makes it a centennial summit. Tucked in the shadows of larger Mount Elbert and La Plata Peak, Lackawanna can sometimes go unnoticed. But this high summit offers some good backcountry skiing options.

GETTING THERE

From Leadville, head south on US Highway 24 East for 14.5 miles. Turn right (west) onto Colorado Highway 82. If beginning from Buena Vista, head 19 miles north on US 24 West. Turn left (west) onto CO 82, heading toward the town of Twin Peaks and Independence Pass.

Once on CO 82, travel west for 14.5 miles to the La Plata Peak trailhead, which is indicated by a small but obvious parking area on the left (south) side of the road. From there, continue another 1.3 miles west to park at a very small parking area on the left (south) that can hold about five cars. This parking area is not marked and is difficult to find.

Note that Independence Pass is closed during the winter months, typically until around Memorial Day. The winter closure is about 0.5 mile west of the aforementioned parking area, so the seasonal closure does not impact access to this trailhead from the east. However, if you're coming from the west, through Aspen, you will not be able to go over Independence Pass until it is open for the summer season. For the status of Independence Pass, check with the Colorado Department of Transportation (see Resources). During the months that we recommend skiing this route, Independence Pass will likely be closed.

THE ROUTE

From the parking area, walk on the road eastward for about 0.2 mile. There, you will see a south-facing drainage coming down from Lackawanna Peak. Begin ascending this drainage upward. This drainage is usually a snow-filled gully in winter and spring. However, later in the spring, you may need to hike for 1000 vertical feet or so before reaching snow.

Around 12,700 feet, the gully becomes less defined and opens up to more of a bowl-like feature. You should continue to head north to ascend to Lackawanna's south ridge. Follow this ridge to the summit.

Descent. From the summit of Lackawanna Peak, you'll have two options that are typically best for a ski descent. First is to retrace your ascent route. Second is to ski Lackawanna's west face, which is a bit steeper than your ascent route, and exit via a different gulch to the west of where you ascended.

If you choose to ski Lackawanna's west face, be aware that the top of the line does not always have coverage for a descent. Sometimes a downclimb is needed. The best place to enter on to the west face is through a small relief in the rocks immediately north of the summit.

Once you're on the west face, descend about 1500 vertical feet to an obvious gully below (approximate elevation 12,300 feet). You will then follow along this gully as it travels southwest back to CO 82. In order to ensure greater snow coverage, you should remain on the more north-facing terrain just to the south of the gully. Once on CO 82, you'll need to walk about 0.7 mile east along the road back to your vehicle, passing the gate for the Independence Pass road closure along the way.

75 Independence Pass: Mountain Boy Gulch

Starting Elevation	12,095 feet
Finishing Elevation	11,500 feet
High Point	12,812 feet
Vertical Gain/Loss	1600 feet/2200 feet
Ascent Distance	2.5 miles
Descent Distance	1 mile
Time	2 to 3 hours
Ski Skills	Moderate
Fitness Level	Not very strenuous
Technical Skills	Low
Gear	The basics
Best Months	End of May to early June
USGS Maps	Garfield and Pahlone Peak

Normally open by Memorial Day weekend, Independence Pass is a great location for late-season backcountry skiing. A standard must-do tour for the pass, Mountain Boy

Enjoying Memorial Day weekend turns on Independence Pass

Gulch holds a lot of fun easy-access skiing options, but it requires a short shuttle or a quick hitchhike.

GETTING THERE

From the east: If in Leadville, head south on US Highway 24 East for 14.5 miles. Turn right (west) onto Colorado Highway 82. If beginning from Buena Vista, head 19 miles north on US Highway-24 West. Turn left (west) onto CO 82, heading toward the town of Twin Peaks and Independence Pass. Once on CO 82, travel west for 23.5 miles to the top of Independence Pass.

From the west: In Aspen, begin at the intersection of East Cooper Street and South Original Street. Head east on East Cooper Street, which is also CO 82. Follow East Cooper/CO 82 as it exits Aspen. Travel 19.3 miles east to the summit of Independence Pass.

The start of the tour is at the top of Independence Pass, but the end is about 2 miles down on the east side of the pass at the Mountain Boy Gulch switchback at 11,500 feet. You can leave a vehicle at both trailheads and shuttle between them. Hitchhiking is also common for skiers on this pass, so you could choose to hitch from the end of the tour back to the top of Independence Pass.

Note that Independence Pass is closed during the winter months, typically until around Memorial Day. The winter closure on the west side is about 10 miles east of Aspen, approximately 9 miles from the summit of Independence Pass. The winter closure on the east side is a little over 16 miles west of the intersection of CO 82 and US 24, about 7 miles from the summit of the pass. For the status of Independence Pass, check with the Colorado Department of Transportation (see Resources).

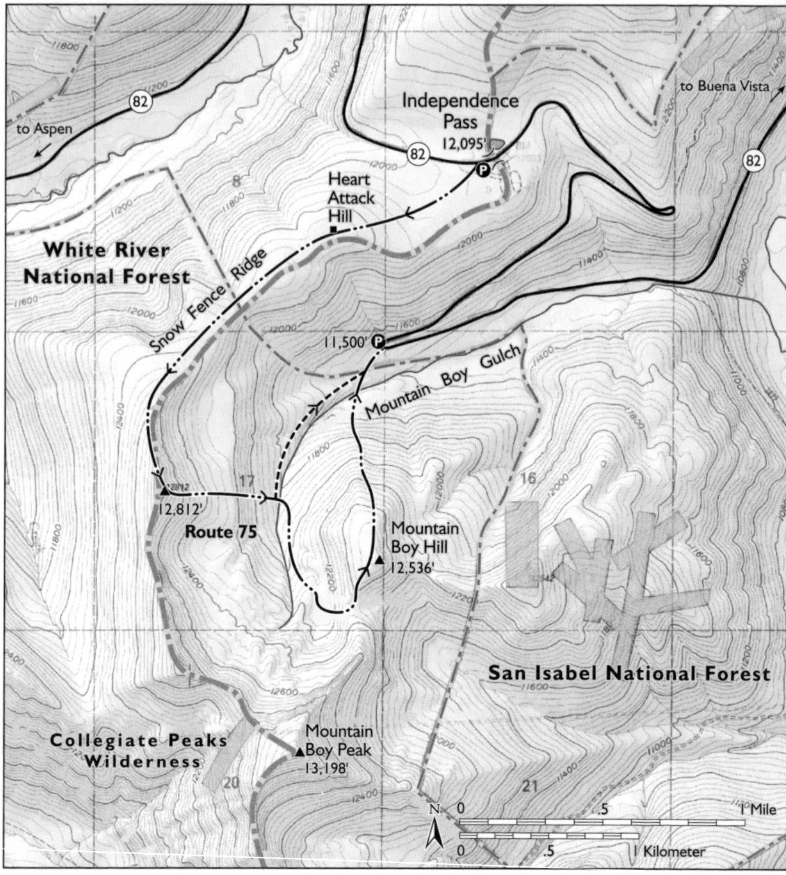

THE ROUTE

Mountain Boy Gulch lies just south of Independence Pass on the east side of the Continental Divide. Begin your tour from Independence Pass (elevation 12,095 feet) and head southwest up a hill, sometimes called Heart Attack Hill. Follow along an obvious ridge with a snow fence, called Snow Fence Ridge, until you see a good point to descend east into Mountain Boy Gulch. Most people follow the ridge about 1.75 miles to Point 12,812 and descend from there.

Descent. Enjoy your turns into Mountain Boy Gulch until about 12,200 feet or a bit lower. From the bottom of the valley, you can choose to follow the drainage north to exit. Or you could go up for another lap on Mountain Boy Hill. To extend your tour, head toward an obvious saddle in the ridge that comes down on the east side of "Mountain Boy Peak." Ascend the saddle, which tops out around 12,350 feet, and then begin heading north to the top of "Mountain Boy Hill" (12,536 feet). Descend the slopes to the north, returning to Mountain Boy Gulch. Cross the gully to reach a big switchback in CO 82 where you have set up a shuttle or can hitch a ride back to the top of the pass.

Extra Credit: After your descent from Snow Fence Ridge into Mountain Boy Gulch, consider climbing and descending the north face of Mountain Boy Peak. The best way to ascend this peak is via the saddle just to the west of the summit, and then following the ridge to the top.

76 La Plata Peak: Southeast Couloir and North Face

Starting Elevation	10,160 feet
High Point	14,336 feet
Vertical Gain/Loss	6000 feet
Ascent Distance	5.6 miles
Descent Distance	5.1 miles
Time	11 to 13 hours
Ski Skills	Difficult
Fitness Level	Very strenuous
Technical Skills	Moderate
Gear	The basics, plus ice and crampons
Best Months	March to May
USGS Map	Mount Elbert

From nearly any peak in the Sawatch to the south of La Plata, the southeast couloir will show itself as a striking line, begging to be skied. The difficult part of this line, however, is the access. While it is possible to approach the line via the Crystal Lake Creek valley, the easiest way to ski the southeast couloir is to summit La Plata via the standard northwest ridge route and then reclimb La Plata to ski the classic north face.

GETTING THERE

Start your odometer at the intersection of US Highway 24 and Colorado Highway 82. Travel west on CO 82 for 14.5 miles to the well-marked La Plata trailhead. This is a year-round trailhead.

THE ROUTE

Starting at the trailhead, take South Lake Creek Road over a bridge until the start of the well-marked La Plata Trail after a quarter mile. Follow the trail over a footbridge crossing South Fork Lake Creek. The summer trail continues up La Plata Gulch before heading up west-facing avalanche slopes near 11,100 feet. The west-facing slopes on the summer route have areas of avalanche danger, and it may

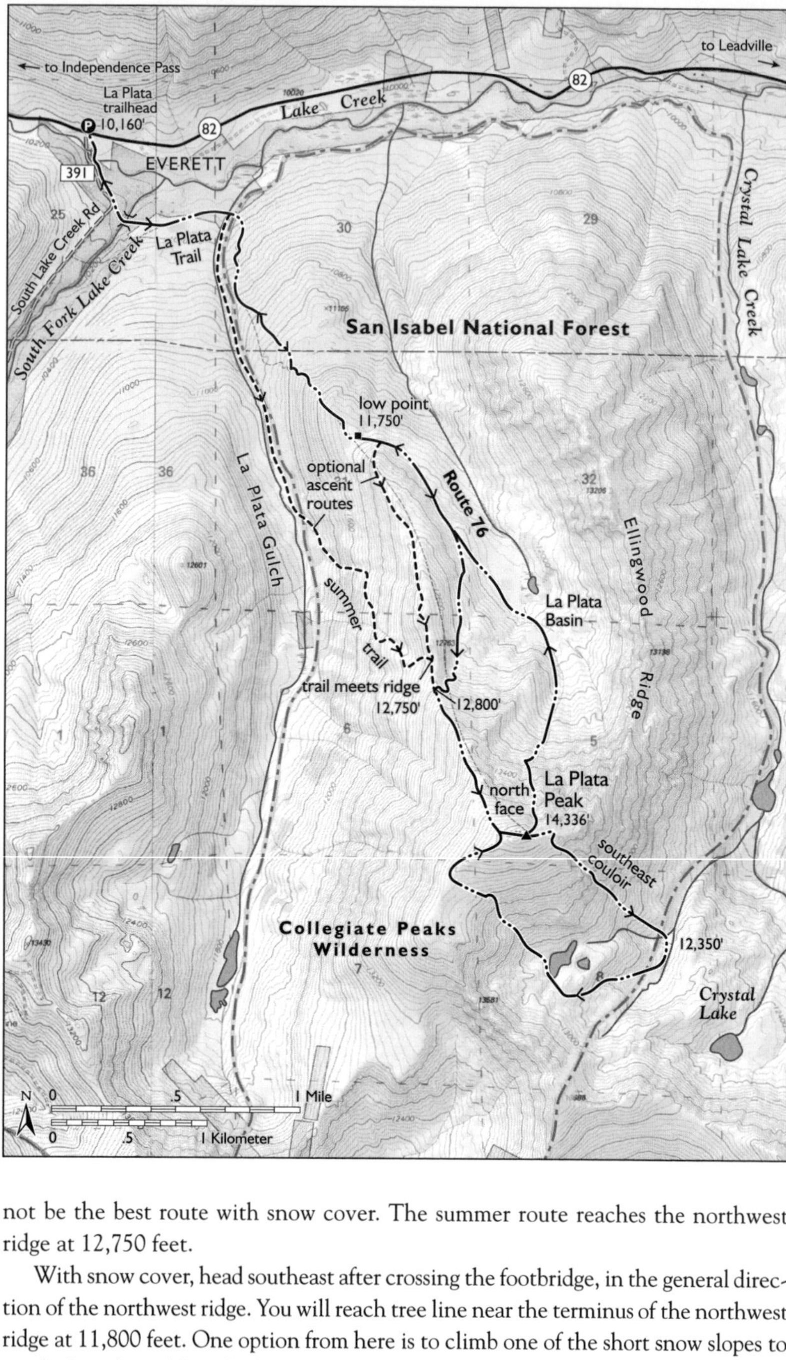

not be the best route with snow cover. The summer route reaches the northwest ridge at 12,750 feet.

With snow cover, head southeast after crossing the footbridge, in the general direction of the northwest ridge. You will reach tree line near the terminus of the northwest ridge at 11,800 feet. One option from here is to climb one of the short snow slopes to reach the ridge, although this may also have significant avalanche danger. The final

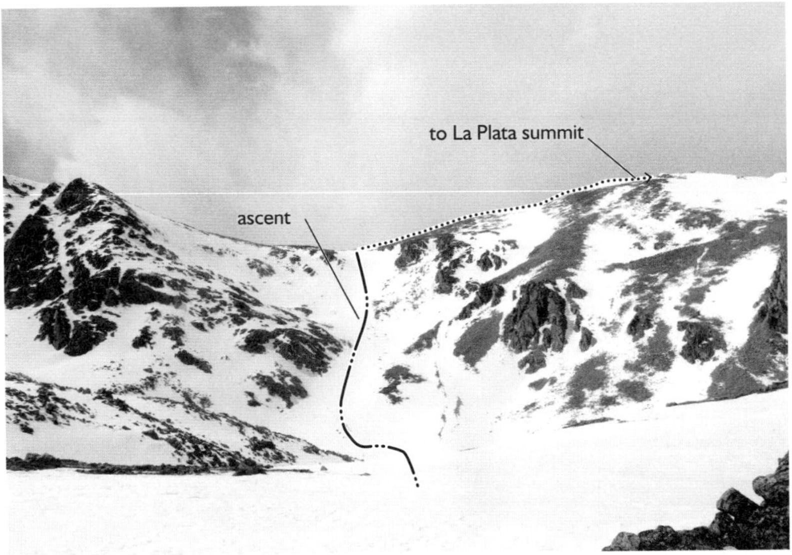

option is to continue southeast into La Plata Basin. Skin up La Plata Basin until you can begin veering to the climber's right to reach the northwest ridge at 12,800 feet. Choosing which of the routes to take will depend on avalanche conditions as well as how late in the season you're climbing La Plata. One other factor to consider is that older maps do not show the newer summer trail. Total mileage for all of these routes is similar, depending on the exact route taken.

Descent. The southeast couloir can be found by heading east on the summit ridge to a small col. Several entrances to the couloir can be found in good conditions. Ski the couloir to the valley floor at 12,350 feet. This magical valley sees few visitors and feels shockingly quiet compared to the busy north side of La Plata. You have two options to regain La Plata's summit. One is to simply climb the couloir you just skied. If you're skiing the couloir in springtime corn conditions, however, thawing conditions may dictate an alternate choice. This choice involves an enjoyable tour up the valley to the southwest ridge of La Plata. Begin by taking the climber's left to avoid steeper terrain in the valley floor. Curve around toward the southern slopes of La Plata and ascend to the southwest ridge and follow the ridge to the summit. If these slopes are also thawing too quickly for your liking, you should be able to find a route on scree and talus to La Plata's summit, on the climber's right of the snow slopes mentioned above.

The north face contains several choices for a ski descent. The easiest involves descending the northwest ridge that you climbed earlier in the day to a broad gully that descends into La Plata Basin. The most popular choice is to once again head east on the summit ridge to identify a steeper couloir.

Whichever route you choose on La Plata's north face, you will need to exit La Plata Gulch near tree line. To do this, descend La Plata Gulch, keeping an eye on the northwest ridge on your left. As the northwest ridge ends, contour toward your left near tree line toward a low point at 11,750 feet. Follow any feasible route toward your ascent route from earlier in the day (assuming you did not ascend the summer trail). Early in the season, you may even find quality turns in the trees on a northwest heading. Once you are back on your ascent route, follow it back to your vehicle.

77 Mount Shimer (a.k.a. Sunshine)

Starting Elevation	8600 feet
High Point	11,950 feet or higher
Vertical Gain/Loss	3350 feet
Ascent Distance	5.6 miles
Descent Distance	4.1 miles
Time	6 to 8 hours
Ski Skills	Moderate
Fitness Level	Strenuous
Technical Skills	Low
Gear	The basics
Best Months	January to May
USGS Map	New York Peak

Contrary to what you may have seen in *Dumb and Dumber*, the mountains that greet you as you drive into Aspen are not the Maroon Bells. It's more likely, in fact, that the mountain you're looking at from Aspen toward the southeast is Mount Shimer, sometimes called "Sunshine." While Aspen is more closely associated with the Elk

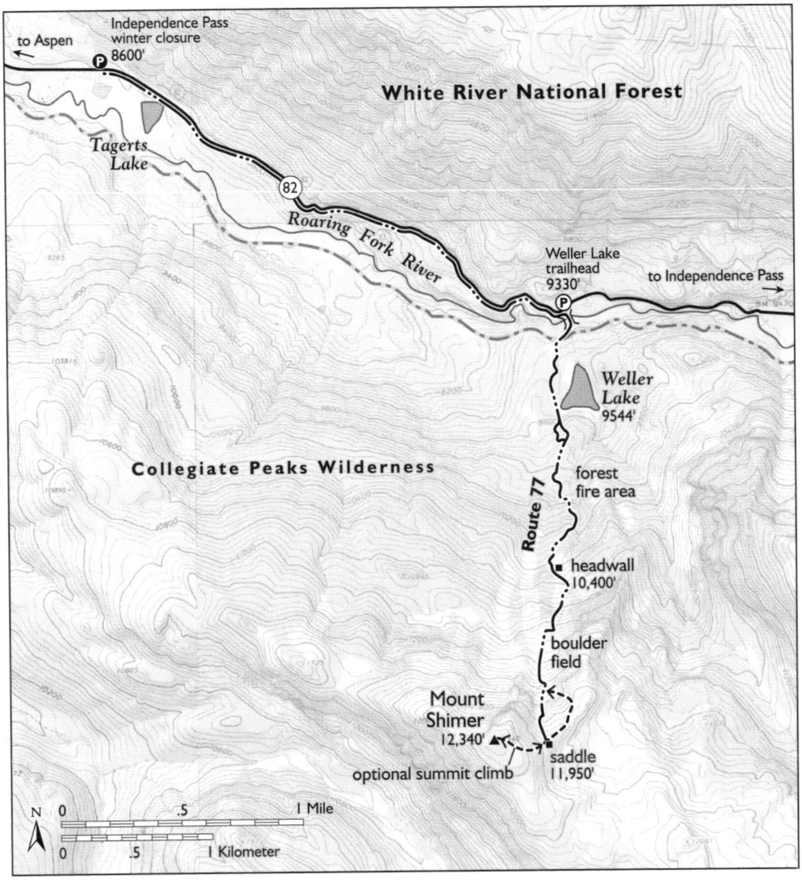

Mountains, the peaks to the east are more accurately categorized as Sawatch Range peaks, including Shimer. With careful routefinding, Mount Shimer can be skied during safer periods, even midwinter.

GETTING THERE

From Aspen, start your odometer at the corner of Cooper Avenue and Original Street. The winter closure of Colorado Highway 82 (Independence Pass) is located 5.4 miles east from this intersection and is the trailhead for this route. Late in the season, you may be able to drive another 2 miles to the Weller Lake trailhead described below.

THE ROUTE

Fom the Independence Pass winter closure at 8600 feet, follow CO 82 east for 2 miles to the Weller Lake trailhead at 9330 feet. Your goal is a small saddle just to the east of Mount Shimer, ascending through undulating terrain between this trailhead and the summit. Head south, immediately crossing the Roaring Fork River over a bridge. Skin through the forest, staying west of Weller Lake. Stay to the climber's right, toward the trees, as you skin past an old forest-fire burn area. At 10,400 feet, a steeper headwall will be encountered, which is also exposed to slides from above. If you're comfortable with conditions, continue up this short section. If not, call it a day. At the top of the steeper section, you will arrive at a field of large boulders, and the upper bowl will be straight ahead. Ascend this shallow feature toward the small saddle east of Mount Shimer. In midwinter conditions, this saddle may make a good stopping point. If conditions continue to be favorable, continue up the broad east ridge to the summit.

Descent. While this is a feasible winter route, it is best suited for experienced backcountry skiers during times of lower danger. If conditions do not seem favorable at any point, the best choice will be to stop and ski some of the lower slopes rather than continuing higher. The terrain from the east saddle makes for excellent, lower-angle skiing. From the saddle, you can descend your ascent route. Alternatively, you can ski a couloir to skier's right of the saddle, which you likely noticed as you ascended. Below the boulder field, the terrain on the skier's left is a playground of pillows. Regain your skin track above Weller Lake, and follow your ascent route back to the trailhead.

78 Anderson Peak: North Face

Starting Elevation	10,575 feet
High Point	13,235 feet or higher
Vertical Gain/Loss	2660 feet
Ascent Distance	5.6 miles
Descent Distance	5.6 miles
Time	8 to 10 hours
Ski Skills	Very difficult
Fitness Level	Moderately strenuous
Technical Skills	High
Gear	The basics, plus ice axe and crampons
Best Months	May to June
USGS Maps	New York Peak and Independence Pass

The opening of Lincoln Creek Road is eagerly awaited by Colorado backcountry skiers every spring. This road provides easy access to a rugged area of the Sawatch Range as well as the classic north couloir of Grizzly Peak (not the same Grizzly Peak as the one in this book). While 95 percent of skiers will head to Grizzly, skiers looking for something a little steeper and less crowded should head toward the amazing north face of "Anderson Peak," which hosts several steep couloirs to choose from.

GETTING THERE

From the east, reach Lincoln Creek Road by driving 33.2 miles over Independence Pass (after it opens for the summer, see Route 71) from the intersection of Highway

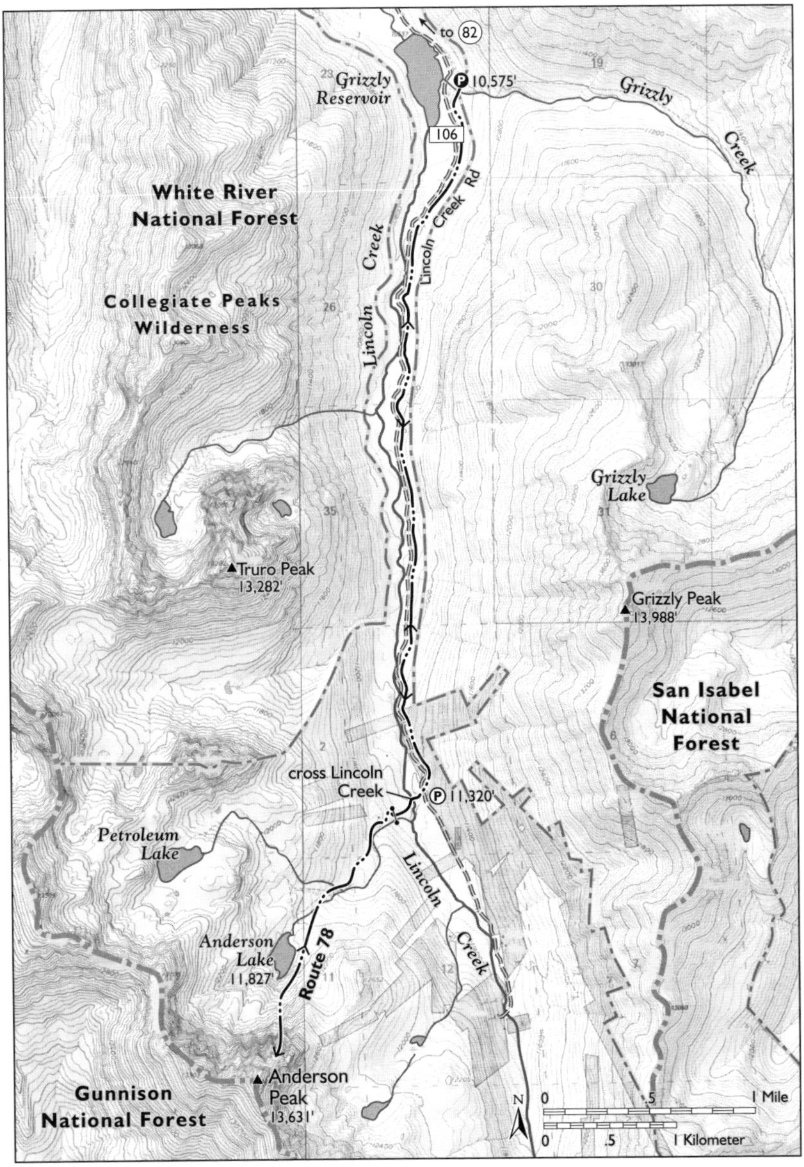

24 and Colorado Highway 82 near Twin Lakes. From Aspen, start your odometer at the corner of Cooper Avenue and Original Street. Head east on CO 82 for 9.6 miles to the turnoff for Lincoln Creek on the south side. From the Lincoln Creek Road turnoff, it is 6.4 miles to the Grizzly Reservoir trailhead. This road is passable for high-clearance 2WD vehicles but is better suited to 4WD. Lincoln Creek Road (Forest Road 106) is often plowed but remains gated in late spring well past the opening

Skiing down to the shores of Anderson Lake

of Independence Pass, so eager ski mountaineers have been known to hike or bike the road to Grizzly Reservoir.

THE ROUTE

Starting at Grizzly Reservoir (elevation 10,575 feet), continue up Lincoln Creek Road (FR 106) for 3.2 miles to the trailhead for Anderson Lake and Petroleum Lake at 11,320 feet. This point can be reached with a high-clearance 4WD vehicle if the road from the reservoir is free of snow. There is no bridge at the start of the trail toward Anderson Lake, so you will need to wade across Lincoln Creek. Immediately after the creek crossing is a closed gate, barring vehicles from continuing any farther. Follow this old road/trail to Anderson Lake at 11,827 feet, which may also require small creek crossings depending on conditions.

At least four distinctive couloirs dot the north face of Anderson Peak, making this area ideal for a base camp if you're interested in several high-quality ski descents. Plan your route from Anderson Lake. The couloir on the far climber's right may offer the easiest access to Anderson's summit from a saddle. The statistics for this route assume a ski descent of the couloir that is second from the climber's left, which is a steep, narrow, and twisting line that stops almost 400 feet short of the summit. Survey conditions, and then climb the couloir or couloirs of your choice.

Descent. Ski your chosen couloir, then retrace your approach back to your vehicle.

79 Jenkins Mountain: Steeple Couloir

Starting Elevation	10,290 feet
High Point	13,432 feet
Vertical Gain/Loss	5000 feet
Ascent Distance	3.2 miles
Descent Distance	3.2 miles
Time	7 to 9 hours
Ski Skills	Difficult
Fitness Level	Strenuous
Technical Skills	Moderate
Gear	The basics, plus ice axe and crampons
Best Months	May to early June
USGS Map	Pieplant

At the northwest end of a wall of mountains above Taylor Park Reservoir sits Jenkins Mountain. From this angle, it's an unassuming mountain with a large south-facing bowl. On the hidden north side, however, sits the diagonal gash known as Steeple Couloir, which drops into Church Basin. Several other couloirs grace the north side of the mountain, making Church Basin a fine place to visit on Sundays, or any other day for that matter.

GETTING THERE

After spring melt-off, start your odometer at the intersection of Cottonwood Pass and Taylor River Road in Taylor Park, which is thirty minutes northeast of Gunnison and

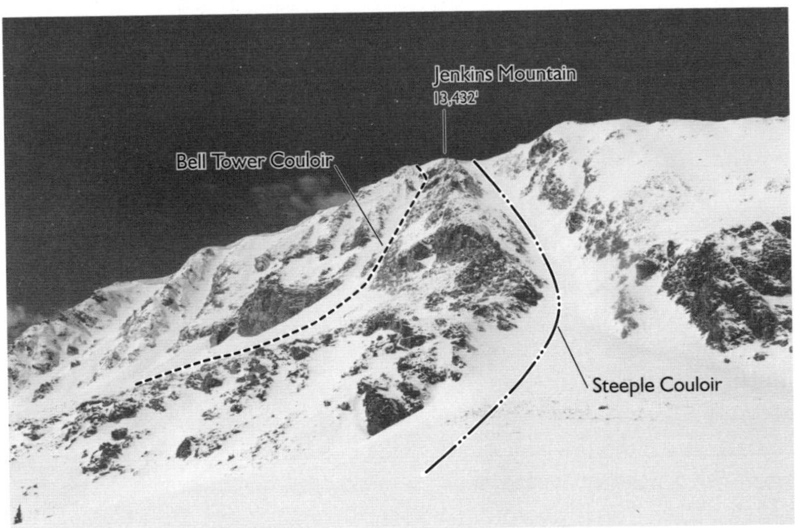

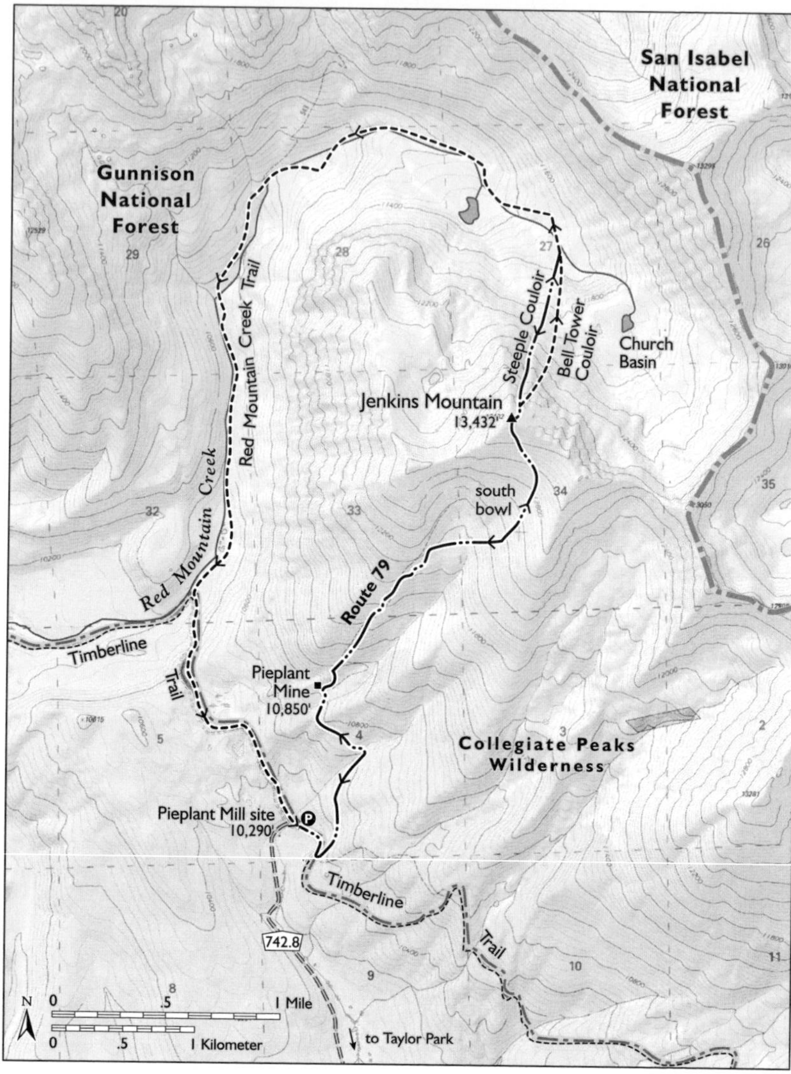

west of Cottonwood Pass. Head north on County Road 742 for 4.3 miles, to CR 742.8 (Pieplant). Turn right and follow this road for an additional 3.8 miles to the end of the road and the Pieplant Mill trailhead, located at the old Pieplant Mill.

THE ROUTE

Head southeast from the trailhead on the Timberline Trail for 0.4 mile to an unnamed and overgrown road that heads north to the Pieplant Mine. Take this road to the large south bowl of Jenkins Mountain. Ascend this bowl to the summit.

Descent. Slightly east of the summit, at a small depression, lies the top of the north-facing Steeple Couloir. Farther east lies a shorter and steeper couloir known as the Bell Tower, which may have a few melted-out sections late in the season or after a poor snow year. Descend the Steeple or Bell Tower couloir to the valley floor, nearly 2000 feet below.

If conditions allow, switch to crampons and reverse your route back up the Steeple Couloir to the summit of Jenkins for a second time. This is probably the fastest way back to the trailhead, and the turns in Jenkins's south bowl are great—in fact, intermediate skiers may simply want to do this bowl and skip the couloir. The statistics for this route assume that you climb Steeple Couloir and ski Jenkins Mountain a second time down the south bowl.

If the south bowl of Jenkins has no snow or temperatures are rising too quickly for your liking, descend Church Basin to the Red Mountain Creek Trail. Continue down valley to the intersection with the Timberline Trail, and then head left (southeast) back to the trailhead on the Timberline Trail.

80 Park Cone

Starting Elevation	9200 feet
High Point	12,100 feet
Vertical Gain/Loss	2900 feet
Ascent Distance	3.6 miles
Descent Distance	1.6 miles
Time	4 to 5 hours
Ski Skills	Moderate to difficult
Fitness Level	Moderately strenuous
Technical Skills	Low
Gear	The basics
Best Months	December to April
USGS Map	Taylor Park Reservoir

Roughly thirty minutes northeast of Gunnison, Park Cone sits quietly by itself at the southwest corner of Taylor Park. Gunnison-area backcountry skiers have enjoyed its slopes for years, which range from mild to surprisingly wild. As an added bonus, the trailhead is at a fishing area known for some of the state's largest trout, right below the Taylor dam. Bring your rod and reel for a classic Colorado two-sport day.

GETTING THERE

From the town of Almont, between Gunnison and Crested Butte, drive 19.9 miles on County Road 742 (Taylor River Road). Park at the obvious parking area below the dam (elevation 9200 feet), which will often be crowded with fishing enthusiasts. This

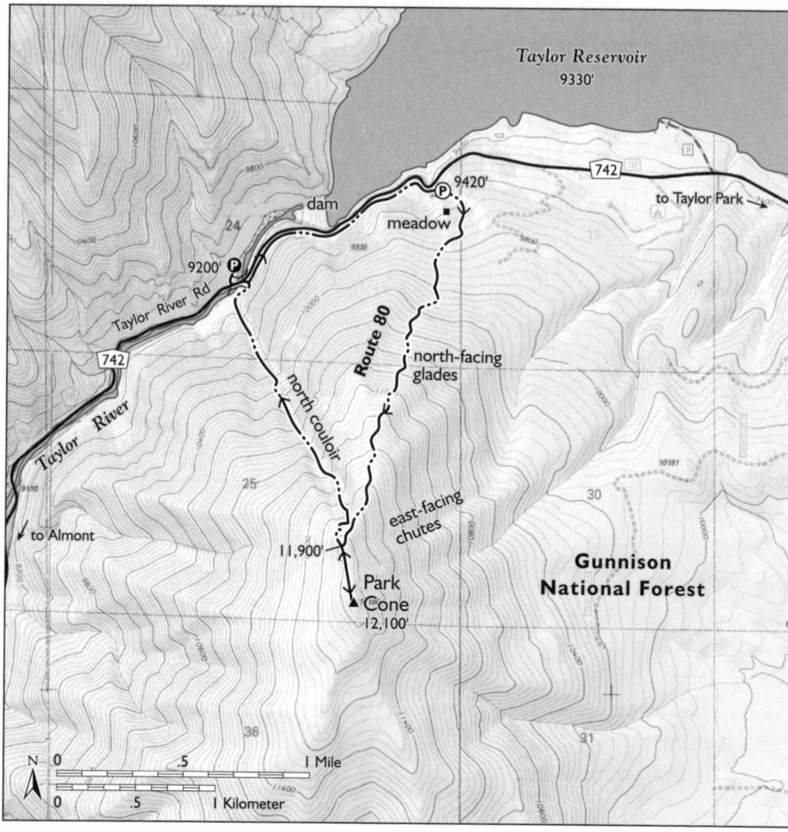

is a year-round parking area. Alternatively, continue 0.9 mile up the road to park at a pullout at 9420 feet.

THE ROUTE

Directly above the trailhead at 9200 feet is the north couloir of Park Cone, which is the primary route described here. This route is sometimes called Catch and Release, inspired by the fishing area at the bottom of the route. Begin the tour by hiking up the lightly traveled CR 742 for 0.9 mile. This section can be eliminated if you are planning on skiing routes other than the north couloir, or if you run a shuttle to one of several roadside pullouts. Leave the road at 9420 feet, where there is a small meadow on the north side of the road. Begin skinning up this meadow, and then trend slightly to your right through the trees on a more south-southwest heading. You will pass through several gladed areas higher on the mountain as you follow a slight ridge south to the summit (12,100 feet).

Descent. From the summit, several choices await backcountry skiers. Two huge east-facing avalanche paths are considered springtime classics. Midwinter skiers will

Skinning up the north glades of Park Cone, which are a safer descent choice during midwinter

probably opt for the safer north-facing glades in the vicinity of the skin track. Both of these options can be accomplished with a higher trailhead and less vertical gain.

The most aesthetic line might be the north couloir, which should only be skied in safe spring conditions. From the summit, follow the flat north ridge, which begins to curve slightly to the northeast. Identify the north couloir near tree line at 11,900 feet. Remember that any full-length avalanche will threaten anyone fishing in the river below. The first 500 feet of this route is quite steep before mellowing out to the mid-30-degree range for the rest of the 2700-foot couloir. When you reach the Taylor River, a short traverse to the skier's right will lead you to the bridge and back to your car.

81 Emma Burr Mountain: Northeast Face

Starting Elevation	11,400+/- feet
High Point	13,538 feet
Vertical Gain/Loss	2200+/- feet
Ascent Distance	3.5 miles
Descent Distance	3 miles
Time	4 to 6 hours
Ski Skills	Difficult
Fitness Level	Moderately strenuous
Technical Skills	Moderate
Gear	The basics, plus ice axe and crampons
Best Months	May and June
USGS Maps	Cumberland Pass, Tin Cup, Mount Yale

Chances are you've never heard of Emma Burr Mountain. Tucked deep in the Sawatch Range, this beautiful peak can be difficult to access early in the season. Ranked the 229th highest peak in Colorado, Emma Burr Mountain also happens to be the tallest peak along the Continental Divide for over 160 miles. If you've spent some time in the southern Sawatch, you've probably spotted her from afar. While the naming origins of Emma Burr seem to be as unknown as the peak itself, this mountain holds some wonderful ski lines that can be easily accessed in mid- to late spring.

GETTING THERE

From Colorado Highway 24 in Buena Vista, turn west onto Main Street. As this road leaves town it becomes County Road 306 (Cottonwood Pass Road). Follow this road for about 6 miles and then turn left (south) at CR 344, where you will see a sign that indicates Cottonwood Lake. If traveling from the west over Cottonwood Pass, this intersection is about 12 miles from the top of the pass just past Rainbow Lake.

Head south on this dirt road for 3 miles to Cottonwood Lake (9553 feet), a popular summer destination. Typically, this stretch of road is fine for passenger cars. Once past Cottonwood Lake, keep following CR 344. It will become increasingly rough and a mid- to high-clearance vehicle is recommended. How far you can drive on this road depends on the capabilities of your vehicle, as well as snowmelt. In late spring, a typical stopping point is at 11,400 feet where the road begins to curve to the south, 6.5 miles up from Cottonwood Lake.

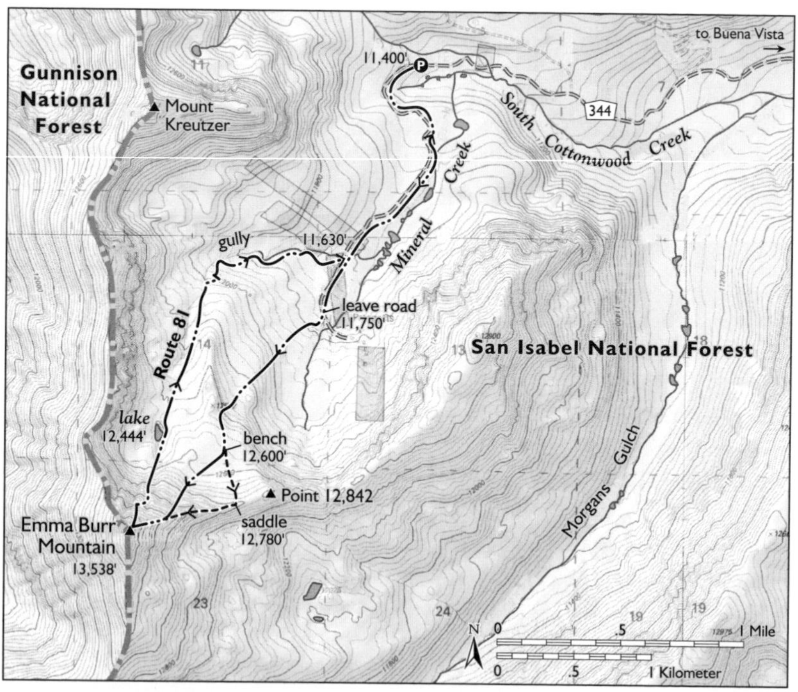

You may not have heard of Emma Burr, but chances are you'll find some good skiing on her northeast face.

CR 344 is not maintained in winter and does have seasonal road closures. Snowmobiles are often used to access the area earlier in the season. To inquire about the status of the road, call the Salida Ranger District (see Resources).

THE ROUTE

From your parking location on CR 344 at 11,400 feet, continue to follow the road up valley west and then south. Shortly after, the trees will begin to thin and you will have a good view of Emma Burr straight ahead. While you may find it tempting to veer off the road, stay on it for more efficient travel. At approximately 11,750 feet, the road begins to curve to the southeast to cross Mineral Creek. Leave the road here and head in a southwest direction toward the looker's left side of Emma Burr.

At 12,600 feet, you will find yourself on a large flat bench where you will need to decide whether to head to the saddle on the left (12,780 feet), just to the looker's right of Point 12,842, or head up steeper slopes on your right to gain the east ridge of Emma Burr. The saddle is recommended if the steeper slopes closer to Emma Burr are devoid of snow. Once on the east ridge, follow it west to the summit. You may encounter some class 3 moves along the way.

Descent. The northeast face of Emma Burr contains a few different chutes that make prime ski descents. From the summit, you may need to downclimb approximately 100 vertical feet to reach the snow. Descend your line of choice to the small lake below at 12,444 feet. Continue following the drainage down and to the northeast, remaining on the skier's right side of the gully, until it intersects with the road at 11,630 feet. If the basin has no snow, you may want to climb over the ridge on your right to reach the road sooner. Follow CR 344 back to your vehicle.

82 Tabeguache Peak: North Face

Starting Elevation	8910 feet
High Point	14,155 feet
Vertical Gain/Loss	5300 feet
Ascent Distance	7.5 miles
Descent Distance	7.5 miles
Time	10 to 12 hours
Ski Skills	Difficult
Fitness Level	Very strenuous
Technical Skills	High
Gear	The basics, plus ice axe and crampons
Best Months	April and May
USGS Maps	Saint Elmo and Mount Antero

From the town of Salida, Mount Shavano dominates the western skyline while Tabeguache Peak sits in its shadows, seemingly unnoticed. Tabeguache Peak is part of the Sawatch Indian Group, along with neighboring Shavano and Antero, and it is named after a band of Utes who were led in the late 1800s by Chief Shavano, who sympathized with the settlers. Ranked the twenty-fifth-highest peak in Colorado, Tabeguache is certainly one of the lesser-known Colorado fourteeners. But it does offer 2500 vertical feet of great skiing on its infrequently visited north face.

GETTING THERE

From Buena Vista, drive south on US Highway 285 for approximately 9 miles and turn west onto County Road 270. From Poncha Springs, 5 miles west of Salida, drive 12.7 miles north on US 285 to reach CR 270.

Once on CR 270, drive west for 1.5 miles at which point the road becomes CR 272. Follow CR 272 for 2 miles until an intersection. Take the left fork, remaining on CR 272 another 1.6 miles to the Browns Creek trailhead (elevation 8910 feet) and park.

THE ROUTE

Take the Browns Creek Trail as it heads west and then south, following to the north of Little Browns Creek and then Browns Creek. If the trail is not dry or compacted, take care not to follow the Little Browns Creek drainage west at an elevation of 9635 feet. Instead, head south following on the west side of Browns Creek. Shortly after, the trail begins veering southwest, remaining on the north side of the creek.

After 5.5 miles, you will arrive at Browns Lake (11,286 feet). Here you will start to see the north face of Tabeguache Peak appearing to your left (south). Pass along the north shore of the lake, paying attention to possible ascent and descent options. About 0.5 mile after the lake, look for a place to cross Browns Creek, which can be difficult during spring melt-off. Begin ascending the apron of the north-facing slopes. The easiest

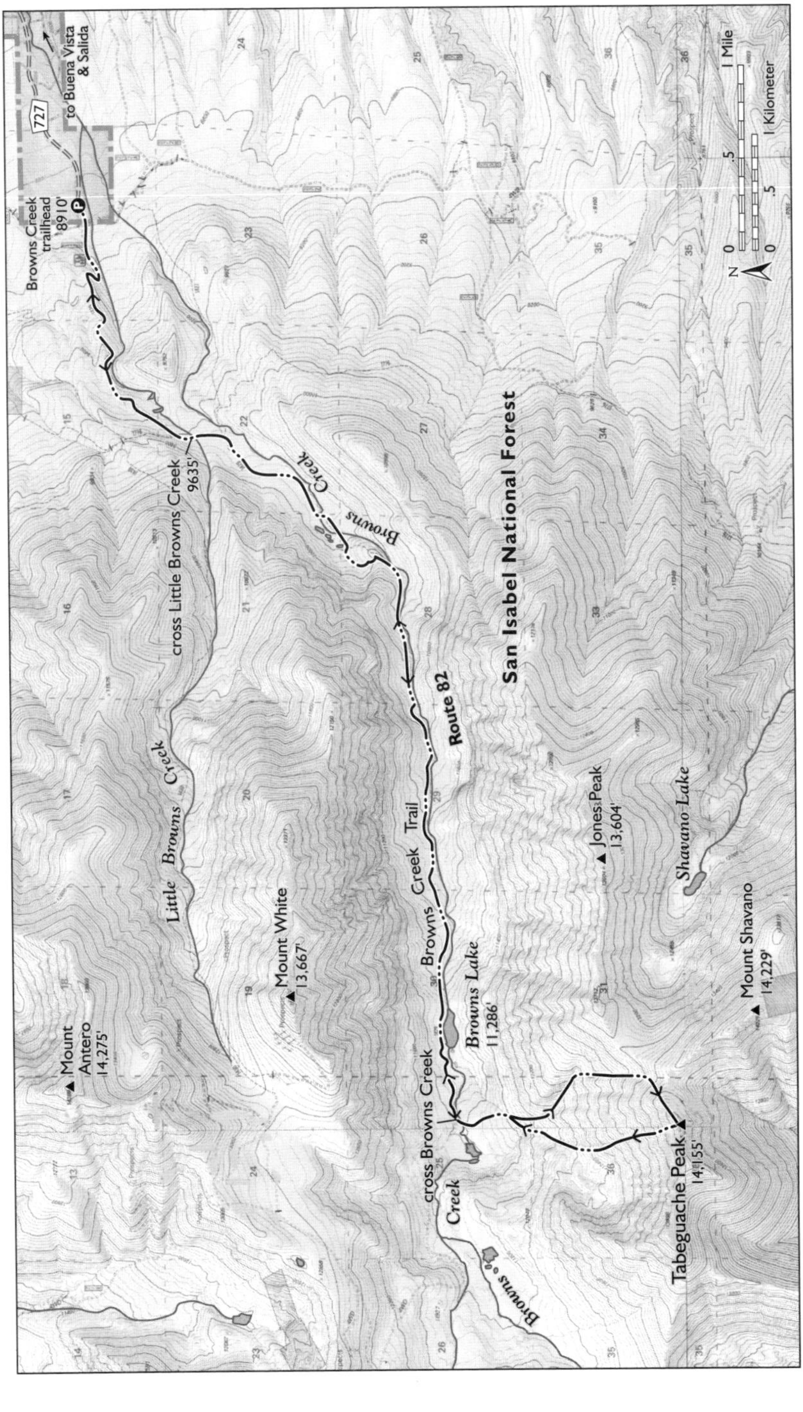
727
to Buena Vista
& Salida
Browns Creek
trailhead
8910'
cross Little Browns Creek
9635'
Browns
Creek
Little Browns Creek
Route 82
San Isabel National Forest
Browns Creek Trail
Mount White
13,667'
Mount
Antero
14,275'
Browns Lake
11,286'
cross Browns Creek
Creek
Browns
Jones Peak
13,604'
Shavano Lake
Mount Shavano
14,229'
Tabeguache Peak
14,155'
N
0
.5
1 Mile
0
.5
1 Kilometer

ascent route follows a gully to the climber's left that drains down to Browns Lake. This gully will lead you to the northeast ridge of Tabeguache, and you will need to follow that ridge southwest to the summit. Otherwise, climb your intended descent route.

Descent. Descend one of the many choices down the north face. Cross Browns Creek and return to the Browns Creek Trail. Follow your ascent route back to the trailhead.

83 Monarch Pass: Perfect Trees

Starting Elevation	11,312 feet from Monarch Pass or 10,995 feet from old Monarch Pass (Low point: 10,800 feet)
High Point	11,700 feet
Vertical Gain/Loss	900 feet
Ascent Distance	1 mile
Descent Distance	1 mile
Time	1.5 to 2 hours
Ski Skills	Moderate
Fitness Level	Not very strenuous
Technical Skills	Low
Gear	The basics
Best Months	January and February
USGS Maps	Garfield and Pahlone Peak

One of Colorado's major passes that sits on top of the Continental Divide, Monarch Pass can catch a surprising amount of snow from storms that seem to leave others

Plunging into powder on a ridiculously deep day in the Perfect Trees

wanting. The ski area of Monarch Mountain sits just below the pass on the east side, but the best zones are left for the backcountry skiers. Perfect Trees lives up to its name, with perfectly spaced pines on a moderately steep slope—a perfect playground to enjoy some serious powder turns on a storm day.

GETTING THERE

Monarch Pass is located on US Highway 50, roughly 22 miles west of Salida and 42 miles east of Gunnison. Park in the large parking lot on the southeast side of the road at the top of Monarch Pass (11,312 feet). During storm days, this lot may not be plowed very well, in which case you may choose to park at the start of Old Monarch Pass Road (10,995 feet) just 1 mile down US 50 on the east side of the pass.

While Monarch Pass is less susceptible to closure than some of Colorado's other high passes in winter, the Colorado Department of Transportation typically closes the pass for scheduled avalanche control during storms (see Resources).

THE ROUTE

From the top of the pass, look for a skin track that begins left of the building for the summer tourist tram. This skin track should head to the northeast, contouring the slope until you reach the ridge north of the peak where the upper tram building sits.

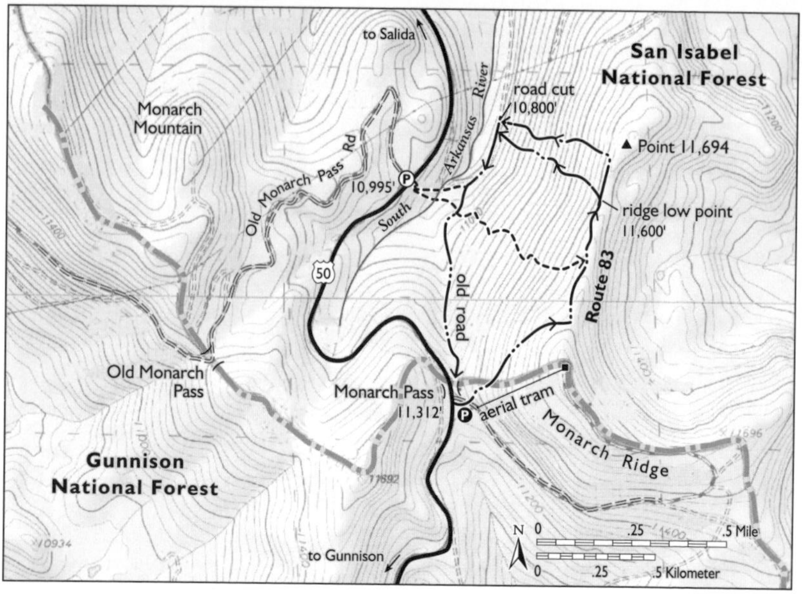

Follow the ridge north, gradually descending, until you reach a low point just over 11,600 feet. Most skiers descend the northwest-facing slopes that lie off the ridge between this low point and Point 11,694 just a little to the north.

If you are starting from Old Monarch Pass Road, cross the road and find a reasonable place to descend from the highway to the drainage below. Begin skinning up the slopes to the southeast until you reach the ridge mentioned above.

Descent. Descend the northwest-facing slopes until you reach a road cut at roughly 10,800 feet. Head south (skier's left) on the road cut. Find a skin track, or make your own, to go up for a second lap if you desire. To return to Monarch Pass, follow an old road cut south, which leads directly to the parking lot at the top of the pass. To return to Old Monarch Pass Road, follow along the road cut until you find your route where you descended from the highway. Use this route to return to your vehicle.

84 Mount Ouray: Devil's Armchair

Starting Elevation	9660 feet
High Point	13,971 feet
Vertical Gain/Loss	4311 feet
Ascent Distance	3.6 miles
Descent Distance	3.1 miles
Time	7 to 8 hours
Ski Skills	Difficult

The east ridge ascent option is on the left in this view of Devil's Armchair.

Fitness Level	Strenuous
Technical Skills	Low to moderate
Gear	The basics
Best Months	March to May
USGS Map	Mount Ouray

Standing proudly at the southern end of the mighty Sawatch Range, Mount Ouray offers commanding views into three major valleys: the Arkansas River, the Gunnison, and the San Luis. More importantly for backcountry skiers, the immense cirque known as the Devil's Armchair harbors a number of fine ski descents. The southern Sawatch Range is not known for high snowfall amounts, so during drier years this route may not be filled in. With good snow cover, however, the Devil's Armchair is one of the best descents in the range.

GETTING THERE

Begin measuring from the intersection of US Highway 285 and US 50 in downtown Poncha Springs. Head south on US 285 for 4.9 miles to the well-marked sign for Marshall Pass on Chaffee County Road 200. Turn right and head southwest. At 6.1 miles, turn right onto Forest Road 202 near a sign displaying the history of "A Town Called Shirley." At mile 8, turn right on FR 200. Continue past O'Haver Lake (good

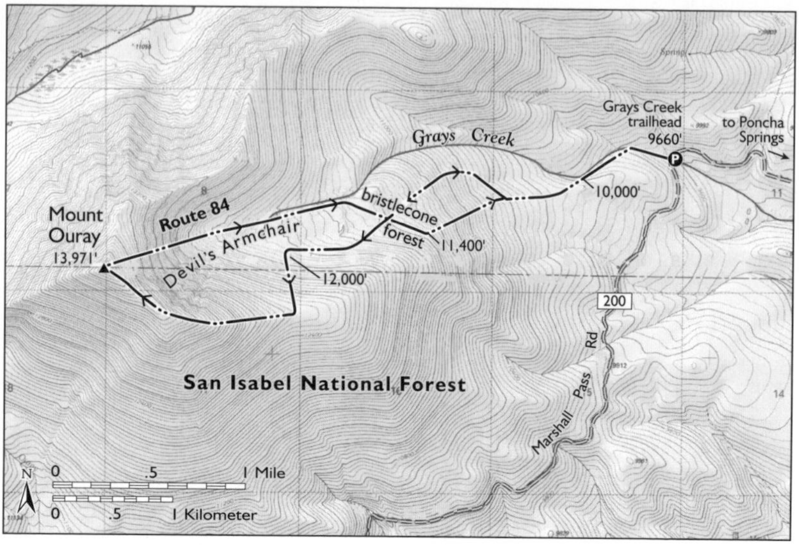

camping can be found here). Mile 11.9 marks the trailhead, a sharp left hairpin turn with a small sign saying "Grays Creek" (elevation 9660 feet). There is a small pull-off here for parking but no winter maintenance. Once the road is clear, 2WD vehicles will not have trouble accessing this trailhead. Until the roads are melted off, a longer tour will be necessary to reach this trailhead, closer to US 285.

THE ROUTE

From the trailhead at 9660 feet, head west up Grays Creek. Most skiers will find that the trailhead has already melted out, in which case an unmarked trail will help guide the way. The trail will frequently cross over downed logs and may be faint, but follow it as best you can. Around 10,000 feet, begin staying to your left, following a smaller creek slightly to the southwest. This area is the most difficult of the tour to follow, but trust your instincts and you'll find yourself at flattening terrain around 11,400 feet, with a good view of the cirque ahead. At this point, you're at the somewhat famous bristlecone pine forest. These remarkable trees are some of the oldest life forms on Earth, and they make for a dramatic backdrop as you continue your way toward the Devil's Armchair. Survey the routes ahead of you; there are a number of possibilities as well as a number of lines that cliff out. Some climbers may want to "climb what you ski," in which case you will want to have crampons and an ice axe and head straight for your intended ski line.

Otherwise, near 12,000 feet, begin heading to your left (south) to gain the east ridge of Mount Ouray. With careful routefinding and good snow cover, you may be able to skin the entire way to the summit, but it may be necessary to cross the occasional bit of talus along the way. The true mass of this mountain will become apparent, and it will take quite some time to reach the summit.

Weaving through incredible bristlecone pines while approaching the Devil's Armchair

Descent. As mentioned previously, care must be taken when choosing a descent route to avoid a line that cliffs out above the valley floor. Generally speaking, lines on the skier's left will be the best bets. Depending on the exact line choice, terrain in the Devil's Armchair can reach or even exceed 45 degrees, and it predominantly faces east. Time your descent for early in the morning before the snow becomes too soft and avalanche prone.

From the bottom of your line, reenter the bristlecone pine forest and consider your options. With good snow cover, one option is to trend skier's right to take advantage of north-facing trees above Grays Creek. By linking traverses and short descents, a savvy skier may be able to reach the trailhead entirely on skis. If there is less snow cover, you will likely prefer to retrace your ascent route to find the trail.

Opposite: Finding recycled powder in the dark confines of the Dead Squirrel couloir

SAN JUAN MOUNTAINS

THE SAN JUAN MOUNTAINS represent Colorado's largest range. Standing on a central San Juan summit, the ski mountaineer can gaze in any direction and see a lifetime's worth of possible ski descents. Nearly half of Colorado's summits over 13,000 feet can be found in the San Juans.

The San Juans were primarily formed by volcanic activity, but peaks in the range run the gamut from sharp pointy peaks, such as Wetterhorn and Sneffels, to the gentler peaks north of Creede in the La Garita subrange.

Access in the San Juans is better than many other ranges. Durango is the southern gateway of the range, Telluride sits in the heart of the west, and Lake City and Creede are nestled at the range's eastern end. But the central towns of Silverton and Ouray provide the best access. With aggressive plowing from both San Juan and Ouray counties on their dirt roads beginning in early spring, the peaks that surround these quaint locales become a ski mountaineer's paradise.

Mining activity was extensive throughout the San Juans, and that legacy has one important result for ski mountaineers: roads. As rugged and vast as the San Juan Range is, miners pushed roads into the most improbable of places. Once springtime rolls around, local county governments plow many of these old mining roads, and the end result is that the San Juans have some of the best springtime access around.

As one might expect of such a large range, weather and snowfall varies widely across the range. Wolf Creek Pass, in the southern part of the range, is well known for being one of the snowiest parts of the state. On the eastern side, the La Garita Mountain subrange sits in the rain shadow of the highest San Juans and tend to receive less snow as a result. On the western side, well-known passes, including Red Mountain and Molas, also tend to be blessed with prodigious snowfall.

With good snowfall and generally easy access, many skiers will proclaim the San Juan Range to be their favorite. Around every turn and atop every mountain, skiers will find themselves adding to their skiing wish list, and will return for another adventure time after time.

85 Unnamed 13,299: Dead Squirrel Couloir

Starting Elevation: 9600 feet
High Point: 13,299
Vertical Gain/Loss: 3680 feet
Ascent Distance: 4.8 miles
Descent Distance: 3.2 miles
Time: 6 to 8 hours
Ski Skills: Difficult
Fitness Level: Strenuous
Technical Skills: Moderate
Gear: The basics, plus ice axe and crampons

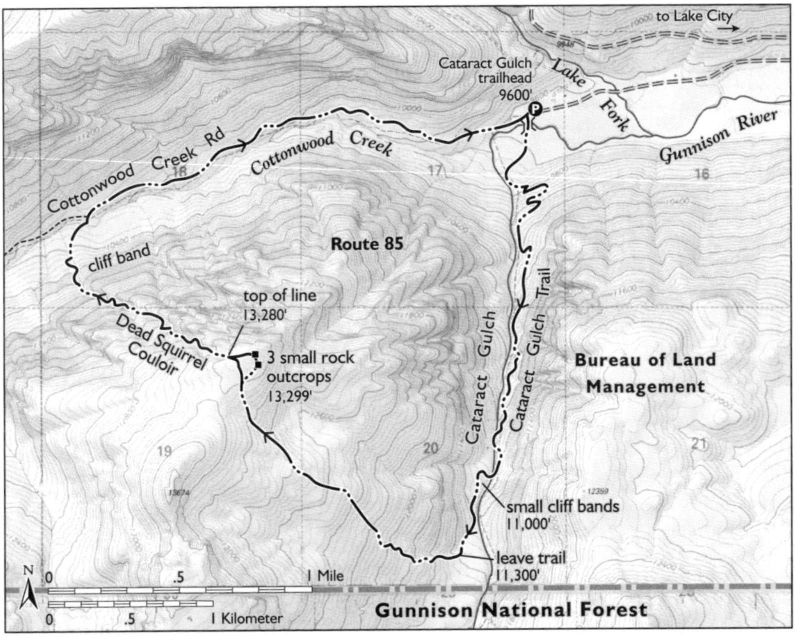

Best Months : March to early May
USGS Map : Redcloud Peak

The Lake City zone of the San Juans may not get a lot of snow or a lot of press, but the hidden couloirs in this area are some of the best you can find. Nearly 3000 feet from top to bottom, the Dead Squirrel Couloir is an absolute gem in a remote setting.

The couloir earned its unofficial name when some friends of ours found a dead squirrel at the top of this line and accidentally knocked it down. As they skied, the frozen squirrel tumbled down the chute with them, thus the name.

GETTING THERE

Start your odometer at the corner of 4th and Gunnison in Lake City. Head south on Colorado Highway 149 for 2.5 miles to the well-marked turn for Lake San Cristobal and County Road 30. At 14.6 miles, you'll stay left at a **Y** intersection heading toward the ghost town of Sherman. Park at the marked Cataract Gulch trailhead (elevation 9600 feet) at mile 17.3. This trailhead has year-round access.

THE ROUTE

Follow the well-signed Cataract Gulch Trail south, crossing Cottonwood Creek on a bridge near the trailhead. This trail sees a fair amount of foot and snowshoe (and moose) traffic, which may make it icy and punchy but also easy to follow. The route

This skier has a long, long way to go to reach the bottom of the Dead Squirrel Couloir.

will cross Cataract Creek on a few occasions, and you may need to do a bit of route-finding around small cliff bands as you approach at 11,000 feet. After approximately 3 miles, make your way through one more group of trees before entering the alpine at 11,300 feet. There you should leave the valley and begin ascending west and eventually northwest. Your goal is the northern end of the broad and flat ridge above you, where three small rock outcrops are visible at Point 13,299 feet. Take a break at the outcrops, and then identify the top of the Dead Squirrel Couloir a short distance to the west. The top of the couloir is usually bare and will probably require easy but rocky downclimbing for 100 vertical feet or so.

Descent. The Dead Squirrel Couloir is surprisingly straightforward as it descends toward Cottonwood Creek far below. While there are a handful of steeper rollovers, much of this route is in the low 40-degree range. When you finally exit the couloir, take the skier's left to avoid a small cliff band, and then continue descending to Cottonwood Creek. Find a snow bridge or log across the creek, and then climb up to Cottonwood Creek Road. Descend the road east for roughly 2 miles back to the trailhead.

86 Mount Sneffels: Snake Couloir

Starting Elevation	9700 feet (Camp Bird Road intersection), or 10,700 feet (2WD parking), or 11,400 feet (4WD parking)
High Point	14,150 feet
Vertical Gain/Loss	4300 feet
Ascent Distance	2.3 miles
Descent Distance	3.8 miles
Time	6 to 8 hours
Ski Skills	Very difficult
Fitness Level	Strenuous
Technical Skills	Very high
Gear	The basics, plus skins; ice axe and crampons may be needed, plus two 50-meter ropes for a rappel and anchors
Best Months	March to May
USGS Maps	Mount Sneffels and Ironton

Mount Sneffels is a highly visible peak in the northern San Juans that dominates the view while driving south on US Highway 550. On a clear day, portions of the Snake Couloir are visible from US 550 and Dallas Divide, on Colorado Highway 62. But due to its twisting nature, the entire line is not visible from any single point. Being the highest point in Ouray County and of the Sneffels subrange, Mount Sneffels catches the eye of every ski mountaineer.

GETTING THERE

Yankee Boy Basin generally allows for the easiest access to this area because the road is regularly plowed early in the spring, even though it is not the most direct route to the Snake Couloir. The lower trailhead for Yankee Boy Basin is accessible with a 2WD vehicle. Four-wheel-drive vehicles can often travel farther, depending on snow conditions. The road to Yankee Boy Basin is typically plowed to the Camp Bird Mine through much of the winter. However, thanks to mining operations, the road might not be open to public vehicles during this time. For the current road status, call the Ouray County Sheriff Department or Road and Bridge Department (see Resources).

At the time of writing, the road was open to public vehicles beginning May 1. If the road is not open to public vehicles, you will need to be creative. Avid skiers could choose to hike or bike the road. Or a different approach could be made from Blaine Basin, not described in this book.

From the town of Ouray, follow US 550 south. At 0.25 mile from the southern edge of town, turn right onto County Road 361. Travel 4.7 miles on this road to the intersection of CR 26. The left fork on CR 361 heads toward the Camp Bird Mine. It's possible that the right fork, CR 26, might not be plowed, and you may need to

Skiing the middle part of the Snake Couloir on Mount Sneffels

park here (elevation 9700 feet). If the right fork is plowed, take CR 26. After 1.5 miles, there will be a junction with the Imogene Pass Road. Stay right on CR 26. After another 0.75 mile, the road forks again. Two-wheel-drive vehicles will need to park around this area (elevation 10,700 feet). However, those with high-clearance 4WD can continue on the right fork, if snow conditions permit. The Yankee Boy Trail begins another 1.3 miles after this intersection (elevation 11,400 feet). A vault toilet is located at this trailhead.

THE ROUTE

All specifications for this route begin at the 4WD parking at 11,400 feet. Parking at the 2WD parking at 10,700 feet adds 1.4 miles (one way) and 700 vertical feet to your route. Parking at the intersection of CR 261 (Camp Bird Road) and CR 26 at 9700 feet adds 3.5 miles (one way) and 1700 vertical feet to your route.

From the 4WD parking at 11,400 feet, head northwest on the Yankee Boy Basin Road on foot until it ends at Wrights Lake at 12,180 feet. From there, continue traveling northwest along the right side of the drainage until you are nearing the end of the valley, following the Blue Lakes Trail if it is not snow covered. There are many impressive peaks in this area that can easily be mistaken for Mount Sneffels, which is not visible until you reach the end of the valley. Be careful not to leave the drainage too soon.

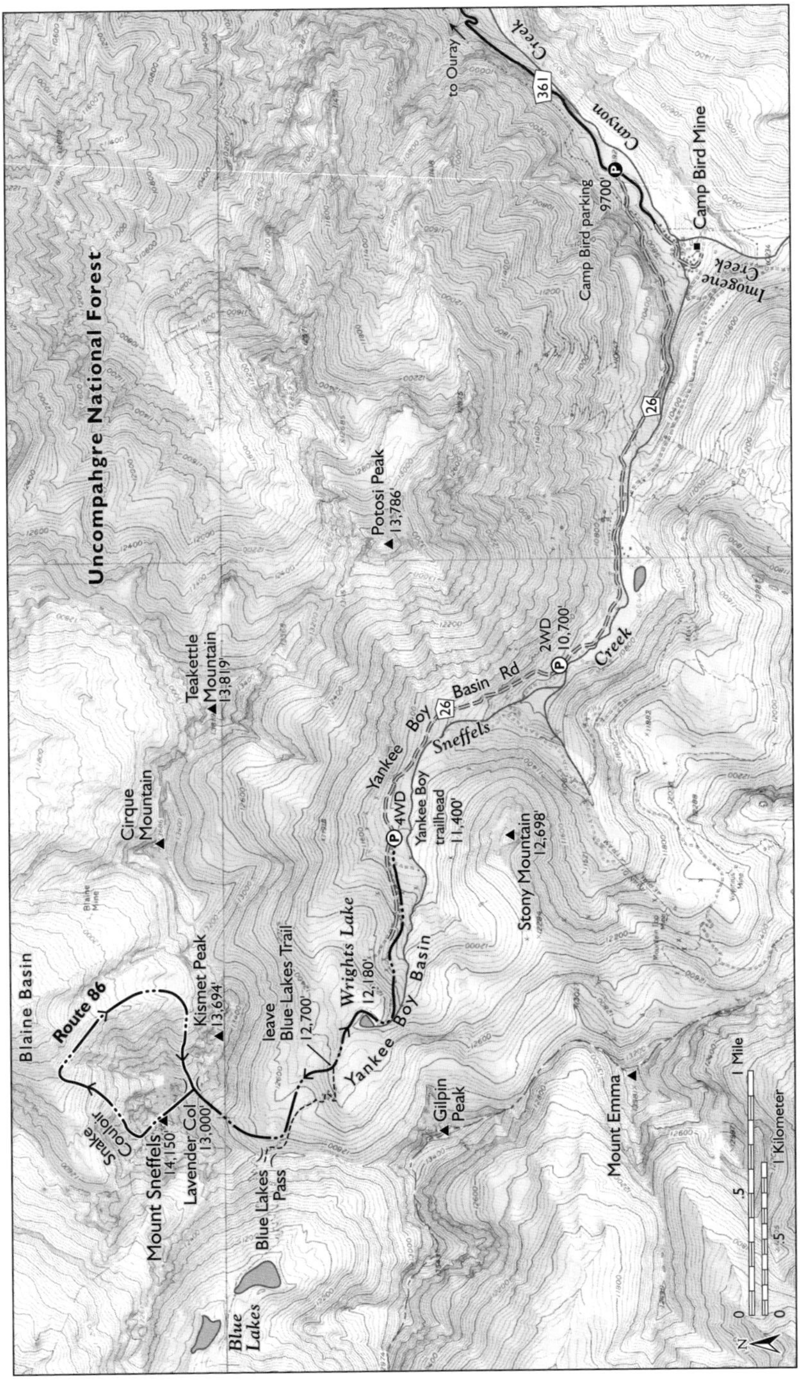
Uncompahgre National Forest
to Ouray
361
Canyon
Creek
Camp Bird parking
9700'
Camp Bird Mine
Imogene
Creek
26
Potosi Peak
13,786'
Teakettle
Mountain
13,819'
Cirque
Mountain
2WD
10,700'
Yankee Boy Basin Rd
Sneffels
Creek
4WD
Yankee Boy
trailhead
11,400'
Stony Mountain
12,698'
Blaine Basin
Route 86
Kismet Peak
13,694'
leave
Blue Lakes Trail
12,700'
Wrights Lake
12,180'
Yankee Boy Basin
Snake
Couloir
Mount Sneffels
14,150'
Lavender Col
13,000'
Blue Lakes
Pass
Gilpin
Peak
Mount Emma
Blue
Lakes
1 Mile
1 Kilometer
N

Around 12,700 feet, the south side of Mount Sneffels becomes visible as well as a snowfield following upward to its east. Leave the Blue Lakes Trail and travel northward up this snowfield to an obvious saddle on the southeast ridge of Mount Sneffels at 13,000 feet. This saddle, called the Lavender Col, connects Mount Sneffels with Kismet Peak. Upon reaching the Lavender Col, continue upward through an obvious southeast-facing couloir that leads toward the summit. Just before you reach the ridge, find a route through the cliff band to the left. This cliff band is typically the crux of the ascent. Once past the cliff band, follow the ridge another 100 feet to the summit.

Descent. The Snake Couloir begins straight off the north side of the summit of Mount Sneffels. The rocky, corniced entrance typically requires a rappel. There often are rappel anchors directly on the summit, but they may be buried under snow. Two thirty-meter ropes or one sixty-meter rope are recommended at a minimum for the rappel from the summit. Longer ropes will get you to a more comfortable place to transition from your rappel to skis or snowboard.

After the rappel, the ski route begins by slanting off to the left, toward the northwest. Around 13,600 feet, the route then doglegs off to the right. At this point, the route steepens and narrows to a tight crux. The crux can be icy and runnelled at times, so beware. Once you are past the narrow crux, the route becomes less steep and opens up again.

Ski this route until between 12,000 and 11,500 feet. At that point, a snowfield to skier's right, facing north, leads back up around the looker's left of Mount Sneffels. Begin climbing up this snowfield. At 12,500 feet, the route veers to the looker's right, facing more eastward. Continue following this route all the way back to the Lavender Col at 13,000 feet. Beware of your timing when climbing this east-facing zone as the snow can be particularly warm and wet.

From the Lavender Col, follow your ascent route back to the trailhead and your vehicle.

Extra Credit: When the Snake Couloir doglegs to the right at 13,600 feet, a short climb above a cornice will take you to the second of three couloirs that comprise a route known as the Trilogy. This tremendous route requires careful routefinding and a long car shuttle.

87 Chicago Peak: Lightning Bolt Couloir

Starting Elevation	10,200+/- feet
High Point	13,385 feet
Vertical Gain/Loss	3185+/- feet
Ascent Distance	3.5+/- miles
Descent Distance	3.5+/- miles
Time	6 to 8 hours
Ski Skills	Difficult
Fitness Level	Moderately strenuous

Technical Skills : Moderate
Gear : The basics, plus ice axe and crampons
Best Months : March to early May
USGS Maps : Telluride and Ironton

The Lightning Bolt Couloir (see map in Route 88) is visible from the Telluride Ski Area and is, not surprisingly, shaped a bit like a lightning bolt. This route takes you past the historic Tomboy Mine, with some of the best views of Telluride. Chicago Peak occupies a high point between the towns of Ouray and Telluride, and even the peaks near Red Mountain Pass are clearly visible from the summit. In other words, it's a great introduction to the San Juan Range.

Sitting more than 3000 feet above Telluride, the Tomboy Mine is one of the more famous mines in Colorado thanks to a memoir written by Harriet Fish Backus called *Tomboy Bride*. A seemingly harsh place, the town once contained luxuries such as tennis courts and a YMCA. The mine operated from 1880 to the mid-1920s when the ore ran out. Today, this ghost town is worth a visit even if you're not making turns in the area.

GETTING THERE

As you enter the town of Telluride from Colorado Highway 145, you'll be on Colorado Avenue. Take a left on Aspen Street, a right on Galena Avenue, and then a left on Oak Street. The north end of Oak Street turns into Tomboy Road. Tomboy Road is not plowed in winter, so your exact starting point will depend on how much of this

Making the final steps toward the summit of Chicago Peak

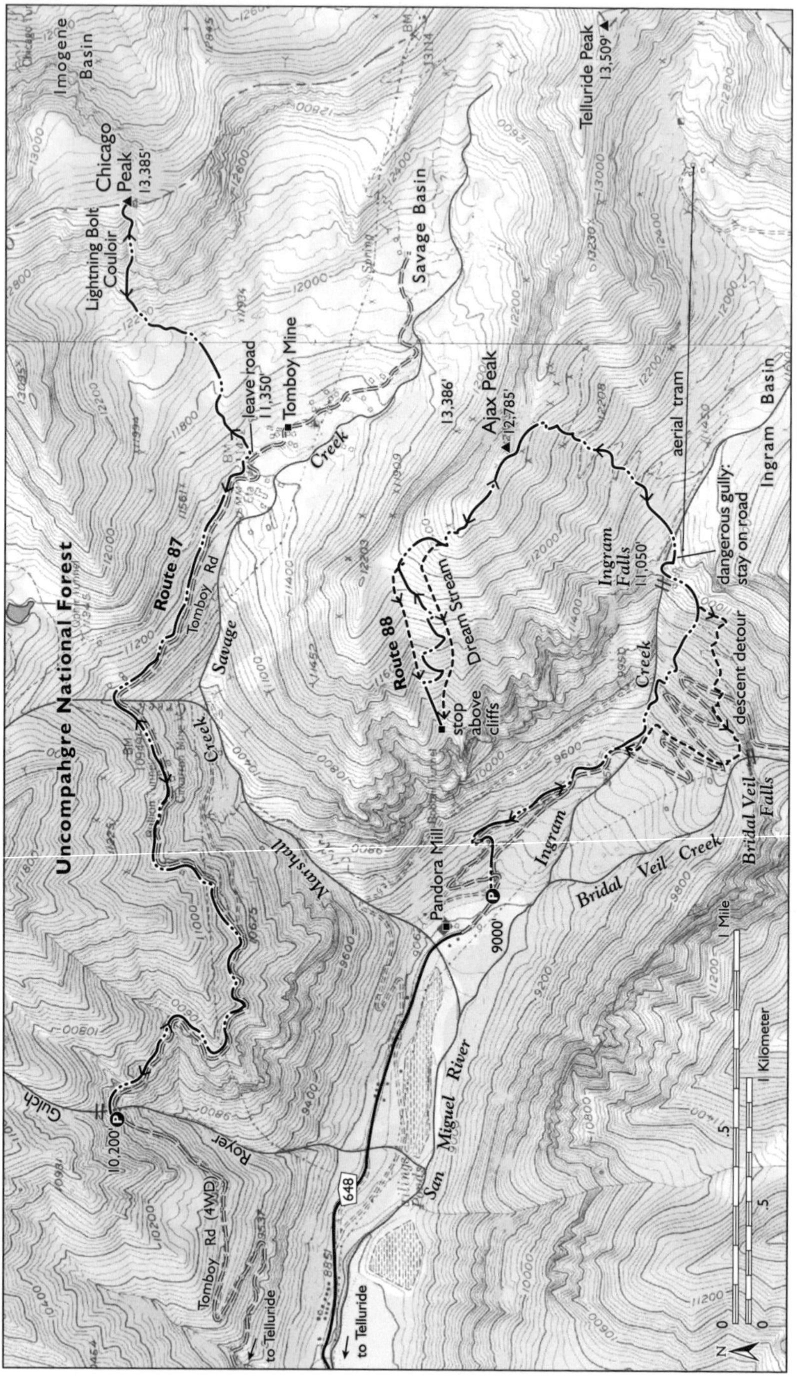
Uncompahgre National Forest
Route 87
Tomboy Rd
Savage Creek
Marshall Creek
Royer Gulch
Tomboy Rd (4WD)
to Telluride
10,200'
648
to Telluride
San Miguel River
Pandora Mill
9000'
Ingram Creek
Bridal Veil Creek
Bridal Veil Falls
Route 88
stop above cliffs
Dream Stream
Ajax Peak
12,785'
13,386'
Ingram Falls
11,050'
dangerous gully: stay on road
descent detour
aerial tram
Ingram Basin
Telluride Peak
13,509'
Savage Basin
Tomboy Mine
leave road
11,350'
Lightning Bolt Couloir
Chicago Peak
13,385'
Imogene Basin
0
.5
1 Mile
1 Kilometer
N

mostly south-facing road has melted. You may be able to drive a high-clearance 2WD vehicle on this road for a short distance, but 4WD is recommended. Commonly, avalanche debris near some waterfalls at 10,100 feet will block upward progress at Royer Gulch. Our route description assumes a starting point near these waterfalls.

THE ROUTE

Wherever you start on Tomboy Road, the tour begins by following the road as it makes its way above Telluride. You will begin to see the Lightning Bolt along the way. Leave the road near the Tomboy Mine at roughly 11,350 feet and continue toward the couloir. Transition to crampons at the bottom of the couloir and begin climbing the Lightning Bolt. Near the summit, a cliff band blocks the direct line to Chicago Peak's summit, but it can be easily bypassed on either side.

Descent. From the summit, you can look down the Camp Bird Mine Road straight into the town of Ouray. The Lightning Bolt averages 45 degrees or so and totals approximately 1000 vertical feet. Descend the couloir and retrace your approach back to your vehicle.

88 Ajax Peak: The Dream Stream

Starting Elevation	9000 feet
High Point	12,785 feet
Vertical Gain/Loss	5400 feet
Ascent Distance	3.7 miles
Descent Distance	3.7 miles
Time	7 to 9 hours
Ski Skills	Moderate
Fitness Level	Strenuous
Technical Skills	Moderate
Gear	The basics
Best Months	March to early May
USGS Map	Telluride

Standing on Telluride's Colorado Avenue, it's impossible to miss the avalanche path known as the Dream Stream on Ajax Peak. After large storm cycles, this route is occasionally avalanche controlled from a helicopter, resulting in spectacular footage from downtown Telluride. This route was first skied by Steve Moose and Scott Burbank in 1977. Because this route terminates at a large cliff band, most skiers will reascend Ajax Peak and descend the south side in addition to the Dream Stream. As an added bonus, this route takes you right past the magnificent Bridal Veil Falls.

The Dream Stream as seen from downtown Telluride

GETTING THERE

As you enter the town of Telluride from Colorado Highway 145, you will be on Colorado Avenue. Simply follow Colorado Avenue through town toward Bridal Veil Falls, and the road becomes County Road 648. Park just past the Pandora Mill at a parking area near the first switchback.

THE ROUTE

Head southeast toward Ingram Falls and Ingram Basin by either following Forest Road 648 or climbing directly up snow, depending on coverage. Follow the road cut near Ingram Falls at approximately 11,050 feet and avoid the temptation to ascend the gully, as it may be dangerously undercut by flowing water. Once in the basin, the terrain eases and you will be in an area with significant mining history, including an old aerial tramway. Ascend Ajax Peak's southwestern slopes to the summit.

Descent. From the summit, descend the broad ridge toward the northwest. As the bowl to your left opens up around 12,400 feet, start trending left toward the Dream Stream slide path while the terrain gradually steepens. There are two main paths, and the Dream Stream is the one on the skier's left. Descend until the large cliff band near 11,000 feet. Transition back to skins and make your way back toward the summit of Ajax. From Ajax's summit, descend the same southwest slopes that you used earlier on your first ascent of the peak. From Ingram Falls, you may want to traverse skier's left to visit beautiful Bridal Veil Falls, one of the main tourist attractions in Telluride. Descend northwest back to your vehicle.

89 Sheep Mountain: Sheep Chute

Starting Elevation: 10,250 feet
High Point: 13,188 feet
Vertical Gain/Loss: 2938 feet
Ascent Distance: 3.5 miles
Descent Distance: 3 miles
Time: 5 to 7 hours
Ski Skills: Difficult
Fitness Level: Moderately strenuous
Technical Skills: Moderate
Gear: The basics, plus ice axe and crampons
Best Months: March to early May
USGS Map: Mount Wilson

From the top of Lizard Head Pass, Sheep Mountain is the closest mountain to the southeast. You can't tell from the highway, but a strikingly aesthetic couloir hides on the mountain's north side. From the summit of Sheep Mountain, the views of the Wilson Group of fourteeners as well as other San Juan Mountains are tough to beat.

GETTING THERE

The trailhead is on top of Colorado Highway 145's Lizard Head Pass, which can be reached from Telluride to the north or Rico from the south. Park in one of the many lots at the top of the pass.

Looking back up Sheep Chute

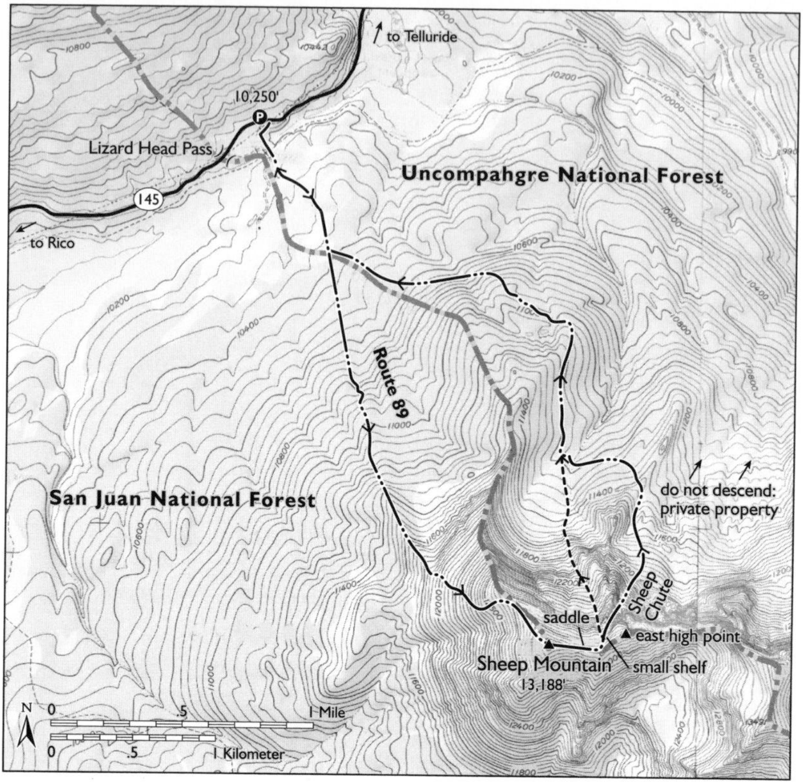

THE ROUTE

From trailhead parking lot at Lizard Head Pass (elevation 10,250 feet), head southeast toward Sheep Mountain, crossing some Nordic trails near the highway. Your goal is to access the south side of Sheep Mountain's northwest ridge, which will allow you to bypass some easily identifiable cliff areas. Most of this will be skinnable, but in some conditions bootpacking may be necessary and crampons or an ice axe may be wanted. Once on the ridge, it's an easy skin to Sheep Mountain's summit, which is the westernmost of two high points. The eastern high point is slightly higher, but the western point is marked Sheep Mountain on maps.

Descent. From the western summit at 13,188 feet, ski down toward the 13,120-foot saddle between Sheep's two summits. This saddle marks the beginning of the route. After approximately 100 vertical feet, there is a small shelf that divides the Sheep Chute from another skiable route that heads skier's left. Stay right and ski the chute for 1000 vertical feet, and then ski the aprons that head down and to the skier's left. As tempting as skiing toward the valley may be, private property blocks access toward Trout Lake Road. Once you reach the forest near 11,500 feet, begin a left contour back toward Lizard Head Pass. With careful navigation and a bit of sidestepping, you should be able to reach your vehicle without putting your skins back on.

90 Gladstone Peak: North Face

Starting Elevation	9700 feet
High Point	13,913 feet
Vertical Gain/Loss	4200 feet
Ascent Distance	6 miles
Descent Distance	6 miles
Time	10 to 12 hours
Ski Skills	Very difficult
Fitness Level	Very strenuous
Technical Skills	High
Gear	The basics, plus ice axe and crampons
Best Months	April to early June
USGS Map	Mount Wilson

Standing tall in the southern San Juans, Gladstone Peak is often overshadowed by its larger 14,000-foot siblings, Mount Wilson, El Diente, and Wilson Peak. Just shy of ranking as a fourteener, Gladstone Peak still ranks as one of the top 100 highest peaks in Colorado, a centennial summit. Simply said, Gladstone is a black sheep among giants. But it is a beautiful peak with steep skiing, accessed through the beautiful Bilk Basin. This summit should pique the interests of all ski mountaineers!

GETTING THERE

From the roundabout at the intersection of Mahoney Drive and Colorado Highway 145 on the western edge of Telluride, head west on CO 145 South for 5.5 miles until

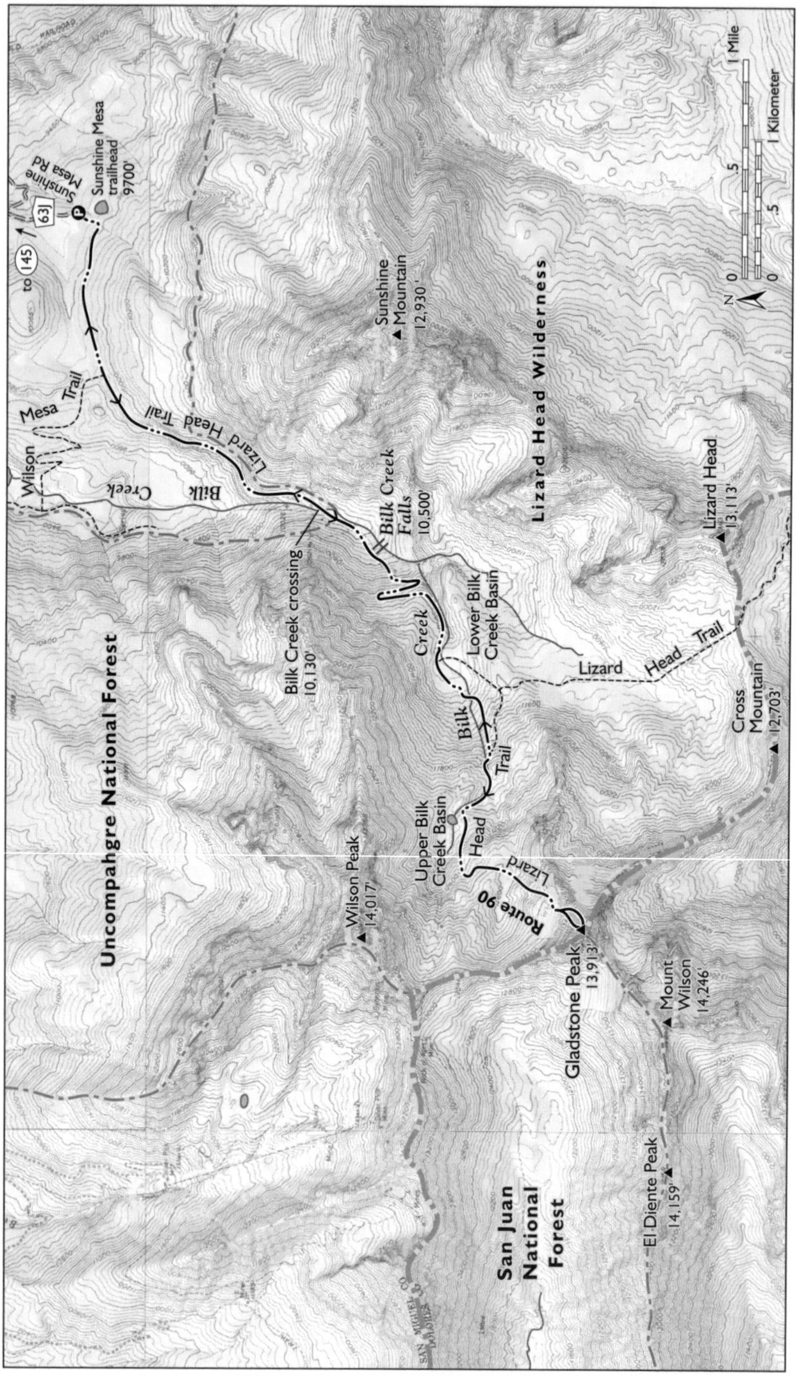
Uncompahgre National Forest
Lizard Head Wilderness
San Juan National Forest
to 145
631
Sunshine Mesa Rd
Sunshine Mesa trailhead 9700'
Wilson Mesa Trail
Lizard Head Trail
Bilk Creek
Bilk Creek crossing 10,130'
Bilk Creek Falls 10,500'
Sunshine Mountain 12,930'
Lower Bilk Creek Basin
Upper Bilk Creek Basin
Lizard Head Trail
Lizard Head 13,113'
Cross Mountain 12,703'
Route 90
Wilson Peak 14,017'
Gladstone Peak 13,913'
Mount Wilson 14,246'
El Diente Peak 14,159'
N
0 .5 1 Mile
0 .5 1 Kilometer

you reach South Fork Road. South Fork Road is also 2.5 miles west of Society Turn and 6 miles east of Sawpit.

Turn south onto South Fork Road (County Road 63L). After crossing the San Miguel River, head south on this road for a total of 2.2 miles, where you will turn right (west) onto Sunshine Mesa Road (CR 63J).

Sunshine Mesa Road is a dirt road usually passable by mid-clearance vehicles. Climbing steeply up through the forest, you'll pass private property and several driveways along the way. You will travel just over 5 miles on Sunshine Mesa Road until the road ends at the Sunshine Mesa trailhead. When you reach an obvious large flat clearing with some old buildings, you'll know you are about a half mile from the trailhead.

During winter months, some of the private property lower on Sunshine Mesa Road may be plowed, but it is unlikely that the upper portion of the road is clear. For information on the road status, call the Norwood District Office (see Resources).

THE ROUTE

From the Sunshine Mesa trailhead, begin following the Lizard Head Trail (Morning Star Trail) southwest. This trail begins fairly flat, following the path of an old mining access road now closed to motorized traffic. After traveling for just a little under 1 mile, you will reach an intersection with the Wilson Mesa Trail. Do not take this trail north. Instead, continue straight, heading southwest along the Lizard Head Trail as it contours around Sunshine Mountain.

Just after 2 miles, you will start traveling alongside Bilk Creek, which you will need to cross in just a bit. The original trail crosses around mile 2.3, but at the time of writing, there was an easier crossing at a logjam about 0.2 mile upstream from that point. To access the logjam, travel south along the eastern banks of Bilk Creek for 0.2 mile, past where the official trail crosses Bilk Creek. You will pass through willows and a scree field to get there.

After crossing, continue following the Lizard Head Trail as it continues southward along the western side of Bilk Creek for another quarter mile before beginning to climb up steeply toward Bilk Basin. You will begin to see Bilk Creek Falls up valley, on the eastern side of the drainage.

You will emerge out of the forest at about 11,060 feet, after traveling for about 4 miles from the trailhead. In this clearing, you can see the prominent and pointy Gladstone Peak to the southwest. Hopefully, snow will be covering the ground by the time you reach this clearing, if not earlier, to make your travel easier.

If snow is present, begin following the obvious valley through Lower Bilk Creek Basin and gully up the valley to Upper Bilk Creek Basin at just over 12,000 feet.

Otherwise, continue following the Lizard Head Trail along the north side of the basin another 0.6 mile up the valley to about 11,400 feet, about 50 feet or so north of the creek. Here, take an unmarked trail that travels north and west. Look for the cairn there, and the trail will go to your right. It starts out faint, but gets more defined, and actually follows a road as it switches back and forth heading up to the Upper Bilk Creek Basin at just over 12,000 feet.

By the time you've reached Upper Bilk Creek Basin, you'll be gazing upon Wilson Peak on your right (northwest) and the north face of Gladstone Peak on your left (southwest).

Climb Gladstone's north face to gain the northeast ridge around 13,670 feet. Follow the ridge southwest a few hundred vertical feet to the summit.

Descent. From the summit, begin descending via the northeast ridge. You may choose to descend through a small couloir that faces a bit more east on the skier's right side of the ridge, just a hundred feet below the summit. If you ski this, be aware that the terrain that rolls over below you around 13,200 feet is laden with cliffs. Due to these cliffs and the rapid warming typical of east faces, we do not recommend that you descend this east face entirely. At the bottom of the short couloir, veer a hard left to get back to the ridge.

Once on the ridge, descend the north face back to Upper Bilk Creek Basin. Follow your ascent route back to the Sunshine Mesa trailhead.

91 Sam's Trees

Starting Elevation	10,250 feet
High Point	11,700 feet
Vertical Gain/Loss	1550 feet
Ascent Distance	1.5 miles
Descent Distance	1.5 miles
Time	2 to 3 hours
Ski Skills	Moderate to difficult
Fitness Level	Not very strenuous
Technical Skills	Low
Gear	The basics
Best Months	December to March
USGS Map	Silverton

Some of the best tree skiing in the Red Mountain Pass area can be found in this zone. If you're looking for tree skiing with a nice pitch, Sam's Trees is your best bet. With a very direct 1500-vertical-foot gain, this line gives you a great bang for your buck. This area faces east and can therefore get crusty after long dry spells or later in the season.

GETTING THERE

From the intersection of US Highway 550 and Greene Street in Silverton, head north on US 550 6.4 miles to find a large parking area on the west side of the road. The parking area is 1.7 miles past the Ophir Pass turnoff and just short of the obvious Chattanooga hairpin turn on US 550.

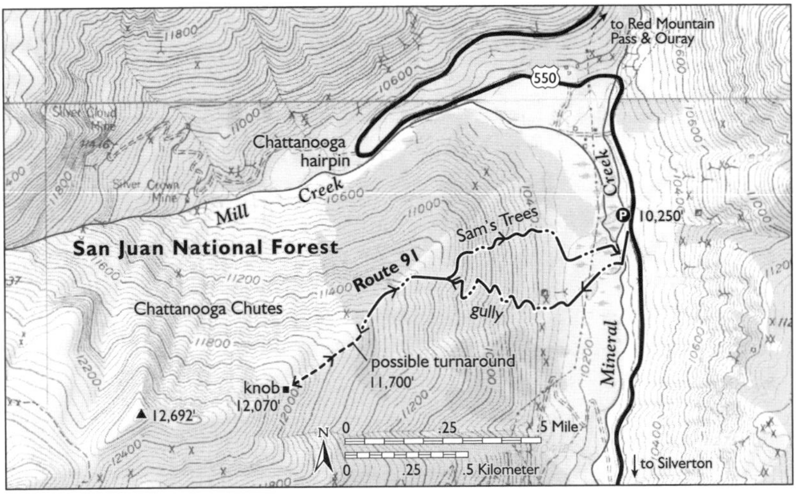

If accessing from the north, the parking area is 3.2 miles south of the summit of Red Mountain Pass, just after the Chattanooga hairpin turn.

THE ROUTE

The parking area provides a nice view of Sam's Trees. As you look east, you'll notice an obvious gully on the looker's left, and various tree shots on either side of the gully. The skin track usually hugs the looker's right of the gully until it reaches the ridge. Any of the tree shots you see are skiable, and you might even pick out one that you would like to ski.

From the south end of the parking area, continue south, dropping about 50 feet down to cross Mineral Creek on a snow bridge and enter the lower part of the valley. Once you've crossed Mineral Creek, head southwest across the valley toward the northern end of the gully mentioned above. Hug the looker's right side of the gully as you ascend, reaching a northeast ridge around 11,350 feet.

Once you gain the northeast ridge, follow it southwest to tree line at 11,700 feet. You may want to transition to ski down from here. In clear conditions and when the avalanche danger is not too high, you may want to venture above tree line, 270 feet higher to a knob at 12,070 feet.

Descent. Follow the northeast ridge downward until you reach a desired area where you want to ski down. Your descent options primarily face east, although you can work the terrain to get slight changes in aspect. Once on the valley floor, head toward the area where you crossed Mineral Creek and follow your path back to the parking area.

Extra Credit: This same approach can be used in safe springtime conditions to reach the north-facing Chattanooga Chutes off Point 12,692. These steep chutes are visible from the Chattanooga hairpin turn—keep in mind that some of these cliff out.

92 Red Mountain No. 3: West Face

Starting Elevation	11,130 feet
High Point	12,890 feet
Vertical Gain/Loss	1760 feet
Ascent Distance	2.9 miles
Descent Distance	2.1 miles
Time	4 to 6 hours
Ski Skills	Difficult
Fitness Level	Not very strenuous
Technical Skills	Low
Gear	The basics; crampons or ski crampons may be helpful at times
Best Months	Late March to April
USGS Map	Ironton

One of the most classic ski routes on Red Mountain Pass between Ouray and Silverton, the west face of Red Mountain No. 3 is a 2000-foot descent. Easily viewed from the highway, "Red 3" is a good starting point for skiers exploring the vast backcountry in this part of the San Juans. The area was heavily mined and, as such, private property is plentiful, and backcountry skiers should take care to obey posted private property signs. Red Mountain No. 3 is occasionally skied during the winter, although it is certainly safer to ski this route with a consolidated springtime snowpack.

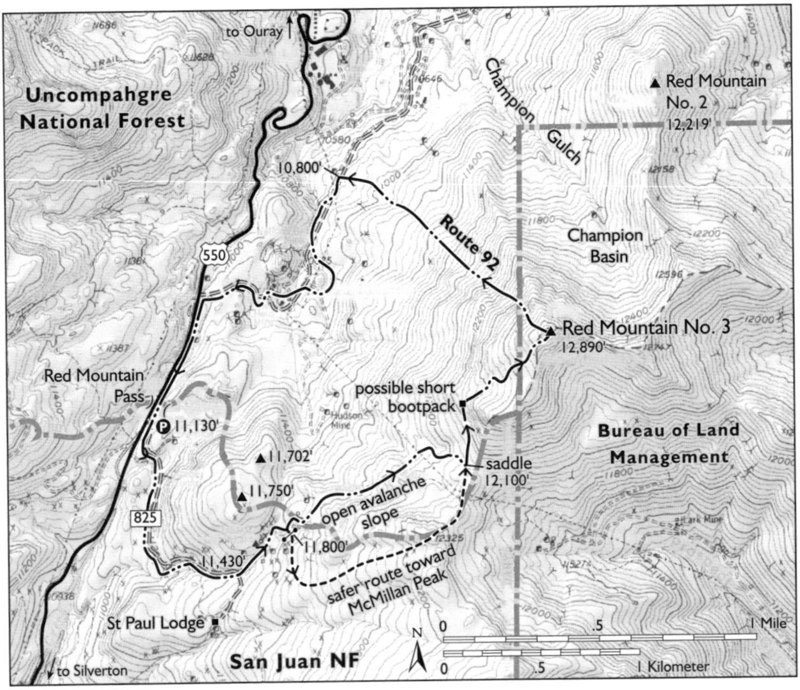

GETTING THERE

Park on the east side at the top of Red Mountain Pass. The pass is located 13 miles south of Ouray on US Highway 550, or 10.5 miles north of Silverton.

THE ROUTE

The top of Red Mountain Pass contains several parking areas, and multiple mining roads and skin tracks originate there. The goal is to circle around a small 11,750-foot hill, which blocks your view of Red Mountain No. 3. Two roads start roughly 50 yards southeast of the pass. Head east on either one until you run into another road after a short distance. Turn right on this road, Forest Service Road 825, and head south. Follow FR 825 as it curves to the east, and then continues to curve to the northeast. At 11,430 feet, stay left at a road junction—turning right would take you to the St. Paul Lodge. Continue heading northeast past several other spur roads until the terrain opens up at a gate at 11,800 feet.

The road here traverses across an open slope with avalanche potential. If conditions seem at all questionable, a safer route choice would be to head southeast toward McMillan Peak and then head north to rejoin the route described here. Past the open slope, trend slightly east as you climb this basin toward a saddle. Just shy of this saddle, near 12,100 feet, turn sharply left to the north and aim to the climber's left of broken

cliffs on Red 3's south side. This area may be icy and require crampons or ski crampons. A short bootpack near the cliff bands will deposit you into a shallow flat basin to the south of the summit. Climb these slopes to the summit.

Descent. The north face of Red Mountain No. 3, dropping into Champion Basin, is also a popular ski, so take note of it from the summit. The west face can be skied right off the summit, although you may need to descend a short distance on foot if winds have scraped it clean. Descend this open face into the glades at tree line until you reach a road at the 10,800-foot level.

Follow this road south and west back toward the highway. You may need to put skins back on, as the road is just slightly steep enough at times to make skinning more enjoyable than sidestepping or skating. Reach the highway a short distance to the north of your parking area, and then walk the road back to your parking spot.

93 Clear Lake: South Lookout Peak and V2

Starting Elevation	9800+/- feet
High Point	13,309 feet (V2)
Vertical Gain/Loss	3500 feet
Ascent Distance	5.3+/- miles
Descent Distance	5.3+/- miles
Time	5 to 7 hours
Ski Skills	Moderate to very difficult
Fitness Level	Moderately strenuous to strenuous

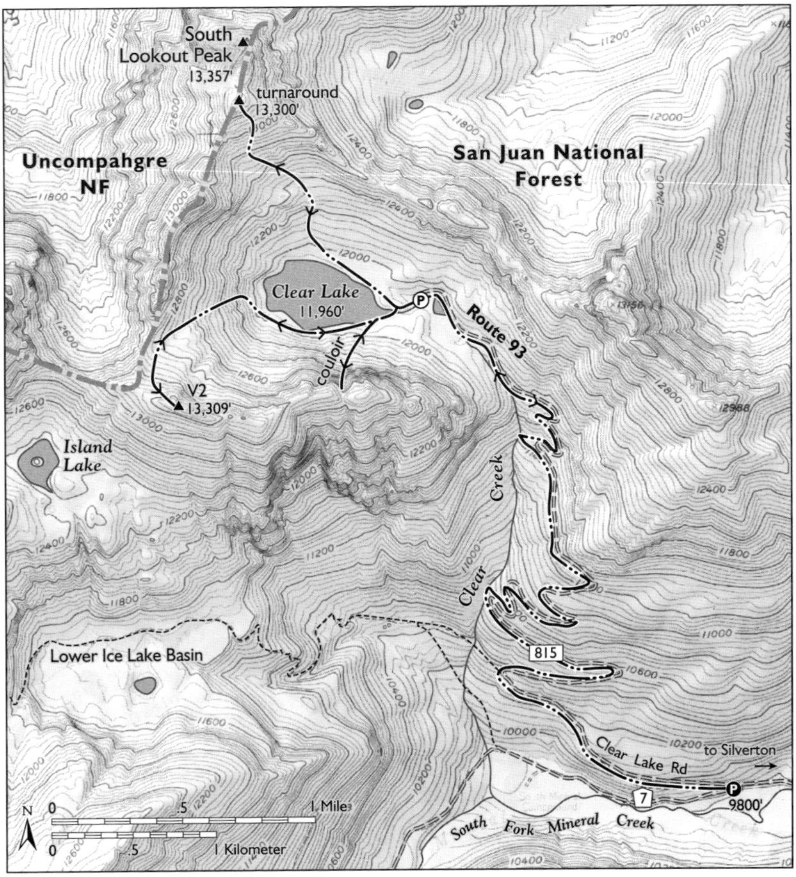

Technical Skills	Moderate to high
Gear	The basics, plus ice axe and crampons
Best Months	May to June
USGS Map	Ophir

If you're looking for a basin in the San Juans that offers easy access and lines that range from mild to wild, look no further than Clear Lake Basin. Better still, the basin contains a number of different aspects, allowing motivated backcountry skiers the ability to follow the sun from one line to another. On top of all that, it's a beautiful spot that has great views of other San Juan favorites, such as Ice Lake Basin.

GETTING THERE

From the intersection of US Highway 550 and Greene Street on the southwest edge of Silverton, turn right to head north onto US 550. Travel 2 miles and then turn left (southwest) onto South Mineral Road (County Road 7 [Forest Road 585]),

Ascending the southern slopes of South Lookout Peak, with Clear Lake and the steep north-facing couloir off of V2's ridge visible behind

which is usually plowed in the springtime. Shortly after turning, you will pass the Kendall Campground and then the Sultan and Anvil campgrounds. After 3.7 miles of dirt road, turn right onto the well-signed Clear Lake Road (FR 815). Park at this junction or continue driving up the 4WD Clear Lake Road as far as conditions allow. If you're able to park at the lake, subtract 2150 feet from your vertical gain and 4.4 miles each way.

THE ROUTE

Follow FR 815 north to Clear Lake at 11,960 feet if you have been unable to drive all the way to the lake. From the lake, survey conditions. The southeast slopes of South Lookout Peak will be the first aspect to warm up and can be reached by skinning or booting up the face. Reaching the summit of South Lookout from here involves class 5 climbing, but the ski route stops on a high point around 13,300 feet, short of the summit. Across the valley, the northwest slopes of "V2" are the next area to corn up and may require a mixture of skinning and bootpacking to reach the summit at 13,309 feet. Finally, the king line of the basin is the steep north-facing couloir off V2's east ridge, and it will require an ice axe and crampons.

Descent. Ski one, two, or all three of the routes described. All of the routes above will lead back to Clear Lake. From the lake, return to your vehicle.

94 Tower Mountain: North Face

Starting Elevation	10,550+/- feet
High Point	13,552 feet
Vertical Gain/Loss	3002+ feet
Ascent Distance	3+ miles
Descent Distance	3+ miles
Time	4 to 6 hours
Ski Skills	Difficult
Fitness Level	Moderately strenuous
Technical Skills	Moderate
Gear	The basics, plus ice axe and crampons
Best Months	April to early June
USGS Maps	Howardsville and Handies Peak

The highest point to the immediate northeast of Silverton is Tower Mountain, and it offers a commanding view of the vicinity. Its long summit ridge protects a large north-facing cirque with several choices for springtime skiers. Silverton Mountain Heli Skiing uses Tower Mountain as a landing zone, but it begins winding down its season in April at about the same time conditions begin to trend toward safer springtime conditions for backcountry skiers.

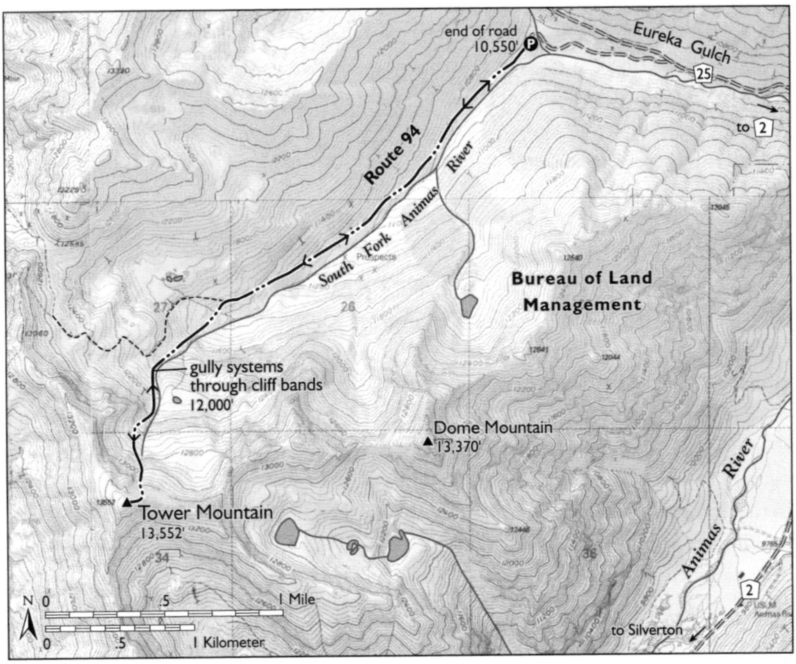

A skier makes her first turns of the day on Tower Mountain in front of the San Juan Mountains.

GETTING THERE

From downtown Silverton, head northeast on Greene Street, and then turn right on County Road 2. Follow CR 2 northeast for 7.9 miles to the ghost town of Eureka (9860 feet) and the distinctive stair-stepped slopes of the Sunnyside Mill. The road is generally open this far in winter. After spring melt-off, turn left (west) on CR 25 just past the mill. At 1.2 miles from the CR 2 and CR 25 intersection, stay left at the fork and follow the road as it parallels the south fork of the Animas River. Reach the end of the road (elevation 10,550 feet) 1.9 miles past the intersection of CR2 and CR 25 near Eureka. This 1.9-mile section requires 4WD.

THE ROUTE

If you do not have 4WD or snow remains on CR 25, begin the tour by walking or skinning to the trailhead described above. From the end of the road, head southwest up the valley, either on the marked trail or on snow, staying on the north side of the south fork of the Animas River. The trail gets rather faint, so you may end up walking off trail. After 2 miles, you will be underneath Tower's north face, near tree line. The entire approach to this point is threatened by numerous slide paths, so only tackle this route during safe periods. Continue up the valley until you can spot a way through small cliff bands low on the face around 12,000 feet. Climb gully systems through these cliff bands to the upper basin below Tower's summit. Pick any snow route on the north face toward the summit that seems feasible and is not blocked by a cornice.

Descent. Descend your ascent route. It may be worthwhile to ski multiple laps on the upper face. Follow the valley back to your vehicle.

95 King Solomon Mountain: North Face

Starting Elevation	9875 feet
High Point	13,185 feet
Vertical Gain/Loss	3310 feet
Ascent Distance	2.5 miles
Descent Distance	2.5 miles
Time	5 to 7 hours
Ski Skills	Difficult
Fitness Level	Moderately strenuous
Technical Skills	Moderate
Gear	The basics, plus ice axe and crampons
Best Months	March to early May
USGS Map	Howardsville

King Solomon Mountain is indeed regal, with three summits strung out along a long summit ridge. This route descends the steep and inviting north face of the central 13,185-foot subsummit (the southern summit, at 13,220 feet, is slightly higher). Over 3000 feet of high-quality skiing awaits skiers who tackle the King. Keep in mind that late in the season, the lower slopes may be choked with small trees and avalanche debris.

Can you spot the skier in the couloir below King Solomon's summit?

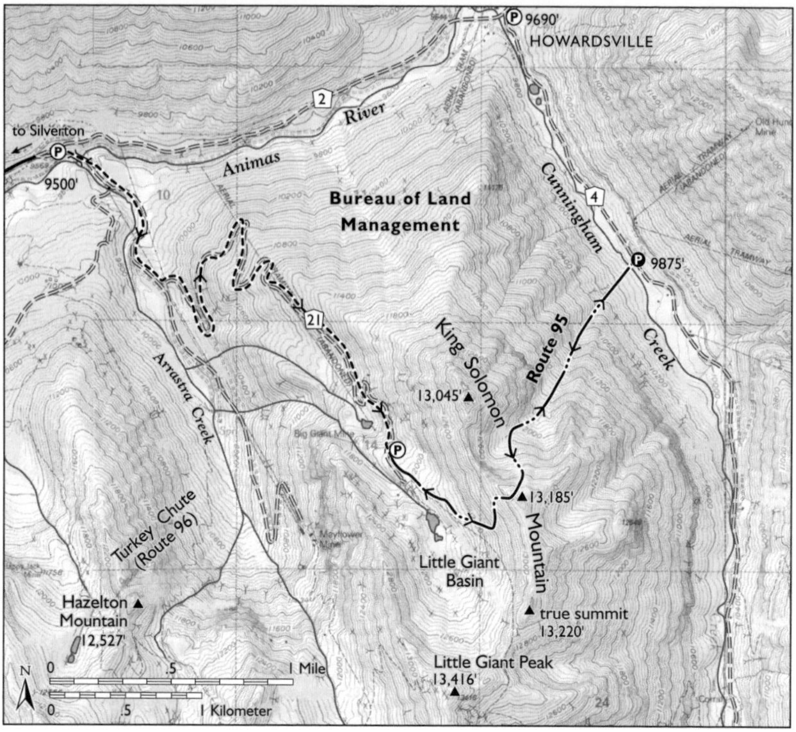

GETTING THERE

From downtown Silverton, head northeast on Greene Street, and then turn right on County Road 2. Follow CR 2 northeast for 4 miles to CR 4 and Cunningham Gulch (9690 feet). Park here or continue driving southeast for 0.9 mile on the lower CR 4 to the base of the route near mining ruins at 9875 feet if the road is clear. Most 2WD vehicles can reach this point.

THE ROUTE

From the parking area at 9690 feet, follow the road to the mining ruins mentioned above. The ascent route can be seen from here, starting with the lower avalanche path all the way through the alpine and the 13,185-foot summit. The best couloir off the summit is slightly hidden, however, and may be hard to identify from the valley floor. Cross Cunningham Creek, which you may need to wade across if you are unable to find a snow bridge. Make your way up the avalanche path until you are below the north face. Climb the couloir, which starts off skinny with a couple of turns before transitioning into a more broken face above.

Alternatively, you can climb the grassy western slopes of King Solomon on CR 21 and Little Giant Basin if you want to do a shuttle. CR 21 is located off CR 2, 2.1 miles before the intersection with CR 4 (see Route 96, Getting There). The couloir described above may be difficult to identify from the summit if you ascend King Solomon's backside, however.

Descent. Ski your ascent route back to Cunningham Gulch.

96 Hazelton Mountain: Turkey Chute

Starting Elevation	9500 feet
High Point	12,300 feet
Vertical Gain/Loss	2800 feet
Ascent Distance	3.5 miles
Descent Distance	2.5 miles
Time	4 to 6 hours
Ski Skills	Difficult
Fitness Level	Moderately strenuous
Technical Skills	Moderate
Gear	The basics
Best Months	November; March to early May
USGS Maps	Howardsville and Silverton

Easy access, an incredibly aesthetic couloir, and a spectacular location make the Turkey Chute (see map in Route 97) a Silverton classic. The Turkey Chute is often skied by Thanksgiving, hence the local name.

GETTING THERE

From downtown Silverton, head northeast on Greene Street, and then turn right on County Road 2. Follow CR 2 northeast for 2.1 miles to CR 21 at Arrastra Gulch. An old mining tramway remains above the trees. Find a parking spot near the bridge over the Animas River, just past the junction at 9500 feet.

THE ROUTE

Immediately after the Animas River is the marked CR 20A. Be aware that online maps may incorrectly place CR 20A closer to Blair Gulch. Skin up CR 20A as it winds through the forest. Continue heading southwest through a maze of side roads until approximately 10,600 feet, when you should leave the road and begin heading south toward Blair Gulch. Leave the forest near the 10,900-foot level, and ascend the steep headwall in Blair Gulch on the climber's left. Above the steep headwall, continue up the valley in easier terrain, looking for a slightly hidden notch (12,300 feet) in the ridge just north of Hazelton's summit. This notch marks the top of the Turkey Chute and may require a short bootpack to reach.

Descent. The Turkey Chute drops away diagonally to the northeast into Arrastra Gulch. Ski the chute, and then enjoy beautiful open terrain to the valley floor. Following this valley will lead you back to your vehicle, but private property blocks the

Chuting the Turkey

way. Avoid the posted no trespassing areas by ascending slightly to the skier's right to reach public county roads.

97 Kendall Peak: Northwest Couloir

Starting Elevation	9500 feet
High Point	13,451 feet
Vertical Gain/Loss	3951 feet
Ascent Distance	4.6 miles
Descent Distance	3.3 miles
Time	7 to 9 hours
Ski Skills	Difficult
Fitness Level	Strenuous
Technical Skills	High
Gear	The basics, plus ice axe and crampons
Best Months	March to early May
USGS Map	Howardsville

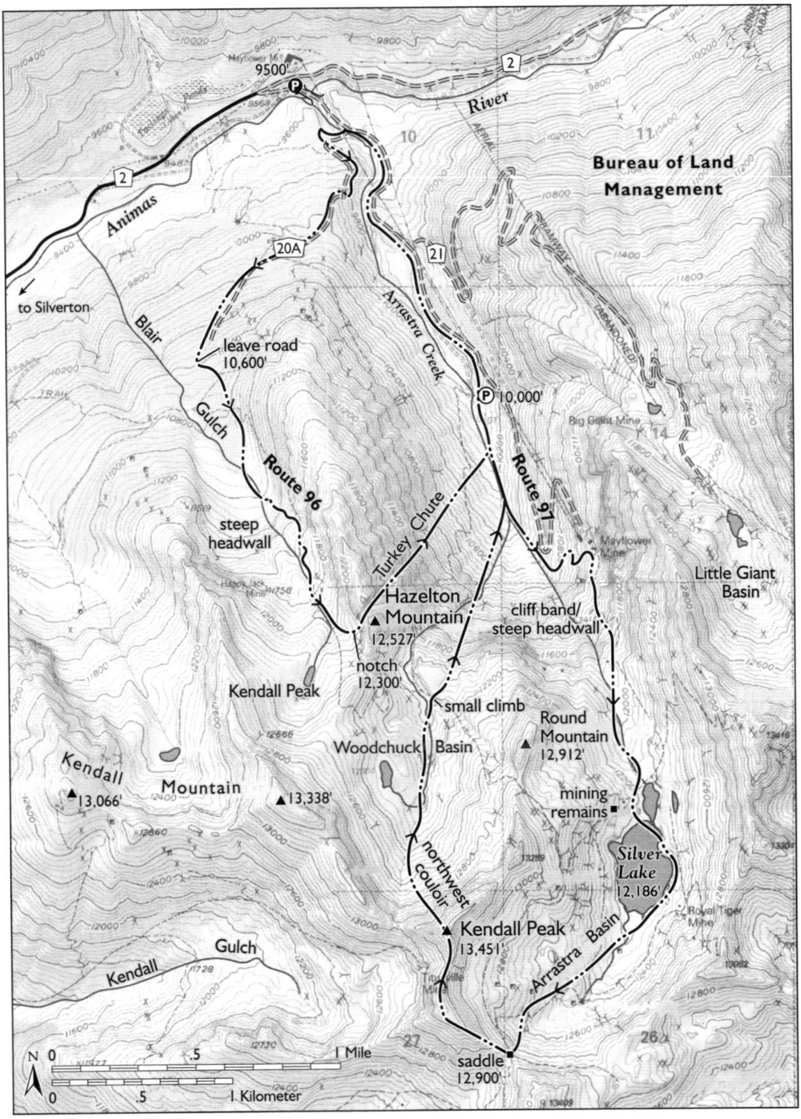

Kendall Mountain towers over the town of Silverton, while the higher Kendall Peak hides behind it. This tour takes you up a steep headwall, past an amazing high alpine lake complete with a ghost town, gains a summit, and finishes with a steep, narrow couloir down to the valley.

GETTING THERE

From downtown Silverton, head northeast on Greene Street, and then turn right on County Road 2. Follow CR 2 northeast for 2.1 miles to CR 21 at Arrastra Gulch.

An old mining tramway remains above the trees. Find a parking spot near the bridge over the Animas River just past the junction at 9500 feet, or continue up the road if you're skiing this route later in the season after snowmelt. The road ends at 10,000 feet, approximately 1.3 miles from the bridge.

THE ROUTE

Follow CR 21 southeast as it ascends Arrastra Creek. The steep headwall straight ahead is the crux of this route. Your ascent route will take the climber's left of Round Mountain, while the end of your tour will descend one of the steep, narrow couloirs to the looker's right of Round Mountain—so take note of your descent route for later in the tour. The easiest way to reach the upper Arrastra Basin is to take the climber's left around the initial cliff bands. This will lead you to a hanging snowfield that you can traverse to the final exposed moves. The terrain abruptly flattens out past the final steep moves, and you will once again be skinning rather than climbing. Another, steeper, option is to climb a narrow strip of snow, possibly with water ice, directly to Arrastra Basin.

Skin south to Silver Lake and what's left of the mining structures surrounding the lake before heading to the east shore. This is a beautiful spot to be! Continue up Arrastra Basin, first to the south before curving toward the southwest. Kendall Peak is on your right, and you should aim for the saddle (12,900 feet) on the south ridge. Gain the summit at 13,451 feet via the south ridge.

Descent. The northwest couloirs roll over steeply from the vicinity of the summit. There are a couple of variations to choose from, so take your pick from the top. From the bottom of the couloir, descend Woodchuck Basin to the north. As you near the bottom of the basin, keep right, possibly even sidestepping up a short distance to reach the narrow exit couloir that you hopefully took note of during your ascent earlier in the day. From the bottom of the couloir, retrace your approach route and obey "No Trespassing" signs lower in the valley.

98 Grand Turk: Zipper Couloir

Starting Elevation	10,480 feet
High Point	12,930 feet
Vertical Gain/Loss	2450 feet
Ascent Distance	1.8 miles
Descent Distance	1.6 miles
Time	4 to 6 hours
Ski Skills	Very difficult
Fitness Level	Not very strenuous
Technical Skills	High
Gear	The basics, plus ice axe and crampons
Best Months	March to April
USGS Map	Silverton

The Zipper Couloir is the roadside attraction clearly visible from Molas Pass, on the southeast face of Grand Turk's 13,015-foot subsummit. With an early start, you should be done well before noon, leaving plenty of time to drive home to the Front Range or perhaps ski another more shaded line in the afternoon. The southeast aspect of this line heats up quickly and may be runnelled later in the season. Other lines abound in the area, including the Fingers, the Wishbone couloirs, and routes off nearby Sultan Mountain. Views of the Needles and Grenadiers from this route are some of the best anywhere.

The Zipper Couloir as seen from Snowdon Peak (Route 99)

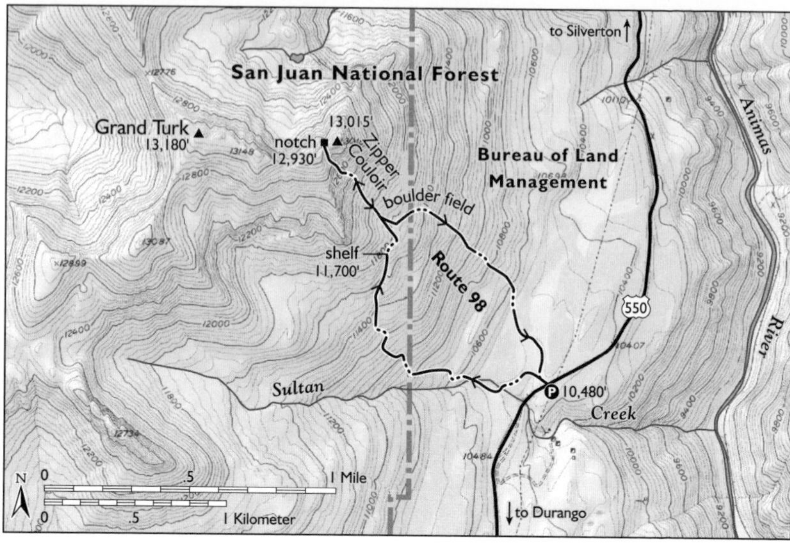

GETTING THERE

Molas Pass is more of a high plateau than a sharp mountain pass, so there are a number of different pullouts as well as camping areas to choose from. You're looking for a small U-shaped parking area on the south side of the highway at an elevation of 10,480 feet. This parking area is near the point where Sultan Creek crosses US Highway 550. This point is 4.4 miles south of Silverton, and 44 miles north of Durango. If you don't find the exact same parking area that is described here, don't worry about it too much. As long as you can see the Zipper Couloir straight ahead, any parking area will work.

THE ROUTE

From the north side of Molas Pass at 10,480 feet, head west/northwest near Sultan Creek. There is a bit of a maze of roads in this area, so take whatever seems like the path of least resistance in this direction. Near 10,800 feet, begin trending to the north. You're aiming for an 11,700-foot shelf that will allow you to make an ascending traverse more to the northeast. This traverse will take you to a boulder field below the Zipper Couloir. Skin as high as you can below the couloir, and then switch to bootpacking up this steep and narrow couloir as it zigs and zags upward. The couloir ends at a notch around 12,930 feet, below the 13,015 high point to climber's right.

Descent. From the top of the Zipper Couloir, the true summit of Grand Turk is to the west and Sultan Mountain is northwest. Both of these are also popular ski descents. Ski the Zipper Couloir, but skip your traverse along the shelf from the ascent route. Instead, continue to the southeast, through a playground of boulders and small drops. When the terrain flattens out, head in a slightly more south/southeast direction to return to your vehicle.

99 Snowdon Peak: Naked Lady Couloir

Starting Elevation : 10,675 feet
High Point : 13,077 feet
Vertical Gain/Loss : 2402 feet
Ascent Distance : 2.9 miles
Descent Distance : 2.9 miles
Time : 4.5 to 6.5 hours
Ski Skills : Extremely difficult
Fitness Level : Moderately strenuous
Technical Skills : High
Gear : The basics, plus ice axe and crampons
Best Months : March to May
USGS Map : Snowdon Peak

The Naked Lady Couloir is the striking gash on the highly visible Snowdon Peak south of Molas Pass. Savvy skiers can often find powder conditions hanging on in the

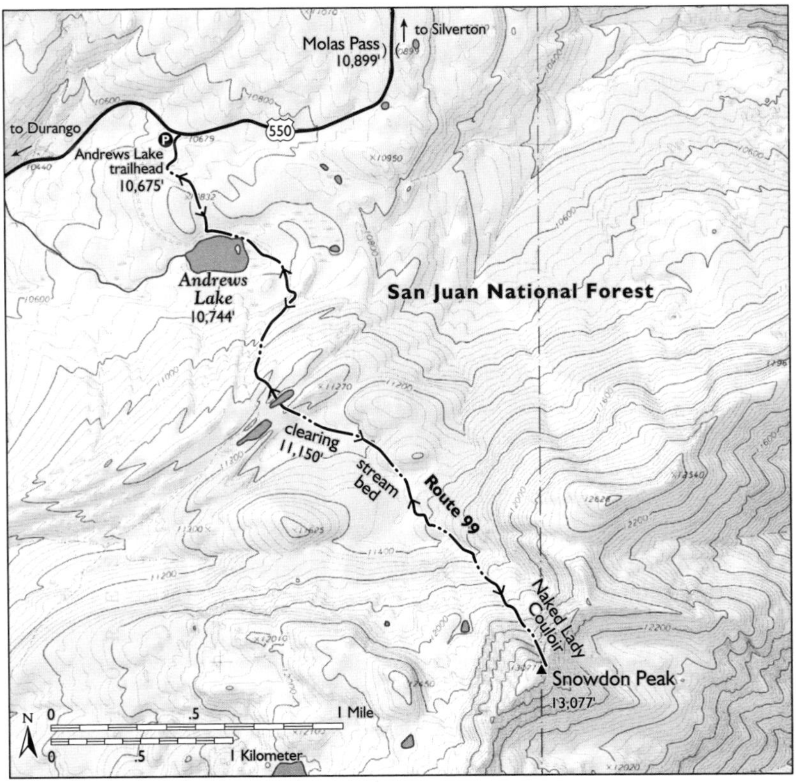

Nearing the upper reaches of the Naked Lady Couloir

protected and north-facing Lady. Easy access from a major highway only adds to the classic nature of this route.

GETTING THERE

The Andrews Lake trailhead is a small, well-marked pull-off roughly 1 mile south of Molas Pass. The pull-off is located 40 miles north of Durango on US Highway 550 and 8 miles south of Silverton on the same highway.

THE ROUTE

Starting at the Andrews Lake pull-off (10,675 feet) on the side of the highway, begin the tour by following the road toward the lake. After only 0.2 mile, a wide alleyway through the trees heads southeast, allowing you to cut off some road mileage toward the lake if it is still snow covered. Continue heading southeast toward Snowdon. The undulating terrain in this area is frustrating, and you will almost surely find yourself cresting small hillsides only to be forced to descend them on the other side. Persevere until you reach a large clearing at 11,150 feet. From here, the route gets a bit more straightforward, as you follow a deep streambed, still in a southeast direction. Stay on the north side of this stream until you reach open terrain and Naked Lady's apron around 12,000 feet.

Transition to bootpacking and begin your way up the couloir. Two-thirds of the way up the couloir, you may encounter a small rock band in lean snow years. Continue up the couloir as it gets both steeper and narrower near Snowdon's northeast ridge. At the ridge crest, difficult and exposed climbing will take you to Snowdon's summit. Many skiers will simply choose to skip the summit and gear up for the descent at the top of the couloir around 13,000 feet.

Descent. Ski the couloir and follow your approach route back to the trailhead.

100 Wolf Creek Pass

Starting Elevation	10,840 feet
High Point	11,750 feet
Vertical Gain/Loss	2000+/- feet
Ascent Distance	3+/- miles
Descent Distance	1.5+/- miles
Time	4 to 6 hours
Ski Skills	Easy to moderate
Fitness Level	Not very strenuous
Technical Skills	Low
Gear	The basics
Best Months	November to April
USGS Maps	Wolf Creek Pass and Mount Hope

Wolf Creek Pass has long been known as one of the snowiest locations in Colorado, and in good years, there may be a four-foot base by Halloween. The original ski lifts at Wolf Creek Pass were located on the north side of the pass near Lobo Overlook, which is described here. Short pitches are the norm at the pass, so plan on making several laps once you've reached the run of your choice.

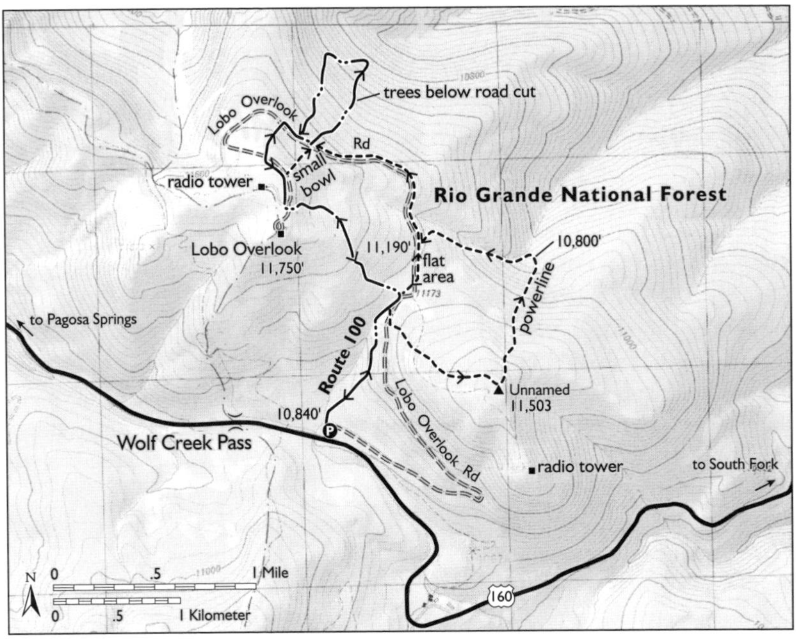

Typical terrain at Wolf Creek Pass

GETTING THERE

Wolf Creek Pass is located on US Highway 160, 23.5 miles from Pagosa Springs on the west side, or 19 miles from South Fork on the east. Parking for these routes is located 0.2 mile east of the pass, at a large parking area north of the highway.

THE ROUTE

The best way to start exploring Wolf Creek terrain is to ascend to Lobo Overlook. To do so, head north from the parking lot, staying climber's right of a small creek. This direct route cuts off a big switchback on the Lobo Overlook Road. Intersect the road again near a flat area at 11,190 feet. The road curves around toward the west on the way to the summit, passing under a small bowl with avalanche potential on the north side of Lobo Overlook. You may choose to leave the road here and take a more direct route to Lobo Overlook, thus avoiding the terrain below the bowl, and shortening the route by about a 0.25 mile. This route also makes a good descent.

Descent. Survey the terrain—there are many possibilities beyond what is discussed here. One good place to start is the trees below the road cut near the small bowl mentioned above. Ski the bowl back to the road cut if avalanche conditions allow; otherwise, ski the flatter terrain to the west of the bowl. The trees below the road cut offer perfectly spaced alleyways, which slowly grow steeper. Ski these for approximately

800 to 1000 vertical feet before turning around and setting up a skin track back to the road cut. Lapping this area once you have a skin track put in makes a lot of sense.

Ski the east slopes of Lobo Overlook back to the 11,190-foot flat area. If you're calling it a day, ski back down the south-facing, possibly icy, slopes back to the trailhead. Another possibility is to ascend to the summit of Unnamed 11,503 near the radio tower. Find the powerline on the north side of this summit and ski this to the northeast. This can be skied to the highway, miles away from the trailhead. If you do this, beware a terrain trap gully at the bottom. But logistically it may be easier to stop near 10,800 feet, put your skins back on, and climb west for roughly 200 vertical feet back to the 11,190-foot flat area. As before, ski south slopes back to your vehicle at the end of the day.

101 Tomahawk Basin

Starting Elevation	9900 feet
High Point	13,050 feet
Vertical Gain/Loss	3150 feet
Ascent Distance	3.2 miles
Descent Distance	3.2 miles
Time	5 to 7 hours
Ski Skills	Difficult
Fitness Level	Moderately strenuous
Technical Skills	Moderate
Gear	The basics, plus ice axe and crampons
Best Months	May
USGS Map	La Plata

Tomahawk Basin is the gem of the La Plata subrange of the San Juan Mountains. This island of peaks sits northwest of Durango, and once the access road melts off they offer great access for spring skiing. Tomahawk Basin is oriented from east to west, so savvy springtime skiers will work the aspects, starting on east faces in the morning and ending with north faces in the afternoon.

GETTING THERE

Set your odometer at the intersection of US Highway 160 and US 550 in Durango. Travel west on US 160 for 11 miles, and then turn right on well-marked County Road 124 (La Plata Canyon Road). This road starts off paved, and then turns into gravel and gets gradually rougher as you approach the trailhead—possibly requiring 4WD for the last half mile. It is 10.1 miles from the highway to Basin Creek at 9900 feet, assuming the snow has melted. Park alongside the road at an appropriate pullout. La Plata Canyon is popular with snowmobiles when snow covered, which may aid your approach earlier in the season.

Approaching Tomahawk Basin with the ridge connecting Mount Moss and Diorite Peak on the right

THE ROUTE

Follow Basin Creek Road in a westerly direction toward Tomahawk Basin. Reach the Tomahawk Mine at 10,600 feet, and follow a climbers' trail up the tailings to regain the road at 10,700 feet. Continue into the upper basin and survey your options. Straight ahead, the ridge connecting Babcock Peak and Mount Moss contains a number of east-facing slopes, all of which are good choices for early morning springtime skiing. Meanwhile, the ridge connecting Mount Moss and Diorite Peak is a good choice for more southerly exposures later in the day. Most of these slopes are in the 30- to 40-degree range, and roughly 1000 vertical feet, so making yo-yo laps is your best plan of action. Your final line of the day should be the north-facing dogleg couloir on Babcock Peak, which is slightly hidden until you are in the upper reaches of Tomahawk Basin. This route may require crampons and an ice axe.

Descent. All of the routes mentioned above will drop back into the main Tomahawk Basin. Retrace your approach back to your vehicle.

102 Babcock Peak: South Couloir

Starting Elevation : 9300 feet
High Point : 13,050 feet

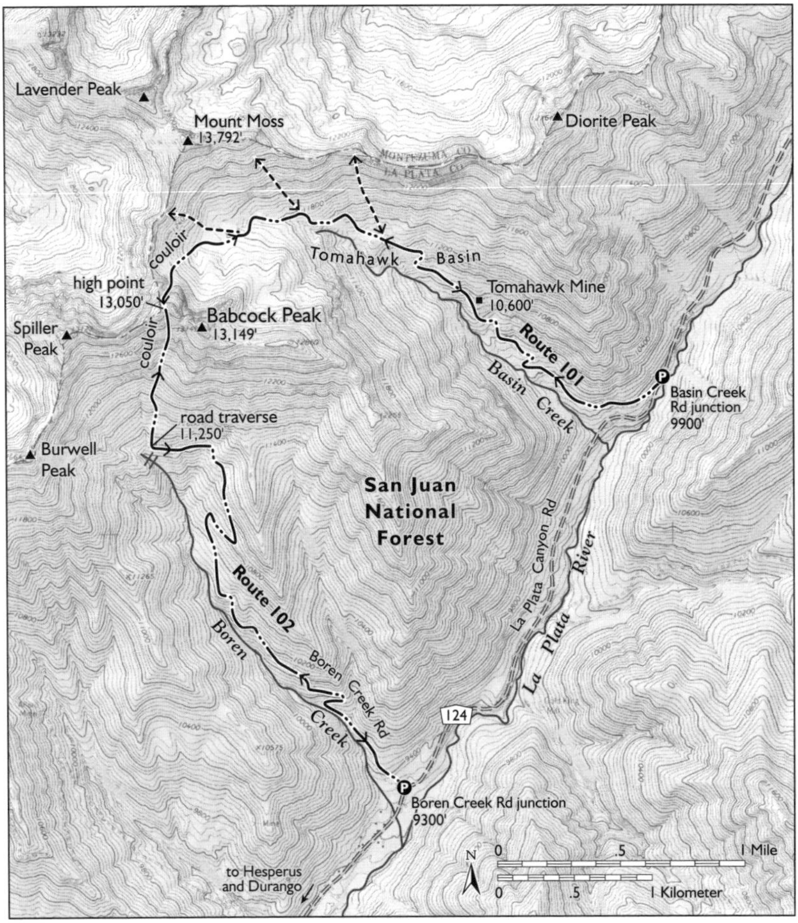

Vertical Gain/Loss	3750 feet
Ascent Distance	4 miles
Descent Distance	3.8 miles
Time	5 to 7 hours
Ski Skills	Difficult
Fitness Level	Moderately strenuous
Technical Skills	Moderate
Gear	The basics, plus ice axe and crampons
Best Months	May
USGS Map	La Plata

Babcock Peak is one of the higher and more easily accessed peaks in the La Plata Range. The north side can be part of a tour in Tomahawk Basin (Route 101), but the south couloir is another aesthetic choice accessed from a different basin.

A skier approaches the south couloir from the basin.

GETTING THERE

Set your odometer at the intersection of US Highway 160 and US 550 in Durango. Travel west on US 160 for 11 miles, and then turn right on well-marked County Road 124 (La Plata Canyon Road). This road starts off paved, and then turns into gravel and gets gradually rougher as you approach the trailhead, although 4WD should not be necessary to this trailhead. It is 8.3 miles from the highway to the marked Boren Creek Road (marked on maps as either Forest Service Road 794 or FR 061), which is narrow and rough. Park at this intersection (elevation 9300 feet). La Plata Canyon is popular with snowmobiles when snow covered, which may aid your approach earlier in the season.

THE ROUTE

Follow Boren Creek Road as it winds northwest up the valley. The road traverses at 11,250 feet to get into the main basin. Several different couloirs will be visible once you've reached the basin. Perhaps the most distinctive route on the south face of Babcock Peak is the small, skinny couloir that constricts and holds a bit of ice at the bottom. The couloir that you're aiming for is immediately climber's right from the icy dead-end couloir described above. This couloir doglegs to the left, so you will not be able to see the entire couloir from below. Take a look around the basin while you're there, since there are several other worthwhile objectives to come back for, such as the southeast face of Spiller Peak.

Descent. Descend the couloir to the bowl below, which harbors great corn skiing in the springtime. The main drainage leads to an impassable waterfall, so be sure to use the same 11,250-foot traverse that you used on the ascent. Follow your ascent route back to your vehicle.

RESOURCES

AVALANCHE INFORMATION AND EDUCATION

Avalanche Education Providers, American Institute for Avalanche Research and Education Courses, http://aiare.info/providers_list.php

Colorado Avalanche Information Center, http://avalanche.state.co.us/

Crested Butte Avalanche Center, http://cbavalanchecenter.org/

GUIDING SERVICES

The American Mountain Guides Association is a central resource for finding certified guides, https://amga.com/

ROAD, WEATHER, SNOW, AND SKI CONDITIONS

Colorado Department of Transportation, www.cotrip.org/home.htm

Ouray County Road and Bridge Department, (970) 626-5391, http://ouraycountyco.gov/151/Road-Bridge

Ouray County Sheriff Department, (970) 325-7272

Ski conditions, http://coloradoski.com/

SNOTEL automated snow sensors, www.wcc.nrcs.usda.gov/snow/

Weather, www.weather.gov/

Weather, trailhead, and conditions for some routes may be found at www.14ers.com

NATIONAL PARKS

Great Sand Dunes National Park
and Preserve
Visitor Center
11999 State Highway 150
Mosca, CO 81146
www.nps.gov/grsa/index.htm

Rocky Mountain National Park
1000 US Highway 36
Estes Park, CO 80517
(970) 586-1206
Trail Ridge Road Status
(970) 586-1222
www.nps.gov/romo/planyourvisit/road_status

NATIONAL FORESTS

Arapaho and Roosevelt
National Forest
2150 Centre Avenue, Building E
Fort Collins, CO 80526
(970) 295-6600
www.fs.usda.gov/arp

Boulder Ranger District
2140 Yarmouth Avenue
Boulder, CO 80301
(303) 444-6600

Canyon Lakes Ranger District
2150 Centre Avenue, Building E
Fort Collins, CO 80526
(970) 295-6700

NATIONAL FORESTS (CONTINUED)

Clear Creek Ranger District
Located at the Idaho Springs
Visitor Center
2060 Miner Street
Idaho Springs, CO 80452
(303) 567-4382

Sulphur Ranger District
P.O. Box 10
9 Ten Mile Drive
Granby, CO 80446
(970) 887-4100

Grand Mesa, Uncompahgre and
Gunnison National Forest
2250 Highway 50
Delta, CO 81416
(970) 874-6600
www.fs.usda.gov/gmug

Grand Valley Ranger District
2777 Crossroads Boulevard, Suite 1
Grand Junction, CO 81506
(970) 242-8211

Gunnison Ranger District
216 North Colorado Street
Gunnison, CO 81230
(970) 641-0471

Norwood Ranger District
P.O. Box 388
1150 Forest
Norwood, CO 81423
(970) 327-4261

Ouray Ranger District
2505 South Townsend
Montrose, CO 81401
(970) 240-5300

Paonia Ranger District
P.O. Box 1030
North Rio Grande Avenue
Paonia, CO 81428
(970) 527-4131

Pike and San Isabel National Forests
2840 Kachina Drive
Pueblo, CO 81008
(719) 553-1400
www.fs.usda.gov/psicc

Leadville Ranger District
2015 North Poplar
Leadville, CO 80461
(719) 486-0749

Pikes Peak Ranger District
601 South Weber Street
Colorado Springs, CO 80903
(719) 636-1602

Salida Ranger District
325 Rainbow Boulevard
Salida, CO 81201
(719) 539-3591

San Carlos Ranger District
3170 East Main Street
Cañon City, CO 81212
(719) 269-8500

South Park Ranger District
320 Highway 285
Fairplay, CO 80440
(719) 836-2031

South Platte Ranger District
19316 Goddard Ranch Court
Morrison, CO 80465
(303) 275-5610

Rio Grande National Forest
1803 West Highway 160
Monte Vista, CO 81144
(719) 852-5941
www.fs.usda.gov/riogrande

Conejos Peak Ranger District
15571 County Road T5
La Jara, CO 81140
(719) 274-8971

Divide Ranger District
13308 West US Highway 160
Del Norte, CO 81132
(719) 657-3321

Creede Office
304 South Main Street
P.O. Box 270
Creede, CO 81130
(719) 658-2556

Saguache Ranger District
46525 Colorado Highway 114
Saguache, CO 81149
(719) 655-2553

Routt National Forest
2468 Jackson Street
Laramie, WY 82070
(307) 745-2300
www.fs.usda.gov/mbr

Hahns Peak/Bears Ears
Ranger District
925 Weiss Drive
Steamboat Springs, CO 80487
(970) 870-1870

Parks Ranger District
P.O. Box 158
612 Fifth Street
Walden, CO 80480
(970) 723-8204

Yampa Ranger District
P.O. Box 7
300 Roselawn Avenue
Yampa, CO 80483
(970) 638-4516

San Juan National Forest
15 Burnett Court
Durango, CO 81301
(970) 247-4874
www.fs.usda.gov/sanjuan

Columbine Ranger District
367 South Pearl Street
Bayfield, CO 81122
(970) 884-2512

Dolores Ranger District
29211 Highway 184
Dolores, CO 81323
(970) 882-7296

Pagosa Ranger District
P.O. Box 310
Second and Pagosa
Pagosa Springs, CO 81147
(970) 264-2268

White River National Forest
900 Grand Avenue
Glenwood Springs, CO 81601
(970) 945-2521
www.fs.usda.gov/whiteriver

Aspen-Sopris Ranger District
Aspen Ranger Station
(open July–October)
806 West Hallam
Aspen, CO 81611
(970) 925-3445

Carbondale Office
620 Main Street
Carbondale, CO 81623
(970) 963-2266

Blanco Ranger District
317 East Market
Meeker, CO 81641
(970) 878-4039

Dillon Ranger District
680 River Parkway
Silverthorne, CO 80498
(970) 468-5400

Eagle–Holy Cross Ranger District
Eagle Office
125 West Fifth Street
Eagle, CO 81631
(970) 328-6388

Holy Cross Office (Vail area)
24747 US Highway 24
Minturn, CO 81645
(970) 827-5715

Rifle Ranger District
0094 County Road 244
Rifle, CO 81650
(970) 625-2532

STATE PARKS

Pearl Lake State Park
P.O. Box 750
Clark, CO 80428
(970) 879-3922
http://cpw.state.co.us/placestogo/Parks/pearllake

State Forest State Park
56750 Highway 14
Walden, CO 80480
(970) 723-8366
http://cpw.state.co.us/placestogo/Parks/stateforest

SKI AREAS

Arapahoe Basin, www.arapahoebasin.com/
Aspen Highlands, www.aspensnowmass.com/
Aspen Mountain, www.aspensnowmass.com/
Beaver Creek, www.beavercreek.com/
Breckenridge, www.breckenridge.com/
Buttermilk, www.aspensnowmass.com/
Copper Mountain, www.coppercolorado.com/
Crested Butte, www.skicb.com/
Eldora, www.eldora.com/
Granby Ranch, www.granbyranch.com/
Hesperus, www.ski-hesperus.com/
Howelsen Hill, www.steamboatsprings.net/
Keystone, www.keystoneresort.com/
Loveland, www.skiloveland.com/

Monarch, www.skimonarch.com/
Powderhorn, www.powderhorn.com/
Purgatory, www.purgatoryresort.com/
Silverton, www.silvertonmountain.com/
Ski Cooper, www.skicooper.com/
Snowmass, www.aspensnowmass.com/
Steamboat, www.steamboat.com/
Sunlight, www.sunlightmtn.com/
Telluride, www.tellurideskiresort.com/
Vail, www.vail.com/
Winter Park, www.winterparkresort.com/
Wolf Creek, www.wolfcreekski.com/

OTHER USEFUL RESOURCES

10th Mountain Division Hut Association
1280 Ute Avenue, Suite 21
Aspen, CO 81611
(970) 925-5775
www.huts.org

Boulder County Road Department
(303) 441-3962
www.bouldercounty.org/roads/pages/default.aspx

Friends of Berthoud Pass, www.berthoudpass.org/

Friends of the Colorado Avalanche Information Center,
https://avalanche.state.co.us/donate/

Friends of the San Juans, www.thesanjuans.org/

Gunnison–Crested Butte Tourism Association
202 East Georgia Avenue
Gunnison, CO 81230
(970) 379-5498
(877) 213-5375
www.gunnisoncrestedbutte.com

Pearl Lake Yurts
(800) 678-2267
http://cpw.state.co.us/placestogo/parks/PearlLake/Pages/CampingYurts.aspx

Seedhouse Guard Station
400 Seedhouse Road
Clark, CO 80487
(877) 444-6777
www.recreation.gov

Shrine Pass Hut
www.huts.org/Reservations/Vail_Pass_Taskforce.php

FURTHER READING

History

BOOKS

Bueler, William M. *Roof of the Rockies: A History of Colorado Mountaineering*. Golden, CO: Colorado Mountain Club, 2000.

Dawson, Louis W. *Wild Snow: A Historical Guide to North American Ski Mountaineering*. Golden, CO: American Alpine Club, 1997.

Fay, Abbott. *A History of Skiing in Colorado*. Ouray, CO: Western Reflections, 2003.

Huntford, Roland. *Two Planks and a Passion: The Dramatic History of Skiing*. London: Continuum, 2011.

Stanko, Jim, Sureva Towler, Judy Seligson, and Arianthe C. Stettner. *The Historical Guide to Routt County*. Steamboat Springs, CO: Tread of Pioneers Museum, 2010.

WEBSITES

Gilmore, Susan. "Masontown's Rise and Fall above Frisco." *Summit Daily*. Swift Communications, 13 June 2016. www.summitdaily.com/explore-summit/history/masontowns-rise-and-fall-above-frisco/.

"The Home of Colorado's Highest Peaks." *14ers.com: Home of Colorado's Fourteeners and High Peaks*. 14ers Inc. www.14ers.com/.

"Lists of Peaks." *Lists of John*. Lists of John. http://listsofjohn.com/.

McAdams, Daniel. "The Abandoned Magnolia Mill Is Rich with Colorado Mining History." *OnlyInYourState*. Only in Your State, 16 June 2016. http://www.onlyinyourstate.com/colorado/abandoned-magnolia-mill-co/.

Mehlberg, Adam. "Champion Mine." *4X4Explore.com*, 6 Jan. 2014. www.4x4explore.com/rds/c_rds/champn_mine.html.

"Montgomery--Colorado Ghost Town." *Montgomery--Colorado Ghost Town*. Atjeu Publishing. www.ghosttowns.com/states/co/montgomery.html.

Route Information

BOOKS

Bronski, Peter. *Powder Ghost Towns: Epic Backcountry Runs in Colorado's Lost Ski Resorts*. Berkeley, CA: Wilderness Press, 2008.

Conners, Ben, and Brian Miller. *Climbing and Skiing Colorado's Mountains: 50 Select Ski Descents*. Guilford, CT: Globe Pequot Press, 2014.

Davenport, Chris, Art Burrows, and Penn Newhard. *Fifty Classic Ski Descents of North America: A Visual Tribute to North America's Finest Ski Descents*. Silt, CO: Capitol Peak, 2010.

Dawson, Louis W. *The Northern Peaks: The Complete Mountaineering Guide to Colorado's High Peaks, Technical Routes, Snow Climbs, Ski Descents, Classic Hikes*. Monument, CO: Blue Clover, 1994.

———.*The Southern Peaks: The Complete Mountaineering Guide to Colorado's High Peaks: Technical Routes, Snow Climbs, Ski Descents, Classic Hikes*. Monument, CO: Blue Clover, 1996.

Haddad, Ron, and Eileen Faughey. *Front Range Descents: Spring and Summer Skiing and Snowboarding in Colorado's Front Range*. Boulder, CO: Sigma, 2003.

———.*Indian Peak Descents: Ski Mountaineering and Snowboarding in Colorado's Indian Peak*. Boulder, CO: Sigma, 1996.

Kelly, Mark. *Backcountry Skiing and Ski Mountaineering in Rocky Mountain National Park*. Edgewater, CO: Giterdun, 2013.

Lipp, Jordan. *Backcountry Skiing Berthoud Pass: A Guidebook to Skiing and Snowboarding Berthoud Pass, Colorado*. Denver, CO: Summit Guide, 2005.

Roach, Gerry. *Colorado's Fourteeners: From Hikes to Climbs*. Golden, CO: Fulcrum Pub., 2004.

———.*Colorado's Indian Peaks: Classic Hikes and Climbs*. Golden, CO: Fulcrum Pub., 1998.

Roach, Gerry, and Jennifer Roach. *Colorado's Thirteeners, 13,800 to 13,999 Feet: From Hikes to Climbs*. Golden, CO: Fulcrum Pub., 2001.

Sovick, Andy. *An Essential Guide to Backcountry Skiing: Silverton Zone*. Gunnison, CO: Off-Piste Ski Atlas, 2014.

———.*An Essential Guide to Backcountry Skiing: Crested Butte, Colorado*. Gunnison, CO: Off-Piste Ski Atlas, 2013.

Sperry, Fritz. *Making Turns in Colorado's Front Range*. Edgewater, CO: Giterdun, 2014.

———.*Making Turns in Colorado's Tenmile-Mosquito Range*. Edgewater, CO: Giterdun, 2012.

Van Tilburg, Christopher. *Backcountry Ski and Snowboard Routes: Oregon*. Seattle: Mountaineers Books, 2011.

Volken, Martin. *Backcountry Ski and Snowboard Routes: Washington*. Seattle: Mountaineers Books, 2014.

WEBSITES

Dawson, Louis. "Backcountry Skiing Colorado." *Backcountry Skiing Colorado Guidebook*. www.backcountryskiingco.com/.

"Teton Gravity Research Forums." *Teton Gravity Research Forums RSS*. Teton Gravity Research. www.tetongravity.com/forums/.

Writz, Rob. "Main." *Front Range Ski Mountaineering*. AlpInIsmo. www.frontrangeskimo.com/.

Skills

BOOKS

Fredston, Jill A., and Doug Fesler. *Snow Sense: A Guide to Evaluating Snow Avalanche Hazard*. Anchorage, AK: Alaska Mountain Safety Center, 2011.

The Mountaineers. *Mountaineering: The Freedom of the Hills*, 9th Edition. Seattle: Mountaineers Books, 2017.

Tremper, Bruce. *Staying Alive in Avalanche Terrain*. Seattle: Mountaineers Books, 2014.

Twight, Mark, and James Martin. *Extreme Alpinism: Climbing Light, Fast, and High*. Seattle: Mountaineers Books, 2006.

Wilkerson, James A., Ernest E. Moore, and Ken Zafren. *Medicine for Mountaineering: And Other Wilderness Activities*, 6th Edition. Seattle: Mountaineers Books, 2010.

WEBSITES

"A Compendium of Knowledge for Backcountry Skiers and Snowboarders." *Colorado*. www.backcountryrecon.com/.

"Climbing, Hiking, Mountaineering : SummitPost." *SummitPost.org*. Summit Post. www.summitpost.org/.

ACKNOWLEDGMENTS

First and foremost, we would like to thank our parents for introducing us to skiing at an early age as well as our instructors, coaches, and mentors who helped us develop into the skiers we are today. Additionally, we would like to thank the team at Mountaineers Books for giving us the opportunity to write this guidebook. We were looking for another adventure, and you gave us one.

Thank you, Lou Dawson, for the advice and encouragement as we began our work on this book.

A heartfelt thanks to Chris Davenport for writing the foreword.

Ben Pritchett and Zach Guy, thank you for your review and advice for the avalanche forecasting and education sections of this book.

We were graciously supported by a number of companies while conducting research. In no particular order, we would like to thank Blizzard, Tecnica, Leki, Smith, Fritschi, Black Diamond, La Sportiva, Honey Stinger, Big Agnes, Intuition, and Backcountry Access.

Finally, this book would not have been possible without the help and support of our friends and ski partners. Thank you for skiing with us, sharing your knowledge, and sharing your photos. In no order of any kind: Jarrett Luttrell, Dave Bourassa, Pete Sowar, Sven Brunso, Josh Macak, John Jasper, Natalie Moran, Susan Mol, Matt Kamper, Gary Fondl, Keith Spargo, Larry Fontaine, Forrest Thorniley, Colin McKernan, Jordan White, Ann Driggers, Mark Cavaliero, Cory Thibodeau, John DiCuollo, Marko Ross-Bryant, Cory Lowe, Sam Coffey, Nate Rowland, Ben McShan, Will Herringer, Scott Edlin, Zach Taylor, Dan Bowers, Kim Ross, Frank Stern, Alex Riedman, Fritz Sperry, Chris Webster, Ben Morello, Chris Miller, Pam Rice, Brad Bond, and Lance Waring.

INDEX

Wolf Creek Pass 280, 315–317

ABOUT THE AUTHORS

Brittany Walker Konsella is an avid outdoors enthusiast who began skiing at age four on the slopes of Ohio. In 2011, she became the second woman and ninth person overall to ski Colorado's 14,000-foot peaks. A former freestyle skiing competitor and coach, Brittany now spends her free time skiing, backcountry skiing, hiking, and mountain biking. Brittany pieces together multiple jobs that allow her schedule to remain flexible to maximize her time outdoors, including website development and tutoring middle school and high school math and science.

Frank Konsella grew up in Golden, Colorado, and began skiing at age three. A former ski racer and International Freeskiers and Snowboarders Association Big Mountain competitor, Frank found himself indulging in the backcountry surrounding Crested Butte on an increasingly regular basis. In 2008, he finished his goal of skiing all of Colorado's 14,000-foot peaks, the fourth person to do so. His favorite part about backcountry skiing is the freedom to tackle any line that catches his eye. Frank is a real estate agent in Crested Butte, where he and Brittany make their home.

Frank and Brittany both write frequently about their outdoor adventures on their blog, www.14erskiers.com.

MOUNTAINEERS BOOKS

SKIPSTONE BRAIDED RIVER

recreation • lifestyle • conservation

MOUNTAINEERS BOOKS is a leading publisher of mountaineering literature and guides—including our flagship title, *Mountaineering: The Freedom of the Hills*—as well as adventure narratives, natural history, and general outdoor recreation. Through our two imprints, Skipstone and Braided River, we also publish titles on sustainability and conservation. We are committed to supporting the environmental and educational goals of our organization by providing expert information on human-powered adventure, sustainable practices at home and on the trail, and preservation of wilderness.

The Mountaineers, founded in 1906, is a 501(c)(3) nonprofit outdoor activity and conservation organization whose mission is "to explore, study, preserve, and enjoy the natural beauty of the outdoors." One of the largest such organizations in the United States, it sponsors classes and year-round outdoor activities throughout the Pacific Northwest, including climbing, hiking, backcountry skiing, snowshoeing, bicycling, camping, paddling, and more. The Mountaineers also supports its mission through its publishing division, Mountaineers Books, and promotes environmental education and citizen engagement. For more information, visit The Mountaineers Program Center, 7700 Sand Point Way NE, Seattle, WA 98115-3996; phone 206-521-6001; www.mountaineers.org; or email info@mountaineers.org.

Our publications are made possible through the generosity of donors and through sales of more than 800 titles on outdoor recreation, sustainable lifestyle, and conservation. To donate, purchase books, or learn more, visit us online:

MOUNTAINEERS BOOKS
1001 SW Klickitat Way, Suite 201 • Seattle, WA 98134
800-553-4453 • mbooks@mountaineersbooks.org • www.mountaineersbooks.org

Mountaineers Books is proud to be a corporate sponsor of the Leave No Trace Center for Outdoor Ethics, whose mission is to promote and inspire responsible outdoor recreation through education, research, and partnerships. The Leave No Trace program is focused specifically on human-powered (nonmotorized) recreation. • Leave No Trace strives to educate visitors about the nature of their recreational impacts and offers techniques to prevent and minimize such impacts. • Leave No Trace is best understood as an educational and ethical program, not as a set of rules and regulations. • For more information, visit www.lnt.org or call 800-332-4100.